Class Issues

Class Issues

Pedagogy, Cultural Studies, and the Public Sphere

Edited by Amitava Kumar

NEW YORK UNIVERSITY PRESS
New York and London

NEW YORK UNIVERSITY PRESS
New York and London

Library of Congress Cataloging-in-Publication Data
Class issues : pedagogy, cultural studies, and the public sphere /
edited by Amitava Kumar.
p.   cm.
Includes bibliographical references (p.   ) and index.
ISBN 0-8147-4696-9 (cloth : acid-free paper). — ISBN
0-8147-4697-7 (pbk. : acid-free paper)
1. Critical pedagogy.   2. Intellectuals—Political activity.
3. Class consciousness.   4. Culture—Study and teaching.
5. Socialism and education.   6. Postmodernism and education.
I. Kumar, Amitava, 1963–
LC196.C53   1997
370.11'5—dc21   97-4773
                        CIP

New York University Press books are printed on acid-free paper,
and their binding materials are chosen for strength and durability.

Manufactured in the United States of America

10 9 8 7 6 5 4 3 2 1

Contents

Acknowledgments

I would like to thank all the contributors, who made this work a pleasant learning exercise for me. In addition to those who wrote for this volume, several members of the Marxist Literary Group sent me syllabi or otherwise participated in conversations about this collection: Fred Pfeil, Andrew Parker, Jean Howard, Elayne Tobin, Matt Ruben, and Hap Veeser. Special thanks to Lisa Frank, savvy sub-commandante of left publishing. Several deep bows in the direction of Norman, Oklahoma, from where Dan Cottom continues to operate by the high standards he set in these parts as a scrupulous reader and friend. My thanks also to John Murchek, who shed elegant light on my initial proposal. Jeff Williams provided generous counsel and ventriloquized the "voice of the profession" at every stage of this project. Janet Lyon was simply Janet Lyon. My extreme indebtedness to Ira Livingston, who brings poetics and politics together like no one else I know. Thanks also to two other Stony Brook stalwarts: Mike Sprinker and Tim Brennan.

Henry Giroux and Neil Larsen, along with New York University Press's able editor Eric Zinner, provided all kinds of advice and encouragement; in a fair world, all three of them would have to share the responsibilities for the failures of this volume. I also want to express awe at Despina Gimbel's professionalism at NYUP.

Biju Mathew and Vijay Prashad, through their new initiatives on behalf of the Forum of Indian Leftists, provide exemplary instances of the efforts required to create democratic and well-informed public spheres of dissent. The same can be said about my other comrades in the diaspora: Anannya Bhattacharjee, S. Shankar, Vivek Bald, Gayatri Gopinath, Shishir Jha, Chandan Reddy, Aamir Mufti, Milind Wakankar, Gurleen Grewal, Raji Mohan, Qadri Ismail, Purnima Bose, Arun Agrawal, and Sanjeev Chatterjee. "Mere seené mein nahin to tere seené mein sahee/ Ho kahin bhi aag, lekin aag jalni chahiye."

It is to the collective labors of these young oppositional intellectuals, working in what Ché Guevara called "the belly of the beast," that this book is dedicated. In solidarity and with greatest affection. "Jiyein to apné bageeché mein gulmohar ke talé/ Marein to gair ki galiyon mein gulmohar ke liye."

Introduction

Amitava Kumar

Op-Ed

In 1995, inside a Pennsylvania prison, the black activist and Peabody Award–winning journalist Mumia Abu-Jamal awaited his execution, which had been set for August 17. A few months before that, in May, when the Marxist Literary Group (a small group of almost entirely U.S.-based academics who practice leftist cultural criticism) met for its Summer Institute in Pittsburgh, there was a panel organized to strategize the mobilization of resistance against a racist judicial system that appeared intent on carrying out this modern-day lynching.

An organizer from the Committee to Save Mumia Abu-Jamal repeatedly told the audience at the Summer Institute that they needed to write letters and articles in newspapers. (Protests, processions organized worldwide by a broad coalition of democratic forces, and, yes, national and international appeals in the media did

1

manage to block Abu-Jamal's execution.) Perhaps the organizer was proffering this particular piece of advice to her audience because they were, after all, a "literary group." And yet here was a matter of general importance that couldn't be disregarded. The next day, during a session entitled "Pedagogy and the Public Sphere," the conversation returned to the political organizer's remark in order to underline the historical relationship between literary criticism in English and the rise of the admittedly limited, liberal bourgeois public sphere in the early eighteenth century. Peter Hohendahl has written in this context, "In the Age of Enlightenment, the concept of criticism cannot be separated from the institution of the public sphere. Every judgement is directed toward a public; communication with the reader is an integral part of the system."[1]

In this post-Enlightenment age, leftist intellectuals rightly aim to present a conflictual rather than a consensual public sphere. But how often do we proceed in search of our publics, and, equally important, what role have we allowed our teaching to play in this scenario? The need for this volume emerged with these basic questions.

In recent years, threatened by financial marginalization and gross vilification at the hands of a reactionary, anti-intellectual political machinery, some in the academy have responded with combative zeal. Michael Bérubé, author of a book tellingly entitled *Public Access*, has argued that cultural critics cannot forgo the task of making popular interventions intelligible to a nonacademic public. "Popularizing academic criticism therefore means, among other things," Bérubé writes, "struggling for the various popular and populist grounds on which the cultural right has been trying to make criticism unpopular."[2]

What critics like Bérubé represent, for me at least, is at once an extension and transformation of the tasks prescribed by an earlier generation of critics like Edward Said. When Said enjoined postcolonial peoples to engage in the task of "diffusing a different form of history, a new kind of sociology, a new cultural awareness," he was demanding that we present counternarratives to contest what he rightly described as "crude, essentialized caricatures."[3] In the aftermath of the attacks on "political correctness" and now the so-called Newt Revolution, it is the status of academic work itself that is under immense scrutiny and the threat of endangerment. Another way of putting this would be that we are faced with the loss of schools and universities as a viable public sphere. For progressive intellectuals at the current juncture, the constitutive entry into the public sphere is as much about constructing the proper object of criticism as it is about protecting it. In short, it is a struggle for survival.

It is not enough for me, answering Said's call, to write a column in the local paper in the days preceding the Atlanta Olympic Games, telling viewers that the next time they heard the NBC commentators go gaga over a U.S. victory against another small Third World nation, they should remember to ask preliminary questions like, when was the last time Bush bombed that country, or Reagan imposed an embargo against it, or whoever else named Rockefeller or Guggenheim stole copper from its shores. (Think of the feeling of silly triumph after the U.S. "dream team"'s victory against Angola in the Barcelona Games. Angola has only two modern indoor gyms and its professional basketball is still sustained entirely through its absorption in the markets of its former colonial master, Portugal.) Instead, for cultural critics and intellectuals, it has become vital to inform the reading public of the devastation wrought by the economic and political priorities of the ruling elite. That, for example, the state of Florida spends more on its 56,000 prisoners than its 220,000 university students or 300,000 community college students. That we must wage battles against a corporate culture and its minions in the legislature who are imposing massive cuts in the funds for education. (Surely, a Mississippi state legislator's malaprop "More education is not a pancreas" quite effectively reveals that those who do the hurting are also getting hurt.)[4]

The grim alienation that many of the essays in this volume convey are the effects of the contempt in which the dominant ideology holds all efforts at securing a real education. The scars revealed by some of these writers are also the signs of many battles successfully engaged and the considerable possibilities opened up by collective, innovative struggles both inside and outside the classroom. In other words, for many readers and potential writers, these essays will provide materials—and certainly reasons—for engaging in a public defense of education and the values threatened by a dangerous culture of corporate downsizing.

All the contributors to this volume may not put the same value on the fight for a place for our opinions in the public sphere; none among them, however, I'd be prepared to argue, would doubt that such an effort must be a part of a broader strategy or movement. The need to theorize and understand in some careful and elaborate ways the strategies as well as the goals of a progressive academic project might be defined as the more central concern of the essays that follow.

While none of these essays are even in the slightest sense quarantined from contact with the world outside, their focus is determinedly on the classroom space and the practice of teaching. In fact, it is precisely from the position of pedagogy that aspects of the broader culture are engaged. In this regard, this volume signals an unwillingness to surrender to that kind of disciplinary terrorism, holding sway over left intellectuals in the past, that has dictated a silence on issues of one's own self-formation as well as a lingering inattentiveness to the operations of power in and through the production of values, identities, and social relations.

This "odd reluctance," as Neil Larsen comments in his excellent essay in this volume, is odd not only because teaching is what most left intellectuals do in this country, but also because a relation of theory to pedagogy, in Marxism at least, is "an internal, dialectical necessity." Tough Marxists, who see their own positioning in the academy as a retreat from the real battles outside, are often too dismissive of their work in the classroom and shamefaced about cultural struggles to give much thought to pedagogy. On the other hand, there are those who, every time they toss another oppositional reading of a text or uncover the contradictions cleaving the dominant discourse, rather easily assume swift reversals without being forced to think through questions of real gains and popular mobilization. In either case, seriously assessing what one does in the classroom—and how—is a task that remains largely ignored.

In the introduction to his new book, *Fugitive Cultures*, Henry Giroux (also a contributor to this anthology) rightly notes that "cultural studies often fails to address how the politics of pedagogy actually operates within schools and other educational sites."[5] The writers in this volume grapple with the problems and the histories that, as Raymond Williams would put it, "make learning a part of the process of social change itself."[6] Not simply learning in the classroom, but learning from reading this book too. In that sense, this volume inaugurates a dialogue, not through metacommentaries on the politics in education via the P.C. wars, but through its addressal of the ordinary politics of everyday teaching, curricular reform, local activism, and global shifts.

This turn, in itself, reflects a change: we are learning to invent our publics and ourselves: as teachers, as students, as activists, as global workers. Or not. Which means we are learning about the fatal errors of dominant assumptions that "the essence of knowledge is knowledge about knowledge, and if you know the right thing your mind will change, and if your mind changes you will do good." As Gayatri Chakravorty Spivak writes in her essay in this collection, "We must remind ourselves that knowledge and thinking are halfway houses, that they are judged when they are set to work. Perhaps this can break our vanguardism that knowledge is acquired to be applied."

The essays in part I open our interest to the altered space of the classroom, showing how the category of literature has been replaced by a set of concerns

about culture. George Lipsitz identifies the different vocabularies that help articulate, in the classroom, life experiences defined by social class; Bruce Robbins
introduces a concept of "fraught aesthetics" to reexamine the mediations
between the literature classroom and the world around it; Maria Damon presents
for us the irruption of micropoetries that have inaugurated new, alternative public spheres; John Mowitt, in his approach to literature, examines the pedagogical
limitations of an instrumentalized classroom; and Donald Hedrick argues for a
popular (rather than elitist) notion of history in the teaching of literature involving early modern periods.

In complicated meditations on what one might call a specifically Marxist theory
of teaching, Neil Larsen and Gayatri Chakravorty Spivak put forward arguments
for a critical internationalism. While Larsen offers a historical contextualization of
pedagogies of theory and theories of pedagogy as practiced in the U.S. academy,
Spivak clearly instantiates her call—issued some years ago—for Marxism to
reinvent itself "in the pores of feminism." Here, her report on a course on global
feminist theory, accompanied by a working class-syllabus, offers a stringent critique of "remote-control bleeding-heart feminism." These two essays are comple-
mented in part 2 by a philosophical contribution by Peter Hitchcock on how a
cultural studies pedagogy can approach, following Marx, "the enigma of value."
Alan Wald undertakes a detailed survey of a "pedagogy of unlearning" in the
combined personal and political histories of recent radical teaching in the United
States. Similarly, Mike Hill's essay sketches a genealogy of cultural studies and its
relation to such aspects as mass culture and the labor crisis. Ronald Strickland's
essay recuperates the term "accountability" in order to produce a model of pedagogy and public service that holds the university and its practices answerable
ultimately to the laboring public.

In part 3, forceful attempts are made to assess the role of intellectuals and produce contestatory agendas for mobilization. Henry Giroux's broad-ranging essay
on the role and relevance of public intellectuals critiques the celebratory corona-
tion of certain black intellectuals. Rachel Buff and Jason Loviglio enter into dialogue on the prevailing political and cultural backlash, in their classrooms,
against the idea of "the public." Carol Stabile contests the conflation of professional and political practice: a deliberation on the limits of the classroom. Timothy Brennan offers an alternative genealogy of cultural studies, locating in the
process global resources of cultural resistance. Last, Jeffrey Di Leo and Christian
Moraru collaborate on a list of necessities for a pedagogy to suit a "posttheory"
generation.

The essays in part 4 represent new, divergent challenges for left pedagogy in this country. Included in this section are Vijay Prashad's essay arguing that a dialectical principle of teaching must present contradictions—"the other worlds"—in the classroom; Judith Halberstam's injunctions for a radical transformation of queer studies in favor of transgender studies; Gregory Ulmer's use of the avant-garde family album to produce an alternative public sphere; John P. Leavey's meditation on the pedagogy of the apostrophe, a pedagogy out of joint with any settled assumption; and Jeffrey Williams's frankly cynical view of the current interest in pedagogy. Each of these essays, in their particular ways, expands and lends specificity, in the current conjuncture, to the search for oppositional pedagogies and oppositional public spheres.

NOTES

1. Peter Uwe Hohendahl, *The Institution of Criticism* (Ithaca: Cornell University Press, 1982), 52.
2. Michael Bérubé, *Public Access: Literary Theory and American Cultural Politics* (London: Verso, 1994), 176.
3. Edward Said, *Covering Islam* (New York: Pantheon, 1981), 63, 26.
4. See Amitava Kumar, "Education Priorities Out of Reach," *Gainesville Sun*, May 4, 1996, 6A; and idem, "The Real Meaning of the Olympics," *Gainesvile Sun*, July 6, 1996, 6A.
5. Henry A. Giroux, *Fugitive Cultures: Race, Violence, and Youth* (New York: Routledge, 1996), 18. See also Amitava Kumar, "In Praise of the Consciousness Industry," *American Quarterly* 47, no. 4 (December 1995): 750–55.
6. Raymond Williams, quoted in Giroux, 20.

Part I

Literature and Beyond

Class and Consciousness
Teaching about Social Class in Public Universities

George Lipsitz

1

If nothing else, the Republican "freshman class" elected to Congress in the 1994 elections has made valuable contributions to the folklore of the future. Certainly the "tall tales" and exaggerations in traditional U.S. folk stories about Paul Bunyan or John Henry pale in comparison to the yarn spun by Representative Fred Heineman of North Carolina about social class in America. Heineman observed that "someone who is making anywhere from $300,000 to $750,000 a year, that's middle class. When I see someone above that, that's upper middle class."[1] Since 96 percent of Americans earn less than $100,000 a year, we might conclude from the congressman's comments that almost no one in the United States is middle-class, that poverty is more widespread than even the most alarmist critics have noticed. More plausibly, we might take this comment as evidence of how parochial and isolated rich people are in our society, how dwelling in isolated enclaves, talking mostly to one another, and living lives organized

9

exclusively around the love of gain leaves them with a completely false understanding of their own status, privileges, and advantages.

Of course, Representative Heineman probably did not intend his remarks to be
taken as a statistical description of the U.S. class structure. To be charitable and to
give him the benefit of the doubt, we should recognize that while false in statistical terms, his formulation captures an important aspect of our society's ideology
about social class: it does not exist. Our shared social language about wealth,
reward, status, and stratification encourages everyone to think of themselves as
middle-class. We are taught to desire riches and flaunt the symbols of wealth
without ever admitting that anyone is actually rich. We are taught that labor is
honorable in the abstract but in actuality something to be imposed on others
whenever possible. We are taught that individual ingenuity and effort will enable
us to secure rewards proportionate to our social contributions, yet never to speak
about the ways the distribution of education, assets, and opportunities is severely
skewed along class lines. We might from time to time talk about "disadvantaged"
populations, but almost never do we connect their disadvantages to their
exploitation, subordination, and suppression as low-wage or unemployed laborers, as people taken advantage of or as people whose "disadvantages" secure
pleasant and profitable advantages for others.[2]

As educators, we are implicated in our society's erasure of class. In a singu-
larly important essay in *College English* some years ago, Linda Brodkey asked
teachers why the realities of social class that are so pervasive in American society
remain largely unaddressed in the classroom. Brodkey speculated that prevailing
classroom practices and pedagogies contain an institutionalized allegiance to
middle-class norms and ideologies that suppress any direct acknowledgment of
class divisions.[3] Educators, students, and parents rarely recognize the role of the
classroom as a place where labor is socialized, where people learn the requisite
values, attitudes, and behaviors needed to make them docile, compliant, and
productive workers and citizens. Instead, the classroom in our culture is seen as
a site for upward mobility, a place where workers might gain the resources
needed to make themselves supervisors, where entrepreneurs might become professionals, where professionals might join the ranks of upper management. This
creates a "hidden curriculum" that influences every aspect of learning and
teaching.

We know from detailed sociological studies that the ideals of meritocratic
upward mobility bear little relation to actual social experience.[4] Yet, while
rarely accomplished in fact, the mere promise of upward mobility depends on

the suppression of class tensions, the erasure of class differences, and the con-struction of an ideological "middle-class" identity that is not so much a descrip-tion of actual social roles or status as an affirmation of allegiance to competition, individual ambition, and the pursuit of personal material gain as the center of the social world. As a result, our pedagogical practices privilege activities that encourage students to distinguish and differentiate themselves from their class-mates, to pretend that knowledge is an atomized individual activity rather than a shared social act. Destructive as process, these practices also have negative con-sequences for the production of knowledge. By reinforcing ideologies that see social existence as primarily private and personal, our teaching discourages social theory. Just as we divide knowledge into separate subjects, departments, and classrooms, our students compartmentalize the things they learn into dis-crete and disconnected fragments. This way of knowing about the world is a deficient approach to all subjects, but it is particularly inadequate for under-standing social relations and the connections that link individual lives to broad social structures.

The study of social class as an element of classroom instruction can offer important opportunities to create a more dynamic, productive, and useful learn-ing process. But it is difficult to do. Students may not enjoy reading and writing about other kinds of social identities like race and gender. Their inquiries into these areas may raise painful, divisive, and difficult discussions. Yet to most stu-dents, race and gender are legible as social identities and legitimate as social issues. The existence and importance of gender and race are recognized, rein-forced, and represented repeatedly in political and journalistic discourse as well as in advertising and entertainment. But social class is another matter. In my experience, my students have found it nearly impossible to identify the vocabu-laries and grammars they would need in school to articulate and analyze experi-ences and perspectives defined by social class, at least at first. In contrast, their out of school experiences often offer rich storehouses of evidence, insight, and eloquent expression about social class, most of which they judge inappropriate for discussions in school, where the language of civics instruction and the imper-atives of optimistic discourse about one's life chances reign largely unchallenged.

Most discussions of curriculum and pedagogy suffer from a lack of specificity. We know that there are many kinds of students, many kinds of teachers, and many kinds of classrooms, yet we sometimes act as if these diverse situations can be addressed by one kind of curriculum or one kind of pedagogy. My teaching experiences have spanned a broad range of contexts, from elite private schools to prison education programs, from correspondence courses to classes in community centers, from advanced graduate courses to museum lectures for the general public. The study of social class has presented problems in each of these sites, albeit for vastly different reasons. In this essay, I want to focus on one particular context that has occupied most of my attention for the past ten years—teaching undergraduate and graduate courses at large public universities. I present my efforts to end the silence about class in my classroom not as an all-purpose model capable of implementation in any teaching situation, but rather as an intervention in one particular context with its own specific needs and demands.

At a university where all that most students know about the working class is that they do not want to be a part of it, my strategy has been to ask my students to study the history of how working people in the United States have struggled to represent themselves and their experiences. In one sense of the word "representation," this means the translation of experiences, actions, ideas, and aspirations into artistic forms—literally to "re-present" something in another form. Yet these struggles for artistic representation have also been part and parcel of a desire for political representation, an effort to build structures and institutions of power capable of addressing and redressing the indignities and alienations of working-class life. In order to capture both senses of the word "representation" and to explore both the structural and cultural dimensions of social class, my curriculum revolves around an examination of "proletarian" fiction, social history, and labor law of the 1930s.

We begin with an illustrative anecdote presented near the end of Jack Conroy's Depression-era "proletarian" novel, *The Disinherited*. During much of the novel up to that point, Conroy's narrator has been struggling for upward mobility, striving to leave behind the working-class world of his parents and to enjoy the rewards and benefits of "white-collar" work. He attends night school, apprentices himself to a successful executive, and reads self-help literature assiduously. But all his efforts have been in vain. He finds himself instead working on a highway construction crew in a small Midwestern town on a hot summer day. The unrelenting demands of hard physical labor have taken a toll on the members of the road crew; their muscles ache, their nerves are frayed, their tempers are short. It is not just that they have to do unpleasant work for little reward, their plight embarrasses them, it reminds them of the lost dreams and blasted hopes of their youth, it seems to mock them for ever having wanted something better.

Finally, their frustration erupts into some boisterous and rambunctious horseplay. During a break they begin pushing and shoving and pelting each other with rocks and dirt. But their fun ends when a well-dressed woman nearby gathers her young son in her arms and tells him not to be afraid, that she will protect him from the "bad men." Hearing her words, the workers feel a mixture of resentment and shame. They know that they are not "bad men," that their behavior stems from how they have been humbled by poverty and humiliated by the indignities of low-wage labor. Yet they also feel ashamed and guilty. They know how they look to the woman and her son; inside each of them an inner voice says that she is correct. But then Conroy's narrator makes an interesting leap. He connects the contempt he feels from this protective mother to his relationship with his own mother, a "coal camp" wife who cleaned other people's homes all day and then came home to do her own family's chores. He recalls how the skin on her hands cracked open from the abrasive lye soap she had to use in her own work. He muses that the "canned" sentiments in Mother's Day messages on greeting cards or Western Union telegrams are intended for mothers like the one shielding her son from the road gang, that "motherhood" itself is a middle-class category accessible to some mothers and not to others. Through this realization, Conroy's narrator sees that social class is a system, that the distance between classes can be measured by his own shame in knowing how he looks to the middle-class woman, by the distance between his own mother's life and the middle-class motherhood constructed in popular culture, and by the inarguable legitimacy of the middle-class mother's contempt for men who have no way to argue the injustice of their own circumstances.[5]

Raised on Horatio Alger stories about upward mobility, pluck, and luck, surrounded by sentimental stories representing love, affection, and mutuality as available only in the middle-class family, Conroy's narrator feels a gap between his own social experience and the representations that strike him as "true" even when they conflict with his own experience.[6] These stories make his life seem wrong because his experiences do not conform to the contours of his society's dominant cultural ideals. They sting because he knows them from the inside, having once believed in them himself. They conform to what political scientist James C. Scott calls the "public transcript"—the representation of reality favored by dominant groups and performed endlessly by members of oppressed groups as evidence of their desire to share in the rewards and benefits apportioned out by those in power.[7]

Yet while Conroy's narrator defers to dominant ideologies, he cannot quite accept them. The gap between his experiences and the stories told about them eventually leads him to participate in politics, in collective mass action. Toward the end of the novel he confronts the organizing drives and mass mobilizations that will eventually produce the Congress of Industrial Organizations and its efforts to win collective bargaining rights for workers in heavy industry. His sympathy for the union comes as much from his feelings of exclusion from the messages in Mother's Day cards as it does from an understanding of union politics, as much from a redeployment of the shame and humiliation he experiences in the disapproving gaze of the middle-class mother as from concrete trade union policies about wages or working conditions. The narrator of the novel identifies the inner life of the worker as an important terrain of class struggle; whatever it does in the way of redistributing resources and opportunities in society at large, collective mass action also silences inner doubts and reworks old identities in ways that are both therapeutic to the individuals involved and subversive to prevailing power relations in society at large.

Rich as it is, Conroy's text does not present transparent truths about working-class life. Constructed as propaganda by a worker-intellectual sympathetic to the Communist Party, *The Disinherited* represents working-class life through stories that are every bit as partial, perspectival, and interested as those they critique. The book is a product of the social movement it describes; Conroy's role as worker-writer emerged from his own life experience, but he found institutional support and outlets for publication through the organized activity of the Communist Party and the broader social movement of which it was an integral part. It is this social movement that is left untheorized in the book. The mass activity central to CIO organizing appears as a *deus ex machina*, "a storm about to break," rather than the product of concrete conditions and practical politics.

Like other texts of its time, *The Disinherited* makes defense of working-class interests a matter of defending masculinity. It presents its discussions of social class by coasting on preexisting languages about gender. Conroy's dramatic contrasts—between the boisterous male horseplay and the disapproving middle-class mother's gaze, between the virile working class and the bourgeois feminized family, between working-class men robbed of their ability to protect women or children and the middle-class female's privileged role—all rely on sexist and gendered hierarchies that flow more from the masculist language of class struggle than from the actual realities of working-class life where, after all, women are workers too.[8]

Conroy's perceptive account of how workers come to think of themselves as part of a class remains incomplete because he does not probe adequately the political processes, social structures, and gendered categories that shaped the actual historical events that *The Disinherited* both envisions and enacts. We need to turn to social history to connect Conroy's text to its full historical context. Recent works by Lizabeth Cohen and Vicki Ruiz, for example, provide indispensable insights that amplify Conroy's analysis and augment his arguments about class and class consciousness. Their research reveals the broader social and political matrices in which workers like Conroy's narrator were located during the Great Depression, how class consciousness emerged out of more than individual alienation and transformation, but rather from the collective consequences of broader social changes in the identities and institutions central to working-class life.

In *Making a New Deal*, Cohen shows how the Great Depression damaged ethnic institutions and discredited their leaders in Chicago.[9] The wave of business and bank failures, mortgage foreclosures, pay cuts, layoffs, and evictions that characterized the Depression overtaxed the resources of ethnic self-help and charitable associations, called attention to class differences within ethnic communities, and encouraged the growth of political and cultural alliances along ethnic lines. The narratives of nationality that had previously been so effective in explaining and ordering much of working-class life in a land where so many workers had been immigrants and so many immigrants had been workers gradually gave way to class-wide identities. Cohen explains how trade union organizing by the Congress of Industrial Organizations revolved around a "culture of unity" that stressed the ways people from different ethnic groups could work together for common goals.

This culture of unity did not arise spontaneously from a shared relationship to the means of production; it was created through collective mass action. Workers decided to emphasize the things that united them instead of those that divided them because they became convinced it was in their collective interest to do so. Cohen points out that capitalists made their task somewhat easier through rationalization of production and consumption that gave previously divided workers similar if not identical experiences with the same chain grocery stores, motion pictures, and automated work sites. Yet those commonalities could just as easily have become the basis for even greater fragmentation and differentiation based on segmented markets and job opportunities.

During the 1930s, interethnic political mobilizations made Anton Cermak mayor of Chicago and propelled Fiorello La Guardia to the same post in New York. The journalism of Louis Adamic celebrated the Statue of Liberty in order to circulate a new image of America as a land of immigrants whose descendants built a unity based on open acknowledgment of their differences. In *Cannery Women/Cannery Lives*, Ruiz tells a similar story about Los Angeles. She shows how women workers from diverse ethnic backgrounds found common ground in CIO organizing efforts, how interethnic unity in urban neighborhoods translated into class solidarity and pro-union consciousness at work, and how in turn, collective bargaining and trade union representation gave them an institutional protection against distinctly gendered oppressions, like sexual harassment at work.

In their accounts, Cohen and Ruiz show that class consciousness does not arise solely from the inner life of the worker or from injustices at the point of production. They show how the Great Depression damaged previous identifications with ethnicity as the primary locus of individual and collective identity, how political mobilization enabled workers to experience new identities, and how cultural practices helped define the content of class consciousness. Most important, they identify class not only as a structural relationship with the means of production, but also as an individual and collective form of self-definition forged through practice on many fronts. These studies from social history underscore the connections between political representation and cultural representation. They show how working-class people have had to struggle to defend their interests and define themselves. They illustrate the importance of institutional resources, political processes, and cultural categories in enacting imagined class solidarities. But they also show that class consciousness is more than a state of mind, that physical force and legal repression always stand in the way of any potential class unities and identifications.

Social historians Cohen and Ruiz offer important insights into the process of class formation during the 1930s, but their inspirational accounts of successful organizing drives by CIO unions tell only part of the story. Even during the Great Depression and World War II, trade union membership in the United States has never involved even half of the working class, and perhaps even more significant, the gains made by organized workers have come at the expense of those who are unorganized. Rather than victories for the working class as a whole, trade union triumphs have all too often created new stratifications within the working class itself. To understand how the emancipatory hopes and democratic practices detailed by Conroy, Cohen, and Ruiz have failed to realize their own best instincts, we need to turn to labor law, to the processes by which direct action and mass mobilization have become institutionalized in labor-management relations and in working-class life.

During times of social crisis like the Great Depression, insurgent movements can win concessions from elites that promise to institutionalize in law the gains they have made through direct action protests. In 1935, Congress passed the Wagner Act, legislation that created the National Labor Relations Board, enumerated fair labor practices, recognized the rights of workers to secure representation for collective bargaining purposes, and involved the government in fashioning relative equity at the bargaining table between labor and management. Yet the ideological assumptions encoded within the law worked to insulate rather than institutionalize the victories won by mass struggle. Careful scrutiny of this law and its implementation exposes another important dimension of the relationships linking representation and social class.

The Wagner Act establishes labor unions as administrative units under federal supervision, unlike business corporations, which enjoy status as "legal persons" under the law.[10] The Wagner Act poses the right to organize a union and bargain with employers as an individual "civil right" created by this act alone and subject to its specific conditions and restrictions. Yet workers clearly had this "right" long before passage of the Wagner Act. How could unions have existed and functioned as representatives of workers if they had no right to do so? What unions historically lacked was the power to compel business to bargain with them. During the Depression, the success of union organizing drives and the defensiveness of capital combined to pose a real threat to capital, and it was at this point that leaders of business and government consented to place labor-management relations under federal supervision.

The Wagner Act gave no new rights to workers, but it did employ a doctrine of countervailing power in an attempt to insure relatively equal bargaining power between unions and businesses. However, only those unions sufficiently positioned to disrupt production in key industries could actually take advantage of the procedures and protections enumerated in the Wagner Act. These unions could force company representatives to come to the bargaining table or they could involve government officials in efforts to secure social peace and uninterrupted production. The Wagner Act did not even cover farmworkers or domestics, and it was of no real practical use to workers and unions who did not already have the power to compel employers to bargain. Smaller groups of less strategically located or less actively mobilized workers could be fired and intimidated just as before, despite the existence of the Wagner Act.

Conservative labor leaders from the American Federation of Labor distrusted the Wagner Act from the start, precisely because it refused to acknowledge any existing rights for labor independent of those granted by the act, but the more liberal leaders of the Congress of Industrial Organizations embraced the bill because they saw in it a key resource for institutionalizing the gains workers had won during the 1930s. But while the Wagner Act worked in the short run to secure government protection for union organizing in large industries, it ultimately served as an ideal tool for management efforts to insulate workers from a broader social constituency, to undermine unions by turning them into instruments of industrial discipline. In return for institutional recognition and government supervision, unions committed themselves to giving management a virtually free hand to determine the nature, pace, purpose, and rewards of productions.

From the start, the National Labor Relations Board used the doctrines of "economic duress" and "countervailing power" to hide systematic imbalances in power between labor and capital.[11] The board attempted to protect the institutional power of labor unions and corporations, with little regard for the experiences, opinions, or aspirations of rank-and-file workers. As a result, leaders of unions, business, and government gradually identified labor peace and economic stability as the main goals of the act. Slowdowns and strikes at the point of production and community mass mobilizations away from the factory floor threatened those relations, and consequently came to be seen as practices to be forbidden. NLRB interpretations of the Wagner Act between 1935 and 1947 laid the foundation for the Taft-Hartley Act of 1947. This bill further undercut the power of rank-and-file workers in order to build up the institutional power of trade unions. The new law banned secondary boycotts and general strikes, and it transformed union officials into company agents authorized to police the shop floor. Although many union leaders denounced the bill and applauded President Truman's veto of it, nearly all of Taft-Hartley's antilabor provisions had already been implemented through NLRB interpretations of the Wagner Act. In addition, labor leaders put up only token resistance to the bill once it was passed, disciplining workers and local union leaders who wanted to use direct action strikes and demonstrations to defeat the new law. After Congress passed the bill over Truman's veto, labor leaders used it effectively to consolidate their institutional power at the expense of dissident locals and shop floor factions.[12]

The Wagner and Taft-Hartley Acts insulated the trade unions from broader social mobilizations and made them agents of increased production on the factory floor. But in addition, like other aspects of U.S. labor law, these legal acts made much of working-class life disappear from legal scrutiny. The mass uprisings and general strikes that forced concessions from business and government in the first place often originated in responses to alienated labor, in recognition of the common goals and ambitions of diverse groups of workers, in the aggressive festivity of mass action. Labor law, in this case, makes the working class disappear, denies protection to its most important political practices, and places it under the supervision of business, the state, and the trade unions in the service of labor peace and uninterrupted production. It destroys the institutions workers created in the processes of mass struggle, but more important, it seeks to supervise the sites and proscribe the practices where the articulation of class identity emerged in the first place.

By combining *The Disinherited, Making a New Deal, Cannery Women/Cannery Lives,* and close examination of the Wagner Act, students may get an understanding of how complicated the category of class can be. They may view it as something created by both human agency and social structure, by social institutions and social imagination, by direct solidarity and sophisticated coalition building. Of course, they will respond to Conroy's fiction, the social histories by Ruiz and Cohen, and the letter and substance of the Wagner Act in diverse ways. Some of my students see Conroy's narrator as a whiner and complainer, someone who would succeed if he would only persist in the practices of self-help, hard work, and individualism. Others find the mass struggles described by Cohen and Ruiz nothing to celebrate; they see them as mob actions responsible for the creation of a welfare state that unnecessarily inhibits capital accumulation by individuals and corporations. Some students view the idea of working-class self-activity and self-representation as unreasonable and utopian, something too complicated and sophisticated to be accomplished by ordinary workers. Others view the mystifications of labor law as necessary and inevitable structures for insuring stability, predictability, and security for investors. Yet even these responses entail an engagement with the realities of social class, the struggle for self-representation, the history of class mobilizations, and the institutional practices of class control. For other students, these explorations unmask the illusion of a classless society, explain important aspects of the history of individual and collective identities, and uncover the institutional barriers to a politics of class. They provide an in-school language for the class consciousness and conflicts they encounter repeatedly as gendered subjects, citizens, consumers, and community members.

My goal is not to create one idealized curriculum or one true representation of social class. But I do wish to show how every representation leaves something out, how every struggle to tell a story is also a struggle to displace a story. Most important, I hope to engage my students in processes that will lead them to understand and analyze the nature of social class today, to understand that they live the lives they do because other people have to clean their classrooms, grow their food, build their houses, and sew their clothes under conditions they do not control for rewards that increasingly do not allow them to meet their own basic needs. I hope to show that identities of race and gender always intersect with class, that unlikely coalitions across identity categories have succeeded in the past, but only when people honestly acknowledged the things that divided them and created actual practices and structures of inclusion rather than just abstract calls for unity.

The ever increasing economic power of multinational corporations, the stagnation of real wages in the United States and the growth of low-wage labor jobs, the evisceration of the welfare state and the social wage, the austerity that drives people to migrate far from their homes looking for work, and the destructive polarities of wealth and poverty that characterize contemporary urban life all demand a theoretical and practical understanding of class often absent in our classrooms. The erasure of social class is one of the limitations of meaning that Michael Ryan identifies as central to education's unfortunate role in curtailing social possibilities and eliminating "potential political alternatives."[13]

History shows us how hard people have had to fight for the most elementary resources—food, a place to live, a job. But the fight for knowledge, for the right to know and the right to act on that knowledge, is no less important. Our students will come to their own conclusions when they read texts about social class. But whatever they conclude, they will be better prepared for the future if they know that for many people at many different times there has been a class struggle even more important than the one between the teachers and the students.

NOTES

1. "Go Back to Class," *Dollars and Sense*, no. 203 (January–February 1996): 4.
2. What would happen, for example, if all of the unemployed population found jobs tomorrow? Would they be welcomed into the workforce? Or would Alan Greenspan and the Federal Reserve Board decide that full employment was inflationary, that it threatened management control over the pay, pace, and purpose of production? I think it is clear that Greenspan would raise interest rates until unemployment reached 5 or 6 percent. Yet our public policy discussions would continue to blame the

internal character, family experiences, and work ethic of the unemployed for what is obviously a structured as well as structural crisis.

3. Linda Brodkey, "On the Subjects of Class and Gender in *The Literacy Letters,*" *College English* 51 (1989): 125–41.

4. See, for example, Melvin L. Oliver and Thomas M. Shapiro, *Black Wealth/White Wealth* (New York: Routledge, 1995), chapter 4 especially. Frank S. Levy, *Dollars and Dreams: The Changing American Income Distribution* (New York: Norton, 1987).

5. Jack Conroy, *The Disinherited* (Westport, CT: Lawrence Hill, 1982).

6. See Richard Weiss, *The American Myth of Success: From Horatio Alger to Norman Vincent Peale* (New York: Basic Books, 1969).

7. James C. Scott, *Domination and the Arts of Resistance: Hidden Transcripts* (New Haven: Yale University Press, 1990).

8. See Paula Rabinowitz, *Labor and Desire* (Chapel Hill: University of North Carolina Press, 1991) for a detailed analysis of the relationship between gender and genre in 1930s leftist fiction.

9. Lizabeth Cohen, *Making a New Deal* (Cambridge: Cambridge University Press, 1991). See also George Sanchez, *Becoming Mexican American* (New York: Oxford University Press, 1993).

10. Christopher L. Tomlins, *The State and the Unions: Labor Relations, Law and the Organized Labor Movement in America, 1860–1960* (Baltimore: Johns Hopkins University Press, 1989), 101–2.

11. Roberto Mangabeira Unger, *The Critical Legal Studies Movement* (Cambridge: Harvard University Press, 1986), 70–71.

12. George Lipsitz, *Rainbow at Midnight: Labor and Culture in the 1940s* (Urbana: University of Illinois Press, 1994).

13. Michael Ryan, *Politics and Culture* (Basingstoke, England: Macmillan, 1989), 169.

The Return to Literature

Bruce Robbins

In the fall of 1995 I taught an undergraduate comparative literature course on upward mobility narratives that began by linking Jonathan Demme's film *Silence of the Lambs* to Balzac's novel *Le Père Goriot*. The hinge I was most interested in was the figure of the mentor or mediator, Hannibal Lecter in *Silence of the Lambs* and Vautrin in *Le Père Goriot*, and the point I most wanted the students to get was that it was this figure, a criminal, indeed a murderer, a figure of sexual as well as moral ambiguity, and in some sense a very attractive figure, who presided over the protagonist's social ascent and did most of the work of filling in its unexpectedly ambiguous meanings.

I offer this as an example of benign coexistence between the literary and the nonliterary within a frame that might as well be called cultural studies—that is, an example of a kind of work that I hope those who want us to return to literary studies in an older, more restrictive sense will not succeed in shutting down. But

I also offer these morally and erotically ambiguous mediators of upward mobility—figures who perhaps lurk behind the influence of Michel Foucault over aspiring students of cultural studies today—as a metaphor for the institutional and affective reality of both literary and cultural studies, a metaphor that's meant as a somewhat sobering alternative to the many passionate avowals of "love for literature" that have been urging us to put the literary back in its proper place in our hearts.

Even the most cautious supporters of the "back to literature" movement seem unable to explain themselves these days without recourse to a provocative lexicon of passion or sensuality. I'll cite one example, among many, from a representative argument by Elaine Marks. Complaining about "the deadly weight imposed on literary texts by the insistence on 'relevant' moral and social issues" (3), Marks writes as follows: "I must confess that what continues to stir my imagination and even to turn me on" is literary masterpieces. "I came into our profession through a passionate curiosity about and love for a modern language and literature. . . . This curiosity and this love have not faded."[1]

There is no need to doubt the genuineness of the passion thus displayed in order to be a bit uncomfortable with the meaning of the display itself. The rhetoric of confession at first seems timid, as if (like literature itself in one of its better known definitions) it dared to affirm nothing at all beyond the truth of its own feelings. But it is better described, I think, as passive/aggressive, for the apparent timidity (this is only what I feel) protects from reasoned argument assertions that have a hidden sting. Like displaying an American flag on my bumper, displaying my love for literature implies that unnamed others do not love literature, or do not love it passionately or faithfully enough. It is as if we were offered the following parody of a syllogism: I love literature, and there's no denying the authenticity of my feelings; I love literature, and that's how I got into this profession; I love literature, and there's no denying that the true essence of this profession is what provokes and nourishes my unarguable feelings: literary criticism is what I love to do. Literary criticism: love it (love what I loved when I first entered it) or leave it.

I myself do not love the nativist, Moral Majority tone of this, with its strong suggestion that an ethical or political criticism, say, would be adulterous or unfaithful criticism. I'm not against the offering of feelings as evidence, or against acknowledging how much feelings have to do with our profession. On the contrary. However, there are feelings and there are feelings. In a response to Marks, Jonathan Culler noted that "Love without aggressivity, transference, sadomasochism, identification, or fetishization is scarcely love at all."[2] Mediatory terms like transference have the virtue of reminding us that when I say that I love literature, other people and other feelings are also involved.[3]

If critics tend to use the vocabulary of eroticism when they describe an initial attraction to their discipline, it is perhaps because disciplines seek to reproduce themselves, and because the process of reproduction, in disciplines as in couples, requires the mobilizing of libidinal energy. This is true for all legitimizing discourse aimed at the public, but the moment of greatest libidinal drama for a discipline, its equivalent to the adventure of sexual bonding that structures so many novels, is the moment of recruitment—the moment when a member of the public is picked out and drawn toward the disciplinary community. From the point of view of the recruit, it's a moment that has something in common with falling in love. And all the more so to the extent that disciplinary or professional communities, dispersed geographically in networks across the nation and now across the world, take over some of the emotional functions of families and residential communities, which are more localized.[4]

It was exactly this zone of cultural history that I wanted to start mapping in the upward mobility course. My speculative hypothesis, developed from an argument by Gayatri Chakravorty Spivak about *Jane Eyre*, was that since the nineteenth century such narratives have tended to replace a problematic of "companionate love," that is, the reproduction of the family, with a problematic of what Spivak calls "soulmaking," a sort of nonbiological reproduction that is centered outside the family, in civil society.[5] That is, narratives begin to take as their problematic the reproduction of institutions other than the family, institutions like professions, corporations, and disciplines. When Spivak shows that the marriage plot between Jane and Rochester is interrupted and inflected by Jane's desire for meaningful professional work, a desire that finds expression in the St. John Rivers/"missionary" subplot and the reproduction of British imperialism, I take her to be suggesting that the displacement of erotic energies outside the reproduction of the family, which we see in films like *Silence of the Lambs*, *Interview with the Vampire*, and *Clerks*, is already going strong in the nineteenth-century novel and its ambiguous valuations of "unnatural" mentorship and "unnatural" eroticism.

The hardest part of all this to get at in the classroom was not the idea that literature departments too have their own reproductive erotics, that teaching therefore has its parallels to Vautrin's feeding off the emotions of good-looking young

rastively as that which blocks or diverts us from the simple purpose
nt communication. Literature is a vehicle for the expression and preser
llective experience, among other things. And if this means it shares son
th lots of other sorts of discourse, including historical documents that se
ally sophisticated or self-reflexive or undecidable, it seems to me that the
es can be noted and duly respected without becoming the single, definiti
ion on which we desperately try to base our identity, a sort of excuse fo
nary "identity politics" in the worst sense of the term. If our students
tory from us, or their sociology, or their philosophy, so be it. What we sh
her disciplines counts too. It may not advertise the uniqueness of our pro
it's not a negligible claim for the significance of what we do.

I more time, I would have liked to say more about Michel Foucau
account of the paradox of "commentary" (saying for the first time wh
t had already said, repeating tirelessly what it had never said) belongs
my own stories of disciplinary first love.[14] Students who come to sch
pward mobility on their minds will often find that Foucault is the men
ir mentors, the Matthew Arnold of cultural studies, our most seducti
ter. The figure who described the confessions of Pierre Rivière, nineteen
y parricide, as "beautiful," Foucault is so seductive, I think, because li
n and Lecter he manages to represent both the transgression of power a
r itself, and because both the power and the transgression of power
died in a version of the aesthetic. My concluding question, then,
her this somewhat contradictory ideological content might have anything
ith the upward mobility narratives brought to and read in our classroom
reframe this as a hypothesis, I'm suggesting that the debate over the place
iterary in cultural studies may have more to do than we think with the as
ns of our students. John Guillory, following Bourdieu, distinguishes betwe
rking-class aesthetics of sensual pleasure and a bourgeois aesthetics of dis
stedness: the "deferral of supposedly more immediate gratifications" (29
comes close to Ian Hunter's reading of Foucault, which insists that there is
ificant break between literary studies and cultural studies precisely beca
are committed to a version of the aesthetic. For both, Hunter says, the eff
content of the aesthetics we have taught and continue to teach is a form
berian rationalization—that is, one of the great modern upward mobility n
ves. "In its remorseless problematization of non-aesthetic life, in the state
manent self-critique and self-modification induced in its practitioners . . .
recognize a full-blown rationalization of existence in the Weberian sens

men or Hannibal Lecter's hunger to know Clarice Starling's secrets. Touchy as that might be, the touchiest, at a state university like Rutgers where students often work twenty hours and more a week outside class, was to remember that they are largely if not exclusively animated by a thin hope of upward mobility, which we their teachers can have little assurance of being able to satisfy—and, while remembering this, to maintain at the same time that the parallel with Vautrin and Lecter is not entirely a bad thing. Lecter turns out to be a surprisingly "good" mentor, I told the students, because his hunger can be satisfied, without cannibalism or sex, by Starling's revelation of the "silence of the lambs" story, that is, because he solicits and then approves her nonsexual, morally satisfying allegory of why she wants to do the work she is training to do.[6] Thus Lecter ratifies the work of stopping serial killers like himself.[7] Another analogue to this self-subverting relation to one's own authority might be, in Foucault's discussion of asymmetrical sex between Greek men and boys, the devious return of ethical constraints on aesthetic "self-fashioning." These are not ideal versions of academic work, but they are not merely cautionary either. In a time when expectations are not great, and are diminishing, when illusions are often not there to be lost, the upward mobility of our students, both individual and collective (I'm suspicious of any politics that thinks it can confine itself to the latter), may require cruelty as well as nurturance—the cruelty of inciting or encouraging hopes for which there is so little guarantee.[8]

Now I'm going to move briefly and schematically through a second category of mediated otherness that, like mentorship, is left out of the literature lovefest: disciplines other than English. However one may try to narrow literature down so as to make it distinct and autonomous, one is always carving a space for it out of, and against, the competing and overlapping objects of other disciplines. This is arguably true for even the most closed and purist of definitions, and it is blindingly evident for the more open and interesting ones. John Guillory, one of the more eloquent champions of a return to the traditional humanities canon, argues in *Cultural Capital* that "the specificity of aesthetic judgment is not . . . simply an illusion to be exploded, but rather a privileged site for reimagining the relation between the cultural and the economic in social life."[9] I ask you to stop and think about the phrase "privileged site." A privilege is an advantage enjoyed at someone else's expense. Why should such an advantage, an advantage in the understanding of "social life," of all things, be enjoyed by a literature department at the expense of, say, departments of sociology or history or economics or anthropology? And yet it is these invisible others that are both engaged and dismissed when literary departments, by virtue of the lucky particularity of their object, claim to occupy a "privileged site."[10]

Now this is not an obvious injustice. And the reason is that there is no non- or transdisciplinary standard by which, or even place in which, those who "privilege criticism above contending discourses" (to quote Tony Bennett) have to confront and negotiate with those contending discourses.[11] Where and how could these conflicting claims ever be rationally and impartially adjudicated? Which faculty has the right to interpret the conflict of the faculties? I may feel that criticism is absurd when it makes special claims for literature's formal autonomy, or for that matter claims for the novel as a privileged window onto imperialism. But other disciplines, like literary criticism, submit to pressures to legitimize their disciplinary objects that are no less distorting. Disciplinarily speaking, it's a jungle out there. One cannot take for granted that "contending discourses" or disciplines are like ethical subjects necessarily deserving of equal and unconditional respect. Hence, to recall Hannibal Lecter again, disciplinary cannibalism cannot be ruled out.

Still, this comparative perspective on our local impulse to define and stick to a distinct and autonomous notion of literature makes at least one thing clear: disciplines do not in fact depend on possessing a distinct, autonomous object. Or, more precisely, they depend at least as much on their answers to the "so what?" question. Why should the inquiry be carried out at all? In other words, the claim to *distinctiveness* has to be supplemented and restrained by a claim to *significance*. And it is on the terrain of significance, whatever and wherever that may be, that an eventual discipline of disciplinarity will find some rough version of transdisciplinary adjudication.

What this means, in terms of the current conjuncture in literary studies, is that the messy overlaps and areas of lingering dispute can be seen (for better or worse) as sources of disciplinary strength rather than symptoms of insufficient self-definition. They are signs of what David Simpson calls "the rule of literature."[12] The claim put forward by literature departments, a claim pressed largely but not entirely in terms of theory and cultural studies, has been that we have expertise about problematic conditions of knowledge and discourse, narrative and rhetoric, that are pertinent far outside the boundaries of the canon, however conceived. Though it is not absolutely distinct from a claim to absolute distinctness, I think this is a relatively defensible claim to social significance. If we have not done a great job lately defending it, it's perhaps because we've been too worried about the purity of the distinctiveness claim.

Here I'd like to say a few words about one of the [...] the distinctiveness claim I know, Derek Attridge's acc[...] ature in *Peculiar Language*. Writers since Wordsw[...] Attridge says, that literature "can engage with the [...] everyone who speaks the same tongue, and that it at[...] intervene in the ethical and political life of a communit[...] claim too far, however, is to endanger the existence o[...] tinct entity, for if literature does not employ a special l[...] it derive its appeal and its strength?"[13] Hence there are [...] tent demands—that the language of literature be recogr[...] language we encounter in other contexts, and that it be[...] (3). Attridge's solution to this problem is in effect to defir[...] impossibility of definition.

At least in one sense, it is a happy impossibility, for th[...] dox that literature can call its own. The problem, in my v[...] this paradox its own. What Attridge has done is to specify [...] paradox that is general, a paradox that is built into discip[...] As Attridge himself notes in passing, "the word *literature*"[...] or *law*, capable of destabilizing the discourses and institutio[...] its being" (17). But if literature is like writing or law in thi[...] like rhetoric, or religion, or culture, or space? Is there anythir[...] that could effectively distinguish literature from the objects [...]

In 1996 the National Council of Teachers of English and th[...] ing Association released a document called "Standards for th[...] Arts," which aims to define what English teachers should [...] schools all over the country. This document makes almost no r[...] ness." Works of fiction, works of the past, works from other cu[...] read, of course. But there is nothing about why the goals of lit[...] correct grammar, critical thought, and so on—should be in[...] means and not others. The closest thing to an answer to tha[...] assumption that literature serves as a vehicle for the preserva[...] experience. This is a scandal. Technocratic, speech-communi[...] these are certainly something for boosters of cultural studies a[...] concept of literature to worry about. But—and this is my real [...] threatened dominance of a "communications" model, which som[...] defeat in the conflict of the faculties, is not a reason to fall back in[...] ature's supposed distinctiveness, for example, on literariness conc[...]

(355).[15] Like Foucault's conjoined interests in aesthetic self-fashioning and the "ethical work" of Greek sexual life, to which Hunter is alluding, the aesthetic in other words remains a kind of ethical work ethic: perhaps a way of keeping the work ethic alive in different terms and difficult circumstances.[16]

This difficult, ethical version of the aesthetic, a paraphrase of the more familiar pedagogical goal of "critical thinking" that comes close to Weber on delayed gratification, is clearly a preparation for upward mobility. It also puts a premium on mentorship and mediation. For both these reasons, it should perhaps be contrasted with D. A. Miller's Foucaultian take on upward mobility in Balzac's *Père Goriot*. According to Miller, the central factor in the success story of Rastignac and of Balzac himself is "Vautrin's homoerotic admiration (said to make Rastignac tremble 'in every member')" for Rastignac's seductive "good looks," his *beauté* (681). Or rather, the central factor in that success story is the *sacrifice* of Vautrin. In Miller's version, Rastignac can succeed in Parisian society only by sacrificing the bodily pleasures that Vautrin obscurely promises. "The price of success under Balzac's patriarchal capitalism is a rigorous ascesis."[17] For Miller, Vautrin is not a mediator at all; indeed, the pleasure he promises is immediate, unmediated.

My suggestion would be, on the contrary, that it's not the loss of Vautrin that's essential to upward mobility. Rather, it's Balzac's and Rastignac's persistence in connections that are just as "unnatural," just as external to the domestic narrative of biological reproduction—for example, affairs with "older women," who mediate in turn the power of their husbands—all of which Vautrin stands for, rather than against. In other words, Miller wrongly tries to take mediation out of the upward mobility story. In the United States we often call this the "Horatio Alger story," named incidentally for an author who began his career as a clergyman and was thrown out of his church for dallying with young boys. It is worth noting the extent to which Alger's stories are not about hard work and renunciation, but about seduction of or by mediator/benefactors.[18]

What does all this have to do with the place of the literary? My point, which can only be suggested here in the sketchiest way, is that Miller takes from Foucault a notion of "pleasure" that rewrites the aesthetic as the private, the self-enclosed, the self-sufficient. Pleasure is the immediate: it needs others, perhaps, but it does not need mediators, and it is incompatible with the impurity and inequalities of social climbing. This is a notion of pleasure that I think has a deep appeal right now for our students, a so-called slacker generation tempted to resign itself to the absence of real possibilities for upward mobility. And I think it may have a lot to do with "the aesthetic" in its purist, "back to literature" mood. Perhaps "back to literature" should be seen as a response both to the shrinking market within our institutions and, more disquietingly still, to the declining aspirations of our students.

At any rate, I myself am trying to clarify and, I think, to defend that other aesthetic, mediated and impure, fraught with ethical and political difficulties, that one finds in Balzac and Demme: an aesthetic like the one that in his discussion of unequal sexuality between Greek men and boys Foucault tried to see as free "self-fashioning," but ended up instead seeing as necessarily submitting to ethical limits. An aesthetic that can function for and within narratives of upward mobility precisely because it takes for granted that inequalities of power are real, and are what our supposedly purest aesthetic perceptions are made up of. An aesthetic, therefore, in which mentors and mediation can't be made to go away, as scary as they may be, and in which the scariest or cruelest thing may be that, as a starting point for our students, even aspiration can't be taken for granted.

Notes

1. Elaine Marks, "In Defense of Modern Languages and Literatures, Masterpieces, Nihilism, and Dead European Writers," *MLA Newsletter*, fall 1993, 2–3. Note the double irony that anti-totalizing theory, with its praise of the local, here turns back against itself, as well as the way the new authority of autobiographical feeling and confession is here mobilized against the innovations that made it possible.

    A similar argument against cultural studies in the name of feeling can be found in Stanley Fish, *Professional Correctness: Literary Studies and Political Change* (Oxford: Clarendon, 1995). Fish writes about literary interpretation, "I do it because I like the way I feel when I'm doing it" (110).

    This section of my essay is adapted from an essay published electronically, entitled "Literature, Localism, and Love," *Surfaces* 4, 3 (1994).

2. Jonathan Culler, "Lace, Lance, and Pair," in *Profession 94* (New York: Modern Language Association, 1994), 5.

3. This excess of otherness is present even when the primal moment recalled is not an immediate relation to literature but an immediate relation to a given teacher. John Guillory writes,

    The wish to recapture the moment of "surprise" is only a wish to experience once again the first and freshest moment of the transference. It is that moment which seems in retrospect to have no relation to the "institution," to exist entirely in a private space between the master and the disciple, and

men or Hannibal Lecter's hunger to know Clarice Starling's secrets. Touchy as that might be, the touchiest, at a state university like Rutgers where students often work twenty hours and more a week outside class, was to remember that they are largely if not exclusively animated by a thin hope of upward mobility, which we their teachers can have little assurance of being able to satisfy—and, while remembering this, to maintain at the same time that the parallel with Vautrin and Lecter is not entirely a bad thing. Lecter turns out to be a surprisingly "good" mentor, I told the students, because his hunger can be satisfied, without cannibalism or sex, by Starling's revelation of the "silence of the lambs" story, that is, because he solicits and then approves her nonsexual, morally satisfying allegory of why she wants to do the work she is training to do.[6] Thus Lecter ratifies the work of stopping serial killers like himself.[7] Another analogue to this self-subverting relation to one's own authority might be, in Foucault's discussion of asymmetrical sex between Greek men and boys, the devious return of ethical constraints on aesthetic "self-fashioning." These are not ideal versions of academic work, but they are not merely cautionary either. In a time when expectations are not great, and are diminishing, when illusions are often not there to be lost, the upward mobility of our students, both individual and collective (I'm suspicious of any politics that thinks it can confine itself to the latter), may require cruelty as well as nurturance—the cruelty of inciting or encouraging hopes for which there is so little guarantee.[8]

Now I'm going to move briefly and schematically through a second category of mediated otherness that, like mentorship, is left out of the literature lovefest: disciplines other than English. However one may try to narrow literature down so as to make it distinct and autonomous, one is always carving a space for it out of, and against, the competing and overlapping objects of other disciplines. This is arguably true for even the most closed and purist of definitions, and it is blindingly evident for the more open and interesting ones. John Guillory, one of the more eloquent champions of a return to the traditional humanities canon, argues in *Cultural Capital* that "the specificity of aesthetic judgment is not . . . simply an illusion to be exploded, but rather a privileged site for reimagining the relation between the cultural and the economic in social life."[9] I ask you to stop and think about the phrase "privileged site." A privilege is an advantage enjoyed at someone else's expense. Why should such an advantage, an advantage in the understanding of "social life," of all things, be enjoyed by a literature department at the expense of, say, departments of sociology or history or economics or anthropology? And yet it is these invisible others that are both engaged and dismissed when literary departments, by virtue of the lucky particularity of their object, claim to occupy a "privileged site."[10]

Now this is not an obvious injustice. And the reason is that there is no non- or transdisciplinary standard by which, or even place in which, those who "privilege criticism above contending discourses" (to quote Tony Bennett) have to confront and negotiate with those contending discourses.[11] Where and how could these conflicting claims ever be rationally and impartially adjudicated? Which faculty has the right to interpret the conflict of the faculties? I may feel that criticism is absurd when it makes special claims for literature's formal autonomy, or for that matter claims for the novel as a privileged window onto imperialism. But other disciplines, like literary criticism, submit to pressures to legitimize their disciplinary objects that are no less distorting. Disciplinarily speaking, it's a jungle out there. One cannot take for granted that "contending discourses" or disciplines are like ethical subjects necessarily deserving of equal and unconditional respect. Hence, to recall Hannibal Lecter again, disciplinary cannibalism cannot be ruled out.

Still, this comparative perspective on our local impulse to define and stick to a distinct and autonomous notion of literature makes at least one thing clear: disciplines do not in fact depend on possessing a distinct, autonomous object. Or, more precisely, they depend at least as much on their answers to the "so what?" question. Why should the inquiry be carried out at all? In other words, the claim to *distinctiveness* has to be supplemented and restrained by a claim to *significance*. And it is on the terrain of significance, whatever and wherever that may be, that an eventual discipline of disciplinarity will find some rough version of transdisciplinary adjudication.

What this means, in terms of the current conjuncture in literary studies, is that the messy overlaps and areas of lingering dispute can be seen (for better or worse) as sources of disciplinary strength rather than symptoms of insufficient self-definition. They are signs of what David Simpson calls "the rule of literature."[12] The claim put forward by literature departments, a claim pressed largely but not entirely in terms of theory and cultural studies, has been that we have expertise about problematic conditions of knowledge and discourse, narrative and rhetoric, that are pertinent far outside the boundaries of the canon, however conceived. Though it is not absolutely distinct from a claim to absolute distinctness, I think this is a relatively defensible claim to social significance. If we have not done a great job lately defending it, it's perhaps because we've been too worried about the purity of the distinctiveness claim.

Here I'd like to say a few words about one of the most compelling versions of the distinctiveness claim I know, Derek Attridge's account of the concept of literature in *Peculiar Language*. Writers since Wordsworth have always claimed, Attridge says, that literature "can engage with the language and thoughts of everyone who speaks the same tongue, and that it attains thereby the power to intervene in the ethical and political life of a community or a nation. To push this claim too far, however, is to endanger the existence of literature itself as a distinct entity, for if literature does not employ a special language, from what does it derive its appeal and its strength?"[13] Hence there are "two mutually inconsistent demands—that the language of literature be recognizably different from the language we encounter in other contexts, and that it be recognizably the same" (3). Attridge's solution to this problem is in effect to define literature as this very impossibility of definition.

At least in one sense, it is a happy impossibility, for this appears to be a paradox that literature can call its own. The problem, in my view, is that it can't call this paradox its own. What Attridge has done is to specify criticism's version of a paradox that is general, a paradox that is built into disciplinary objects as such. As Attridge himself notes in passing, "the word *literature*" is "a term like *writing* or *law*, capable of destabilizing the discourses and institutions within which it has its being" (17). But if literature is like writing or law in this respect, isn't it also like rhetoric, or religion, or culture, or space? Is there anything in this description that could effectively distinguish literature from the objects of other fields?

In 1996 the National Council of Teachers of English and the International Reading Association released a document called "Standards for the English Language Arts," which aims to define what English teachers should teach in secondary schools all over the country. This document makes almost no mention of "literariness." Works of fiction, works of the past, works from other cultures should all be read, of course. But there is nothing about why the goals of literary pedagogy— correct grammar, critical thought, and so on—should be inculcated by these means and not others. The closest thing to an answer to that question is the assumption that literature serves as a vehicle for the preservation of collective experience. This is a scandal. Technocratic, speech-communication allies like these are certainly something for boosters of cultural studies and critics of the concept of literature to worry about. But—and this is my real point—even the threatened dominance of a "communications" model, which some would see as a defeat in the conflict of the faculties, is not a reason to fall back in a panic on literature's supposed distinctiveness, for example, on literariness conceived narrowly and contrastively as that which blocks or diverts us from the simple purpose of transparent communication. Literature is a vehicle for the expression and preservation of collective experience, among other things. And if this means it shares something with lots of other sorts of discourse, including historical documents that seem less formally sophisticated or self-reflexive or undecidable, it seems to me that these differences can be noted and duly respected without becoming the single, definitive foundation on which we desperately try to base our identity, a sort of excuse for a disciplinary "identity politics" in the worst sense of the term. If our students get their history from us, or their sociology, or their philosophy, so be it. What we share with other disciplines counts too. It may not advertise the uniqueness of our product, but it's not a negligible claim for the significance of what we do.

Had I more time, I would have liked to say more about Michel Foucault, whose account of the paradox of "commentary" (saying for the first time what the text had already said, repeating tirelessly what it had never said) belongs to one of my own stories of disciplinary first love.[14] Students who come to school with upward mobility on their minds will often find that Foucault is the mentor of their mentors, the Matthew Arnold of cultural studies, our most seductive recruiter. The figure who described the confessions of Pierre Rivière, nineteenth-century parricide, as "beautiful," Foucault is so seductive, I think, because like Vautrin and Lecter he manages to represent both the transgression of power and power itself, and because both the power and the transgression of power are embodied in a version of the aesthetic. My concluding question, then, is whether this somewhat contradictory ideological content might have anything to do with the upward mobility narratives brought to and read in our classrooms.

To reframe this as a hypothesis, I'm suggesting that the debate over the place of the literary in cultural studies may have more to do than we think with the aspirations of our students. John Guillory, following Bourdieu, distinguishes between a working-class aesthetics of sensual pleasure and a bourgeois aesthetics of disinterestedness: the "deferral of supposedly more immediate gratifications" (291). This comes close to Ian Hunter's reading of Foucault, which insists that there is no significant break between literary studies and cultural studies precisely because both are committed to a version of the aesthetic. For both, Hunter says, the effective content of the aesthetics we have taught and continue to teach is a form of Weberian rationalization—that is, one of the great modern upward mobility narratives. "In its remorseless problematization of non-aesthetic life, in the state of permanent self-critique and self-modification induced in its practitioners . . . we can recognize a full-blown rationalization of existence in the Weberian sense"

(355).[15] Like Foucault's conjoined interests in aesthetic self-fashioning and the "ethical work" of Greek sexual life, to which Hunter is alluding, the aesthetic in other words remains a kind of ethical work ethic: perhaps a way of keeping the work ethic alive in different terms and difficult circumstances.[16]

This difficult, ethical version of the aesthetic, a paraphrase of the more familiar pedagogical goal of "critical thinking" that comes close to Weber on delayed gratification, is clearly a preparation for upward mobility. It also puts a premium on mentorship and mediation. For both these reasons, it should perhaps be contrasted with D. A. Miller's Foucaultian take on upward mobility in Balzac's *Père Goriot*. According to Miller, the central factor in the success story of Rastignac and of Balzac himself is "Vautrin's homoerotic admiration (said to make Rastignac tremble 'in every member')" for Rastignac's seductive "good looks," his *beauté* (681). Or rather, the central factor in that success story is the *sacrifice* of Vautrin. In Miller's version, Rastignac can succeed in Parisian society only by sacrificing the bodily pleasures that Vautrin obscurely promises. "The price of success under Balzac's patriarchal capitalism is a rigorous ascesis."[17] For Miller, Vautrin is not a mediator at all; indeed, the pleasure he promises is immediate, unmediated.

My suggestion would be, on the contrary, that it's not the loss of Vautrin that's essential to upward mobility. Rather, it's Balzac's and Rastignac's persistence in connections that are just as "unnatural," just as external to the domestic narrative of biological reproduction—for example, affairs with "older women," who mediate in turn the power of their husbands—all of which Vautrin stands for, rather than against. In other words, Miller wrongly tries to take mediation out of the upward mobility story. In the United States we often call this the "Horatio Alger story," named incidentally for an author who began his career as a clergyman and was thrown out of his church for dallying with young boys. It is worth noting the extent to which Alger's stories are not about hard work and renunciation, but about seduction of or by mediator/benefactors.[18]

What does all this have to do with the place of the literary? My point, which can only be suggested here in the sketchiest way, is that Miller takes from Foucault a notion of "pleasure" that rewrites the aesthetic as the private, the self-enclosed, the self-sufficient. Pleasure is the immediate: it needs others, perhaps, but it does not need mediators, and it is incompatible with the impurity and inequalities of social climbing. This is a notion of pleasure that I think has a deep appeal right now for our students, a so-called slacker generation tempted to resign itself to the absence of real possibilities for upward mobility. And I think it may have a lot to do with "the aesthetic" in its purist, "back to literature" mood. Perhaps "back to literature" should be seen as a response both to the shrinking market within our institutions and, more disquietingly still, to the declining aspirations of our students.

At any rate, I myself am trying to clarify and, I think, to defend that other aesthetic, mediated and impure, fraught with ethical and political difficulties, that one finds in Balzac and Demme: an aesthetic like the one that in his discussion of unequal sexuality between Greek men and boys Foucault tried to see as free "self-fashioning," but ended up instead seeing as necessarily submitting to ethical limits. An aesthetic that can function for and within narratives of upward mobility precisely because it takes for granted that inequalities of power are real, and are what our supposedly purest aesthetic perceptions are made up of. An aesthetic, therefore, in which mentors and mediation can't be made to go away, as scary as they may be, and in which the scariest or cruelest thing may be that, as a starting point for our students, even aspiration can't be taken for granted.

Notes

1. Elaine Marks, "In Defense of Modern Languages and Literatures, Masterpieces, Nihilism, and Dead European Writers," *MLA Newsletter*, fall 1993, 2–3. Note the double irony that anti-totalizing theory, with its praise of the local, here turns back against itself, as well as the way the new authority of autobiographical feeling and confession is here mobilized against the innovations that made it possible.

   A similar argument against cultural studies in the name of feeling can be found in Stanley Fish, *Professional Correctness: Literary Studies and Political Change* (Oxford: Clarendon, 1995). Fish writes about literary interpretation, "I do it because I like the way I feel when I'm doing it" (110).

   This section of my essay is adapted from an essay published electronically, entitled "Literature, Localism, and Love," *Surfaces* 4, 3 (1994).

2. Jonathan Culler, "Lace, Lance, and Pair," in *Profession 94* (New York: Modern Language Association, 1994), 5.

3. This excess of otherness is present even when the primal moment recalled is not an immediate relation to literature but an immediate relation to a given teacher. John Guillory writes,

   > The wish to recapture the moment of "surprise" is only a wish to experience once again the first and freshest moment of the transference. It is that moment which seems in retrospect to have no relation to the "institution," to exist entirely in a private space between the master and the disciple, and

therefore to be subversive of institutionality per se. Yet the desire to repeat that moment of quasi-exteriority to the institution is hardly incompatible with the institution of a methodology: it *is* methodology.

John Guillory, *Cultural Capital: The Problem of Literary Canon Formation* (Chicago: University of Chicago Press, 1993), 243–44.

In a different vein, Adela Pinch notes that one motive for literary study is "deeply anti-social, a way of avoiding other people" (personal communication).

4. It is in the battles over institutional reproduction that this fight (not too strong a word) is already being waged: battles over hiring, over tenure, over whether the slots that need filling must be defined as "period" slots or not, and so on.

5. Gayatri Chakravorty Spivak, "Three Women's Texts and a Critique of Imperialism," *Critical Inquiry* 12 (autumn 1985): 243–61.

6. Remember that Lecter, the reader, is also a figure of the aesthete. Aesthetics, in this popular view, is exemplified by Lecter creating a thing of beauty by means of inhumanity and anaesthesia: for example, the winged victory erected in his Nashville cell out of a policeman's corpse. I discuss *Silence of the Lambs* at greater length in "Murder and Mentorship: Advancement in *The Silence of the Lambs*," *UTS Review* 1, 1 (August 1995): 30–49, and *boundary 2* 23, 1 (spring 1996): 71–90.

7. Note the "it takes a thief to catch a thief" parallel with Vautrin/Vidocq.

8. I am not suggesting, as one might reasonably infer, that higher education in the humanities ought to tend toward an endpoint of direct vocational placement. But the complacency with which humanists (and post-humanists) see their goal as on the contrary something like "critique" seems to me equally untenable, especially if you consider how well it coexists with the exploitation of increasingly insecure and underpaid graduate student labor.

9. Guillory, *Cultural Capital*, xiv.

10. My own position is close to that of Francis Mulhern:

> Literature, in its ordinary sense of an inherently valuable canon of imaginative writing, has been and remains a potent cultural value. As a norm, it has been institutionalized in public bodies and internalized by countless individuals, organizing the whole culture of writing and reading, inflecting the course of practice in other media, and validating major traditions of discourse. An enormous amount of important work has been done under its sign. The historical reality and productivity of "literature" are not in dispute. The interesting question is, rather, whether it can make a legitimate claim of *privilege* [my emphasis] either as an object of analysis or as a norm of subjectivity. Balibar, Macherey, Bennett and Williams have been notable in maintaining—correctly—that it cannot. The claim that the study of written culture should continue as the study of "literature" is dogmatic and

obscurantist. Literary studies so conceived are an authoritarian defense of
certain received cultural values, within preset limits of debate and discovery.
[But note: isn't this so for all disciplines at all times?] "Literature gives us wisdom," goes one definition-cum-defense I have personally encountered. It is
memorable as an act of self-exposure: the verb erases reading as an active
process; "wisdom" replaces debatable knowledge in favour of humbling revelation; and the appeal to an indeterminate "us" simply cancels the existing
order of human relations and interests. Procedural openness to the whole
field of writing and a pluralist corporate ethos are the minimum conditions of
genuinely "critical" literary study. It may be that there are important and
very general qualitative distinctions to be made within the material range of
writing, yet it is doubtful whether "literature" will feature among them.

Francis Mulhern, ed., *Contemporary Marxist Literary Criticism* (London: Longman,
1992), 19–20.

11. Tony Bennett, *Outside Literature* (London: Routledge, 1990), 196. For Fredric Jameson, Bennett notes, criticism is "a privileged site of ethical, cognitive and political
totalisation" (195). Bennett also quotes, approvingly, Bourdieu on Kant.

12. David Simpson, *The Academic Postmodern and the Rule of Literature: A Report on
Half-Knowledge* (Chicago: University of Chicago Press, 1995).

13. Derek Attridge, *Peculiar Language: Literature as Difference from the Renaissance to
James Joyce* (London: Methuen, 1988), 1.

14. In "The Order of Discourse," Foucault says that this division, of which literature and
criticism clearly form one example, allows the primary text to be both a source or occasion for the production of new words and a restraint on them. It is credited with "multiple or hidden meaning," an "essential reticence and richness," which is "the basis for
an open possibility of speaking": "By a paradox which it always displaces but never
escapes, the commentary must say for the first time what had, nonetheless, already been
said, and must tirelessly repeat what had, however, never been said." Foucault had
explained not what literature is, perhaps, but what it is *for criticism*, the essential motor
of its academic being. The best English translation is in Robert Young, ed., *Untying the
Text: A Post-Structuralist Reader* (Boston: Routledge and Kegan Paul, 1981), 48–78.

15. Ian Hunter, "Aesthetics and Cultural Studies," in *Cultural Studies*, ed. Lawrence
Grossberg, Cary Nelson, and Paula Treichler (New York: Routledge, 1992), 347–72.

16. Michel Foucault, *The Use of Pleasure*, vol. 2 of *The History of Sexuality*, trans. Robert
Hurley (New York: Random House, 1985), 27.

17. D. A. Miller, "Body Bildung and Textual Liberation," in *A New History of French Literature*, ed. Denis Hollier (Cambridge: Harvard University Press, 1989), 681–87.

18. The "how-to" book, for example the *ars erotica*, is Foucault's alternative discourse:
Alger's genre, and America's.

Postliterary Poetry, Counterperformance, and Micropoetries

3

Maria Damon

> Yes, pappy, i went to kollage, but what the Hell has
> that to do with poetry?
>
> —*Stephen Jonas*

> Should I sing a requiem as the trap closes?
> Perhaps it is more fitting to shout nonsense.
>
> —*Bob Kaufman*

> Jokingly invoking the death of Jimi Hendrix
> I find myself vomiting all over my copy
> of the *Princeton Encyclopedia of Poetry and Poetics*.
>
> —*Ed Morales*

Creating new interlocutors in and out of the academy strikes me as an apt description of what we do when we teach. In the academy—at the graduate level, since at least in theory many of our students are training for an academic life. Out of the academy—at the undergraduate level, since—at least in the public institution I'm in—our students are bound by and large for lives of bare and secular survival (as, in fact, we and our graduates are as well in these anti-intellectual times). If they can carry into those bare survivalist lives a kinetic memory of exultation occasioned by the poetic and by exercising their own apperceptive faculties at large, and if they can find resonating experiences in their intimate, public, or professional lives, the revolution in poetic language can claim another victory by stealth, however subtle, diffuse, and even invisible to the instrumentalist eye.

The inarticulable poetic experience I want to facilitate in students has everything to do with empowering citizenry. At the same time, I'm not making the
argument that Stanley Aronowitz warns against in his essay "Is a Democracy
Possible?"—the argument made by Jefferson, Dewey, and Walter Lippman that a
people imbued with high culture through a formal education constitute the
entirety of those fit to govern themselves. On the contrary, as I hope will be
demonstrated by my examples, the poetry that inspires this putatively charged
citizenry does not have to be academic or even the product of educated literacy.
What I hope to accomplish in the academy is to create an environment in which
these expressions can be understood and reflected on as poetry.

Another element in this discussion is not a revision—because many of us
understand what I'm about to say as axiomatic—but an *emphasis* on the audience (listenership) as cocreator—as makers—as poets. The concept of new audiences implies new interlocutors, new conversations, emergent communities of
urgency, that can't necessarily, as Giorgio Agamben has observed, correspond to
any current understanding we have of the word *community*. And not that newness is new—newness itself is infinitely renewable. Dante's "De Vulgari Elo-
quentia," written almost a millennium ago, is rewritten by every avant-garde and
every ideology of salvation, only to be recuperated and rearticulated—and each
time, with threads that can't be woven neatly into the juggernaut of normative
text; shreds of resistance, of quirky paths out of centricity, hang off the edges
and await our engagement.

Mixed feelings and multiple, mutually canceling self-critiques always accom-
pany citing student work. Everybody's going on and on about pedagogy these
days, from the most rigorous radical theorists to the back-to-basics Bennettites on
the far right—not to mention the in-between liberal touchy-feelies as well. The
reason is clear: with the utter disappearance of a meaningful public sphere that
includes an operative democracy, people turn to the classroom as the putative site
of conflict and change. The problem with this model, however, is that it is already
nondemocratic. The etymology of the word *pedagogy*—to lead children—betrays
a discourse founded on condescension and self-aggrandizement, to which even
those of us who work with adults over eighteen can fall prey. One troubling
aspect of "pedagogy" is that when it comes to poetry and, I suspect, most other
things, it's backwards. The poet Jack Spicer said, "Poetry comes to us through the
young . . . and that is why we need them." Students, our structural if not chronological juniors, are producers, conduits, and rapt consumers of the poetic. As
such, they lead us and sharpen our sensibilities. They're the ones constructing

and instantiating new publics, new republics that tease Plato's poetry out of hiding and make it/or him—Plato—queen of the garden. They are themselves a defense of poetry.

POSTLITERARY POETRY

I will start with delineating the contours of what I call postliterary poetries and counterperformance. In so doing I want to showcase examples from these realms of gold. It's hard to convey in academic prose unaccompanied by videos and other evidence the passion one can feel from and for language that bridges the vernacular and the literary. Nonetheless I want to turn my workplace—the academy—into a place where this language is valued. And part of this project, as it has been for other subjects under revision such as identity, means challenging the category of poetry itself, and how poetry is conceived of in a liberal humanist context.

My epigraphs are such examples. The first two are from poets who, despite the decorousness of these particular lines, were street poets whose stints in prison, the merchant marine, psychiatric hospitals, and the military gave their lives what institutional contours they had. Both here call into question the relationship between formalism, the academy, poetry, and the sense of urgency that compels that poetry. So does Ed Morales, a NuYorican poet in both senses of the word (he is a New York Puerto Rican who writes poetry, and he is associated with the Lower East Side's NuYorican Poets' Cafe), who did go to college but clearly maintains a fine sense of irony about its benefits. Perhaps it *is* more fitting to shout nonsense. What the Hell's kollage to do with poetry indeed? This is a question that I face daily as an associate professor whose department has allotted me the field labeled contemporary poetry to graze in. My approach is not primarily formalistic, and academic poetry is almost unspeakably boring to me; yet poetry itself blazes through my waking and sleeping mind like a comet so large my head can't hold it, my tongue can't tell it, and my body dies when I can't get it. So this essay is a first move of someone into a new perceptual field unbounded by discipline, where we have all moved all along with muscles we may have forgotten but poetry hasn't. With respect to postliterary poetry, performing in the border means performing in the zone where vernacular meets the academy, where disciplines are undone, where street and workshop are one.

John Beverley's *Against Literature*, whose subject is Latin American literature, offers a roadmap that gets close to what I think should be done for poetry in the United States. Beverley investigates the ways nonliterary genres like *testi-monio* and revolutionary poetry throw into crisis the tight and cofoundational relationship between official politics, nationalist self-representation, and literary production, even in as revolutionary a context as the Nicaraguan revolution, in which most of the key players were poets as well as military or political actors. Their poetry and their understanding of what poetry (and all of literature) is was formed by a classically oriented literary education; and, paradoxically, Ernesto Cardenal's Solentiname experiment faced a crisis when these classically trained revolutionary literati couldn't handle the so-called crude poetics of the newly lit-erate peasantry they had given their lives to uplift. *Unlike* literature in Latin America, which has always been explicitly understood as a nation-building enterprise, Anglo-American literature and its critical apparatus have posited themselves—at least in the last several generations—as resolutely disinterested, apolitical, and esoteric (pace Kennedy/Frost and Clinton/Angelou inaugural spectacles). To some extent, even by those of us who came up intellectually in an era that proclaimed that everything was guided by a politics, this political infl-uence or agenda was assumed to be tacit—the elitism and racism of the New Critics had to be teased out through attending to and eventually condemning their silences. Thus, we used the close(d) reading skills we'd learned from the New Critics and Agrarian poets to flush out their unspoken faith in class, gender, and racial hierarchy. This technique continues to validate poetry that needs "unpacking" or decoding. Even in the wake of canon wars and poststructuralist or materialist critical incursions into the world of discourse, there remains an anachronistic reluctance to speak of poetry in other than formal or thematic terms. The narrative arts on the one hand, like novels or film, and mass-pro-duced mass culture on the other have been the beneficiaries of the innovations of a politically charged cultural studies, while poetry—especially, I'm sorry to say, contemporary poetry—seems to still be encased in its golden cage, with the most adventurous work limited to close readings of heretofore neglected women poets—and "neglected" means that fewer poems of theirs than of their male coevals and friends appear in the standard teaching anthologies.

And while in other circles cultural studies is already being mourned as having become trivialized, having abandoned its class-based analysis and its political commitments in favor of Shakespeare with a twist or the playful deconstruction performed by subaltern subject Imelda Marcos on the Filipino people, it has steered clear of poetry, leaving it in the hands of the critically undead. The fact that a biography of Elizabeth Bishop or a critique of anthologies is big news in the poetry world, that people are still arguing the viability of Anne Sexton as a poet because of her popularity, and that Adrienne Rich is seen as revolutionary are cases in point. Only the author-based, canonical offspring of cultural studies has been incorporated into poetic studies: "homosociality among the Romantics"; "T. S. Eliot—was he really anti-Semitic?" This year's National Poetry Foundation conference was arranged by author (three or four panels on Ezra Pound in the 1950s!), as is the American Literature Association. The MLA newsletters for several years ran ads for an MLA panel on "Reassessment of the Official Frost Biography"—finally in 1994, it made it to be number 466 in the program schedule, which contained other stirring topics such as "Poetries of the Isles of California" (in which latter I participated with an essay on the multicultural "third world" poetry scene in the San Francisco Bay Area, following poet Ed Dorn's diatribe against "bootlicking fascists of multiculturalism"). I don't mean to assert unilaterally that this kind of poetic scholarship cannot be imaginative, rigorous, exciting, insightful, or profound. But it tends, on sum, to contribute to the existing matrix of dominant literary texts and critical practices rather than challenging it, reinforcing a static conception of what literary studies is, can be, ought to be. I think the fate of New Historicism (complete absorption into the normative textile of literary discourse, like a stain that didn't) is a good cautionary tale illustrating the limits of the Shakespeare-with-a-twist orientation.

In terms of aesthetic representation of nontraditional or heretofore noncanonical writers, the scene is no more promising. As for poets of color, if their work is formal and decorous in the lyric tradition, like Rita Dove or Michael Harper, their work can be tokens in this matrix of dominant literary texts, but no more. Check this out: There is less Black nationalist verse in the second (1988) *Norton Anthology of Modern Poetry* than there was in the first (1974) edition. Incredible but true. As for vernacular poetry by people of color, that's called folklore. Even Henry Louis Gates, Jr.'s *Signifying Monkey*, a brilliant argument for the foundational significance of a piece of vernacular poetry, is primarily cited for its insights into the already-deemed-literary work of Ishmael Reed and Zora Neale Hurston. Small wonder, for Gates frames his own work this way. Even his foray into the world of "Spoken Word" (performance poetry castrated of scary P-words) is tinged with a distant, be- and a-mused professional condescension; remarking in the *New Yorker* on a certain orally delivered poem: "I don't see it making the Norton Anthology, but it has a certain vigor, and the crowd cheers and whistles its approval." With the exception of a handful of texts dubbed folkloric or ethnographic (such as Steven Caton's and Lila Abu-Lughod's studies of poetry as social practice among Northern Yemeni men and Bedouin women respectively), poetry studies is still in the lite ages, up where the aether is pure — it clings to its isolation as if that loneliness made it pure.

It takes this loneliness, in fact, as testimony to its prophetic, specialized role as chosen genre. See, for example, Jorie Graham's interview in *A View from the Loft*, a Minneapolis literary organ. She discusses very intelligently her own latest work, which apparently draws heavily on a rich polyvocal chorus of competing voices, including those of Wittgenstein, Benjamin, Plato, and Brecht; she then tries to refute the claim that contemporary American poetry is "elitist." She says,

> What can I say to that? A country becoming increasingly poorly educated, producing some of the most culturally illiterate children in the world — a country willingly narcotizing itself via radio and television — should pray desperately that some few crazed idealists might devote their lives (on behalf of the culture I might add . . .) to raising the consciousness, the aural and sensate capacities, of their culture. Or no, not raising it, but restoring gifts truly innate though repressed by corporate rapacity and the willingness of people to be raped.

This is the quintessentially liberal plaint and appeal to high culture as socially salvific, of which Aronowitz complains in the essay alluded to earlier. It is possible to make the argument for poetry as counterdiscourse or antidiscourse without divorcing it so radically from the concerns of everyday life, and the realities of everyday habit and practice. To suggest, furthermore, that people are willingly deprived of their oral and literary traditions is to overlook the tremendous resistances that have been raised against co-optation, the flexibility and ingenuity of living traditions struggling to thrive in hostile circumstances, and the social, communal, and often oral/performative traditions that constitute much of poetry's origins. Television, radio, and other public venues can indeed be stultifying, but they can also be reimagined as dynamic contributors to a social renaissance of poetry and poetic activity. As in the work of poet Paul Beatty, the media can become subject matter and suggest formal techniques (like flow, rupture, etc.) for much brilliant verbal play. The image of the anonymous masses, drugged by a debased culture, in need of rescue from themselves suggests a very narrow, self-aggrandizing conception of what poetry, poets, and poetry scholars must be.

Cultural studies, in turn, has written poetry off as a priori high cultural, ergo unrecuperable. Irony of ironies, because, far more than narrative written genres poetry — ritually charged incantation — has been central to the cultural traditions of many subordinate peoples in the United States. Nonetheless, because of a perception that poetry belongs to an elite, as well as "poetry anxiety" even on the part of professional literati, the standoff between cultural studies and contemporary American poetry continues. Given this situation, I hope to be forgiven some general, provocative-to-some, old-hat-to-others statements like "academic poetry is dead on arrival" (this line was considered a challenge within my own department; at SUNY-Albany people yawned). Performance studies, cultural studies, and ethnic studies are more fitting arenas for the study of poetry. It is more fitting for academics to shout nonsense. In postliterary poetry studies, the cries of infants with fetal alcohol syndrome and drug addiction, meetings of Persons with AIDS support groups and settings where it's not permitted to transcribe or even recount personal narratives and anecdotes, slams in bars and community centers, writings on housing project walls will compel our attention. And we'll be attending as participant subjects, not simply as scholars who want to support, document, and study people who are not us. Our investment in these practices is not simply for the aesthetic frisson these languages elicit but for what they can tell us about our own human situations—they'll be our sustenance because we're those PWAs and the parents of addicted infants. Many of us already engage in these life-sustaining verbal processes, protesting, as many of my students do, "but I don't *do* poetry," "but I can't *read* poetry." Well. We can shout nonsense, and if we can't yet, then we teach what we need to learn.

Conversely, the artifacts I describe are not compelling for merely ideological reasons, though in both cases the content could be described as touching on "political" issues such as class, labor, racial violence. And of course, since words refer, the content at the crudest level of comprehension can't not be the partial subject of a receptive analysis. Rather, like the intensity one feels from some indigenous musics, or from authentic conversation, there's a tonal quality—of close attention and respect—that compels our audience—for these resonant and audient performances. To listen to someone who's really listening is the beginning of collaborative intellectual communities. The claim I'd like to make for certain texts that appear to be conventionally representational—and they've even, in some contexts in which I've presented them, been derided as crude social realism of the most falsely conscious stripe, which is, I think, to miss the point completely—is one that the "language poets" have foregrounded through their practice and critical writings: it is a useful exercise to listen to these apparently semantically overdetermined texts, attending to the degree to which, to paraphrase Bob Perelman's description of an early language-poetic principle,

"semantics are definitely softpedaled but not inaudible"(315). Simply by virtue
of trying to articulate some powerful apperceptive experience that does not
reside in representation alone, or in sonic beauty in a conventional lyrical sense,
I may be verging on invoking what in the 1960s was called "authorial voice," a
concept that has rightly been criticized as a mystification of the writing process,
and a prescription for the subservience of reader to writer. This is not my intention; rather, I want to understand the degree to which all writing bears traces of
a push against the limits of the rationally known, and to delineate, as grace-
lessly as a drunken boat afloat on the big fat poem of the sea, some thoughts on
how to facilitate a receptivity in ourselves, a precise receptivity to hearing that
push limits.

Amiri Baraka writes in "SOS,"

> Calling black people,
> calling all black people, man woman child,
> Wherever you are, calling you, urgent, come in
> Black People, come in, wherever you are, urgent calling
> you, calling all black people
> calling all black people, come in black people, come
> on in.

If you think this is a call to poetic activity, for poetic activity, come on in.

A postliterary poetry is one that is comfortable with its own politicization,
not necessarily thematically but in its production, distribution, and reception.
Its producers will not necessarily receive MacArthurs, though they may; there
will not be one name on everyone's lips—"oh, that's the postliterary poet." In a
postliterate world, letters speak and there is writing without words, sidewalks
will burn with language. Textiles whisper names of the dead, and the wearers of
mass-produced or handcrafted garments hear these names in their sleep or as
they walk, legs chafing in pants made in Singapore, in the Philippines, in Macao.
More modestly, the postliterary indicates a new orality: slams, 'zines and open-
mike readings with their underground cachet and unpredictable energy. It can't
be contained; there isn't a single bordered field large enough to feed a world that
hungers for poetry like bread. But *in* the borders there's poetry enough for
everyone. Who knows what perpetually liminal utterance will sound or look
like. Academics are at the (sub-liminal) threshold of the threshold of this inquiry.
But poetry itself is already revolutionary—the academy can only gain by loosening its bleeding grip on a thorny and withering bouquet.

COUNTERPERFORMANCE

Counterperformance operates on several levels, especially as practiced by marginalized poets in American culture—young people, Black people, street people, female people, various combinations thereof, and so on: how proper notions of public declamation are subverted by performance itself, and how performance signifies differently when the performing subject is a traditionally subjugated person. BlacQ, a nineteen-year-old freshman at Macalester College when he performed this poem in November 1993, won the series of poetry slams that accompanied the NuYorican Poets' residency. His poem, briefly paraphrased, concerns his move from an intensely urban 'hood scene to the "gentle college land" of a Midwestern dorm lounge, where the luxuries of uninterrupted study and protected youth are available to him. He puzzles over the vast gulf separating his two worlds, thinking that perhaps he has really escaped the former, when "It came to me"—he takes a break from reading Whitman, Keats, and Baraka to check out television's offerings and finds himself attacked as an African American youth: "they killed me on the tv." The power of his performance lay in the collision of hard-hitting verse delivered with traditional "hip-hop" gestures and inflections with his relatively low-key vocal style, in the beauty of his committed language (which rhymed "drama" and "bomber"), and the timbre of his voice (untransmittable in print, but soft and young).

When Walter Benjamin, in the late 1930s, protested that to give the masses a chance to express themselves without giving them their rights was the foundation for fascism, he was not speaking about the contemporary multiculturalism vogue. He was speaking about the rise of Nazi Germany, and the self-expressions of the masses against which he warned were mass rallies in which hatred caught fire. However, the extreme separation of the academy from the mainstream and the naïveté of the academy's belief in itself as a standard bearer of and shelter for progressive thought and free and diverse expression portend a need for wariness about its simultaneous fetishizing of and disdain for popular expression. BlacQ's poem both formally and thematically addresses the academic humanities' role in enabling and disabling young people of color's political and expressive aesthetic self-realization; it speaks to the simultaneous proximity and distance of the academy from the street. The poem articulates beautifully the violence of representation from which his new liberal arts home cannot protect him; the TV Guide is a parallel syllabus for Western Civ. Though education is his way to be himself, and though he turns to poetry as a salvific from the ravages of the cartoonlike violence that assails him at home and in the Macalester dorm lounge, there is no less violence in this world than the one in which his homeboys wear gold and patrol their turf. BlacQ's body was younger even than his years, and his baseball cap visor shielded his face from the stage-lights so that he was almost literally self-effacing. The adolescent look and self-presentation enhanced the power of the words, as did the control and precision of delivery. He is and is not literary, as his references indicate; he refers to him-self as a poet of experience, and enjoys critical feedback on form and meter. He values poetry slams in that they echo some of the old rap-off energy from the 1980s. Though he resists the label "hip-hop poet," it is not hip-hop that troubles him so much as labels. Like Duke Ellington, he finds categories and the processes of categorizing to be grand canyons of bombast. BlacQ's poetic analysis of the violence of representation and the representation of violence, the distance and the proximity of the academy to those representations, and the odd disorienta-tion of being a bridge, of participating in multiple spheres demonstrates the power and insight of "student writing" from a young poet whose work bridges in its content the academy and the street. He is himself, as all of us are, a multi-ply constructed subject whose several identities, conflicting but also mutually sustaining, find their poetic expression formally in a vernacular modernism, and publicly at a series of poetry slams that helped to offset the doubt he expressed to his creative writing teacher that his writing was "really poetry" like the lyric verse of the other students in the class.

MICROPOETRIES

The study of micropoetries would sharply revise academic approaches to "poetry," a turn away from formalism and canonicity entirely, toward the micro-genres that permeate our everyday lives. These micropoetries could be graffiti as language, poetry therapies, prison poetry, a relative's topical verse, the history of fortune cookies, the use of modernist conventions (linebreaks, the belief in the sudden private aperçu) to market corporate slogans lasered in gothic script onto wooden plaques . . . they could also be pre-slam colloquial, vernacular poetry (usually contained as "folklore" or colorful ethnographic detail), sound that con-tributes to a texture of living in forgotten places. I borrow the term from ethno-musicologist Mark Slobin, whose study of "micromusics of the west" brings to light new fields for intellectual and emotional play—that is, research. Among his roster of micromusics one could find lullabyes, counting-out ditties, family songs that locate the immigrant family's town of origin generations later. (Think here of W. E. B. Du Bois's essay "Of the Sorrow Songs," which begins as a meditation on a song inherited from his "grandfather's grandmother," whose words he doesn't understand but faithfully transcribes syllable by syllable, and which essay continues to be one of the first and most profound pieces of writing on the cultural, historical, and emotional work accomplished by slave spirituals.)

Approaching these traces, these semiobytes of charged language, with an attention that transgresses solely ethnographic, formalist, or materialist agendas will tell us what we need to know about the hidden life of language, of bodies, of social relations, and of everything in between. Studying these bodies of work is important not because they're whimsical and eccentrically eclectic, or because such scholarship flushes the most obscure verbiage out of hiding (poetics scholarship as ethno-exotica tourism), but because it offers a texture of reality to proclamations such as "poetry is social practice." As George Lipsitz observes in a chapter entitled "This Ain't No Sideshow," what might appear to some as a quaint novelty is heavily saturated with meaning that richly rewards investigation. Such investigative work creates an ever more lively and complete sense of grassroots creative activity. In my undergraduate poetry classes, students must research and document a micropoetry. I've received some brilliant and many perfunctory papers; the following shows pragmatically how poetry research can bridge discourses and concerns within and outside the academy. A friend remarked, apropos this assignment, "It seems your aim is to increase your students' sensitivity to their sociolinguistic environments—but beyond that?" He meant, how do I then make the bridge to "real" poetry? How do I use that "increased sensitivity" to analyze more conventionally conceived-of "poems"? I guess I don't.

Micropoetry Research and Analysis: by DK

A Prestigious Structure

I have heard rumors now and then of
a possible dismantling of the grand
old Williams Arena, formerly the
fieldhouse. I am concerned for this
dear old building because I was a

> bricklayer there during its construc-
> tion in 1927–28.
>
> Few people know of the quality ma-
> terials used and the dimensions. I do
> not remember the overall dimen-
> sions, but I do know of the mam-
> moth steel construction and the solid
> brick walls. The two long side walls
> are 16 1/2 inches thick — four bricks
> wide. The two end walls built to
> follow the round curved steel roof are
> 29 inches thick from bottom to top
> — seven bricks wide. The bricks
> themselves are of the highest quality.
>
>   —Roy Larson, Cumberland, Wis.
>   (letter to *Minnesota Daily*)

This "poem" is about many prominent cultural symbols in America, among them the symbolic importance of the laborer or "blue col-
lar" worker, the edifice and the importance of large public buildings
in the expansion of the United States, the academic institution of the
University, the importance of sports (and the Big Ten) within that academic institution, and most prominently, the brick, a symbol of great
significance regarding the story of development in the United States,
especially in the first half of the Twentieth Century. Finally, this letter
has further significance at this time for the University community in
Minneapolis, where Memorial Stadium has now been destroyed.

One of the most interesting issues raised by this poem is the pride
in craftsmanship expressed by the letter-writer. Seldom are we
afforded the opportunity to read such simply stated, artistic writing
expressing the love of a blue-collar worker for the product that he or
she has helped to create. His simple explication of the dimensions of
the building has a very minimal feeling; no overt political, or even
aesthetic, statement is made, which distinguishes this letter from
most of those printed on editorial pages, which by their nature deal
with overt political themes. This letter seems to have a different
intention; it is documentary, historical, and has more in common

with a statistician's report than a George Will column. Further, the letter-writer admits that he has only a limited amount of knowledge to provide. Being a bricklayer, he does "not remember the overall dimensions"; he can only recall his contribution to the project, the bricks that composed the outer walls. The admission by the letter-writer that he has only a small amount of information to contribute to the debate regarding the fate of Williams Arena, as well as the minimalist, or "simple," descriptions such as "the grand old Williams Arena" and "this dear old building" contribute to the emotional reaction that this letter produces, a feeling of pride and adoration for the product of a blue-collar labor-intensive project and the skill and knowledge required to make such a building.

The importance of these buildings in the life of both the University and the community in general is directly linked to the sporting activities and the overall competitive and commercial aspects of academia in general; it is illuminating that craftsmanship on such a grand scale is devoted to building a "sports" arena. A look at modern buildings like the Hubert H. Humphrey Metrodome and the Target Center indicates that this theme continues to thrive in our urban environment.

Of all the culturally significant symbols in Roy Larson's poem-letter, the most fascinating is the brick. The brick is an ancient form of building material; bricks over 4500 years old have been found in the Indus river valley and other areas. Bricks have many advantages over other materials, being weather resistant and a good form of insulation (two important features for a Minnesota building). The bricks of Williams Arena "are of the highest quality," undoubtedly intended to last as long as the bricks of the Indus civilization. This is one of the important features of the brick; it is not a material used for nonpermanent building—Williams Arena [was] designed to last forever. Until, as with the Memorial Stadium, [it is] torn down out of bureaucratic necessity and changing cultural values.

Bricks have become an important symbol of the expanding size and technological capabilities of the United States. The construction method described eloquently in this letter was a common one; the steel structure supporting solid brick walls. This method of architecture is no longer used, with modern buildings utilizing steel-reinforced concrete and cinder-block walls that sometimes, not always, provide a structure for a brick facade. But the symbolic importance of the material value of the brick is evidenced in the recent razing of Memorial Stadium. The University of Minnesota, in a moment of fund-raising genius, decided to sell the bricks taken from the walls of the stadium for ten dollars each. That anyone would find sentimental value in a brick, especially ten dollars worth of value, is a testament to the import of these symbolic building blocks.

How can poetry, or more specifically, the poetic activity that is a shared project, illuminate our public civic relations? How can the private pleasures of reading this paper, now shared in a circumscribed, though somewhat more public, chapter setting, translate into meaningful activity that intervenes in the machinery of the status quo? The point of bringing poetry into discussions of the public sphere is precisely to counter usefully the divide-and-conquer practice of genre that dictates poetry's irrelevance to the common good because of its subjectivist orientation. I would argue, following Nancy Fraser's call for more and internally heterogeneous publics in which differences are openly articulated, that poetry's *permission* for subjectivity (or hermeticism, if language poets are uncomfortable with an uncritical acquiescence to the convention of lyrical subjectivity) contributes to a rich, ahierarchic heterogeneity of which a (hypothetical?) democracy consists. While Fraser's critique of Habermas's bourgeois public sphere, and most discussions thereof, do not take the aesthetic into account as a meaningful category, this exclusion does not have to be the case. Though I'm barely in a position to elaborate the role of the aesthetic in articulating the academy to its secular counterpart, and in enabling an empowered multiplicity of publics, it seems intuitively obvious that these examples embody such an articulation. The realms of gold are a utopian hetero-democracy made of charged talk-language, but like other alchemical ideals, it's also always already here.

WORKS CITED

Abu-Lughod, Lila. *Veiled Sentiments: Honor and Poetry in a Bedouin Society*. Berkeley: University of California Press, 1986.
Agamben, Giorgio. *The Coming Community*. Minneapolis: University of Minnesota Press, 1994.

Algarin, Miguel, and Bob Holman, eds. *Aloud: Voices from the NuYorican Poets' Café*. New York: Henry Holt, 1994.

Aronowitz, Stanley. "Is a Democracy Possible? The Decline of the Public in the American Debate." In *The Phantom Public Sphere*, edited by Bruce Robbins, 75–92. Minneapolis: University of Minnesota Press, 1993.

Baraka, Amiri. "SOS." In *The Amiri Baraka/Le Roi Jones Reader*. New York: Thunder's Mouth Press, 1991.

Beatty, Paul. *Big Bank Take Little Bank*. New York: NuYorican Poets' Cafe Press, 1990.

Benjamin, Walter. "The Work of Art in the Age of Mechanical Reproduction." In *Illuminations*, translated by Harry Zohn, 217–51. New York: Schocken, 1969.

Beverley, John. *Against Literature*. Minneapolis: University of Minnesota Press, 1993.

Caton, Steven. *"Peaks of Yemen I Summon": Poetry as Cultural Practice in a North Yemeni Tribe*. Berkeley: University of California Press, 1990.

Du Bois, W. E. B. *The Souls of Black Folk*. New York: Signet, 1969.

Fraser, Nancy. "Rethinking the Public Sphere: A Contribution to the Critique of Actually Existing Democracy." In *The Phantom Public Sphere*, edited by Bruce Robbins, 1–32. Minneapolis: University of Minnesota Press, 1993.

Gates, Henry Louis, Jr. *The Signifying Monkey*. London: Oxford University Press, 1990.

———. "Sudden Def." *New Yorker*, June 19, 1995, 33–42.

Graham, Jorie. Interview. In *A View from the Loft*. Minneapolis: The Loft, 1994.

Jonas, Stephen. "Letter to Cid Corman," March 2, 1961. In *that: Shorts Sets of Writing* 23 (July 1994): 1.

Kaufman, Bob. "Perhaps." In *Solitudes Crowded with Loneliness*, 54. New York: New Directions, 1965.

Lipsitz, George. *Time Passages*. Minneapolis: University of Minnesota Press, 1992.

Morales, Ed. "The Last Hispanic." In *Aloud: Voices from the NuYorican Poets' Café*, edited by Miguel Algarin and Bob Holman, 99–100. New York: Henry Holt, 1994.

Morris, Tracie. *Chap-T-Her Won*. Brooklyn: TM Ink, 1993.

Perelman, Bob. "Parataxis and Narrative: The New Sentence in Theory and Practice." *American Literature* 65, 2 (June 1993): 313–24.

Robbins, Bruce, ed. *The Phantom Public Sphere*. Minneapolis: University of Minnesota Press, 1993.

Slobin, Mark. *Subcultural Sounds: Micromusics of the West*. Hanover, NH: Wesleyan University Press, 1993.

Spicer, Jack. Interview by Lew Ellingham with Gail Chugg. Cited in Lew Ellingham and Kevin Killian, *Poet, Be Like God: The Life of Jack Spicer* (Middleton, CT: Wesleyan University Press, 1998).

Survey and Discipline

Literary Pedagogy in the Context of Cultural Studies

John Mowitt

4

BEING THERE *AND* BEING SQUARE

In what could only be characterized as an inauspicious opening, let me begin by recounting a history of failure. Here at Minnesota, as vestiges of the era recently eclipsed by the "new accountability," we offer two campus-wide teaching awards. As is typical of such awards, they are long on cachet (the fact that one is a recipient is flagged in the "course guide" through which undergraduates "shop" for courses each quarter) and short on cash. Fittingly enough, one is nominated to compete for these awards by one's students, and, in fact, usually one student in concert with your chair is centrally responsible for assembling your dossier. Clearly, since bureaucratic labor is involved, one nominates with conviction.

I have twice been nominated for these awards, without yet having received one. Since other colleagues whom I would consider my pedagogical equals have

48

received either one or both awards, you will understand why—when a colleague and friend who served on the review committee offered to explain my failure—I instantly set aside whatever scruples I might otherwise have had about violating professional confidentiality and pricked up my ears. In a cryptic phrase befitting the pseudo-gravity of the moment, my colleague whispered, "the students on the committee thought you were too ideological." Though not entirely surprising, this disclosure immediately prompted me to reflect on the difference between the two groups of students: those who saw fit to nominate me, and those who, no doubt, regarded the former group as essentially "duped" by my effective, though ultimately corrupt, pedagogical powers. To my knowledge, none of the students who judged me "too ideological" were actually past or present students of mine (surely this would have come out in the committee's deliberations), which meant that their assessment was based entirely on the characterization of my pedagogical objectives (goals and methods) contained in my dossier. However, rather than bemoaning the fact that they had never witnessed me "in action" (as though that would make the slightest bit of difference), I found myself acknowledging that, though they were mistaken about the uniquely troubling link between ideology and my teaching, they were certainly right to characterize my work in such terms. In effect, they "knew" that even when I was not teaching leftist ideology (say, the German ideology in "Theories of Culture"), I was teaching ideologically.

In the "statement on teaching" that appears in my dossier I describe my pedagogical approach as one dictated by a commitment to what I have elsewhere characterized as "antidisciplinarity" (Mowitt 1992). I stress the importance of organizing courses (even those that meet major requirements) around questions whose answers oblige one to rethink the framework within which the questions were formulated, a rethinking that allows one to savor the dynamics of deferral (the pleasure of difficulty) while at the same time emphasizing the importance of answers that change the way we think by changing the social conditions under which thinking "takes place." Most immediately, of course, these conditions are disciplinary, at once curricular and extracurricular. In effect, every course is, to some significant degree, a remake of the *Argos*—the ship that must be dismantled and reassembled (I would prefer to say "chopped") while at sea. When teaching is about the subject matter—say, the genre of the essay—as much as it is about the matter of teaching, it is doubly instructive. It is also ideological. To insist on this in a society where, as Walter Benjamin says, "practice is in decline" is to side with all those committed—at some level or other—to the labor theory of value.

Such a perspective is, to my mind, indissociable from the desire, as Fredric Jameson calls it, of cultural studies (Jameson 1995), a desire that has undergone an instructive trauma of late. I am referring, of course, to Alan Sokal's hoax perpetrated on the editors of *Social Text* (a journal on whose editorial board I too once sat). If I characterize this hoax as a traumatization of cultural studies, it is for essentially two reasons: (1) Sokal, as the coauthor of *Random Walks, Critical Phenomena*, and *Triviality in Quantum Field Theory*, represents himself as the standard bearer of precisely the realist epistemology that cultural studies (to the extent that it presents itself on the pages of *ST*) is accused of having forsaken; and (2) Sokal also presents himself as a fellow "fellow traveler," that is, a leftist academic. Though this is by no means the first time that the partisans of cultural studies have been attacked by the left (one thinks here of the acrimony of the comparatively recent debate over "politically correct" cultural criticism), the fusion of realism and Marx in a well-publicized and effective hoax has given this particular attack its unique sting. Since I have no desire to further stir the contents of this proverbial can of worms, let me clarify why I have alluded to it at all. In explaining the "necessity" of his intervention, Sokal writes,

> I say this [presumably the entirety of the preceding article] not in glee but in sadness. After all, I am a leftist too (under the Sandinista government I taught mathematics at the National University of Nicaragua). On nearly all practical political issues—I'm on the same side as the *Social Text* editors. But I am a leftist (and a feminist) *because* of evidence and logic, not in spite of it. Why should the right wing be allowed to monopolize the intellectual high ground? (Sokal 1996, 64)

Quite apart from the invidious characterization of cultural studies as the low ground (a euphemistic evocation of the very deceptive practices Sokal admits to in his article), there is the matter of Sokal's leftist credentials. Even if we take him at his word—and why not, since the left today needs practically every ally it can get—I am struck by his confidence that he can unequivocally establish his credentials merely by invoking his teaching in Nicaragua. As the election that brought Violeta Chamorro to power in 1990 made clear, at least some nonleftists were probably teaching at the National University during the Ortega regime. More important, however, Sokal apparently believes that simply by establishing that he taught in the context of an emergent (and later stunted) socialist society, he *therefore* must be a leftist. Moreover, unless we are to infer that everything a leftist does is itself leftist (an untenable if not finally absurd proposition), then

Sokal's claim makes it impossible to determine in what sense he is a leftist *academic* who, on virtually all practical matters, would indeed side with the editors of *ST*. Lest I be misunderstood here: I have no quarrel with Sokal's desire to invoke his decision to teach in Nicaragua with pride. I respect and even envy him in this regard. My quarrel is with the way he feels entitled to remain silent about his teaching practice, as though *how* he taught mathematics in Nicaragua is irrelevant to whether we ought to consider him a leftist academic. The cartoons (in Spanish, by the way) that punctuate *Random Walks* suggest — at most — that Sokal tries to make his teaching (the book explicitly addresses itself to graduate students and researchers) warm and fuzzy, or as we now say, "user friendly." His silence on the matter of pedagogical practice, coupled with his various disciplinary commitments to epistemological realism (mathematics, physics, etc.), though likely to garner him a teaching award at the University of Minnesota, also implicitly aligns him with those currently monopolizing the real estate on the "high ground," that is, the right. We can justify this assertion — albeit sketchily — by considering the educational agenda of the right over the last two decades.

Contemporary pedagogy (which I understand to include both how and what we teach) either confirms and implements national educational goals or contradicts and challenges them. This is not restricted to a particular "genre" of pedagogy. It is just as true of the sciences (both "natural" and "social") as it is of the humanities. But where exactly do "national goals" intersect educational practices? Put succinctly, this intersection is to be found in the social determination of educational priorities. When educators in this country are publicly scolded for having contributed to our national loss of "competitiveness," it is clear that, from the perspective of the admonishers, the social function of education is to be defined in strictly economic terms. Moreover, this is not a matter of economic terms *in general*, since competition functions as an unequivocal evaluative concept primarily, if not exclusively, within the context of the economic practices that have been central to the national ambitions of the United States for the better part of two centuries. This preoccupation with competitiveness should not be surprising. It is, after all, the logic of capitalism to subsume all experience (including that associated with leisure and pleasure) within the economic sphere.

When educators seek to address such a situation by conceding the priority given to instruction in mathematics (theoretical and applied) and science, thereby underscoring our already massive epistemological commitment to, broadly speaking, "realism," we are explicitly cooperating with a national political agenda and, in effect, surrendering education to the complex and uneven task of social reproduction. The fact that instruction in the fields of mathematics and science (some obviously more than others), particularly at the postsecondary level, is expensive (not everyone can afford, say, a particle accelerator) means that the priority given these fields will *necessarily* be at the expense of other fields since, despite all its highly concentrated abundance, North American capitalism is *still* an economy of scarcity. In fact, it must remain one if competition is to continue functioning as its premier motivational device. "Downsizing" is thus little more than a spectral avatar of scarcity. To insist then, even strategically, on supporting competitiveness by privileging the production of scientific and mathematical knowledge (even when this is done in the name of understanding the "real world") is to adopt a political position that is indistinguishable, at the level of educational policy, from the traditional conservative legitimations of capitalism. Often such legitimations openly claim that this knowledge can be produced *only* within the context of capitalism (or, to use Karl Popper's formulation, "a free society"), thereby implicitly threatening those critical of capitalism with the "global" implications of a cessation of the production of scientific and mathematical knowledge. Despite what many may think, the survival of capitalism is not a natural phenomenon—it is a sociopolitical achievement. One ought not, therefore, pretend that education—especially in the so-called value-neutral fields of the sciences—can be understood independently of the political interests that traverse the social field in which it is taking place. Of course, good socialists will need to excel at mathematics, but recognizing this in no way clarifies how instruction in mathematics per se contributes to building socialism in the United States. Thus, my point is not that the link between the sciences and national economic policy is *necessary*, but rather that because this link exists, academics, especially those on the left, must articulate what it is they are doing at the level of pedagogy that exposes and challenges it.

This general state of affairs prevails equally, though differently, within the humanities. Since the early eighties we have seen a virtual barrage of works that address what was once referred to as the "crisis of the humanities." Under the first Reagan administration the neo-Arnoldian William Bennett launched an assault on humanities educators, chiding them not for contributing to our loss of competitiveness (at least not directly), but for undermining the enabling conditions of "intellectual authority" (Bennett 1984). Somewhat more recently Allan Bloom, in *The Closing of the American Mind*, pursued a similar line of reasoning to argue that humanities educators, entranced by the theories and objects of what was becoming cultural studies, were leading us to squander what capitalism had given us, namely, the world hegemony of Western cultural values (Bloom 1988). In effect, on Bloom's reading, the problematization of the Western canon has indeed contributed to our loss of competitiveness because it has made it harder to indulge in entrepreneurial exploitation and plunder with a clear cultural conscience. This, apparently, is the one "entitlement program" the right cannot support strongly enough.

Is it any wonder then that the spate of so-called curriculum wars has been so acrimonious? What conservatives have perceived with admirable clarity is that teaching cultural interpretation has explicitly political implications. Challenging the incontestable value of a tradition and the intellectual convictions that have supported it is rightly seen to have a social meaning. Those who obscure this meaning by referring to what is at stake in such a challenge as "curricular innovation" (whether affirmed or denied) sacrifice their analyses to an imprudently apolitical view of culture. By the same token—as John Guillory has convincingly shown—it is equally problematic to interpret debate over the literary canon as synonymous with a cultural revolution (Guillory 1993). After all, who could be more politically ineffectual than a radical intellectual convinced that an unpublished deconstructive reading of *Paradise Lost* is *in fact* the death knell of the West? There is absolutely no point in identifying with the corrosive efficacy attributed to such a critique by one's opponents, opponents whose ultimate form of guile may consist precisely in luring one into just such an identification.

The irony that haunts Bloom's title (after all, what does it mean for a diagnosis of American intellectual decay to become an American bestseller?) infects the entire conservative position. The more they attempt to pass the ideological buck, as it were, while fretting about the decline of the West, the more conservatives make it obvious that Western culture is ideological through and through. Conservatives simply don't like the fact that the humanistic alibi for capitalist rapacity is being systematically undermined. While one might well want to debate the virtues of Soviet-style Marxism, there is no point in denying that capitalism and its cultural logic are ideological. The real question has to do with whether the ideological values celebrated within capitalist societies actually contribute to the general realization of the experiences those values claim to celebrate.

Stuart Hall, in "The Emergence of Cultural Studies and the Crisis of the Humanities," has, to my mind, established with compelling clarity the contentious status of cultural studies in the current conjuncture. Though only toward the end of his remarks does he seek to extrapolate their implications for the U.S. scene, the following citation elucidates nicely the historico-political link between cultural studies and the problematization of Western humanism.

> When cultural studies began its work in the 1960s and '70s [in Britain], it had, therefore, to undertake the task of unmasking what it considered to be the unstated presuppositions of the humanist tradition itself. It had to try to bring to light the ideological assumptions underpinning the practice, to expose the educational program . . . , and to try to conduct an ideological critique of the way the humanities and the arts presented themselves as parts of disinterested knowledge. It had, that is, to undertake a work of demystification to bring into the open the regulative nature and role the humanities were playing in relation to the national culture. (Hall 1990, 15)

Perhaps because Hall's remarks were addressed to an audience gathered to consider the general topic of social technologies and the humanities, he posits as the catalyst for his assumption of the enumerated tasks "the manifest breakup of traditional culture," in postwar Britain, a breakup made explicit in the impact of the mass media on working-class life. Though one would be hard pressed to characterize "traditional culture" in the United States as sharing some deep affiliation with working-class life, Hall himself sees that the reaction against cultural studies here is tied to its role in the struggle to reexamine our cultural heritage, a heritage deemed by the right as crucial to the legitimacy of the "American way of life."

Of predictable interest to me is Hall's later discussion of pedagogy, where he characterizes it as thoroughly reflective of the interdisciplinary and critical character of the cultural studies enterprise. Hall expresses the fact that cultural studies courses at Birmingham were presented to their students as effectively "made up as they went along," and dissertators, when it came time to designate thesis topics, were routinely instructed to work on issues that presented themselves in the world outside academia. To some degree, of course, this amounts to little more than acknowledging the "emergent" character of cultural studies, but to Hall's credit (as well, by the way, as Jameson's), he also recognizes that there is something vital about this form of reflexive pedagogy, especially as a means to articulate the intellectual and political agenda of cultural studies. Thus, in addition to wishing to suggest that this is one of the chief reasons the defense of the traditional humanities has been so vigorous of late, I also want to underscore the extent to which Sokal *appears* committed to a project consistent with the broad cultural agenda of the right. What the right hypocritically insists on, namely, the depoliticization of pedagogy, Sokal takes for granted. That is, by proceeding as though there is nothing politically important to say about his pedagogical practice, Sokal effectively concedes the point to the right, which, of course, claims there *shouldn't* be. This, coupled with his aggressive defense of epistemological realism, invites one to conclude that he would never countenance a form of instruction that "made it up as it went along," because, presumably, to do so would be tantamount to denying that we really know certain things about our subject matter. Though, of course, neither Hall nor I mean to suggest that people in cultural studies teach out of ignorance, I would contend that to teach people what you *do* know about what virtually no one will pay you to know requires an approach that is ideological through and through, one that might even be effectively pursued in the "belly of the beast."

"WE'VE BEEN THINKING . . ."

But what does this have to do with teaching literature? Everything. When we talk about literary pedagogy we have to begin by acknowledging the sociohistorical circumstances under which the question—how should literature be taught?—arises. Prior to any meaningful response to this question must come the further questions—what is the teaching of literature for? what aim does such teaching have? The traditional Leavisite answer—to make us better people—is unsatisfactory because it presupposes the very consensus belied by the question. We need to know what we want people to be better at, or what we want them to be better in relation to. As should be apparent from the preceding remarks, I do not think we should simply be trying to make people better at competing with each other. In fact, competition strikes me as precisely the wrong way to carry out the necessary conceptual and practical task of affirming differences. Instead—and I offer this as an opening gambit—I think we ought to be trying to make people better able to comprehend the conditions and limits of their lives, and better able to translate this comprehension into the practical structuring of daily life at both the local and global levels. Teaching literature, therefore, must assume its form and content from this unabashedly insurgent aim. What does this mean?

To begin with it is important to recognize that literature is tied to the social fate of the humanities. This is true not simply because most of the more publicized quarrels over the humanities have centered on the issues of cores and canons (often explicitly literary), but because the ideological values that are at stake in such quarrels grip the very heart of literary study, namely, the practice of interpretation. Let us not forget that canons are not simply lists of books; they are more fundamentally the standard points of reference that bound the field of cultural interpretation. Canons, as anyone teaching literature at the postsecondary level knows, are typically used to test the merits of an interpretive approach, whether this be at the level of a preliminary exam or at the more quotidian level of a student's written interpretation of a particular piece of writing. It is because of this that in the last twenty years there has been a parallel development between the revision of the Western literary canon and the diversification of interpretive practices—a process closely tied to the multifarious developments in what we conveniently refer to as critical theory.

As is evident from the preceding discussion of Hall, the humanities—and therefore the study of literature—has been deeply transformed by its antagonism with cultural studies. Being no more eager than Hall himself is to "define" cultural studies, I will suggest that its various intellectual, political, and disciplinary currents share, among certain other things, a rejection of the "instrumentalization" of scholarly research. By instrumentalization I mean, as did those who coined the term, the tendency to equate thinking with problem solving, where reflection is subordinated to the requirement of efficacy (Adorno and Horkheimer 1972; Horkheimer 1974). Contrary to what is typically assumed, this instrumentalization has not, however, involved a "dehumanization" of the humanities. Instead, instrumentalization has involved three related trends: (1) the enervation of rigorous intellectual scholarship in the humanities due to pseudo-pluralistic demands for accessibility and relevance that date from the sixties; (2) the "positivization" of humanistic research, where uncritical reliance on "social scientific" paradigms has displaced hermeneutical complexity with a quasi-juridical obsession with critical evaluation and the search for facts—an overcompensation for the effects of enervation; and (3) the sanctification of humanistic research, which aims to protect the Western tradition by artificially severing it from, and thus making it utterly vulnerable to, the historical context of capitalistic patriarchy. The latter trend in particular resists being read as a dehumanization because by insisting on the transcendental character of Western "man" it seeks to recapture precisely what contemporary life has threatened to deprive humanism of, namely, its subject. What nevertheless keeps this trend within the orbit of instrumental reason is its refusal to ground cultural interpretation in the political struggles that traverse and constitute the social—a refusal it shares, in different ways, with both other trends, and which marks all three as signs of instrumentalization. Though this may not seem immediately applicable to the trend toward positivism in humanistic research, it is only the veneer of anti-theoreticism that sustains this illusion. Social scientism is just as instrumental as unbridled humanism in that it, too, typically bases its epistemological authority on an implicit, ahistorical ontology.

Crucial to the critique of instrumental reason is the recognition that it thrives on the segmentation and hierarchization of fields. Only when certain "ways of knowing" become dominant, that is, not just practically reliable but — for that very reason — the very model of what thought in general ought to strive for, is it possible for problem solving to transcend the disciplinary field in which it operates. Thus, one of the decisive contributions of cultural studies has been the extrapolation of the interdisciplinarity cortical to the traditional humanities — an extrapolation that has required that the humanities be seen as a field that not only borders on other fields, but also is internally structured by the presence of many different borders. Instead of reading this relation as essentially benign, however, cultural studies has defined itself by insisting on the reciprocally constitutive aspect of the relations among fields. Precisely because we must oppose instrumentalization, then, it becomes crucial to oppose the segmentation of fields that supports both sanctification and positivization: the former, in that segmentation permits one to believe that a domain can be transcendentally separated from other domains; the latter, in that positivization requires that "data" be so delimited as to permit factual conclusions (i.e., conclusions no longer meaningfully subject to interpretation). What nevertheless differentiates this refusal of segmentation from traditional models of interdisciplinarity is the fact that within cultural studies, discipline itself has become problematical. It is no longer enough to insist on breaking down the barriers between disciplines, what has become urgent now is the need to examine how disciplines have *always* been traversed by one another. Such an examination reveals that the important struggle is against disciplinarity as such. Insofar as cultural studies engages this struggle, it articulates less an interdisciplinary than an antidisciplinary activity.

If we situate the teaching of literature in such a context, it becomes important to abandon any notion of the "properly literary" that would constitute the object of such teaching. This does not mean that the specificity of "literary language" has to be ignored or forsaken. It simply means that this specificity is perhaps better comprehended as an effect of an intertextual field of discourses, rather than as the mystical property of certain speech acts. What constitutes this intertextual field? Obviously, it is necessary to move beyond the opposition between literary and nonliterary discourses and include in the analysis of "literature" the institutions that reproduce the opposition between elite and popular culture as well as the multifarious cultural practices that articulate the social divisions of race, class, and gender. Of course, once one adopts such a perspective the question of pedagogy is immediately posed in sociopolitical terms. Either we seek to conduct our classes in a manner that is consistent with this sense of the object of cultural studies, or we proceed otherwise. The latter option can be accomplished in one of two ways: either by openly rededicating oneself to the instrumentalization of the humanities, or by teaching cultural studies in a manner that sacrifices what is potentially distinctive about it to the pedagogical limitations of an instrumentalized classroom.

What constitutes an instrumentalized classroom? Perhaps one of the most conspicuous signs of such a classroom is the subordination of the instructional materials to the survey paradigm. A feature of postsecondary education in the United States since the forties, a survey course, regardless of discipline, almost invariably means that a wide range of materials will be examined from an unspecified vantage point for the duration of the course. In literary departments, surveys typically function to introduce students to national, historical, or generic fields ("Survey in British Literature," for example). The paradigm recommends itself for its efficiency. The survey course covers a lot of ground quickly, and it can be taught with an incredibly high student-to-teacher ratio. Moreover, it encourages precisely the sort of histrionics on the part of teachers that create the impression of pluralism and the "free marketplace of ideas" for students — people who are regarded by their teachers as simultaneously empty vessels and indisputable authorities on "what they like." To be sure, students often enjoy such courses, but less because they are indeed successful than because their "exposure" to a field of knowledge can be orchestrated so that the discovery of their "ignorance" becomes indistinguishable from the pleasure their instructors take in being smarter than those who are, by their instructor's own definition, incapable of seriously evaluating his or her intelligence. This, of course, does not distinguish survey courses from other large lecture courses.

What makes survey courses particularly problematic is their basic structural character. According to the *Oxford English Dictionary*, the notion of a survey course depends heavily on two semantic fields: (1) where the accent falls on a comprehensive *mental* view of something; and (2) where "survey" refers to the process of measuring a tract of land from a particular vantage point. If we think these fields simultaneously (and the institutional history of this paradigm encourages us to do so), we recognize that there is an implicit convergence between the mind (of someone) and the vantage point from which a land measurement is taken. Instead of immediately stressing how important it is for "ignorant" students to have an "overview" of a field (in order, presumably, to prepare themselves for a more in-depth sounding later in life), let us consider the implicit assumptions behind the very model of a survey as a way to educate people.

As those of us familiar with them well know, most survey courses consistently bite off more than they can chew. There is simply no way to responsibly cover what might be deemed significant about a century of world history in ten to sixteen weeks. Obviously, one must select from an overwhelming field of materials. This, in itself, is not a tremendous problem—even an advanced seminar on Virginia Woolf's periodical essays will have to select from among them in order to read any of them carefully enough to say something pertinent about them. But what one can do in an advanced seminar, namely, situate Woolf's essays with regard to a particular problematic, cannot be accomplished in a survey—regardless of the intentions of the instructor. Why? When we speak of situating a text, it is apparent that there are many ways to do this. In survey courses, because they stress an impossible comprehensiveness, the task of situating is typically carried out by establishing how various artists or authors "influenced" one another. What is the medium of this influence? Ideas.

Even in the best of survey courses the relations among the figures covered are established not simply in the *mind* of the person responsible for the syllabus, but in the sphere of ideas. The point is not that the figures actually exchanged thoughts—this is far too vulgar a connection for most practitioners of survey courses—but that it is in the sphere of ideas that the coherence of the time covered in the survey is to be located. One need not appeal to the dubiously Hegelian notion of the *Zeitgeist* in order to affirm such a position. Anytime one organizes a course around figures who are imagined to be elaborating different opinions about some shared intellectual concern, and affirms that on the basis of this exchange of opinions these figures *belong* to the period covered by the survey, s/he is confirming the survey paradigm. Though most partisans of survey courses would scoff at the suggestion, there is little that separates their courses from the thankfully short-lived talk show hosted by Steve Allen, *The Meeting of the Minds.*

Latent within survey courses is a form of idealism that is not merely incidental to the instruction that goes on within such courses. This idealism need never be presented as such to be passed along to the students, who are thus encouraged to

accept this undefended intellectual perspective as being as "obviously" true as
their own attendance. In effect, students are being taught a double lesson: one
about the content of the course; the other about the "necessary" nature of their
relation to these contents. In surveys, regardless of what one learns about British
literature, one also learns that what is worth knowing circulates as ideas, and that
it is in the sphere of ideas that history takes place. This is not an innocent lesson.
It is not a lesson that is simply "compensated" for at the intermediate and
advanced levels of the curriculum. Learning to survey is a political lesson that
those involved in cultural studies ought to be attempting to undermine.

What gives the idealism latent in the survey paradigm its political charge is
the fact that, in the name of providing a general exposure to a subject area that
should open up students' choices, it consolidates and gives institutional legitimacy to the epistemological assumptions students have been hailed with since
elementary school—assumptions that are demonstrably narrow and thus incapable of promoting open choices. The assumptions animating idealism are
restrictive because they contain as an implicit foundational claim the notion that
the sphere of ideas is autonomous (i.e., separate from society and material history) and determinant in the last instance (i.e., ideas make the world go around).
It is because ideas are assumed to make the world go around that partisans of
survey courses believe that it is responsible to present the sphere of ideas as that
which enables a historical period to cohere. It is not a compromise for the sake of
pedagogical expediency that motivates this focus—after all, other sorts of
courses and major requirements *can* be imagined—what motivates this focus is a
belief in idealism as such. And while it is true that surveys often deal with history, they do so in a manner consistent with the tenets of idealism. This means
two things: on the one hand, it means that history is reduced to what we refer to
as intellectual history—a reduction that automatically privileges the experiences of those able to give their experiences intellectual expression, and that
simultaneously excludes or renders impertinent all otherwise contemporaneous
experiences. On the other hand—and this is perhaps the most decisively restrictive aspect of idealism—its approach to history requires that the discourses of
intellectual expression be seen as instruments of an intelligence that manipulates
them from an ontological elsewhere. In other words, cultural discourse is not
only treated as merely historical in the sense of engaged in the day-to-day struggle for existence, but it is also seen as ultimately incapable of infecting the mind
with matter. In effect, survey courses, even when they are historical at the level
of content, are ahistorical at the level of pedagogical articulation because they

proceed as though "great ideas" engage other "great ideas" in some timeless sphere where material history never enters. When this arrangement is mapped onto the typical format of an undergraduate lecture, where the mind of the teacher expresses itself in front of what is, on one level, a secretarial pool devoted to materializing his/her ideas (one thinks here of Saussure's students), the problematic political effects of survey courses are made particularly clear.

In learning to survey, students absorb a lesson about their relation to knowledge, a lesson that, not surprisingly, is fully coincident with capitalist ideology: those who are in a position to sense the truth of the idea that mind dominates matter learn not only that this idea has always been true, but that it must be true—for if it were not simply a matter of truth (a concept that ambiguously and therefore conveniently refers both to a place and a condition), then one would have to come to terms with the power relation within which this idea has been made to appear true. Idealism is designed to shield truth from power by making the former apply to a sphere of existence that maintains what power it has by denying that power affects this sphere in any way. This is how even the most radical critiques of capitalist patriarchy are instantly neutralized—they are treated as more "great ideas," a fact that suggests yet another way surveys are inherently restrictive, namely, they are incapable of being effectively critical of the context in which they are offered. For if we agree that being *effectively* critical has something to do with empowering students to change their social relations, then a course that essentially reproduces the existing social relations within its own organizational dynamics not only cannot be critical, but actively contributes to a maintenance of the status quo. Such a result can hardly be construed as either neutral or open, and in this respect survey courses are indeed problematic even on their advocates' own terms. To insist, as some proponents of survey courses no doubt will, that one can override the limits of the model through "creative" design, is to fall back into idealism. Specifically, such an insistence relies on the notion that one can simply escape the history embedded in the model, bypassing the domains of the term's derivation, the relations implicit in the very concept of an overview, the tradition of its institutionalization, and so forth, merely by *thinking* about things differently. This is not to say that educators are purely passive bearers of what has preceded them, but if we are in some sense capable of historical agency, why should we waste our energies trying to revitalize a patently deficient paradigm? It is time to do something else.

This is, in effect, the impulse that cultural studies has attempted to respond to. In closing I will suggest how this response might affect literary pedagogy. To begin, literature can no longer adequately be taught in isolation. Literature ought to be seen as a complexly negotiated phenomenon that is traversed by multiple interests and forces. Even, as I said before, if we want to understand how Elizabethan prosody emerged as a distinctive practice, this has to be done contextually, since it, unlike Athena, did not emerge fully formed from Zeus's brain. The only way contextualism can be responsibly pursued is interdisciplinarily. If a literary scholar wants to know about the impact of minstrel rhythms on verse patterns, then s/he ought to consult the disciplines of ethnomusicology and linguistics. But it is not enough to elaborate the contexts of formal (or other) innovations interdisciplinarily. One must also question the limits imposed on such an elaboration by the social relations inscribed in disciplinary power.

Foucault, in his suggestive discussion of criminology (an interdisciplinary fusion of psychiatry, psychology, sociology, and architecture), has shown that certain disciplines within the social sciences developed in close proximity to the specifically bourgeois institutions of surveillance and punishment. His point is not that this proximity is evil (though he is not happy about it), but that the disciplines and institutions organized by it gave expression to a socially sanctioned way of treating human beings as subjects. Though it is true that one must fill in the links between this process and the disciplines of the humanities (both the social sciences and the humanities share an instrumentalized concept of humanity), doing so would only tend to confirm the fact that the internal structures of educational institutions derive their stability from the modes of power that bind these institutions to the societies they serve. Education, even a so-called liberal education, does not take place in a vacuum, but nor is it merely benignly related to its context. This is why teaching students about the limits or conditions of their experience must include an interrogation of disciplines.

Such an interrogation cannot be carried out in a survey course. This is because a survey *presupposes* a discipline, portions of which can be "panoptically" scrutinized. Thus, literary pedagogy within the framework of cultural studies should abandon the survey paradigm and the curriculum that derives from it. If a faculty deems it urgent to familiarize students with a broad range of developments (historical, social, generic, stylistic, etc.), then it should design courses that seek to specify the heterogeneity of discourses that articulate such developments, thereby refusing to treat ideas as self-generating phenomena destined to be "thought" at some later point and cognitively secreted into the minds of students. Moreover, such courses must be capable of reflecting on their own contextual preconditions—well-educated students ought to know something about the discipline into which they are implicitly being initiated. Obviously, this will mean that fewer "facts" are likely to be communicated, but this can be addressed in alternative ways. Courses can be longer, smaller, and differently coordinated than they are at present. In fact, since one hears continually about the pathetic advising students receive, perhaps it would make sense to have students and their advisers, to whatever extent possible, select courses each term that go together—either because they "teach the conflicts," as Gerald Graff says, or because they supplement each other in productive, that is, "dangerous" ways. Perhaps "internships" should be redefined as well. Instead of simply being ways to receive academic credit for professional training, perhaps they could become a way to locate "education" in the context of community activism. In my own courses I have "assigned" students interventions in the local public sphere (both print media and radio).

Why should educators begin with the assumption that they need to tailor their curricula to meet the needs of students, when all they are really doing is desperately trying to find a way to bring educational rhythms and structures into line with the social psychology of capitalism? It is time to transform a general acknowledgment of the political character of education into a movement to radicalize it. Why should corporations and professional and state agencies be the chief benefactors of the traffic between educational institutions and society? Let us drop the traditional obsession with being "well-rounded," and replace it with the aim of being "well-grounded." By which I mean that students, particularly in "humanities" programs, ought to be sufficiently grounded in their "situation" (as Sartre might say) that their interpretations of the world can engage it in a manner that allows them to change it. Anything short of this is not really worth our labor and our passion. Moreover, it can be done right here, right now.

WORKS CITED

Adorno, Theodor, and Max Horkheimer. *Dialectic of Enlightenment*, trans. J. Cummings, chap. 1. New York: Continuum Books, 1972.

Benjamin, Walter. *Charles Baudelaire: A Lyric Poet in the Age of High Capitalism*. London: Verso, 1983, 145–46.

Bennett, William. " 'To Reclaim a Legacy': Text of a Report on Humanities in Higher Education." *Chronicle of Higher Education*, Nov. 28, 1984, 16–21.

Bloom, Alan. *The Closing of the American Mind*. New York: Simon and Schuster, 1988.

Foucault, Michel. *Discipline and Punish: The Birth of the Prison*, trans. Alan Sheridan, pt. 3. New York: Pantheon, 1978.

Graff, Gerald. *Professing Literature: An Institutional History*. Chicago: University of Chicago Press, 1987, 258.

Guillory, John. *Cultural Capital: The Problem of Literary Canon Formation*. Chicago: University of Chicago Press, 1993.

Hall, Stuart. "The Emergence of Cultural Studies and the Crisis of the Humanities." *October* 53 (1990): 11–23.

Horkheimer, Max. *The Critique of Instrumental Reason*, trans. Matthew J. O'Connell. New York: Continuum Books, 1974.

Jameson, Fredric. "On Cultural Studies." In *The Identity in Question*, ed. John Rajchman, 251–95. New York: Routledge, 1995.

Mowitt, John. *Text: The Genealogy of an Antidisciplinary Object*. Durham: Duke University Press, 1992.

Popper, Karl. *The Open Society and Its Enemies*. Vol. 2, *The High Tide of Prophecy*. London: Routledge, 1945.

Sokal, Alan. "A Physicist Experiments with Cultural Studies." *Lingua Franca*, May–June 1996, 62–64.

Dumb and Dumber History
The Transhistorical Popular

5

Donald K. Hedrick

> It may be better not to know so many things than to
> know so many things that are not so.
>
> —*Felix Okoye,*
> The American Image of Africa

About that "history," so called. I begin by pairing two moments, one pedagogical and one textual, which together may install brakes on the accelerating
progress of cultural studies pedagogy. Their pairing helps me think about what
ought to be a chief question, at least for pedagogy involving early modern periods:
Is there or ought there to be a historical competency that is popular rather than
elitist? Although my concluding pedagogical suggestions require Marxist cultural
theory about our sense of the past, my trajectory leads me to be critical of the
Jamesonian Prime Directive to "always historicize." A different posture, constituting something of a formalist anticipatory critique of emerging practices, may help
us out of a certain impending impasse of cultural studies, particularly in its customary allegiance to intellectual critique as opposed to performative experience.

Teaching *Henry IV, Part 1* to an introductory Shakespeare class years back, I
needed an example to bring alive the factoid that Shakespeare's audience would
not have had a close familiarity with the distant history represented in the play.

Casting for a handy and forceful American parallel, I asked, "For Shakespeare's audience to look back some two hundred years earlier would be comparable to our looking back to what period from our history, class?" Assuming this to be a Socratic rather than a real question, I found, even before I had time to regret its condescending tone, that it had drawn blank looks and resentful silences. A lone voice eventually peeped, "The Civil War?" I realize this moment would be a choice bit for an NAS cocktail chat swap of Declining Academic Standards anecdotes. But I too share our pain. Nevertheless, the incident raised real questions for me about what history my students ought to be expected to know, not merely for "coverage" of Shakespeare but in the larger interests of a more public sphere. The fact that most students in American high schools cannot identify which half of the nineteenth century the Civil War occurred in (and my anecdote suggests the real situation may be worse) could throw curves to a cultural studies pedagogy grounded in a Marxism grounded in history, even before we ever reach "critical pedagogy."

My initial scandal, moreover, was tempered somewhat by the fact that the point of my comment in the first place was to show that the popular theater of Shakespeare's time demanded from its audience only a rough, working familiarity with the past rather than a historian's knowledge. Why then should I expect differently from my students? Should I not rather condone in them the spectacular cheek of Stanley Fish, who once declared (at the English Institute, no less), "I hate history. History makes me fall asleep." Rightly assailing some received pieties of new historicist enthusiasm, Fish's remark also made me confess to myself, and now to you, that in my own career origins, while it was Marxism that brought me to history, it was not history that brought me to literature. Was not a rough, working knowledge of a certain piece or pieces of history what my students most needed? How much history, for that matter, did I need?

We need here a history of the use-value of history, particularly one designed to consider "good enough" popular and democratic uses. For all the agonized journalistic head-scratching over increasing American ignorance of the past, the more available Marxist alternative to lamenting "standards" would be to recognize a current material condition now obtaining in the United States: if you are someone with wealth and power, or else someone with thwarted hope of getting them, in either case you don't need history to take you anywhere. And if recent history often has less value for the underfranchised, the situation makes early modern cultural studies even less urgent; if "critical pedagogy" for a Henry Giroux intends to unpack the ideological constructions of the contemporary popular, what is the payoff of doing that for a popular four hundred years old?

Perhaps as leftists and as cultural studies teachers we may even have something to learn from the plays themselves, as Fredric Jameson contends in a
review of "materialist" essays on Shakespeare. What he calls the "permanent
revolution" in Shakespeare studies (i.e., no more romantic genius, no more privatized artistic production, no more apologetics for the aristocratic class) has direct
consequences for pedagogy, particularly if organized into a radical account of
Shakespeare rather than a liberal pluralist one (although it is worth considering
that the distinction between these accounts may not always translate into a
direct political consequence).

In the plays themselves, then, Shakespeare explores history's use-value for
different kinds of historical information. I take one moment from the same play
as an example, a scene reminding us that the need for history occurs as the selection of a historical archive. In this comic moment set pointedly at the start of the
rebellion, the fuming Hotspur cannot recall the name of the castle where he first
met Henry Bolingbroke, the future king of England and his present opponent:

> Hotspur: In Richard's time—what do you call the place?—A plague
> upon it, it is in Gloucestershire—'Twas where the madcap duke
> his uncle kept—His uncle York—where I first bow'd my knee.
> Unto this king of smiles, this Bullingbrook—'Sblood! When
> you and he came back from Ravenspurgh—
> Northumberland: At Berkeley castle.
> Hotspur: You say true. (*Henry IV, Part 1*, 1.3.242–45)

Hotspur's irritation at the ingratitude of the same person his own family helped
raise to the throne becomes intermixed with his irritation at forgetting the name
of the castle. History is thus represented not as a neutral collecting of data, but as
a process within inspiration, intermingling fact and use, and even as a forgetting.
Indeed, in this case it is a forgetting that looks like the sort of derailment of a train
of thought that my own pedagogical experience imitated when I discovered a
crippling lack of common knowledge among my students. In Hotspur's case, it is a
father who provides the historical name (to be used to uncrown a father), a little
monument of reference allowing Hotspur back on his original narrative track.

In its gloss of this passage, one teaching edition of the play is instructive for
our consideration of history's pedagogical use, particularly in the distinction
between popular and elitist use. In its extensive references to Shakespeare's
source in Holinshed, the *Riverside Shakespeare* glosses the name of the castle,
although not in this scene but rather in *Richard II*, 3.2., as if assuming the reader

will absorb and reapply the knowledge for future reference to another play, ho ho. In the textual note we learn that "Barkloughly" was "Shakespeare's version of Holinshed's Barclowlie, itself an error for Hertlowi, i.e., Harlech, a castle in Northern Wales built by Edward I in 1285"—an elucidation, moreover, oblivious to the Elizabethan era's indifference toward spelling, and thus only selectively drawing from historical experience. Even more interesting about this gloss and its continuation is how, like a reader-response "garden path" strategy, it leads the reader in one direction of needing to know (a comprehension-based need), immediately catching her up by new information that manages to remove any need to know whatsoever: "Actually, when Richard returned from Ireland in July 1399 he landed at Milford Haven in southern Wales." Huh? The original "fact" is progressively stripped of possible purposes, remaining utterly mute and presumably "objective." As if to compensate for a reader's futile investment in following the "facts" in this rhetorical bait and switch, it adds a little new info—Richard's return in 1399. Even so, we might then wonder whether we are going to be fooled again by another gloss that will take away what we now "know." The political performative here is a ritual exorcism of contemporaneous political relevance.

Shakespeare toys with the very sort of conservative deployment of historical information that his editors unwittingly mimic in glossing him, a historical deployment I hereby term "the-Name-of-the-Castle." The significance of this is that while a cultural studies pedagogy still needs shared knowledge, and thus the form of the gloss, this should rather be a gloss of the transhistorical popular, avoiding the implicit elitism of the Riverside text, or sometimes of new historicist knowledges often almost as obscure. "The Name-of-the-Castle" signifies the pointlessness of its applicability, an implicit stigmatization of the sorts of "uses" a popular agenda might seek. Uselessness thus stands as the guarantor of objectivity. While any information could in theory be available for a progressive use, what is maintained here is undoubtedly Foucault's rejected "monumental history"—of battles, heroes, victories—against which a form of countermemory needs to be found.

What, again, do they (we) need to know? It is not enough to take a low-level poststructuralist dodge here by asserting that "facts" are only motivated historical reconstructions. For if the impossibility of determining "facts" much less master facts is undermined by poststructuralist quotation marks, one could simply defer the question to another level by asking what "perceived facts" it would be good to know. Of course, Hotspur's own example provides something of a popular countermemory in seeking the name in order to uncrown rather than legitimate this monarch (though in this case the popular energies are

absorbed within the form of a dynastic struggle among nobles rather than commoners). What his example of a political parapraxis provides, more importantly
than something about historiographic relativism, is what might be thought of as
a more popular form, deriving from a more popular use, of the historical archive.

In all of this I concur with Cary Nelson's call to include within historical pedagogy "current debates and social practices" (281) and to "rearticulate" the past to
"current interests" (282). What I am trying to get at here, however, goes beyond
Nelson's framing of this in terms of intellectual critique. To elaborate, what I mean
particularly by attention to Hotspur is that his moment of anger, grasping at a
name his tongue won't afford, reminds us of Walter Benjamin's noted discussion
of history, when he asserts that articulating the past means "to seize hold of a
memory as it flashes up at a moment of danger" (255). It is some sense of danger,
then, together with a sense of the cost of materials in the archive, that is required
for the cultural studies classroom, all the more so for an early modern period. The
reason for this requirement is, moreover, as much for the sake of better historical
sense as it is for more political commitment. As if to underscore this understanding of the dramatic moment in representing history as what one needs, Shakespeare has Hotspur stumble over a history that he comically didn't really need, a
pointlessly aristocratic residue providing an obstacle to rebellion.

If the classroom and textual examples I have given are juxtaposed, we find that
progressive historical use may itself call for "competency," but one associated
with a sense of urgency rather than of complacency and depoliticization. To call
up an image from the past, moreover, may entail particularity instead of "coverage," although which particularity may not always be known in advance. Indeed,
the epigraph of this essay, invoking the case in which less is more, may suggest
that what we need to promote above all is a certain form of committed historical
imagination of a certain form (although the case may be somewhat different for
graduate study). Drawing from Benjamin's observations on a real sense of history,
we can have this truth without requiring as an ideal the universal collection of the
chronicler, since only a "redeemed" society has what in pedagogical terms might
be called historical "coverage," that is, "only for a redeemed mankind has its past
become citable in all its moments" (254).

What this means in practice, for one thing, is an awareness of materials for a
common countermemory. For students of Shakespeare there may be a historical
competency that is not monumental or elitist. What I am calling for here is
admittedly to some extent already occurring, whether or not in a specifically
"cultural studies" classroom, but as a function of increasingly "contextualized"

liberal classroom practices. In fact, most teachers of Shakespeare now undoubtedly make pointed reference to the rebellion by the earl of Essex, who hired
Shakespeare's theater company for a private performance of *Richard II*—a play
whose deposition scene was itself censored—on the eve of his attempt to topple
Elizabeth, in a realization of Benjamin's notion of a history of need. While it may
be argued that, as in Hotspur's case, such rebellion is merely among aristocrats, it
is also the case that it specifically drew a consciousness-raising power from the
popular energies of the new commercial, transclass theater. With transhistorical
value at the general level of "resistance" (a value in term limited by the circumstances of any historical moment), the fact becomes indispensable, though not
"essentialist," knowledge.

Although the antimonarchical certainly appears to lack the requisite sense of
danger for students presently, it may be a danger at least imaginatively repro-
ducible. Besides, one is not limited to historical materials based on power from
the top down—a familiar critique of the way that new historicism tends to select
out its historical archive. (I might note, however, that an important, often ignored
value of the new historicism from the present perspective is that it opened up the
possibility of practicing history without a license, a useful disciplinary disruption.) Other materials may also have such a transhistorical character, as in the case
of the early seventeenth-century pamphlet debates about the nature of women
and women's roles in society, the "protofeminism" of writers such as "Jane
Anger," which most introductory students are extremely surprised to find out
existed at all. Or one might intervene in present censorship and information control debates by way of the Elizabethan censorship practices and antitheatrical
tracts, again indispensable for a historical reconstruction of danger.

While such primary information and materials are undoubtedly becoming
common, a cultural practice in the classroom must keep in mind Benjamin's central implications about transhistoricality, so as not to let such materials dwindle
into a mere syllabus (the original source of the Leavisite "canon"). One must especially be alert, moreover, to distinguish popular materials, whether literary or
nonliterary, from a kind of "pseudopopular" based on the current marketing of
the Renaissance, through star-system phenomena like Kenneth Branagh and
theme park-style Renaissance festivals. Attending a workshop for high school
teachers of literature, I encountered an enhanced version of this in an elaborate
"mini Renaissance Festival" held at one school, an event involving literature and
drama teachers in a yearlong series of projects related to Shakespeare. The teachers were so enthusiastic about their students designing costumes, creating models

of castles and catapults and the like, that I soon became the critical, even cynical academic throwing cold water on their historical party. Of course, I sometimes find such hands-on projects useful myself, but primarily in the context of the students putting on Shakespeare scenes. What occurs there without prompting or "pedagogy," I find, is that its license affords an occasion for students to call up their own images of the past that resonate with the present, often appropriating the historical material for a topical comment. At any rate, one of these teachers admitted that a project of reading or writing about Renaissance history usually did not appeal to students, and that in any case she didn't even encourage them to do such a project. The entire school got into the heady "spirit" of this revelry, with lesson plans from class to class made fully interdisciplinary. Students dressed up in costume for the occasion, although a disturbing exception was mentioned in passing about two young men who, not much liking the idea of doing this, after continual pressure from other students went along with the game — and enjoyed it, too! Here we have a commercially based popular (one piece of the increasing encroachment of capitalism and the entertainment industry directly into classroom experience, not a discourse but a deliberate marketing strategy), destructive of real historical knowledge. Indeed, with its emphasis on the castle, not to mention the castle-building project, this is really just a miniaturization of the monumental history a cultural studies practice should oppose. While festivals, as we know historically, have often been, especially in the early modern period, sources of popular and even revolutionary energy and social unrest, these "mini-festivals" are festivals designed to be, in Victor Turner's distinction, "liminoid" rather than truly liminal, that is, they are only productive of luxury simulacra of history. If history is to be dumbed down, reduced to a minimum, it ought to be done in the name of the truly popular and democratic or the effort to identify them.

Of course, my own posture in this symptomatizes what is nevertheless a real failure of most progressive university academics to establish real ties with secondary teachers, a situation especially lamentable since our shared, direct connection with the public sphere is in teaching. If history is the ground of a Marxist-informed cultural studies pedagogy, we should not only resist such appropriations, but also actively intervene in how history is taught. While many were engaged in what might be called "left-spectacle" issues, we in the United States lost one major opportunity for direct involvement in the failure of coalition with the National History Standards project. This was the large-scale project that backfired on Congress and Lynne Cheney (then head of the sponsoring National Endowment for the Humanities) when it produced not a "cultural literacy" list of

Important Dates like Columbus's "discovery," but an immensely informed and intelligent set of outlines and principles for students to explore, as the consensus terms of the program describe, not just the ideals of our country but where, importantly for left political purposes, we have failed at those ideals. (The long collaboration process between secondary and university teachers, many years of waste, nevertheless produced the now abandoned and unauthorized texts, of which copies are still available if you contact the authors privately.) Its criteria—"to read historical narratives imaginatively," to consider "multiple perspectives" and "competing historical narratives," to "identify gaps in the available records" (such as a popular voice in the past), and to "marshal contextual knowledge" are as appropriate to a cultural studies pedagogy as to a merely liberal one. Often, there may be for us a "good enough" pedagogy, as there is a "good enough" historical competency for progressive ends, as long as the past remains not "citable in all its moments." Of course, it may be objected that what I have described is not fully distinguishable from a merely liberal pedagogy rather than a radical one. That objection has merit.

This leads me, in another direction, to consider how the phenomenon of "miniaturization" affects us in a different way in classroom practice, especially in our radical experiments. That is, our progressive instincts lead us not only away from "good enough" history, but also away from a "good enough" classroom in terms of its own democratic practices. While the utopian impulse underlies both our sense of injustice and the radicalization of teaching styles, I think the latter is ultimately more privatized and always already less of a permanent revolution than other disciplinary ones. Radicalizations, moreover, have a way of conforming to the appropriations of flexible domination and the ever new needs of the global, corporate state, as we now see from "student-centered pedagogies" that easily map onto the corporate model of consumerism and are therefore often readily embraced by administrators, or from the other direction, in the new corporate movements to "manage diversity," to develop postmodernist management styles, and the like. Disney will forever be our forefather in such advances. In the context of such developments and their effect on the Castle Cultural Studies, awareness of the historical moment of teaching and what would constitute an intervention within it might, rather than lead us to permanent innovation, return us to former practices that acquire some new purchase in a new context: I am being only slightly teasing to suggest that, to my way of thinking, such a stigmatized form as the lecture (presumably a mode in which Marx himself got radicalized) might be an example of a form that can be progressively used or rethought. While I only suggest this example as provocation, it may be the case that no model or general form of critical pedagogy is inherently progressive and hence unavailable for appropriation for capital-ist profiteering or its cultural equivalent. Furthermore, there is no mode of knowl-edge that does not in turn form the basis for producing social stratifications, in our distinguishing and sorting by means of shifting standards of classroom discrimina-tion, the good from the bad workers of the future.

Can we have, then, a popular competency with a progressive edge, arrived at through rejection of forms of the monumental? Once again, I urge emphasis of Benjamin's insights as a corrective to a vague advocacy of a universalized "resis-tance" (which is not to throw out the concept at all). The latter is the occupa-tional hazard of a progressive pedagogy that, as Barbara Foley has observed, is in danger of turning some historicizations into dehistoricizations. But if that sce-nario is possible, the present formal critique suggests that its opposite is as well, namely, that some dehistoricizations, or apparent dehistoricizations, could turn into a better historicization. Even a mere historical analogy, or less, might serve to call up an image of the past in a moment of danger. In effect, my initial call for a transhistorical popular competency has been somewhat prematurely tempered, since the discussion has revealed that it is more important to recognize the grounds of such shared knowledge in present moments of danger, and to con-sider what makes any historical archive more truly democratic.

A concluding example of one classroom exercise in "good enough" history might suggest one of many ways to put such reflections to practice. In fact, it is somewhat more of an extreme case of providing minimalist history, since it pro-vides no actual historical materials at all, but rather the form of historical knowl-edge and historical consciousness. What I do is an adaptation of Raymond Williams's discussion of "residual, dominant, and emergent" structures of feel-ing available at any particular moment, a model essential for unpacking the con-tradictions of the art or projects of a particular era. I ask the students simply to discuss ideas of a play that are either old-fashioned, current, or contemporary, exploring who holds them and in what contexts or oppositions. Thus, one might ask in *Measure for Measure*, for example, which of the ideas or characters repre-sent old-fashioned, which current, and which progressive notions about sexual-ity (or ask for outdated, current, or progressive views of love and marriage in *As You Like It*). A kind of prelearning for a Marxist critical thinking, the exercise seems in my experience to produce a real gain in historical acuity, even without primary materials or a clearly defined sense of difference between the values of the text in its era and those of our own contemporary era. It teaches how the past feels, prior to a critical unpacking of its "ideas." Indeed, it may make gains even if a student simply projects his current values onto those of the play, a practice that the professional historian might declare to be anathema.

   Ultimately, our cultural studies classrooms need not fear the tactical presentation of less rather than more history, even as our practice and motives are defined by the possibilities of historical change. It may be that while our analysis and research must be grounded in as fully contextualized an object of inquiry as possible, as if we already inhabited the redeemed society, our teaching, on the other hand, needs to be grounded in Benjamin's more dramatized or perhaps performative sense of historical consciousness for citable moments from the past, not simply in ideological "critique." If our teaching is to be truly popular in the sense of democratic, then it might pay to consider in advance what and how little ought to be the popular historical grounds of our subject. It is to this end that I propose limitations on history, history that, while popular and sometimes a bit crazy, is not dumb, and indeed has the linkage with contemporaneity that will make the events of the past refuse to be as mute as the names of the castles of our fathers. Jameson's directive to us can now be updated: No longer "Always historicize"; rather, "Sometimes dehistoricize."

WORKS CITED

Benjamin, Walter. *Illuminations*. New York: Schocken, 1969. Reprint, 1978.
Foley, Barbara. "Subversion and Oppositionality in the Academy." In *Margins in the Classroom: Teaching Literature*, ed. Kostas Myrsiades and Linda S. Myrsiades. Minneapolis: University of Minnesota Press, 1994.
Giroux, Henry A. *Disturbing Pleasures: Learning Popular Culture*. New York: Routledge, 1994.
Jameson, Fredric. "Afterword: The Permanent Revolution in Shakespeare Studies." In *Materialist Shakespeare: A History*, ed. Ivo Kamps. New York: Routledge, 1994.
Nelson, Cary. "Always Already Cultural Studies: Academic Conferences and a Manifesto." In *What Is Cultural Studies? A Reader*. London: Arnold, 1996.
Okoye, Felix. *The American Image of Africa: Myth and Reality*. Buffalo: Black Academy Press, 1971. Cited in James W. Loewen, *Lies My Teacher Told Me: Everything Your American History Textbook Got Wrong*. New York: Simon and Schuster, 1995.
The Riverside Shakespeare. Ed. G. Blakemore Evans. Boston: Houghton Mifflin, 1974.
Turner, Victor. "Frame, Flow, and Reflection: Ritual and Drama as Public Liminality." In *Performance in Postmodern Culture*, ed. Michel Benamou and Charles Caramello. Milwaukee: Center for Twentieth Century Studies, University of Wisconsin-Milwaukee, 1977.

Part II

Marxist Practices in the Classroom

Theory at the Vanishing Point

Notes on a Pedagogical Quandary

Neil Larsen

6

I admit to an odd reluctance to take up the subject of pedagogy—odd, because it's one of the few subjects I can speak about with the authority of long practical experience. All things considered, I probably expend more mental labor (and anguish) on the bewildering problem of how to teach my next class than I do on much else. A perhaps even greater reluctance to address the subject in the more "public sphere" of conference panels and published discourse no doubt partakes of an elitist tendency to disdain pedagogy as too technical and vocational, too little taken up with the "theoretical" sorts of discourses required by the rules of intellectual and professional legitimation. Those who do confront pedagogical problems directly—for example, in the area of "composition studies"—turn out to be as engaged with "theory" as anyone else, of course, yet the notion persists that the practical question of how to *teach*, say, the theory of ideology is only casually a question for the "theorists" themselves. The relation of theory to pedagogy itself, that is, still tends to be seen as purely instrumental and contingent, even when the "theory" in question—Marxism, for example—would, in principle, insist on this relation as bearing an internal, dialectical necessity.

There is, as always, a history inscribed in this tendency. I haven't the space or the breadth of knowledge necessary to reconstruct it fully here, but I have the sense of having lived out a version of this history myself over the past two to three decades—as both student and teacher—and so perhaps I can be permitted the attempt to historicize and contextualize my own (mis)adventures in pedagogies of theory—and theories of pedagogy—en route to some more general observations.

I left graduate school in 1983, comparative literature Ph.D. in hand, to take up a job teaching Latin American literature and Spanish in a large, private, urban, mainly undergraduate university. As might be guessed, I arrived armed to the teeth with "theory," literary and otherwise, and as bent on dispensing it in my classes as I was clueless as to how, or whether, it might be possible to do this.

My task seemed to be simplified, in some ways, by the bitter political conflicts then engulfing Central America and by the Sandinista and FMLN "solidarity" movements that had sprung up across college campuses. At least one corner of Latin America itself was the subject of general discussion and even, perhaps, "theoretical" debate in the public sphere. I taught the works of Ernesto Cardenal, Omar Cabezas, Gioconda Belli, Roque Dalton, Manlio Argueta, and Rigoberta Menchú in my classes, and, if the deeper theoretical sorts of questions embedded in them could not surface, at least I thought it possible to deploy their content to convey something of the cultural dimension of anti-imperialist resistance in Central America.

However, I soon came to doubt the efficacy of even this modest form of cultural-political mediation. To utilize, say, Argueta's *One Day of Life* for the mildly critical purpose of providing a more sympathetic portrait of the Salvadoran insurgency presupposed, for example, that the student assigned to read it already possessed some minimal knowledge of what the opposing forces were, both locally and globally, and of what, in broadly political terms, was at stake. This almost always turned out to be a false assumption, and I was faced with the necessity, if my critical pedagogy was to be given even just the chance to work, of supplying the missing context myself. I tried doing this, to some effect possibly, but usually with the sense that I was merely positing the existence of a more general contextual knowledge when, in fact, it too was missing. During the "contra" counterinsurgency in Nicaragua I remember spending the better part of a class explaining the history of *Sandinismo*, the politics of the FSLN, the depredations of the "contra" forces, their direct links to the U.S. government, and so on. When I had finished and was about to return to the contemporary Nicaraguan poetry that had prompted this long supplementary digression, one of my students raised her hand and announced that she now understood it all: the "contras" were the "communists"!

This left me at a complete loss. My aim had been the—as I thought—"theoretically" restricted one of reading literary texts for a "cultural" content that in turn would supply a mediating but hopefully "counterhegemonic" link between the students' spontaneous sympathies for victims of injustice and the conscious, political critique of U.S. imperial policy in Central America.[1] Perhaps some students finally did "read" in this way, but then, if "contras" could be communists, Ernesto Cardenal could be a Reagan appointee. Incredible as it seemed, many of my students really did not know enough to see any contradiction here. Few could fail to feel sympathy for, say, Rigoberta Menchú as victim; but victims could not be "communists." My students, that is, *had* linked culture to politics, even if in a surreal fashion. But the logic of the prevalent hegemony was not fundamentally challenged by this. On the contrary, this hegemony had itself furnished the "theoretical" ground of mediation. Given enough time, no doubt I could have explained how "contras" could be other than communists, but the literary texts I was supposed to be teaching were evidently extraneous to this explanation. Their "cultural" content was not unreadable from a generally ethical, "humanist" perspective. But there was nothing in the texts themselves, or in such a reading of them, to make it necessary for my students to think more critically about their own political views—nothing intrinsically or spontaneously "counterhegemonic."

How—if at all—to find my way out of this pedagogical quandary? I have some further practical experience to relate here, but first I think there are some general, intellectual-historical factors to be adduced from my pedagogical troubles. I propose, in fact, that it is possible to chart in them the recent history of a volatile left-intellectual relation to "theory" itself as preeminent object of classroom instruction.

As I've said, I came out of graduate school in the early 1980s thinking of myself as someone who "did theory." My conventionally "literary" knowledge was not, I think, inconsiderable, but I had come to see literature—whether "comparative," national, canonical, and so on—less as theoretical object than as theoretical anteroom, an ideal point of departure for theory, but not, in most cases, its necessary point of return. In the late 1970s I had, in fact, witnessed—

and welcomed—the uprooting at my university of a Eurocentric, late-New Critical, belletristic comparative literature curriculum (still cast in the mold of Curtsius, Spitzer, Wellek et al.) and the implantation of a curriculum sprung from—to be only slightly reductive—the ur-texts of Freud, Marx, and Saussure and watered by the reading practices of feminism and poststructuralism. It was the notorious *coup-de-tête* now universally abhorred by the cultural right, the fabled "closing of the American mind." Many political-intellectual projects combined to produce this change, some of which—for example, Marxism and poststructuralism—were shortly to fall out. Yet they had all at one point marched together under the banner of "theory."

But what, on its own terms, did it mean to "do theory"? At the outset, it meant actually *reading* the works of Freud, Marx, and others, instead of receiving them—if at all—through the often doubtful medium of academic literary studies. I think no one can gainsay the great boon that this was. One thing it didn't mean, however, at least in my experience, was the development of any sense of what, beyond "reading," the activity of teaching/learning theory might involve. I've remarked already on what I consider to have been the long-term, paradoxical effects of this pedagogical vacuum, and on the particular difficulties I encountered trying to teach theory—or teach literature in a theoretically informed way—to students who could not "read" it. Yet what then had made it possible, at least during the peak moments of the "theory" revolution, to treat theory as if its appropriation—"doing it"—were simply a question of deciding to "read" it—as if, paradoxically, theory needed no theory of itself as a pedagogical subject and object?

My answer, bluntly stated, is that we paid no attention to the pedagogy of theory because, although armed with good political intentions, we had no *theory* of theory itself. Or, if we did have, it was the wrong one. Theory—like revolutionary consciousness according to the popular (and often self-styled "Leninist") misreading of Lenin—had come to us "from without."[2] From the perspective of an academic literary studies still groggily content with the disciplinary self-certainties of neopositivist philology and New Critical formalism, "theory" promised to become a kind of liberating form of higher consciousness, a way of glimpsing the totality of knowledge that we had been assiduously trained to regard as none of our business. Of course, the still fervent political and social energies of the "sixties" rebellions heavily infused this perception, and, if measured strictly against the intellectual narrowness of what was preexisting, the liberatory promise of theory appears largely to have been kept.

But despite the salutary infusion of social and political reality for which "theory" served as an academic wedge, we were nevertheless drawn into the philosophically subjectivist error of supposing theoretical knowledge in its formal abstraction to transcend this reality, and even, in the end, to substitute for it. Understandably impatient with the narrowness of "literature" as a disciplinary object of study, we embraced the much broader, transdisciplinary focus of "theory" as a seemingly natural accompaniment to a new, radical social, sexual and "ethnic" awareness. What we were doing was not about "literature"—or not "just" about it—but about ideology, desire, power, discourse, difference, and so forth. But we failed to supplant "literature" as such a narrow, disciplinary—in effect, *reified*—object (an object supposedly no longer requiring theoretical illumination) with the theory of a dialectically transformed and sublated object, with a "literature" that did not simply dissolve into the theoretical abstractions of ideology, desire, and so forth, but that could be disclosed as their concrete determination. We did not attempt the *immanent* derivation of theory out of the deeper, dialectical reality—the truth—of literature as objective facet of the sociohistorical totality. Rather, we looked to theory itself in its abstract, seemingly fully elaborated and transcendent form to supply the spontaneous antidote to the reified conceptions of philological, New Critical, and belletristic narrowness. In so doing, we simply transferred this reified objectivity directly over into theory itself, where it took on a new, subjective form. *Conceived along radically subjectivist lines, theory inevitably became its own object.*

What, then, determined this subjectivizing approach to theory? To answer this fully would raise in its turn the larger question of the ways the reified structure of "scientific" consciousness in bourgeois society (e.g., as Cartesian *cogito*) results necessarily in a stance of contemplative, abstract subjectivity vis à vis the object. Such a task cannot be undertaken in this brief space. (The reader schooled in "theory" will by now perhaps have detected the echoes of Lukács's *History and Class Consciousness* in the above—and could do worse than proceed directly to that greatly problematic, but ever indispensable, text for the best possible lesson in the "theory of theory.") Suffice it to say that, despite the general skepticism and unconcern of the standard-issue literary "theorist" for the dictates of "scientific" rationality (still typically dismissed these days with some ready-to-hand maxim of Nietzschean/poststructuralist irrationalism), the subjectivist positioning of theory at the site of the cogito as pure, contemplative consciousness is at least as instinctive for literary "theory" as it is for academic, neopositivist thought generally. Even the shrewdest argument for the discursively constructed nature of all so-called objective truth or reality ends up sooner or later wondering how to "apply" itself as "theory" to, say, Hawthorne's *Scarlet Letter*.

But the pertinent question for us here is this: what happens when a "theory" subjectively conceived as, in the last analysis, it own object—"theory" as encapsulating both the subject and object of knowledge—becomes in turn the object of a pedagogy? One result, already familiar to students of my generation, is what might be termed the sheer anti-pedagogy of "theory-speak": for example, the academic who has learned to extemporize in parade-dress Lacanian jargon and who simply converts his or her "theoretical" knowledge into a "lecture" format of unmediated, uninterrupted banter. Here, presumably, one learns "theory" as one would a foreign language in the standard, audio-lingual, total immersion, "sink or swim" classroom. Or one thinks, to cite a more concrete example, of Paul De Man's public lecture style of the 1970s—and of the other thousand and one ministers of deconstruction who tried (and in some few cases still try) their hands at this, with none of De Man's finesse and all of his underlying sectarian arrogance. Of course, Marxist "theory" did not lag far behind here. We mouthed the perhaps even more contemptible "theory-speak" of the Althusserians. This self-caricature has now, unfortunately, become the popular-cultural image of all literary "theory," as propagated by an academic and cultural reaction extending from the relatively innocuous satires of David Lodge to the more vicious diatribes of a D'Souza or the *New Criterion*.

But the grotesque descent into "theory-speak" has not, I think, been so widespread as commonly believed, nor is it really the most symptomatic or significant trend in the pedagogy of "theory." If I may return now to my own classroom misadventures, I suggest that my effectively failed attempt to insert "culture" (as the supposedly given content of a text) consciously into the mediatory space once occupied by "theory" replicates *in nuce* the now dominant theoretical pedagogy. Recall that, faced with the practical impossibility of introducing "theoretical" texts directly to my relatively poorly educated, unread, and "theoretically" illiterate undergraduates, I tried to devise a way to change their consciousness (political, in this case, but "political" in precisely a "theoretical" sense) without the need for the direct introduction ("from without") of theoretical abstractions. My hypothesis was that, without ever exiting the spontaneous and, so to speak, unconscious plane of culture—with its popular notions of "right and wrong"—I could induce, merely by supplying the right sorts of cultural texts or specimens, not a consciousness-"raising" per se, but at least a corresponding shift of cultural or behavioral attitude. Students would read Omar Cabezas's *Fire from the*

Mountain and, without the need for abstract concepts of class, profit, or global division of labor, or the need for a developed historical framework, would join Cabezas's
culturally mediated *Sandinismo* to their own spontaneous, romantic-cultural sympathies for the underdog hero. Since "theory" had become too "abstract" for my
students, my approach could no longer be that of drawing the classroom out of its
spontaneous, immediate—"cultural"—forms of unconsciousness and into the
higher, properly "conscious" sphere purportedly coinciding with "theory." But
perhaps I might find a way to embody these theoretical abstractions directly in a
cultural form. Perhaps, that is, I might be able to hit upon and activate in the
classroom itself not the "higher" consciousness of "theory" per se but something
like its spontaneous, unconscious—"cultural"—equivalent. Unable to pursue a
"theoretical" politics (in which "theory" occupies the site—as imagined by a
"sixties," New Left version of Leninism and Maoism—of "revolutionary consciousness"), perhaps I still might make do with a "cultural" politics.

The nineties radical critic will by now have whispered to herself the name for
this new way of "doing" theory—of which I, in my early-1980s-newly-Ph.D.'ed-
and-exiled-to-the-academic-provinces mindset was only faintly aware: "cultural
studies." Seemingly endless quantities of ink have been poured out in recent
years in speculation and argument over what "cultural studies" really is, where
it came from and is going, and how it might or might not carve out a space for
continued critical-intellectual practice in the academy. I'll spare the reader my
own somewhat jaundiced view on these questions,[3] but will suggest that its
rapid spread in the mid-1980s and early 1990s may have had something to do
with the dispatch of the second "theory generation" to increasingly "theory"-
illiterate classrooms—a politico-cultural *démarche* that repeats the larger, *ex-
cathedra* response of New Left intellectuals to the much hypothesized transfer of
radical energies from sixties-style radical politics to the culture- and "identity"-
based "new social movements." Clearly there is, underlying the general "cultural
studies" style of critique, a sobering recognition that the great "theoretical"
campaigns of yore had isolated us from both society as a whole and the next,
"post-theoretical" generation of students.[4] If "theory" had grown "abstract,
"culture" was the "concrete," the plane on which most people thought, felt, and
were moved to action. So we had better stop poring over Adorno and Lacan,
accept our own pop-cultural pleasures and identities as central to our intellectual practice, and get our theoretical hands dirty.

But this change, while real enough and a welcome relief from the cultishness
of deconstruction, Althusserianism, and so forth, is far less revolutionary than it

appears. "Cultural studies" is still, in practice, held fast within a subjectivist reification of theory—as is readily shown when its pedagogical implications are
thought through. For even admitting the (already questionable) premise that our
students (as representatives of mass society itself) neither can nor need be led
forth from their culturally saturated lifeworlds in order to become potential
agents of social change, we are still left with a "theory" that—as pedagogical
strategy—is responsible for unleashing and directing this unconscious, theory-
less agency. On the one hand, that is, theory demotes itself to unconscious, cultural form, while on the other, and at the same time, it takes upon itself the even
more supremely subjectivist and voluntaristic task of directing this very process
of demotion. Rather than go about the straightforward business of "instilling"
theory "from without," of constructing, like demiurges, the theoretical subjects
of our pedagogy, we propose to do this obliquely—but finally no less consciously—by folding the unconscious energies of culture back on themselves.
We still want to construct a "theoretical" form of subjectivity (modeled on our
own), but one that is "theoretical" only in our—not its own—eyes. "Cultural
studies" denies that the spontaneity of culture can or should be transcended in
the name of an abstract, theoretical "politics," and yet it effectively reproduces
this same "politics" in an even more subjectivized, voluntaristic form. And so it
is that when we actually attempt to carry it out in the classroom, we find, logically enough, that the question of an absent, political-theoretical consciousness
has sneaked up behind us: the "contras" become "communists," or, for example,
the sexual rebel budding inside the Madonna fan just ends up getting married,
doing the dishes every night, and buying all the latest albums.

    Where does this leave us? I'm afraid I haven't got a post-"theory," post-"cul-
tural studies" pedagogy ready to hand. Presented with ever more poorly educated, more intellectually illiterate students, I no sooner devise a new
pedagogical approach than it too becomes obsolete or unworkable. I've had some
modest success, however, by limiting the form of classroom literary and cultural
analysis to one simple conceptual procedure, which is repeated for every successive text or cultural exhibit. For example, I present students with a limited theory of genre, in the form of a classificatory grid. (Believe it or not, I have often
gone back to Frye's neo-Aristotelian theory of "fictional modes" from *The
Anatomy of Criticism* for this purpose.) Classroom discussions of a text, as well as
written assignments, always take this discreet, formal, seemingly context-free
procedure as a point of departure. The result, of course, is a general lack of consensus and a dawning awareness that the classificatory system has no accompa-

nying set of rules for determining once and for all the "right" answer. Is García Márquez's *One Hundred Years of Solitude* a case of the "ironic" or the "low mimetic" mode—or is it a self-conscious return to the "romantic"? And so forth. But the undecidability of the procedure, together with its formally repetitive, constrained, and mechanical aspect, is a small price to pay for making the students conscious of their own conceptual forms of labor and skill. By repeating again and again, in a variety of given contexts, the seemingly simple, formal movement of thought from the particular to the general, from the concrete to the abstract, and back again, the students at least begin to develop a sense of the necessity for theory, and of what its genuine, *immanent* relation to its object is. Theory ceases to be some distant, abstract, inscrutable, and unattainable plane of elaborated doctrine and becomes—conspicuously and self-consciously—that which determines the movement of thought or analysis at every successive step or problem. This all depends, of course, on the strict refusal to reify the classificatory system itself, a refusal to treat its categories as anything more than provisional abstractions useful (or not) for glimpsing the determinate shape of some facet of concrete totality.

I'm reluctant to conclude much from this still experimental approach, but it does appear to point to some general observations, both pedagogical-theoretical and historical. In the former case, it suggests that, just as theory shrivels into its subjectivized, fetish form if it loses sight of its own objective immanence in the concretely real, so too does it become a classroom fetish unless it can be rendered *pedagogically immanent*. Theory must *both* consciously orient the pedagogical process as a whole and also grow spontaneously out of the process itself at each successive phase of development.

Of particular historical significance here is the fact that—at least in my teaching experience—objective circumstances have *forced* the adoption of this pedagogically "immanent" approach to theory. If theory does *not* assume a pedagogically immanent—that is, consciously methodological—form, it simply ceases to be viable as an object of instruction. That this is so, however, is richly reflective of the profound, potentially explosive crisis of the existing social order itself. We teach, increasingly, in an intellectual environment that converges on the theoretical vanishing point, an environment in which there is often no apparent way of mediating our own "theoretical" culture with the "dumbed-down," instrumentalized, consumerist culture of students *except* on the level of the most rudimentary learning—how to read, write, and think. Our classrooms have been or are being stripped of the knowledge needed even to recognize, much less independently construct, the most elementary theoretical postulate. To paint over this severe, really criminal intellectual expropriation with the often glowing colors of "culture" à la "cultural studies" is, in the end, to furnish alibis to the system that has brought it about. Yet this extreme crisis also severely curtails the capacity of this system to legitimate itself theoretically. Those it cheats out of the ability to give theoretical expression to their thinking more readily become the existing order's unconscious agents of reproduction. However, by that same token, this order cannot rely on them to produce, with any intellectual conviction, its own "theoretical" apology. Radical theorists and pedagogues, take note.

NOTES

1. For a full, analytical exposition of this pedagogical approach, see "Teaching Caribbean Texts: Outline for a Counterhegemonizing Pedagogy," chapter 2 of my *Reading North by South: On Latin American Literature, Culture and Politics* (Minneapolis: University of Minnesota Press, 1995), 25–38.
2. See V. I. Lenin, *What Is to Be Done?* As I have taken pains to argue elsewhere, the notorious "from without" refers precisely to the general necessity to open the narrowly constrained "economic" or "trade-union" consciousness of the working class onto the larger, totalizing sphere of the "political." Lenin's reasoning here follows, implicitly at any rate, the dialectical principle of sublation, not some Kantian notion of a transcendental consciousness housed, a priori, in the "vanguard party." But that, clearly enough, is not how many "Leninists"—especially among the student left of the 1960s—have read or interpreted *What Is to Be Done?*
3. See chapters 15–17 of *Reading North by South*.
4. For more on this question, see Jeffrey Williams's valuable essay, "The Posttheory Generation," *Symplokē* 3, no. 1: 55–67.

Diasporas Old and New
Women in the Transnational World

Gayatri Chakravorty Spivak

7

What do I understand today by a "transnational world"? That it is impossible for the new and developing states, the newly decolonizing or the old decolonizing nations, to escape the orthodox constraints of a "neo-liberal" world economic system which, in the name of Development, and now "sustainable development," removes all barriers between itself and fragile national economies, so that any possibility of building for social redistribution is severely damaged. In this new transnationality, what is usually meant by "the new diaspora," the new scattering of the seeds of "developing" nations, so that they can take root on developed ground? Eurocentric migration, labor export both male and female, border crossings, the seeking of political asylum, and the haunting in-place uprooting of "comfort women" in Asia and Africa. What were the old diasporas, before the world was thoroughly consolidated as transnational? They were the results of religious oppression and war, of slavery and indenturing, trade and conquest, and intra-European economic migration which, since the nineteenth century, took the form of migration and immigration into the United States.

These are complex phenomena, each with a singular history of its own. And woman's relationship to each of these phenomena is oblique, ex-orbitant to the general story. It is true that, in transnationality their lines seem to cross mostly, though not always, in First World spaces, where the lines seem to end; labor migrancy is increasingly an object of investigation and oral history. Yet even this tremendous complexity cannot accommodate some issues involving "women in the transnational world." I list them here: 1) homeworking, 2) population control, 3) groups that cannot become diasporic, and 4) indigenous women outside of the Americas.

Homeworking involves women who, within all the divisions of the world, and in modes of production extending from the precapitalist to the post-fordist, embracing all class processes, do piece-work at home with no control over wages; and thus absorb the cost of health care, day care, workplace safety, maintenance, management; through manipulation of the notion that feminine ethics is unpaid domestic labor ("nurturing") into the meretricious position that paid domestic labor is munificent or feminist, as the case may be. The concept of a diasporic multiculturalism is irrelevant here. The women stay at home, often impervious to organizational attempts through internalized gendering as a survival technique. They are part (but only part) of the group necessarily excluded from the implied readership of this essay.

Population Control is the name of the policy that is regularly tied to so-called aid packages, by transnational agencies, upon the poorest women. As workers like Malini Karkal, Farida Akhter, and many others have shown, the policy is no less than gynocide and war on women.[1] It is not only a way of concealing over-consumption—and each one of us in this room is on the average two to three times the size of a person in Somalia or Bangladesh; but it also stands in the way of feminist theory because it identifies women with their reproductive apparatus and grants them no other subjectship.

For "groups that cannot become diasporic" I turn to the original definition of the "subaltern" as it was transplanted from Gramsci:

> . . . the demographic difference between the total . . . population [of a colonial state] and all those who can be described as the "elite." Some of these classes and groups such as the lesser rural gentry, impoverished landlords, rich peasants . . . upper-middle peasants [and now some sections of the urban white- and blue-collar work force and their wives] who "naturally" ranked among the "subaltern," [can

under certain circumstances act for the "elite." . . . —an ambiguity which it is up to the [feminist] to sort out on the basis of a close and judicious reading.[2]

Large groups within this space of difference subsist in transnationality without escaping into diaspora. And indeed they would include most indigenous groups outside Euramerica, which brings me to the last item on the list of strategic exclusions above. Womanspace within these groups cannot necessarily be charted when we consider diasporas, old or new. Yet they are an important part of "the transnational world."

What I have said so far is, strictly speaking, what Derrida called an exergue.[3] It is both outside of the body of the work of this paper, and the face of the coin upon which the currency of the Northern interest in transnationality is stamped. This brief consideration of the asymmetrical title of the conference can lead to a number of labyrinths that we cannot explore. I cut the meditation short and turn to my general argument.

Nearly two years later, as I revise, I will linger a moment longer and inscribe the "groups that cannot become diasporic" more affirmatively, as those who have stayed in place for more than thirty thousand years. I do not value this by itself, but I must count it. Is there an alternative vision of the human here? The tempo of learning to learn from this immensely slow temporizing will not only take us clear out of diasporas, but will also yield no answers or conclusions readily. Let this stand as the name of the other of the question of diaspora. That question, so taken for granted these days as the historically necessary ground of resistance, marks the forgetting of this name.

When we literary folk in the U.S. do multiculturalist feminist work in the areas of our individual research and identity, we tend to produce three sorts of thing: identitarian or theoretist (sometimes both at once) analyses of literary/filmic texts available in English and other European languages; accounts of more recognizably political phenomena from a descriptive-culturalist or ideology-critical point of view; and, when we speak of transnationality in a general way, we think of global hybridity from the point of view of popular public culture, military intervention, and the neo-colonialism of *multi*nationals.

Thus from our areas of individual research and identity-group in the United States, we produce exciting and good work. If we place this list within the two lists I have already made, it becomes clear that we do not often focus on the question of civil society. Hidden and transmogrified in the Foucauldian term "civility," it hardly ever surfaces in a transnationalist feminist discourse. In a brilliant and important recent essay, "The Heart of Ex-nomination: Nation, Woman and the Indian Immigrant Bourgeoisie," Anannya Bhattacharjee has turned her attention to the topic.[4] But in the absence of developed supportive work in the transnationalist feminist collectivity, this interventionist intellectual has not been able to take her hunch on civil society as far as the rest of her otherwise instructive essay.

In an ideal democratic (as opposed to a theocratic, absolutist, or fascist) state, there are structures other than military, and systemic or elective-political from which the individual—organized as a group if necessary—can demand service or redress. This is the abstract individual as citizen, who is "concretely" re-coded as the witness, the source of attestation, in Marxian formulation the "bearer," of the nation form of appearance. This "person" is private neither in the legal nor the psychological sense. Some commonly understood arenas such as health, education, welfare and social security, and the civil as opposed to penal or criminal legal code fall within the purview of civil society. The individual who can thus call on the services of the civil society—the civil service of the state—is, ideally, the citizen. How far this is from the realized scene, especially if seen from the point of view of gays, women, indigenous and indigent peoples, and old and new diasporas, is of course obvious to all of us. However, it is still necessary to add that, within the definitions of an ideal civil society, if the state is a welfare state, it is directly the servant of the individual. When the state is increasingly privatized, as in the New World Order, the priorities of the civil society are shifted from service to the citizen to capital maximization. It then becomes increasingly correct to say that the only source of male dignity is employment, just as the only source of genuine female dignity is unpaid domestic labor.[5]

I write under the sign of the reminder that the other scene, sup-posing any possible thought of civil societies (which is itself race- class- gender differentiated between South and North) of an almost tempoless temporizing, negotiating with the gift of time (if there is any), is not this.[6] It is our arrogant habit to think that other scene only as an exception to the temporizing focussed by the Industrial Revolution, which I pursue below.

I began these remarks by saying that transnationality has severely damaged the possibilities of social redistribution in developing nations. To re-state this in the context of the argument from civil societies, we might say that transnationality is shrinking the possibility of an operative civil society in developing nations. The story of these nations can be incanted by the following formulas since the Industrial Revolution: colonialism, imperialism, neo-colonialism, transnationality. In the shift from imperialism to neo-colonialism in the middle of this century the most urgent task that increasingly backfired was the very establishment of a civil society. We call this the failure of decolonization. And in transnationality possibilities of redressing this failure are being destroyed. I do not think it is incorrect to say that much of the new diaspora is determined by the increasing failure of a civil society in developing nations.

Strictly speaking, the undermining of the civil structures of society is now a global situation. Yet a general contrast can be made: in the North, welfare structures long in place are being dismantled. The diasporic underclass is often the worst victim. In the South, welfare structures cannot emerge as a result of the priorities of the transnational agencies. The rural poor and the urban subproletariat are the worst victims. In both these sectors, women are the super-dominated, the super-exploited, but *not in the same way*. And, even in the North, the formerly imperial European countries are in a different situation from the United States or Japan. And in the South, the situations of Bangladesh and India, of South Africa and Zaire are not comparable. Political asylum, at first sight so different from economic migration, finally finds it much easier to re-code capitalism as democracy. It too, then, inscribes itself in the narrative of the manipulation of civil social structures in the interest of the financialization of the globe.

Elsewhere I have proposed the idea of the rise of varieties of theocracy, fascism, and ethnic cleansing as the flip side of this particular loosening of the hyphen between nation and state, the undermining of the civil structures of society. Here I want to emphasize that, as important as the displacement of "culture"—which relates to the first word in the compound, "nation," and is an ideological arena— is the exchange of state, which is an abstract area of calculation. Women, with other disenfranchised groups, have never been full subjects of and agents in civil society: in other words, first class citizens of a state. And the mechanisms of civil society, although distinct from the state, are peculiar to it. And now, in transnationality, precisely because the limits and openings of a particular civil society are never transnational, the transnationalization of global capital requires a post-state class-system. The use of women in its establishment is the universalization of feminism of which the United Nations is increasingly becoming the instrument. In this re-territorialization, the collaborative non-governmental organizations are increasingly being called an "international civil society," precisely to efface the role of the state. Saskia Sassen, although her confidence in the mechanisms of the state remains puzzling, has located a new "economic citizenship" of power and legitimation in financial capital markets.[7]

Thus elite, upwardly mobile (generally academic) women of the new diasporas join hands with similar women in the so-called developing world to celebrate a new global public or private "culture," often in the name of the underclass.[8]

Much work has been done on the relationship between the deliberate withholding of citizenship and internal colonization. In her "Organizational Resistance to Care: African American Women in Policing," Mary Texeira has recently cited Mike Davis's idea of the "designer drug-busts" in Los Angeles as "easy victor[ies] in a drug 'war' that the LAPD secretly loves losing."[9] Michael Kearney shows vividly how the U.S. Border Patrol keeps the illegal migrants illegal on the Mexican border.[10] The state can use their labor but must keep them out of civil society. In Marx's terms, capital extends its mode of exploitation but not its mode of social production. In Amin's, the periphery must remain feudalized.[11] In Walter Rodney's, underdevelopment must be developed.

In other words, are the new diasporas quite new? Every rupture is also a repetition. The only significant difference is the use, abuse, participation, and role of women. In broad strokes within the temporizing thematics of the Industrial Revolution, let us risk the following: Like the Bolshevik experiment, imperial and nationalist feminisms have also prepared the way for the abstract itinerary of the calculus of capital. "Body as Property" (see note 8) is an episode in "The Eighteenth Brumaire of Bella Abzug."

The study of diasporic women and the ambivalent use of culture in access to a national civil society is a subject of immense complexity whose surface has been barely scratched in terms of such cases as the *hijab*-debates in France. What is woman's relationship to cultural explanations in the nation-state of origin? What is "culture" without the structural support of the state? And, as I have been insisting, the issue is different for women who are no longer seriously diasporic with reference to the modern state. This difference was brought home to me forcefully when a new diasporic student of mine, because her notion of citizenship was related to getting citizenship papers, was unable quite to grasp the following remark by Jean Franco:

> The imperative for Latin American women is thus not only the occupation and transformation of public space, the seizure of citizenship, but also the recognition that speaking as a woman within a pluralistic society may actually reinstitute, in a disguised form, the same relationship

of privilege that has separated the intelligentsia from the subaltern classes.[12]

Franco is suggesting, of course, that even women who resist and reject their politico-cultural description and collectively take the risk of acting as subjects of and agents in the civil society of their nation-state are not necessarily acting for all women.

In the case of *Martinez vs. Santa Clara Pueblo*, where by tribal law the mother cannot claim child custody because her divorced husband belonged to another tribe, and the Supreme Court refuses to interfere, Catharine MacKinnon invokes, among other things, the matriarchal tribal laws of yore.[13] A transnational perspective would have allowed her to perceive this as the colonizing technique of all settler colonies: to create an artificial enclave within a general civil society to appease the rising patriarchal sentiments of the colonized. As the Women's Charter of the ANC pointed out forty years ago, invoking culture in such contexts is dangerous.[14]

I have suggested above that the boundaries of civil societies mark out the state but are still nationally defined. I have further suggested that a hyperreal class-consolidated civil society is now being produced to secure the post-statist conjuncture, even as religious nationalisms and ethnic conflict can be seen as "retrogressive" ways of negotiating the transformation of the state in capitalist postmodernization. Feminists with a transnational consciousness will also be aware that the very civil structure *here* that they seek to shore up for gender justice can continue to participate in providing alibis for the operation of the major and definitive transnational activity, the financialization of the globe, and thus the suppression of the possibility of decolonization—the establishment and consolidation of a civil society *there*, the only means for an efficient and continuing calculus of gender justice *everywhere*.

The painstaking cultivation of such a contradictory, indeed aporetic, practical acknowledgment is the basis of a decolonization of the mind. The disenfranchised new or old diasporic woman cannot be called upon to inhabit this aporia. Her entire energy must be spent upon successful transplantation or insertion into the new state, often in the name of an old nation in the new. She is the site of global public culture privatized: the proper subject of real migrant activism. She may also be the victim of an exacerbated and violent patriarchy which operates in the name of the old nation as well—a sorry simulacrum of women in nationalism. Melanie Klein has allowed us the possibility of thinking this male violence as a reactive displacement of the envy of the Anglos and the Anglo-clones, rather than proof that the culture of origin is necessarily more patriarchal.[15]

The disenfranchised woman of the diaspora—new and old—cannot, then, engage in the *critical* agency of civil society—citizenship in the most robust sense—to fight the depredations of "global economic citizenship." This is not to silence her, but rather desist from guilt-tripping her. For her the struggle is for access to its subjectship of the civil society of her new state: basic civil rights. Escaping from the failure of decolonization at home and abroad, she is not yet so secure in the state of desperate choice or chance as to even conceive of ridding her mind of the burden of transnationality. But perhaps her daughters or grand-daughters—whichever generation arrives on the threshold of tertiary educa-tion—can. And the interventionist academic can assist them in this possibility rather than participate in their gradual indoctrination into an unexamined cul-turalism. This group of gendered outsiders inside are much in demand by the transnational agencies of globalization for employment and collaboration. It is therefore not altogether idle to ask that they should think of themselves collec-tively, not as victims below but agents above, resisting the consequences of glob-alization as well as redressing the cultural vicissitudes of migrancy.

This, then, is something like the situation of diasporas, and, in that situation, of our implied reader. The image of the classroom has already entered as a sort of threshold of description for the latter. Therefore we might well speak of classroom teaching. The so-called immediate experience of migrancy is not necessarily con-sonant with transnational literacy, just as the suffering of individual labor is not consonant with the impetus of socialized resistance. In order that a transnation-ally literate resistance may, in the best case, develop, academic interventions may therefore be necessary; and we should not, perhaps, conflate the two.

Even if one is interventionist only in the academy, there are systemic prob-lems, of course. And I do not intend to minimize them. It is again because of con-straints on time that I am reminding ourselves only of the methodological *problems*. The first one is that the academy operates on the trickle down theory, with rather a minor change in the old dominant, which is that the essence of knowledge is knowledge about knowledge, and if you know the right thing your mind will change, and if your mind changes you will do good. I know how one must fight to change the components of academic knowledge. Nonetheless one cannot fall into the habit of mere descriptive ideology-critical analyses—inci-dentally often called "deconstruction"—and reproduce one's own kind in an individualistic and competitive system in the name of transnationalism. We must remind ourselves that knowledge and thinking are halfway houses, that they are judged when they are set to work. Perhaps this can break our vanguardism that knowledge is acquired to be applied. I have tried to suggest that setting thought to work within the U.S. civil structure in the interest of domestic justice is not necessarily a just intervention in transnationality. Thus we confront an agenda as impossible as it is necessary.

It is in the spirit of such speculation that I will move now to some thoughts about intervention only in the academy. In the Fall of 1993 I attempted to teach a course on global feminist theory. I will share with you some of the lessons I learnt during the semester. My earlier examples from Jean Franco and Catharine MacKinnon are from that class, from the Latin and North American weeks respectively.

This is a list-making kind of essay. This part too will be a list of problems. The book list is long and I will only pick a few items on it. I have generally assigned collective responsibility for the problems. Of course that was not always the case. What I say will seem simple, but to implement what we proposed to ourselves, and to make a habit of it is difficult, certainly more difficult than inspirational political talk in the name of transnationality that silently presupposes a civil structure.

Starting with Ifi Amadiume's *Male Daughters, Female Husbands* we had our first problem: the internalization of European-style academic training.[16] All but one student was against Eurocentrism. But they valued non-contradiction above all else. (Students who come to my poststructuralism seminar can be coerced into relaxing this requirement. But global feminism is a tougher proposition. And, given the subdivision of labor in my institution at the moment and the reputation of the English Department, there were no Black students.) Amadiume, a Nigerian diasporic in London, wasn't doing too well by those standards. The only alternative the class could envision was the belligerent romanticization of cultural relativism. What seems contradictory to Europeans may not to Africans? Nigerians? Ibos? I am not an Africanist and have been faulted for wanting to study African feminism in a general course. But even to me these relativist positions seemed offensive.

A combination of this impatience with illogic hardly covered over with relativist benevolence has now become the hallmark of UN-style feminist universalism.[17] I think it is therefore counterproductive today to keep resistant non-natives or non-specialists from speaking on the obstacles to transnational literacy as they arise with reference to different points on the map. At any rate, I learned to propose that we look always at what was at stake, a question that seemed to be much more practical than the litany of confessional or accusatory, but always determinist, descriptions of so-called subject-positions.

I did not of course have the kind of insider's knowledge of Amadiume's place in the African field that I would have had if I had been an African or an African-ist. It did however seem fairly clear from Amadiume's text that she was pitting her own academic preparation in the house of apparent non-contradiction against "my knowledge of my own people":

> When in the 1960s and 1970s female academics and western feminists began to attack social anthropology, riding on the crest of the new wave of women's studies, the issues they took on were androcentrism and sexism. [She cites Michelle Rosaldo, Louise Lamphere, and Rayna Reiter, among others.] The methods they adopted indicated to Black women that white feminists were no less racist than the patriarchs of social anthropology whom they were busy condemning for male bias.

If we take the magnitude of her predicament into account, we can look at the book as a strategic intervention.

Another problem that some found with Amadiume and that was to surface again and again through the semester with reference to material from different geographical areas was that the traditional gender-systems seemed too static and too rigid. Once again, I asked the class to consider the politics of the production of theory. Amadiume is an anthropologist by training. Africa has been a definitive object of anthropology. Oral traditions do not represent the dynamism of historic-ity in a way that we in the university recognize. And orality cannot be an *instrument* for historicizing in a book that we can read in class. I reminded myself silently of Derrida's tribute to the mnemic graph in orality: "The genealogical relation and social classification are the stitched seam of arche-writing, condition of the (so-called oral) language, and of writing in the colloquial sense."[18] Neither Amadiume nor her readers have at their command the memory active within an oral tradition as a medium. The only kind of thing we are capable of recognizing is where the technical instrument is European and the references alone are bits of "ethnic" idiom, such as Mnouchkine's *Oresteia*, or Locsin's *Ballet Philippine*. But Amadiume is *questioning* the European technical instrument, from within, with no practical access to the instrumentality of her tradition, which makes a poorer showing in a medium not its own.[19] Of course, the traditional gender system will seem "too static" by contrast with the system we fight within.

In addition, as I have pointed out, traditional gender-systems have been used to appease colonized patriarchy by the fabrication of personal codes as opposed to imposed colonial civil and penal codes. They have also been the instrument for working out the displaced Envy of the colonized patriarchy against the colonizer. We must learn to look at customary law as a site of struggle, not as a competitor on a dynamism-count. This became most evident in our readings on Southern Africa.

But let me linger over another moment on the question of what is at stake: who is addressed, within what institution? The class seemed to be most comfortable with the work of Niara Sudarkasa (Gloria A. Marshall), from the Department of Anthropology at the University of Michigan, a woman from an old U.S. diaspora, produced through a reputable U.S. university, who has taken a name from her cultural origin and is explaining that cultural material to other U.S. tertiary students. I am not asking us to denigrate the evident excellence of her work. I am asking us to consider that our approval comes from the comfort of a shared cultural transcription; cultural difference domesticated and transcoded for a shared academic audience. Reading Filomina Steady's *Black Women Cross-Culturally*, I asked the students to read the notes on contributors as texts: what is at stake, who is addressed, what institution, *cui bono*?[20]

Given the difference, for example, between the liberal University of Cape Town and the radical University of the Western Cape, I could not dismiss out of hand a Black man teaching customary law at the former institution as yet another academic. Indeed, the inventive constitutional transmogrification of customary law in some Southern African feminist constitutionalist work, in order that the frontage road to the highway of constitutional subjectship can be left open for the subaltern woman, attempts to face the contradiction which Jean Franco signals. We must learn to make a distinction between the demand, in itself worthy, for the museumization of national or national-origin "cultures" within the instrumentality of an alien and oppressive civil society, and these attempts to invent a gendered civility. In this latter struggle, civil concerns within the new nation under duress must be aware of the threat of economic transnationalization, whose euphemistic description is "Development" capital D, and the lifting of the barriers between international capital and developing national economies, euphemistically known as liberalization. Let us, for example, look at the warning issued by Mary Maboreke, Professor of Law at the University of Zimbabwe:

> Zimbabwe attained independence on 18 April 1980. . . . As of 1 October 1990, Zimbabwe abandoned its strict trade controls over trade

> liberalization. . . . [T]he new economic order flash[es] a warning
> light. . . . All the gains made so far would vanish. . . . Analyses of
> how deregulation programmes affected women should have been
> done before the problems arose. It is now rather late to demand the
> necessary guarantees and protections. As it is we have lost the initia-
> tive and are now limited to reacting to what authorities initiate.[21]

Unless we are able to open ourselves to the grounding feeling, however counterintuitive, that First World diasporic women are, by the principles of the case,
on the other side from Maboreke, we will not be able to think transnationality in
its transnational scope, let alone act upon it. We "know" that to ground thinking
upon feeling cannot be the basis of theory, but that "is" how theory is "judged
in the wholly other," that "is" the "ghost of the undecidable" in every decision,
that "is" how the "truth" of work is set or posited [*gesetzt*] in the work(ing), that
is why logocentrism is not a pathology to be exposed or corrected, that is how
we are disclosed and effaced in so-called human living, we cannot get around it
in the name of academic or arty anti-essentialism.

When a prominent section of Australian feminists claim uniqueness by
virtue of being "femocrats," namely being systemically involved in civil society,
we can certainly learn from them, but we might also mark their "sanctioned
ignorance" of the Southern African effort, sanctioned, among others, by themselves and us.[22] Some of us in the class pointed out that faith in constitutionality
was betrayed after the Civil Rights struggle with the advent of the Reagan-Bush
era. This certainly seems plausible in the U.S. context. But this too is to univer-
salize the United States as ground of evidence, one of the banes of United
Nations feminism. Academic efforts at thinking global feminism must avoid this
at all costs. The ungendered and unraced U.S. constitution was and is widely
supposed to be the first full flowering of the Enlightened State. To be foiled by
its conservative strength is not to be equated with the attempt to put together a
new constitution in Southern Africa—Zimbabwe, Botswana, Namibia, and now
South Africa—and to strive to make it gender sensitive from the start. If the
U.S. experience is taken as *historically* determining, it is, whether we like it or
not, Eurocentric. Philosophically, on the other hand, a persistent critique—
that the subject of the constitution is the site of a performative passed off as a
constative, that the restricted universalism of all ethno-customary systems
shares in some such ruse, that all contemporary constitutions are male-reac-
tively gendered—seems appropriate from those who have earned the right to

practice it, so that a constitution is seen as dangerous and powerful; as a means, a skeleton, a halfway house.[23]

I have repeatedly suggested that the word Development covers over the economics and epistemics of transnationality. "Women in Development" can be its worst scam. Nowhere is this more evident than in Southeast Asia. This taught us (in the class) the importance of checking the specificity of imperial formations in our consideration of the woman of each region. For it is in the clash and conflict of imperial subject-formation, indigenous/customary law, and regulative psychobiographies (the history of which we cannot enter without a solid foundation in local languages) that the track of women in the history of the transnational present can be haltingly followed.

In the case of Southeast Asia, for example, we have to follow the uneven example of U.S. imperialism and the culture of development proper—export-processing zones, international subcontracting, post-fordism and how it reconstitutes women. Aihwa Ong helped us see how the conventional story of colonialism and patriarchy will not allow us to solve the problem.[24] Her most telling object of investigation is so-called examples of mass hysteria among women in the workplace, and her analytical tool is Foucauldian theory. Although Ong herself is impeccable in the politics of her intellectual production, she, like the rest of us, cannot be assured of a transnationally literate audience in the United States in the current conjunctures. The habit of differance between using "high theory" to diagnose the suffering of the exploited or dominated on the one hand, and a self-righteous unexamined empiricism or "experiencism" on the other produces the problem of recognizing theory when it does not come dressed in appropriate language. Foucault is full-dress and we had less difficulty in gaining mastery over our material by way of his speculations, when used by a developing nation-marked U.S. diasporic, especially since the instructor's position of authority was also occupied by a similar subject, namely, Gayatri Spivak. When we resist this within the U.S. field, our only route seems to be an altogether anti-theoreticist position, privileging anything that is offered by nongovernmental activists and their constituencies, not to mention writers who describe them with a seemingly unmediated combination of statistics and restrained pathos. I cannot, at this fast clip, walk with you through learning and earning the right to discriminate among positions offered by "participants." Let me simply say here that out of all the good and fact-filled books on Southeast Asia we read, when we encountered, at the end of Noeleen Heyzer's painstaking book, *Working Women in South East Asia*, full of activist research, words I am about to quote presently, we had difficulty recognizing theory because it was not framed in a Heideggerian staging of care, or a Derridean staging of responsibility.[25] But here is theory asking to be set into — posited in — the work (at least, as long as we are in the classroom) of reading, a task that would inform — and indeed this is what I have been trying to say in these crowded pages — an impossible and necessary task that would inform the overall theme of the conference where these words were first uttered beyond the outlines of the diasporic subject into transnationality; and make indeterminate the borders between the two.

> Women are culturally perceived as really responsible for tasks associated with the private sphere, especially of the family. . . . It is . . . in the public sphere that bonds of solidarity are formed with others sharing similar views of the world. . . . [Yet] many cultures perceive the need to "protect" women from being exposed to these. . . . [By contrast, t]he task ahead is certainly to spread the ethics of care and concern. This concern entails an alternative conception or vision of what is possible in human society . . . a vision in which everyone will be responded to. . . .

Let us linger a moment on the possibility of rethinking the opposition between diaspora and globality in the name of woman, if we can all recognize theory in activist feminist writing (since in the house of theory there is still a glass ceiling). In *Situating the Self*, Seyla Benhabib is clearly looking for a more robust thinking of responsibility to supplement masculist political philosophies that radiate out from social needs and rights thinking.[26]

She cannot, however, conceive of the South as a locus of criticism. Her companions are all located in the North:

> Communitarian critics of liberalism like Alasdair MacIntyre, Michael Sandel, Charles Taylor and Michael Walzer . . . [f]eminist thinkers like Carol Gilligan, Carole Pateman, Susan Moller Okin, Virginia Held, Iris Young, Nancy Fraser, and Drucilla Cornell . . . [p]ostmodernists, . . . by which we have come to designate the works of Michel Foucault, Jacques Derrida and Jean-François Lyotard. . . .

Following the Euro-U.S. history of the division between public and private as male and female, her particular prophet is Carol Gilligan. She cannot find responsibility except in the private sphere of the family, and perhaps, today — though one cannot readily see why this is specifically modern — in friendship.

She cannot, of course, recognize an altogether more encompassing thought of responsibility in what she calls "postmodernism."[27] But neither "postmodernism" nor Benhabib can acknowledge the battering of women in their normality by way of notions of responsibility.[28] It is left to women like Heyzer to recognize that responsibility—the impossible vision of responding to all—has the greatest chance of animating the ethical in the public sphere of women in development, when it becomes another name for super-exploitation, precisely because, in such a case feminine responsibility is conveniently defined, by the enemy, as it were, within the public sphere.[29] Here the incessant movements of restricted diasporas become more instructive than the cultural clamor of Eurocentric economic migration.

When Lily Moya, thwarted in her attempt to move from subalternity into organic intellectuality, runs away into Sophiatown and says, "the witchdoctor is menstruation" and "My life was a transfer," even so astute a writer as Shula Marks looks for a diagnosis.[30] In the comfort of our fourth-floor seminar room, we were learning to recognize theory in unconventional representations, "philosophy in the text of metaphor."[31] Moya's propositions were to us as much of a challenge as "man is a rational animal."

On page 129 of *Beyond the Veil*, a common Arabic women's expression is quoted: *Kunt haida felwlad*.[32] It is rather a pity Fatima Mernissi translates this as: "I was preoccupied with children." If we translate this literally as "I was then in boys," we get a theoretical lever. "Boys" for all "children" packs the same punch as "man" for all persons. And if we take that "in" and place it against the gynocidal thrust of the International Council on Population and Development connected to capital export and capital maximization—the correct description of transnationality—we come to understand the killing schizophrenia which these women suffer, caught in the unresolved contradiction of abusive pharmaceutical coercion to longterm or permanent contraception on the one side and ideological coercion to phallocentric reproduction on the other.[33] And *devenir-femme* in Deleuze and Guattari's *Capitalism and Schizophrenia* can then undergo a feminist reinscription which is para-sitical to the authors' *pouvoir-savoir*.[34]

I touch here upon the crucial topic of the task of the feminist translator as informant. Diaspora entails this task and permits its negligent performance. For diasporas also entail, at once, a necessary loss of contact with the idiomatic indispensability of the mother tongue. In the unexamined culturalism of academic diasporism, which ignores the urgency of transnationality, there is no one to check uncaring translations that transcode in the interest of dominant feminist knowledge.

I began these remarks with a list of the groups that a title such as ours cannot grasp. I then rewrote their name as "those who have stayed in place for more than thirty thousand years," as the limit to the authorized temporizing of our civilization as leading to and proceeding from the Industrial Revolution; the experience of the impossible that opens the calculus of resistance to transnationality. I suggested then that we are called by this limit only by way of battered and gender-compromised versions of responsibility-based ethical systems. Just as for the women of each geopolitical region, we have to surmise some network of response or reaction to hegemonic and/or imperialist subject-constitution, to distinguish the heterogeneities of the repositories of these systems one calculates the moves made by different modes of settler colonizations. And out of the remnants of one such settlement we were able to glean a bit of theory that gave the lie to ontopology and to identitarian culturalisms.

This lesson in theory is contained in the philosopheme "lost our language," used by Australian aborigines of the East Kimberley region.[35] This expression does not mean that the persons involved do not know their aboriginal mother tongue. It means, in the words of a social worker, that "they have lost touch with their cultural base." They no longer compute with it. It is not their software. Therefore what these people, who are the inheritors of settler colonial oppression, ask for is, quite appropriately, mainstream education, insertion into civil society, and the inclusion of some information about their culture in the curriculum; under the circumstances the only practical request. The concept-metaphor "language" is here standing in for that word which names the main instrument for the performance of the temporizing that is called life. What the aboriginals are asking for is hegemonic access to chunks of narrative and descriptions of practice so that a representation of that instrumentality becomes available for performance as what is called theater (or art, or literature, or indeed culture, even theory).[36] Given the rupture between the many languages of aboriginality and the waves of migration and colonial adventure clustered around the Industrial Revolution narrative, demands for multilingual education would be risible.[37]

What will happen to the woman's part in the lost "software," so lovingly described by Diane Bell in *Daughters of the Dreaming*, is beyond or short of verification.[38] For "culture" is changeful, and emerges when least referenced. This lesson I have learned, for example, by way of the displacement of the scattered subaltern anti-colonialist ghost-dance initiative among the First Nations of the North American continent in the 1890s, then into political protest within the civil society at Wounded Knee in the 1970s and its current literary/authentic multiculturalist feminist transformations in Silko's *Almanac of the Dead*.[39]

For reasons of time, appropriate also because of my unease about academic identity politics in these transnationalizing times, South Asia, the place of my citizenship, the United States, the source of my income, and Northwestern Europe, the object of my limited expertise, remained blank on the first time of these remarks. And, apart from reasons of time at this second time, these omissions still seem appropriate. We certainly enjoyed reading some texts of Italian feminism.[40] But it was remarkable that, although diasporic third-world women offer large-scale support, through homeworking, to Italy's post-industrial base, and Benetton is one of the leaders in the field of post-fordist feminization of transnationality, these women and this phenomenon were never mentioned. The class discussions of civil society around the Italian feminists' expressed concerns were therefore interesting, especially since we followed up Swasti Mitter's documentation in her own work on economic restructuring in general.[41] Lack of time will not allow me to touch on the new postcoloniality in post-Soviet Asia and the Balkans; nor on the reasons why East Asia defeated me. These two complex issues do not fit within the broad lines I have laid out. Here's why, briefly.

The historical narratives which constituted "the Balkans" and "inner Asia" as regions are, in themselves, profoundly dissimilar. Yet, by way of their unified definition as Soviet Bloc, and thus their equally single dismantling, albeit into a disclosure of their heterogeneous historicity, they *seem* similar. Our temporizing is organized, not only around the Industrial Revolution, but also around single-nation empires. To see the uneven sovietization of the "Soviet Bloc" in terms of the pre-capitalist multinational empires as well as the Asian bloc, we must examine the difference between Lenin's and Stalin's versions of imperialism and nationalism.[42] Although the unifying bulldozer of financialization is at work in the pores of the Balkans and the Transcaucasus—USAID building a "civic society" in Bosnia, the IMF pressuring Armenia to settle Nogorny-Karabakh before loans are assured—the general question of the diaspora, as perceived by remote-control bleeding-heart feminism, is so patheticized by the human interest that can fill in the loosened hyphen between nation and state that questions of transnationality cannot be considered within a general feminist conference or course. Inner Asia, by contrast, seems only too ready for anthologization into feminism. This may be a result of the existence of a small Russianized corps of emancipated bourgeois women in this sector. But who will gauge their separation from the subaltern, from Asian Islam; how, in more senses than one, they have "lost their language" without being in the almost tempoless temporizing of the aboriginal limit. A new sort of subaltern studies is needed there, for which the appropriate discipline is history and an intimate knowledge of the local languages an absolute requirement. This is all the more necessary because this region's "liberation" comes concurrently with the United Nations' consolidation for a culturally relativist feminist universalism making the world ultimately safe for Capital. My minimal attempts at tracking this region's preparation for the Fourth World Women's Conference organized by the United Nations at Beijing (1995) increases a conviction that the constitution of "woman" as object-beneficiary of investigation and "feminist" as subject-participant of investigation is as dubious here as elsewhere. I have not the languages for touching the phenomenon. And therefore it fit neither my syllabus nor our title.

And East Asia. As controlling capital often a major player with the North. As super-exploited womanspace one with the South and its non-elite networks. Hong Kong unravelling the previous conjuncture, territorial imperialism, the mark of Britain. China unravelling a planned economy to enter the U.S.-dominated new empire. Economic miracle and strangulation of civil society in Vietnam. New World Asians (the old migrants) and New Immigrant Asians (often "model minorities") being disciplinarized together. How will I understand feminist self-representation here? How set it to work? How trust the conference circuit? A simple academic limit, marked by a promise of future work.

To end with a warning. In the untrammeled financialization of the globe which is the New International Order, women marked by origins in the developing nations yet integrated or integrating into the U.S. or EEC civil structure are a useful item. Gramsci uncannily predicted in his jail cell that the U.S. would use its minorities in this way.[43] And remember Clarice Lispector's story, "The Smallest Woman in the World," where the pregnant pygmy woman is the male anthropologist's most authentic object of reverence?[44] It is as if these two ingredients should combine. An example:

A little over a decade ago, I wrote a turgid piece called "Can the Subaltern Speak?", from which I have quoted in note 8. The story there was of a seventeen-year-old woman who had hanged herself rather than kill, even in the armed struggle against Imperialism, and in the act had tried to write a feminist statement with her body, using the script of menstruation to assert a claim to the public sphere which could not be received into what may be called a "speech act." Hence I lamented about this singular (non-)event: "The subaltern cannot speak." Her name was Bhubaneswari Bhaduri.

Bhubaneswari's elder sister's eldest daughter's eldest daughter's eldest daughter is a new U.S. immigrant and has just been promoted to an executive position in a U.S.-based transnational. This too is a historical silencing of the subaltern. When the news of this young woman's promotion was broadcast in the family amidst general jubilation I could not help remarking to the eldest surviving female member: "Bhubaneswari"—her nickname had been Talu— "hanged herself in vain," but not too loudly. Is it any wonder that this young woman is a staunch multiculturalist, wears only cotton, and believes in natural childbirth?

There are, then, at least two problems that come with making the diaspora definitive: first, that we forget that postnationalist (NGO) talk is a way to cover over the decimation of the state as instrument of redistribution and redress. To think transnationality as labor migrancy, rather than one of the latest forms of appearance of postmodern capital is to work, however remotely, in the ideological interest of the financialization of the globe.

And, secondly, it begins from the calculus of hybridity, forgetting the impossible other vision (just, perhaps, but not "pure") of civilization, "the loss of language" at the origin.

Meaghan Morris had apparently remarked to Dipesh Chakrabarty that most trashings of "Can the Subaltern Speak?" read the title as "Can the Subaltern Talk?" I will not improve upon that good word. I will simply thank Meaghan Morris for her witty support, as I will thank Abena Busia, Wahneema Lubiano, Geraldine Heng, Cassandra Kavanaugh, Ellen Rooney, Rey Chow, Jean Franco, and others, for making the syllabus possible; and the members of my seminar at Columbia in Fall 1993 and at the University of California-Riverside in Spring 1994 for teaching me with what responsibility we, women in a transnational world, must address ourselves to the topic: "Diasporas Old and New."

An Unfinishable Syllabus: Always to Be Updated

Spivak   Feminist Theory   Fall 93

I. Sub-Saharan Africa

Ifi Amadiume, *Male Daughters, Female Husbands: Gender and Sex in African Society* (London: Zed Books, 1987).

Filomina Chioma Steady, ed., *Black Women Cross-Culturally* (Rochester: Schenkman, 1981), Introduction, and essays by Sudarkasa, Aidoo, Urdang, Gugler, Pala, Hine and Wittenstein, Terborg-Penn, Staples.

II. North Africa

Assia Djebar, *Women of Algiers in Their Apartment* (Charlottesville: University Press of Virginia, 1992).

Fatima Mernissi, *Beyond the Veil: Male-Female Dynamics in Modern Muslim Society* (London: Al Saqi, 1985).

III. South Africa

Shula Marks, ed., *Not Either an Experimental Doll* (Bloomington: Indiana University Press, 1987).

Susan Bazilli, ed., *Putting Women on the Agenda* (Cape Town: Ravan Press, 1991), Introduction, and essays by Zama, Ginwala, Mabandla, Nhlapo, Gwagwa, Maboreke, Gawanas, Dow.

IV. South Asia

Bina Agarwal, ed., *Structures of Patriarchy: State Community and Household in Modernizing Asia* (London: Zed Books, 1988), essays by Agarwal, Schrijvers, Phongpaichit, Srinivasan.

Kumkum Sangari and Sudesh Vaid, eds., *Recasting Women: Essays in Colonial History* (New Delhi: Kali for Women, 1989), Introduction, and essays by Chakravarti, Mani, Banerjee, Kannabiran and Lalitha, Chatterjee, Tharu.

V. Southeast Asia

Aihwa Ong, *Spirits of Resistance and Capitalist Discipline: Factory Women in Malaysia* (Albany: SUNY Press, 1987), Chaps. 7, 8, 9, 10 (140–221).

Noeleen Heyzer, *Daughters in Industry: Work, Skills and Consciousness of Women Workers in Asia* (Kuala Lumpur: Asian and Pacific Development Center, 1988), Chap. 1 (3–32), Chaps. 8, 9, 10, 11 (237–326), Chap. 13 (356–84).

————, *Working Women in South East Asia* (Philadelphia: Open University Press, 1986), Introduction, and Chaps. 1, 4, 7, 8.

Saskia Wieringa, ed., *Women's Struggles and Strategies* (Aldershot: Gower Publishing, 1988), Introduction, Chap. 5 (69–89).

VI. *West Asia*

Leila Ahmed, *Women and Gender in Islam: Historical Roots of a Modern Debate* (New Haven: Yale University Press, 1992).

Smadar Lavie, *Poetics of Military Occupation: Mezeina Allegories of Bedouin Identity* (Berkeley: University of California Press, 1990).

VII. *Australia*

Diane Bell, *Daughters of the Dreaming* (Minneapolis: University of Minnesota Press, 1993).

Kaye Thies, *Aboriginal Viewpoints on Education: A Survey in the East Kimberley Region* (Needlands: University of Western Australia, 1987).

Selections from John Frow and Meaghan Morris, eds., *Australian Cultural Studies* (Champaign: University of Illinois Press, 1993).

Selections from *Australian Feminist Studies*.

VIII. *Latin America*

Elisabeth Burgos-Debray, ed., *I, Rigoberta Menchú: An Indian Woman in Guatemala* (London: Verso, 1984).

Jean Franco, *Plotting Women: Gender and Representation in Mexico* (New York: Columbia University Press, 1992).

NACLA Report on the Americas 27.1 (1993): 19, 46–47.

Elizabeth Jelin, *Women and Social Change in Latin America* (London: Zed Books, 1990), Introduction, and Part I, Chap. 2.

Jane Jaquette, *The Women's Movement in Latin America: Feminism and the Transition to Democracy* (Boulder: Westview, 1991), Introduction, and 72–148, 185–208.

Selections from Heleieth Saffioti, *Women in Class Society* (New York: Monthly Review Press, 1978).

Steady, *Black Women Cross-Culturally*, essay by Nunes.

Juan Flores et al., eds., *On Edge: The Crisis of Contemporary Latin American Culture* (Minneapolis: University of Minnesota Press, 1993), essay by Franco.

IX. *U.S.*

Catharine MacKinnon, *Feminism Unmodified: Discourses on Life and Law* (Cambridge: Harvard University Press, 1987).

Judith Butler, *Gender Trouble: Feminism and the Subversion of Identity* (New York: Routledge, 1990).

Patricia Hill Collins, *Black Feminist Thought: Knowledge, Consciousness, and the Politics of Empowerment* (New York: Harper, 1991), Chaps. 2, 5, 6, 10.

bell hooks, *Black Looks: Race and Representation* (Boston: South End, 1992).

Steady, *The Black Woman Cross-Culturally*, Part II, Chaps. 2–6.

X. *Italy*

Paola Bono and Sandra Kemp, eds., *Italian Feminist Thought: A Reader* (London: Blackwell, 1991), Introduction, and 33–208, 260–83, 310–17, 339–67, Chronology.

Patricia Cicogna and Teresa de Lauretis, eds., *Sexual Differences: A Theory of Social-Symbolic Practice* (Bloomington: Indiana University Press, 1990).

Mirna Cicogna, "Women Subjects and Women Projects," *Australian Feminist Studies* 4 (Autumn 1987).

Rosi Braidotti, "The Italian Women's Movement in the 1980s," *Australian Feminist Studies* 3 (Summer 1986).

Sheila Allen and Carol Wolkowitz, *Homeworking: Myths and Realities* (London: Macmillan, 1987), 170–71.

Swasti Mitter, "Industrial Restructuring and Manufacturing Homework: Immigrant Women in the U.K. Clothing Industry," *Capital and Class* 27 (1986): 47–49, 62, 75–76.

2 Benetton xeroxes from *Financial Times* and *London Times*. Selections from Enzo Mingione, "Social Reproduction of the Surplus Labor Force: The Case of Italy," in Nanneka Redclift and Mingione, eds., *Beyond Employment* (London: Macmillan, 1985).

XI. *North West Europe*

Toril Moi, ed., *French Feminist Thought: A Reader* (London: Blackwell, 1987), essays by Beauvoir, Leclerc, Delphy, Kristeva, Irigaray, Le Doeuff, Kofman, Montrelay.

Denise Riley, *Am I That Name? Feminism and the Category of "Women" in History* (Minneapolis: University of Minnesota Press, 1988).

Frigga Haug and Others, *Female Sexualization: A Collective Work of Memory* (London: Verso, 1987).

Parveen Adams and Elizabeth Cowie, eds., *M/F* (Cambridge: MIT Press, 1990), 3–5, 21–44, 134–48, 274–82, 315–27, 345–56.

XII. *Post-Soviet Eurasia*

Mary Buckley, *Perestroika and Soviet Women* (New York: Cambridge University Press, 1992).

Nanette Funk and Magda Mueller, eds., *Gender Politics and Post-Communism: Reflections from Eastern Europe and the Former Soviet Union* (New York: Routledge, 1993), Introduction, and essays by Todorova, Harsanyi, Siklova, Kiczkova and Etela Farkasova, Milic, Duhacek, Bohm, Dolling, Adamik, Fuszara, Lissyutkina.

Helena Goscilo, ed., *Fruits of Her Plume: Essays on Contemporary Russian Women's Culture* (Armonk: M. E. Sharpe, 1993), essay by Ivanova.

Barbara Holland, ed., *Soviet Sisterhood* (Bloomington: Indiana University Press, 1985), essays by McAndrew, Allott, Holt.

Selections from Gregory Massell, *Surrogate Proletariat* (Princeton: Princeton University Press, 1977).

Selections from R. Aminova, *The October Revolution and Women's Liberation in Uzbekistan* (Moscow: Nauka, 1977).

APPENDIX

XIII. *East Asia*

(For lack of time, this area was not covered. What follows is a working bibliography on China which I will have to work through. Only one work and one journal covering Japan are included. Since the next time I teach this course, student suggestions will allow me to shorten the reading list, I hope to be more inclusive.)

Margery Wolf and Roxane Witke, *Women in Chinese Society* (Stanford: Stanford University Press, 1975).

Janet W. Salaff, *Working Daughters of Hong Kong* (Cambridge: Cambridge University Press, 1981).

Ono Kazuko, *Chinese Women in a Century of Revolution* (Stanford: Stanford University Press, 1989).

Tonglin Lu, ed., *Gender and Sexuality: Twentieth-Century Chinese Literature and Society* (Albany: SUNY Press, 1993).

Rey Chow, *Writing Diaspora: Tactics of Intervention in Contemporary Women's Studies* (Bloomington: Indiana University Press, 1993).

Yayori Matsui, *Women's Asia* (London: Zed Books, 1989).
Selections from *U.S.–Japan Women's Journal*.

NOTES

This text was published in *Textual Practice* 10 (2), 245–69, © 1996 by Routledge. In that journal the text appears without the syllabus appended at the end of this essay here; that text does appear, however, with the following prefatory note supplied by the author:

> This essay is the text of a talk delivered at Rutgers University on March 1994. The dynamic of women in diaspora is so fast moving that it is hopeless to attempt to update this. The reader might want to check Spivak, " 'Woman' as global theatre: Beijing 1995," *Radical Philosophy*, 75 (January/February 1996), pp. 2–4 for the line of revision that I would take. Increasingly and metaleptically, transnationality is becoming the name of the increased migrancy of labour. To substitute this name for the change from multinational capital in the economic restructuring of the (developed/developing) globe—is to recode a change in the determination of capital as a cultural change—is a scary symptom of Cultural Studies, especially Feminist Cultural Studies.

1. As I will show later, the complexity of Farida Akhter's position is to be understood from the weave (or text-ile) of her work, not merely her verbal texts, which are, like all translations, not a substitute for the "original." Let me cite, with this proviso, Akhter, *Depopulating Bangladesh* (Dhaka: Narigrantha, 1992) and Malini Karkal, *Can Family Planning Solve Population Problem?* (Bombay: Stree Uvach, 1989). The scene has been so Eurocentrically obfuscated that I hasten to add that this is not a so-called pro-life position, but rather a dismissal of Western (Northern) universalization of its domestic problems in the name of woman. See also Spivak, "Empowering Women?" *Environment* 37, 1 (Jan.–Feb. 1995): 2–3.
2. Ranajit Guha, "On Some Aspects of the Historiography of Colonial India," in Guha, ed., *Subaltern Studies: Writings on South Asian History and Society* (Delhi: Oxford University Press, 1982), 8.
3. Jacques Derrida, "White Mythology: Metaphor in the Text of Philosophy," in Alan Bass, trans., *Margins of Philosophy* (Chicago: University of Chicago Press, 1982), 209.
4. In *Public Culture* 5, 1 (Fall 1992).
5. For the usual debate on civil society between left and right, see Justin Rosenberg, *The Empire of Civil Society: A Critique of the Realist Theory of International Relations* (New York: Verso, 1994) and Ernest Gellner, *Conditions of Liberty: Civil Society and Its Rivals* (New York: Allen Lane, 1994).

6. I use "sup-pose" (rather than "pre-suppose," which presupposes the subject's agency) here in what I understand to be Derrida's sense in *The Other Heading: Reflections on Today's Europe*, trans. Pascale-Anne Brault and Michael Naas (Bloomington: Indiana University Press, 1992), 76. The word "suppose" is unfortunately translated "presuppose" in the English version. The imaginary map of geo-graphy as we understand it today has been traced by pushing the so-called aboriginals back, out, away, in. The story of the emergence of civil societies is sup-posed in that movement.

7. Saskia Sassen, *On Governance in the Global Economy* (New York: Columbia University Press, 1996).

8. The argument about feminist universalism propagated through the United Nations is beginning to invaginate this essay in its current revision. I am now convinced that the re-coding of transnationality (an economic phenomenon) as people moving across frontiers is part of this propagation: capital being re-coded into capital-ism. I have proposed elsewhere that these United Nations initiatives in the name of woman have produced feminist apparatchiks whose activism is to organize the poorest women of the developing world incidentally in their own image ("train them to be women," in Christine Nicholls's bitter felicitous phrase), primarily in the interest of generating research fodder according to the old dominant: the essence of knowledge is knowledge about knowledge. As part of this endeavor, some large U.S.-based organizations secure funds for non-elite NGOs in order to enrich their own databases, or to redirect the latters' energies towards activities favored by the former: ideological manipulation of the simplest sort; rather like buying votes (in the interest of "economic citizenship"). Recently I have twice heard this kind of activity described by two different people as "working with" these NGOs. Here again the academic diasporic or minority woman thinking transnationality must be literate enough to ask: *cui bono*, working *for* whom, in what interest? In "The Body as Property: A Feminist Re-Vision" (in Faye Ginsburg and Rayna Rapp, eds., *Conceiving the New World Order* [Berkeley: University of California Press, 1995]), Rosalind Pollack Petchesky almost quotes Farida Akhter, a Bangladeshi activist, for a few lines, only to substitute Carol Pateman, whose "critique" seems to her to have an "affinity" with Akhter but to be "more systematic and encompassing" (395). Not content with silencing Akhter by substitution, she then proceeds to provide a "feminist" alternative to such "essentialism" by way of ethnography (New Guinea tribal women can't be different from women exploited by post-fordism in Bangladesh!), sixteenth century Paris, "the early-modern European origins of ideas about owning one's own body" among the women of the British Levellers, and, finally, the work of Patricia Williams, the African-American legal theorist. Here is her version of Akhter: "Farida Akhter, a women's health activist and researcher in Bangladesh, condemns 'the individual right of woman over her own body' as an 'unconscious mirroring of the capitalist-patriarchal ideology . . . premised

on the logic of bourgeois individualism and inner urge of private property.' According to Akhter, the idea that a woman owns her body turns it into a 'reproductive factory,' objectifies it, and denies that reproductive capacity is a 'natural power we carry within ourselves.' Behind her call for a 'new social relationship' with regard to this 'natural power' of woman lies a split between 'the natural' woman and 'the social' woman that brings Akhter closer to the essentialized embrace of 'difference' by radical feminists than her Marxist framework might suggest" (394–95). In *Capital* I, Marx writes that the pivot of socialist resistance is to understand that labor *power* is the only commodity which is the site of a dynamic struggle (*Zwieschlächtigkeit*) between the private and the socializable. If the worker gets beyond thinking of work as *Privatarbeit* or individual work, and perceives it as a potential commodity (laborpower) of which s/he is the part-subject (since labor power is an abstract average), s/he can begin to resist the appropriation of surplus value and turn capital toward social redistribution. As a person who is daily organizing struggles against transnationalization, Akhter expects familiarity with this first lesson of training for resistance. The trivial meaning of the proletarian is that s/he possesses nothing but the body, and is therefore "free." If one remains stuck on that, there is no possibility of socialism, but only employment on the factory floor. This *Zwieschlächtigkeit* between "private" and "social" (labor and labor power) is Akhter's "split between the 'natural' and the 'social.' " Notice that, in keeping with Marx, she uses "power," where Petchesky substitutes "woman." And indeed, there is a bit of a paradox here: that the "natural" in the human body should be susceptible to "socialization"! Why is Akhter speaking of a "reproductive power"? Because, as a person working against the depredations of capitalist/individualist reproductive engineering, she is daily aware that reproductive labor power has been socialized. When she calls for a "new social relationship," she is using it in the strict Marxist sense of "social relations of production." New because the Marxist distinction between all other commodities and laborpower will not hold here. The produced commodities are children, also coded within the affective value form, not things. U.S. personalism cannot think Marx's risky formulation of the resistant use of socialized labor power, just as it reduces Freud's risky metapsychology to ego psychoanalysis. Further, since its implied subject is the agent of rights-based bourgeois liberalism, it cannot think of the owned body from the proletarian perspective, as a dead end road. It can only be the bearer of the "abstract" legal body coded as "concrete." (It is of course also true that U.S.-based UN feminism works in the interest of global financialization, aka development. Here I should say of Petchesky what I have said of Brontë and Freud in "Three Women's Texts and a Critique of Imperialism," in Henry Louis Gates, Jr., ed., *"Race," Writing and Difference* [Chicago: University of Chicago Press, 1985], 263; and in "Can the Subaltern Speak?" in Cary Nelson and Lawrence Grossberg, eds., *Marxism and*

the Interpretation of Culture [Champaign-Urbana: University of Illinois Press, 1988],
296–97. Akhter expresses similar sentiments more simply in "unconscious mirroring.") Incidentally, it is also possible that the split between "natural" and "social" is
that split between species-life and species-being that the young Marx brings forward
and displaces into his later work as that between the realm of freedom and the realm
of necessity: the limit to planning. But it would take the tempo of classroom teaching
to show how U.S.-based feminism cannot recognize theoretical sophistication in the
South, which can only be the repository of an ethnographic "cultural difference."
Here suffice it to say that Carol Pateman, with respect, is certainly not a more "systematic and encompassing" version of this. And you cannot answer the demand for a
new social relation of production in the New World Order (post-Soviet financialization, patenting of the DNA of the subaltern body for pharmaceutical speculation,
etc.) by citing anthropology and early modern Europe. Indeed, it is not a question of
citing colored folks against colored folks, but understanding the analysis. But perhaps the worst moment is the use of Patricia Williams. I cannot comment on the
ethico-political agenda of silencing the critical voice of the South by way of a woman
of color in the North. It should at least be obvious that the abusive constitution of the
body in chattel slavery is not the socialization of the body in exploitation. The matri-
lineality of slavery cannot be used as an affective alibi for the commodification of
reproductive labor power. Williams herself makes it quite clear that today's underclass African-American wants to *feel* ownership of the body in reaction against her
specific history and situation. And that situation is the contradiction of the use of
chattel slavery to advance industrial capitalism. Patricia Williams writes of this use,
this passage within the U.S. juridico-legal system. She cannot be further used to "disprove" the conjunctural predicament of the South. Women in a transnational
world—notice Petchesky's use of artistic representation as evidence through the
diasporic artists Mira Nair and Meena Alexander, both of Indian origin; not to mention the fact that, in transnationalization, the cases of Bangladesh and India are altogether dissimilar—must beware of the politics of the appropriation of theory.

9. Mike Davis, *City of Quartz: Excavating the Future in Los Angeles* (New York: Vintage
   Books, 1992), 267.
10. Michael Kearney, "Borders and Boundaries: State and Self at the End of Empire,"
    Journal of Historical Sociology 4, 1 (March 1991): 52–74.
11. Samir Amin, *Unequal Development: An Essay on the Social Formations of Peripheral
    Capitalism*, trans. Brian Pearce (New York: Monthly Review Press, 1976); Walter Rod-
    ney, *How Europe Underdeveloped Africa* (Washington, D.C.: Howard University Press,
    1981).
12. Jean Franco, *Plotting Women: Gender and Representation in Mexico* (New York: Colum-
    bia University Press, 1992), 11.

13. Catharine MacKinnon, Feminism Unmodified: Discourses on Life and Law (Cambridge: Harvard University Press, 1987), 63–69.

14. Raymond Suttner and Jeremy Cronin, eds., Thirty Years of the Freedom Charter (Johannesburg: Ravan Press, 1986), 162–63.

15. Melanie Klein, Envy and Gratitude (London: Tavistock, 1957).

16. Ifi Amadiume, Male Daughters, Female Husbands: Gender and Sex in African Society (London: Zed Books, 1987). The passage quoted is from p. 9.

17. A discussion of the impossible situation of the Bangladesh garment industry, caught between World Bank pressure against unionization and post-GATT social dumping, resulting in the fetishization of child labor with a total incomprehension of the situation of urban subaltern children in Bangladesh, drew from a grant-rich "feminist" sociologist colleague, conversant with the depredations upon welfare in New York, the remark that one must of course remember cultural difference! It had quite escaped this intellectual that I was speaking of Northern exploitation, not of some imagined Bangladeshi cultural preference for making children work! It's not much better with Southern academics. A similar discussion in Sri Lanka had elicited from a female graduate student the question, "Is Gayatri Spivak for child labor?"

18. Derrida, Of Grammatology, trans. Spivak (Baltimore: Johns Hopkins University Press, 1976), 125.

19. I have tried to describe a similar predicament for myself in "A Response to Jean-Luc Nancy," in Juliet Flower MacCannell and Lara Zakarin, eds., Thinking Bodies (Stanford: Stanford University Press, 1994), 39–48.

20. Filomina Chioma Steady, ed., Black Women Cross-Culturally (Rochester: Schenkman, 1981).

21. "Women and Law in Post-Independence Zimbabwe: Experience and Lessons," in Susan Bazilli, ed., Putting Women on the Agenda (Johannesberg: Ravan Press, 1991), 215, 236–37.

22. Hester Eisenstein, "Speaking for Women? Voices from the Australian Femocrat Experiment," Australian Feminist Studies 14 (Summer 1991): 29–42.

23. Derrida, "Declarations of Independence," trans. Thomas W. Keenan, New Political Science 15 (Summer 1986): 7–15. But here too we must remind ourselves that the feeling/thinking ground is what makes the critique persistent even as it foils it: disclosure, alas, in effacement. All uses of "deconstruction" as verb or noun are practically breached by this double bind. No use talking about infinite regress, for infinite progress is no different, only differant, in(de)finitely.

24. Aihwa Ong, Spirits of Resistance and Capitalist Discipline: Factory Women in Malaysia (Albany: SUNY Press, 1987), Chaps. 7, 8, 9, 10 (140–221).

25. Noeleen Heyzer, Working Women in South East Asia: Development, Subordination, and Emancipation (Philadelphia: Open University Press, 1986). The passage quoted is from pp. 131, 132.

26. Seyla Benhabib, *Situating the Self: Gender, Community and Postmodernism in Contemporary Ethics* (New York: Routledge, 1992). The passage quoted is from pp. 2–3.

27. Thomas W. Keenan, *Fables of Responsibility: Between Literature and Politics* (Stanford: Stanford University Press, 1996).

28. Frigga Haugg's excellent book, *Beyond Female Masochism: Memory Work and Politics*, trans. Rodney Livingstone (London: Verso, 1992), indispensable for consciousness raising, legitimizes the European history of the compromising of responsibility-in-gender, by a mere reversal. To tease this out for responsibility-based systems requires a different sense of one's own position ("textuality"), a different agenda.

29. I am drawing on a big theme here, which I have merely touched upon by way of the notion of the differance between socialism and capitalism. (See Spivak, "Supplementing Marxism," in Stephen Cullenberg and Bernd Magnus, eds., *Whither Marxism?* [New York: Routledge, 1994], 118–19. Derrida puts these impossibilities in the place of the figuration of the gift, if there is any. But a thinker like Karl-Otto Apel would simply dismiss them as "utopian" ("Is the Ideal Communication Community a Utopia?" quoted in Benhabib, 81). My "experience" here is of young women working in the garment factories in Bangladesh, displaced from their family, seemingly on a superior footing from the unemployed young men on the street, and yet without any care taken to recode their ethical beings into the public. I admire Carol Gilligan, but to cite her here is an insult; for she must retrain herself with a different group under observation and with the instruction of experts in the field such as Heyzer. *Mutatis mutandis*, I encounter a similar problem with the industry in revising Freudo-Lacanian psychoanalysis in the name of feminist cultural studies.

30. Shula Marks, ed., *Not Either an Experimental Doll: The Separate Lives of Three South African Women* (Bloomington: Indiana University Press, 1987), 207, 209.

31. I am of course reversing the subtitle of that essay by Derrida which I cited in note 3.

32. Fatima Mernissi, *Beyond the Veil: Male-Female Dynamics in Modern Muslim Society* (London: Al Saqi, 1985).

33. This contradiction is a gendered displacement of the broader contradiction, which has been pointed out in David Washbrook's essay "Law, State and Agrarian Society in Colonial India" (*Modern Asian Studies* 15, 3 [1981]: 649–721), that if colonial practice operated in the interest of capitalist social productivity, the indigenous practices within which local capitalisms flourished contradicted that interest. See Ritu Birla, "Hedging Bets: Politics of Commercial Ethics in Late Colonial India," Department of History, Columbia University, dissertation in progress. The contradiction we are discussing is also a *classed* displacement of the earlier contradiction between emancipation and culturalism for women in the colonies.

34. Gilles Deleuze and Felix Guattari, *Anti-Oedipus: Capitalism and Schizophrenia*, trans. Robert Hurley et al. (Minneapolis: University of Minnesota Press, 1983).

35. Kaye Thies, *Aboriginal Viewpoints on Education: A Survey in the East Kimberley Region* (Needlands: University of Western Australia, 1987).

36. After the Massacre at Wounded Knee, Sitting Bull's cabin was taken to the 1893 Columbian Exposition at Chicago. This is claiming the right to theatre by the dominant, exactly the opposite of what we are commenting on. Or, not quite exactly. For the historically subordinated "had" the language to lose, which the dominant only destroyed. Somewhere in between is Buffalo Bill Cody, who acquired the freedom of Wounded Knee participants so that they could show "Wounded Knee." Today's restricted multicultural diasporists would find in Cody their prototype. It is Capital in the abstract that "frees" the subject of Eurocentric economic migration to stage "culture" in First World multiculturalism.

37. See Gordon Brotherston, *The Book of the Fourth World* (Cambridge: Cambridge University Press, 1993); and, in the context of contemporary Canadian bilingualist struggle, Merwan Hassan, "Articulation and Coercion: The Language Crisis in Canada," *Border/Lines* 36 (April 1995): 28–35.

38. Diane Bell, *Daughters of the Dreaming* (Minneapolis: University of Minnesota Press, 1993).

39. Leslie Marmon Silko, *Almanac of the Dead* (Harmondsworth: Penguin, 1991).

40. Paola Bono and Sandra Kemp, eds., *Italian Feminist Thought: A Reader* (London: Blackwell, 1991). Patricia Cicogna and Teresa de Lauretis, eds., *Sexual Differences: A Theory of Social-Symbolic Practice* (Bloomington: Indiana University Press, 1990). Mirna Cicogna, "Women Subjects and Women Projects," *Australian Feminist Studies* 4 (Autumn 1987). Rosi Braidotti, "The Italian Women's Movement in the 1980s," *Australian Feminist Studies* 3 (Summer 1986).

41. Swasti Mitter, "Industrial Restructuring and Manufacturing Homework: Immigrant Women in the U.K. Clothing Industry," *Capital and Class* (1986): 27, 47–49, 62, 75–76.

42. See Joseph Stalin, *Nationalism and the Colonial Question: A Collection of Articles and Speeches* (San Francisco: Proletarian Publishers, 1975); and V. I. Lenin, *Imperialism, the Highest Stage of Capitalism: A Popular Outline* (New York: International Publishers, 1939). Although Stalin constantly invokes Lenin in order to legitimize himself, Lenin is speaking of the Northwestern European single nation empires and their connections to the march of Capital, whereas Stalin is speaking of the Russian, Ottoman, and Habsburg empires, and the manipulation of their cultures and identities in the interest of forming something like a future new empire. Thus their lines lead toward finance capital and linguistic and cultural politics respectively; in their current displacements, the economic phenomenon of transnationalization and its re-territorialization into migrant hybridity by multiculturalist diasporists, respectively.

43. See passage quoted in Mahasweta Devi, *Imaginary Maps*, trans. Spivak (New York: Routledge, 1995), 212–13.

44. In Clarice Lispector, *Family Ties*, trans. Giovanni Pontiero (Austin: University of Texas Press, 1972), 88–95.

The Value Of

8

Peter Hitchcock

Etienne Balibar has suggested that philosophy has not forgiven Marx for "ideology" as a concept, as a principle, and as a social phenomenon (43). Yet it seems that philosophers and everyone else have not forgiven him for his elaboration of "value." If, as Steven Connor argues, value is inescapable (8), the irony for Marxism has been that even its putative adherents have fled from the labor theory of value, and indeed use-value, rather than take up the revolutionary prospect of society abandoning its socialization and valorization through exchange. For all the wacky theorizing of Baudrillard that use-value is really only the metaphysical simulacrum of exchange value (Marx puts dialectics on its feet; Baudrillard turns value inside out), his approach is symptomatic of a more general desire to theorize through the signification of exchange, the form of the appearance of value, rather than dwell on the unrepresentability of value in abstraction, in abstract labor, for one. One thing is certain: whether one studies cultural value or value endemic to a particular economic mode of production, the question of value is difficult—

difficult to think, difficult to teach, and difficult to substantiate in a public sphere whose very logic denies its own substantiation.

At the risk of eliding the complexity in Marx's theorization of value, I want to consider a few of the ways "the value of" might be connected to a subject and then a viable and agonistic predicate. The point is to keep the question of value alive in Cultural Studies without ceding the bulk of its critical edge within materialism to the value of culture. Value is too heavy for culture, even if the latter is its most fascinating medium (particularly given the saturating aura of cultural commodification). If the teacher can alert students to the complexity of the subject, perhaps the complexity in the predicate might be more forcefully entertained.

First, the value of value lies in a certain impossibility, a statement that is not a theoretical sleight of hand but is immanent to the problem of value that Marx investigates. In the opening pages of volume 1 of *Capital*, Marx wants us to "see" value, that it "exists"; whereas the commodity relations that he describes precisely render that existence invisible. Certainly, the use-value of a commodity exists—as the ground for exchange, as a function of qualitative difference—but it appears and disappears in the quantitative moment of exchange as if use were not the primary motivation for making a commodity. Of course, within capitalism, exchange value masks use-value, so that the latter might seem inconsequential or a mild irritant to the busy process of capital accumulation. Value itself gets transmogrified into money and the measure of value into price—while capital refutes, denies, or simply forgets what laws might obtain in its very possibility. How to render the invisible, thinks Marx, in order to expound on the law of value that girds a particular regimen of economic activity? At this point Marx is overcome by a desire to represent but, ingeniously some might say (while others dismiss the provocation with the word that is like sunlight to a vampire—"idealism"), he represents the unrepresentable with that which remains. Why is use-value unrepresentable? Because exchange value is the necessary form of its appearance under capitalism. Use-value is defined by what it is not; its existence is indicated by the form of its absence. Use-value is of the commodity but only in terms of its nature: it is cognized through the cognitive logic of lack. Lest the students start remembering dental appointments and head for the door, it is prudent at this point to use the text of *Capital*:

> If then we disregard the use-value of commodities, only one property remains, that of being products of labor. But even the product of labor has already been transformed in our hands. If we make abstrac-

tion from its use-value, we abstract also from the material con-
stituents and forms which make it a use-value. It is no longer a table,
a house, a piece of yarn or any other useful thing. All its sensuous
characteristics are extinguished.

Nor is it any longer the product of the labor of the joiner, the mason
or the spinner, or of any other particular kind of productive labor.
With the disappearance of the useful character of the products of
labor, the useful character of the kinds of labor embodied in them also
disappears; this in turn entails the disappearance of the concrete forms
of labor. They can no longer be distinguished, but are all together
reduced to the same kind of labor, human labor in the abstract.

Let us now look at the residue of the products of labor. There is
nothing left of them in each case but the same phantom-like objectivity; they are merely congealed quantities of homogeneous human
labor, i.e. of human labor-power expended without regard to the form
of its expenditure. All these things now tell us is that human labor-
power has been expended to produce them, human labor is accumulated in them. As crystals of this social substance, which is common
to all of them, they are values—commodity values. (128)

This is not the interpretive key that unlocks Marx's contribution to the
"value of" debate (despite the fact that one could quite easily base a course on
the responses and implications of response to the first few pages of the "Commodity" chapter), but it is a good place to start. The logic of Marx's approach is
not reassuring, yet it is vital to a dialectical understanding of value as he argues
the case. The passage begins with "if," and there can be no viable extrapolation
from Marx's argument if we do not heed the hypothetical condition indicated. *If*
we disregard use-value and *if* we make abstraction from a product's use-value we
realize an interesting discovery: what remains in the product is abstract human
labor—abstract because it is labor that is undifferentiated by the specific form of
a particular commodity. But the present subjunctive makes something appear; if
we do one thing then it causes another and it is this appearance that is otherwise
unimaginable or unrepresentable. This is very tricky because the consequence of
the hypothesis presents a substance that is abstract: we are asked to "look" at a
residue, a congealed or jellied quantity of homogeneous labor. It is an object, but
it is "phantom-like," and anyone with a serious passion for Marx knows that his
specters (as Derrida has more recently discovered) are a vehicle for his sense of

the coming and becoming of social transformation (as in "A specter is haunting Europe"). Objectified labor is not just ghastly (as jelly), but ghostly, a spirit of its laboring self. If there were a substance that would link these mixed metaphors it would be ectoplasm, but Marx expresses this essence in a different way: as a crystal. *There* is value, there in the social substance that is otherwise invisible in the commodity form. *If* we could perform this operation, the diamond would be labor.

But this is not a proof, and the value of Marx's argument lies elsewhere than the formal or normative procedures of logic available to him. The form of value he proposes is immanent to the content of the commodity—the method of subtraction that he uses in his hypothesis is a vehicle for the proposition, not the proof of value itself. Thus, to the first difficulty of visualizing the unrepresentable we must add a second: that the labor theory of value is about a process of valorization that has no proof outside its application to commodity relations where it attempts to calculate the amount of socially necessary labor for a given product. But—and here the teeth begin to gently ache once more—value *is* expressible, and Marx knows it. The problem is that it is expressible as something external to the commodity itself and stands in for the commodity as it stands in for the labor that made it. If labor is made visible by subtraction within the commodity, then it is also made visible by substitution outside the commodity, and more powerfully so. Obviously, this universal equivalent is money: the visible representation of labor, the social expression of the world of commodities—that which can serve as the value form of all commodities. Thus, the problem of labor rendered as an abstraction is connected by Marx to its quantitative substitution by a universal equivalent. Marx, of course, will argue that the substance of value is labor (131), but this is precisely what cannot be grasped in the commodity as an object (the objectivity of commodities as values is not to be found in the commodity's physicality, in its tactile presence). Here then, is the difficulty of thinking "the value of" for Marx. Labor is imagined as a substance; money is a value that substantially represents it. The dialectic of value in commodity exchange is understandable through the magic of this cruel reversal, one in which Marx participates ("Let us look") to accentuate the actual process of commodity production and circulation. Many lessons derive from this, but here let me limit myself to three that might be useful within the pedagogy of Cultural Studies.

"The value of" subject (as that which precipitates a subject, as in a prepositional phrase) disrupts our somewhat tidy discourses on appearance and reality. Here we have a situation where value might be said to "represent" labor, but that is not quite what Marx wants to argue by having us pause over the crystal.

Surely value *is* labor by Marx's account? The problem remains, however, that
the medium of this message is representation and, as Gayatri Spivak has pointed
out, this tends to produce a theoretical distraction from the insight that value is
also always already structured by difference. For Spivak, this provides an
opportunity to emphasize the indeterminacy and open-endedness of the value
form (an opportunity that, strategically, needs to be continually reinscribed).
Perhaps the more modest point at this juncture would be about the critical ability to think the unrepresentable *even when* it offers itself as a determinate form
of representation. Certainly, this accords with Spivak's exegesis on how value
slips the "onto-phenomenological question," but it also draws attention to the
way the metaphors of appearance come to displace the abstractions of reality.
Maybe this adds up to the same point. I would maintain, however, that a close
reading of Marx's polemic on value provides a springboard for discussion of a
cornerstone of materialist critique, namely, that the analysis of real relations
requires an understanding of the ethereal yet concrete nature of abstraction.
The reality of money is the "appearance" of the value form; the abstraction of
labor remains, in large part, its unseen "reality." Once the argument of value is
presented, of course, the debate about the value of value in Marx's formulation
can be enjoined (and here, the "fetishism of labor" as Jean-Marie Vincent calls
it, would have to be addressed). But it might also act as a catalyst (or indeed a
pharmakon) for an approach to the problem of cultural value—a point to which
I will soon return.

The moment of subtraction in Marx's argument predicates the focus on substitution in exchange value. This is not just a rather literal instance of deductive
reasoning but a point in Marx's theory where he attempts to separate essence
from essentialism. To the complaint that there are plenty of instances of value in
use that do not "contain" labor one would have to say something about the
power of appropriation (for instance, one can "make" capital from untilled or
unworked land by appropriating it), but the more interesting question concerns
the nature of the methodology itself, which wants to maintain the compulsive
calculations of the economist with the metaphorical agon of the philosopher-
poet. To calculate the subtraction that will give us value, Marx begins with a
"simple geometrical example" about rectilinear figures composed of triangles,
but this is immediately set aside. Why? Because he realizes that his readers may
associate the invocation of shapes with an actual commodity. What to do? Marx
is insistent on the trope of subtraction because he wants to intimate the real
reduction effected on use-value to produce exchange. As Thomas Keenan has

observed, "No substitution without reduction, without the reduction of the 'manifold ways of using the thing' " (163). But even if the literary critic spies in the process of exchange first synecdoche (the part for a whole) and then metonymy (the substitution of terms [values] in exchange), this is not quite the poetic license that Marx wants to take. For Marx (and here Keenan would agree) is ultimately concerned to show the movement of *abstraction* in his own argument in contrast to the reality of this movement in exchange: there is a descriptive similarity but a necessarily logical contrast without which Marx would be performing the rather dubious practice of philosophy as exchange value (a philosophical and anatomical impossibility). The point would be to underline the necessity of this allusion in the nexus of subtraction and substitution in order to bring the nature of abstraction into focus (and the sight metaphor, of course, is precisely Marx's gambit). But one also has to acknowledge, as Raymond Williams does with Marx's metaphor of the camera-obscura for ideology, that "the emphasis is clear, but the analogy is difficult" (59). Here the lesson of subtraction and substitution is that analogy itself presents an untranscendable danger, that the value of value is always a trope.

This, of course, is the warning of a cultural critic and, if we have learned anything from decades of discursivity (or the discursive turn), it is that a viable politics (or theory of value) does not necessarily derive from tropical delight. Nevertheless, the path to understanding value for Marx lies in extrapolation from his methodology, and this provides, I believe, a useful pedagogical apparatus. After the enigma of value is elaborated (and not merely confirmed), the challenge becomes the sheer preponderance of possible subjects for the prepositional phrase "the value of" (first, value as subject, then the value of). In each we may modify the substance of Marx's example, but not, I would urge, by simply disregarding the difficulty of the mode of substantiality he employs. The complexity of the initial example affects the centrifugal multiplicity of the predicate. One might begin with the thorn in Marxism's side: "the value of" labor as it is interpreted subsequent to Marx's formulation (and even in his own work — in volume 3 of *Capital*, for instance). One could move from this to "the value of" Marxism itself in light of history and its own formulations. But let us skip to another wound, this time in Cultural Studies — somewhere in the region of its heel.

If Marxism stands or falls over the question of value's relation to labor (remove this and the mode of production argument and the edifice of class begin to crumble), then Cultural Studies will expire without continual attention to the concept of value, cultural value in its range of methodologies. Almost every major statement on Cultural Studies has had to reflect on value, since the status of its disciplinary intervention and its logical integrity depend on it. The tremendous work on popular culture, for instance, has not merely opposed the elitism and snobbish pretensions of "high" culture, but affirmed the capacity of the popular to produce its own spheres of value. In this, value performs in a double register. On one level, it may refer to the formation of pleasure that a culture enacts; on another level, it must embody the impossible abstraction that Marx, in his own way, attempts to articulate. The first is the expressive value of this or that culture; the second is its immanent imperative. When we make a value judgment about "the value of" a particular culture we must also respond to its ground for value—not its effects, but the condition for those effects. The problem is that it is usually much easier to grapple with expressive value (which often functions like money in Marx's example) than to struggle over the grounds for a logical integrity in value. And when the first value is taken as an unproblematic epiphenomenon of the second, an old demon inevitably arises: cultural relativism. Here is the irony of the example from Marx. In the nineteenth century, the division between economic and aesthetic value is necessarily sharp, hence the surprise at their proximity in Marx's argument. But in the late twentieth century an aestheticized essence of labor is shocking but not exactly revolutionary, since divisions in value, the whole machinery of discernment, have been almost completely banalized by commodification. The difficulty of value remains, but not its divisions. And this is a political and not just a pedagogical problem.

These are "notes toward a reading" (or at best a detailed footnote about the twist of insubstantiality), and they would not bear the scrutiny that *Capital* still deserves. I do hope, however, that I have indicated the necessity of the subject in "the value of" and the hard work it entails for a radical pedagogy. Marx took the seriousness of value very much to heart, enough indeed to rewrite the first chapter of *Capital* with "greater scientific strictness" (94). Cultural Studies need not attend to that science (it has already proved that it is not Marxism), but it should encourage the "strictness" that is not just a disciplinary zeal, but a cognitive linchpin of its logical integrity. In this way "the value of" studying Marx's extraction as abstraction would foster another subject, "the value of Cultural Studies" itself.

WORKS CITED

Balibar, Etienne. *The Philosophy of Marx*, trans. Chris Turner. New York: Verso, 1995.

Baudrillard, Jean. *For a Critique of the Political Economy of the Sign*, trans. Charles Levin. St. Louis: Telos Press, 1981.

Connor, Steven. *Theory and Cultural Value*. Oxford: Blackwell, 1992.

Derrida, Jacques. *Specters of Marx*, trans. Peggy Kamuf. New York: Routledge, 1994.

Keenan, Thomas. "The Point Is to (Ex)Change It: Reading Capital, Rhetorically." In *Fetishism as Cultural Discourse*, ed. Emily Apter and William Pietz. Ithaca: Cornell University Press, 1993.

Marx, Karl. *Capital*. Vol. 1, trans. Ben Fowkes. New York: Penguin, 1976.

Spivak, Gayatri Chakravorty. *In Other Worlds*. New York: Methuen, 1987.

Vincent, Jean-Marie. *Abstract Labor: A Critique*, trans. Jim Cohen. New York: St. Martin's, 1991.

Williams, Raymond. *Marxism and Literature*. Oxford: Oxford University Press, 1976.

A Pedagogy of Unlearning

Teaching the Specificity of U.S. Marxism

Alan Wald

9

In her recent *Teaching to Transgress: Education as the Practice of Freedom*, bell hooks writes inspirationally of "the pleasure and joy I experience teaching" as an "act of resistance" to racism and sexism (hooks 10). True for me, too, on occasion. But more often classroom teaching seems to be the most complex, enigmatic, and even personally painful issue that the conscientious and self-critical Marxist scholar in the university must confront. Perhaps matters of personal temperament are involved, but I'm more likely to frown quizzically than smile joyfully when reflecting on my life in lecture halls and seminar rooms.

I write this as a teacher-scholar engaged in rather detailed research into the cultural history of the Left, and as an activist in a variety of radical social movements. Although I would like to exclaim that I enter the classroom buoyant and sure-footed about my teaching mission, I have repeatedly concluded that the fear of making a mistake is my predominant concern. I don't mean "mistake" in the sense of an embarrassing blunder. Rather, the notion of my misrepresenting the efforts of those largely forgotten cultural workers whose legacy is in my hands (as a teacher as well as scholar), or of inadvertently misguiding students on knotty political questions of Left history weighs heavily on my every choice of text or pedagogical strategy. There are moments when it seems as if the whole dynamic of our fast-paced consumer society—where culture is linked to entertainment and where sound-byte answers are prized—goes against the grain of any effort to teach with integrity in a conventional educational institution. I can't see myself dressing up, like those popular professors about whom one reads in *Newsweek*, in the costume of a "proletarian" to discuss the excruciating tragedy of William Attaway's *Blood on the Forge* (1941), nor is there a witty one-liner to answer the question, "Were the Rosenbergs guilty?" I'd like my classroom encounters to be fun, but there is a seriousness about my topics, linked to a sense of personal responsibility, that I can't seem to shake off.

Perhaps pedagogy looms so demanding because my expectations are so high. The classroom, after all, is the site of an intense "testing" of the research and theory that one has assembled in the sense that one may receive immediate responses from the classroom community and may also witness firsthand the discussion of one's propositions; even more substantial results may be discerned in the papers and oral contributions of students throughout a semester. Unlike the publication of a book or article, which may be read under unpredictable circumstances that may distort or undercut the impact of one's argument, the situation of presenting analysis in a classroom is relatively more controlled. Also, the radical teacher is in regular contact with the students for at least three months, perhaps longer if one teaches a sequence of courses allowing re-enrollment of the same students. One might actually influence a student in a certain direction; therefore, doesn't one have a personal responsibility in regard to the consequences? This classroom relationship would seem to allow for a high degree of mutual interaction and communication, including many opportunities for students to question one's pedagogical practice and suggest modifications. Yet intimacy with a large number of students in a class is illusory. Even in courses on specialized topics, one confronts a highly diverse audience. The various frames of reference and structures of perception of the situation are largely unknown in advance, if they ever become clearly understood. Moreover, there are nefarious power relations built into the university situation in general and the classroom setting in particular; factors that Henry A. Giroux theorizes as the "hidden curriculum" (Giroux 23).[1] These can precipitate the backfiring of even the most carefully formulated strategies for egalitarian dynamics of communication. The prior inculcation of the student with assumptions of all sorts means that a crucial component of the "learning" experience is that of "unlearning" the hidden curriculum.

Finally, there is the problem of judging how effective one's efforts have been. To me, this remains as mysterious as the search for objective criteria of literary and cultural "value" in contemporary aesthetic debates. Student evaluation forms, today largely multiple choice questions, are usually too standardized to accommodate the convoluted and troubling issues raised by courses that promote nondogmatic critical thought. How does one rank by number the degree to which the classroom experience has successfully disturbed the student's complacent passage through the knowledge industry? Sadly, students are as "human" as their teachers; much student feedback is influenced by subjective factors such as response to personalities, retaliation for alleged slights, and feelings about grades received or that one believes one is about to receive.

Nevertheless, despite the absence of scientific criteria or massive empirical data, we teachers accumulate a backlog of experiences retained in memory and somewhat corroborated by various materials (syllabi, sample exams, assignments, and a large quantity of evaluation forms that at least reveal patterns of contradictory perceptions), allowing for some degree of post facto analysis. Within such limitations, this essay is an attempt to explain how and why one socialist scholar and activist, myself, has developed certain teaching specialities, a corresponding pedagogy, and a Marxist orientation toward the public sphere.

A LIFE OF UNLEARNING

I have taught in an English literature department and American culture program for more than twenty years. Yet even today I recognize that my pedagogical practice in undergraduate as well as graduate classes is decisively informed by my coming of intellectual age among the crosscurrents of the mid- to late 1960s. Of course, that was a time of enormous contradiction; it would be a mistake to assume that any one person's experiences are representative of a larger group when it comes to judging the impact of the 1960s on one's consciousness. Factors such as one's class background, religious (or nonreligious) upbringing, gender, "race," ethnicity, region, sexual orientation, and so forth substantially shaped one's apprehension of the political and cultural upheavals that tumultuously burst forth on the national and international scene.

In retrospect, I have the sense that my attending college for five years from 1964 to 1969 put me in a different situation from many slightly older students, who were, like myself, drawn to literature as the terrain on which to deal with the most pressing personal, philosophical, and social issues in our lives. The older generation—those already in college at the start of the decade and in graduate school at the middle—was surely more fully formed in literary tastes and objectives than myself. Thus there is evidence of their being somewhat "traumatized" by the profound cultural and political questions rising to the fore under the impact of student strikes, ghetto uprisings, mass demonstrations, widespread use of hallucinogenic drugs, qualitative increase in sexual display and disrespectful language, and stark challenges to virtually every aspect of U.S. culture. One variant of this trauma/conversion paradigm can be seen in Bruce Franklin's landmark essay, "The Teaching of Literature in the Highest Academies of the Empire." Here Franklin recalls how, despite some initial resistance stemming from his working-class background, he acquired in his undergraduate years at Amherst College a genuine enthusiasm for Pope, Arnold, the metaphysical poets, and so on, only to realize "one night in the fall of 1967" that he had been fundamentally brainwashed (Franklin 112).

I was young enough so that my own adolescence, in the late 1950s, was already characterized by a steadily increasing adversarial discomfort with the prevailing culture. Alienated from educational, political, and religious institutions, I was not, however, anti-intellectual in the tradition of the classic "Rebel without a Cause." True, I felt no passion for the culture that had become, in the United States, that of the elite (Italian opera, adulation of Shakespeare, the Eurocentric version of "Western Culture"). On the other hand, I was an avid reader of U.S. realists and naturalists (especially Richard Wright and James T. Farrell) and European modernists and existentialists (especially Franz Kafka and Albert Camus), when the high school curriculum was still strictly limited to Shakespeare's *Hamlet*, Sir Walter Scott's *Ivanhoe*, and George Eliot's *Silas Marner*. I was also a devotee of jazz, in a household where classical music reigned unchallenged, and a very amateur jazz musician. But such cultural attractions did not allow me to conceive of a meaningful role for myself, let alone a "profession," inside or out of academe, or pretty much anywhere else.

I wasn't politically active, but this was not due to cynicism or despair. I simply had no vision of politics outside those institutions designed to reproduce the status quo. As a consequence, just as I never underwent the trauma of conversion from canonical to noncanonical literature, so I never experienced the catastrophic disappointment in liberals and the Democratic Party characteristic of older 1960s radicals; the "best and the brightest" of the Kennedy and Johnson administrations never extracted from me any emotional loyalty or illusions whatsoever. In his chapter on "The Decapitation of Heroes" in *The Sixties*, Todd Gitlin describes the dramatic shift from belief in liberal reform to the "rage" that drove radicals like Bernadine Dohrn to the terrorism of "Weatherman"; but the "we" employed by Gitlin in his narrative fails to account for the space where I (and probably many others) stood (Gitlin 311). Prior to my becoming cognizant of the existence of "Beats" or any U.S. counterparts to the Parisian bohemians Jean-Paul Sartre and Simone de Beauvoir, my role models for the life I envisioned were the heroes of a television serial called *Route 66*. The show featured a pair of male buddies who traveled from town to town across the continent each week, avoiding entrapment by particular jobs and routines, and committed only to a never-ending quest for freedom and experience. My own perception of this serial reflects a longing for individual choice, which, although in many respects conventionally masculine, did not translate into a belief in "individualism" as a philosophy of social life.

In sum, the impact of the 1960s on my own developing consciousness was a process closer to a logical progression by which I "unlearned" with relative ease rather than through traumatic disruption/conversion. Of course, I was no doubt traumatized by particular events in my personal life, and certainly by the prospect of being drafted for military service in a war that I opposed, but there was no sense of a wrenching shift from one coherent system of thought to another.

A second legacy of my education in the 1960s that strikes me as important to my pedagogical practice concerns my relation to educational institutions. In contrast to a growing number of students of the next generation, who were often in the new situation of having their teachers share in the countercultural ethos of the 1960s and 1970s, incorporating the fresh sensibility into their selection of texts and classroom presentations, I was able to have the experience of developing my own resources, extra-institutionally. Although I enrolled in the most radical college (Antioch) and university (Berkeley) I could locate, I was unquestionably educationally deprived in that I never once studied with other than white male professors, nor read literary works in a classroom by any people of color, or by a single woman save Emily Dickinson and Jane Austen.

Of course, under the impact of the national and international events of the 1960s, one could see at once the discrepancy between the atmosphere and topics of discussion in the classroom and what was happening in the streets of Detroit and being broadcast each night through television coverage of Vietnam. MIT professor Louis Kampf captured this atmosphere memorably in a 1968 description of himself standing in the hotel lobby of the Modern Language Association convention and, instead of seeing academics, "I kept seeing spectres of Vietnamese villagers being burned by napalm" (Kampf 49).

Such a clear disjuncture between even the most liberal educational environment and my desire for a culture that responded to the important events in the lives of people around me was oddly to my advantage. I early on acquired the habit of locating my own research materials and arguments. Such skills later served as the backbone of my unconventional publishing career as a scholar who has focused on writers and political commitments neglected and even repressed by institutions of knowledge and historical memory. Through a network of radical study groups—involving mainly students, but occasionally a maverick young professor—I and others engaged in the process of developing countercurriculums that spoke to and addressed the "real world" beyond the cultural vision of the university. Our models included the Broadside Press's *Black Poetry: A Supplement to Anthologies Which Exclude Black Poets*, edited by Dudley Randall in 1969, and critiques of leading books in various fields (such as those by Walt W. Rostow, Seymour Martin Lipset, and Daniel Boorstin) made available by the Radical Education Project (REP) of Students for a Democratic Society (SDS). Consequently, as a teacher, I came to prize self-motivated research, even among undergraduates, and still find myself speechless when asked the question, "What do you want from me so that I can get an A?"

From a pedagogical point of view, it is probably even more significant that, under such circumstances, the encounter with "theory" in the 1960s and 1970s evolved bottom-up, from social and historical studies of culture and society. Starting in the mid-1960s, I was encouraged by other radicals to read Lukács, Gramsci, Fanon, and similar thinkers at the same time as we were actively building massive demonstrations against an imperialist war, organizing rallies against political prisoners, and holding moratoriums and counter-educational events at universities to dramatize demands to change the curriculum and alter the composition of the student body and the faculty in an antiracist direction. "Theory" was not an academic demand of our teachers and gatekeepers in order to validate entrance to The Club. The application of theory to literary studies stemmed from the necessity of understanding the integrated and mutually informing aspects of the world. The object of such theory was to clarify, not to dazzle or serve as an alleged mark of sophistication. Finally, while one cannot deny the existence of a 1960s *Zeitgeist*, the rapidity of accumulating changes based on personal, not just intellectual, experience militated against what later became stereotyped as the "radical" and "countercultural" paradigms of political and cultural activity: sharp movements from nonviolence to terrorism, and from chaperoned senior proms to uninhibited sex, drugs, and rock 'n' roll. I don't recall catapulting intellectually and emotionally through a sequence of grand revelations that rapidly produced subsequent behavioral inversions. The memory of my evolution on politics and cultural theory in those years—which I took to be shared among many acquaintances—feels more like a sequence of small but sharp blows and counterpunches. Several such mini-shocks would have an obvious impact on my later classroom teaching:

- No sooner did one come to consciousness of the need for white students to act in solidarity with African Americans, than one came face to face with the demand of African Americans for autonomy. That is, whites seeking interracial unity had to accept a certain degree of a new kind of separatism, but one determined by the targets and not the perpetrators of the prevailing form of racism (white supremacism).
- No sooner did one become convinced of the need for a committed cadre organization to lead the emancipatory struggle, than one was challenged by women who pointed out the masculinist features of such organizations. In other words, the struggle to remake one's life so that one could be "part of the solution" and not "part of the problem" was in no sense an easy switch to behavior winning instant approval by one's allies. Indeed, to live the concept that "the personal is political" meant that one embarked on a journey with little security or certainty in home life as well as political struggle in the streets.
- No sooner did one begin to grasp Marxist categories and methodologies as the most advanced theory of society, than one was met with a host of competing applications and interpretations (via the Frankfurt School, Althusserianism, post-structuralism) of Marxist theory from within the Left. Thus, if one stayed in touch with radical cultural developments, the historical materialism that attracted one to Marxism had little chance of becoming vulgarized.
- No sooner did one begin to formulate a notion of the New Left as a vital force, than one began to discover that its emphasis on spontaneity, its ill-defined notion of "participatory democracy," and its student base all brought about weaknesses rendering it less durable than the much-traduced

Old Left. Hence the legendary binary split between the New Left and Old Left was only partly true. Just as the Old Left anticipated much that became associated with the New Left, so elements of the New Left were impelled to revitalize traditions of the Old Left. Personally, I moved from a general New Left radicalism, somewhat anarchistic and pacifist, to a new appreciation of the legacy of Trotskyism, represented in intellectual circles through the writings of Belgian Ernest Mandel and many contributors to *New Left Review*.

- No sooner did one formulate a program for democratizing literature courses, than it was observed that most of the writers of color were male, that gender and homophobia were hardly addressed, and that literature itself was unfairly privileged over other cultural practices. Thus canon revision became a kind of "permanent revolution"—leaping forward to combine stages, with the study of previously suppressed cultural practices frequently outdistancing what had been known and studied.

In sum, survival then, as now, for radical intellectuals, required the ability to live with unrelenting challenges and chronic instability. Assaults from the Right might threaten one's job possibilities, causing one to feel anger and fear. But assaults from one's own comrades on the Left, sometimes more frequent, caused one to feel guilty and frustrated because they approached the core of one's life work, potentially creating demoralization. Yet many of the latter, as unfair and outrageous as they seemed at the time, were ultimately validated. Who can now deny that much early multiculturalism was patriarchal, or that much early feminism was Eurocentric? Parallel experiences occurred as I pursued my own research into the history of the U.S. cultural Left. Again and again I studied the careers of individuals who set out confidently on a course, only to be surprised by history. Indeed, among the intellectuals, it seemed as if the most cocksure characters among the radicals—people like Max Eastman, James Burnham, Sidney Hook—ended up the most wretched kind of apostates, still proclaiming their certainties even as they lined up on the opposite side of the barricades from where they originally stood. Any moral and intellectual superiority on their part to the die-hard Stalinists became hard to discern. Gradually my sympathies shifted almost entirely toward the lesser-known cultural workers, who often operated quietly behind the scenes, the "rank-and-filers" among the novelists and poets. However, any search for an all-around role model was quickly abandoned. Some of the most impressive writers (such as John Sanford) were deluded by Stalinism, while many with superior political acumen (such as Sherry Mangan) were far less productive in the arts. Moreover, as a steady stream of radicals of my own generation, including some of the most self-righteously "pure," made their separate peace more hastily and under less adverse conditions than many of the Old Left, I became less interested in judging my radical ancestors harshly, with twenty-twenty hindsight; rather, the objective came to be the understanding, in context, of the strengths and weaknesses of those who had survived with their commitments intact.

Indeed, if there was one intellectual lesson that grew steadily out of my personal and scholarly experiences, it was the need for a self-correcting method that I associated with the concept of "unlearning." Of course, I had never felt much attraction to the proselytizing mode, and none at all to any effort by a teacher (the institutionalized authority figure) to turn a classroom into a recruiting ground for social movements; so I happily abandoned what Paulo Freire called the "banking" model of education, even before I began (Freire 2). The object of a university class, in my view, was neither to force-feed opinions nor to cleverly manipulate students toward a desired end. It was to create an environment that I now recognized as a sort of microcosm of the way I saw the 1960s: One in which a spectrum of plausible ideas come into play, so that class members—as well as the person deemed the "teacher"—might enter a collective experience to sort out things anew each term. As bell hooks observes, a radical pedagogy must begin with a "deconstruction of the traditional notion that only the professor is responsible for classroom dynamics" because "Excitement is generated through collective effort" (hooks 8).

I soon found through abundant experience that the most obvious pedagogical requirement for such an approach was the need to abandon the quest for the "standard course," repeated year in and year out. True, such a renowned course was often the hallmark of a "great" teacher, at least in legend; and from a practical experience, mastery of the basic course content would then allow the teacher more free play and interaction with individual students. Still, if 1960s literary (now cultural) studies had been launched on a course of Permanent Revolution, then pedagogy must correspond and follow suit. Unlearning became a principle tantamount to the quest for new experience.

UNLEARNING PARADIGMS

What is a pedagogy of unlearning? If a pedagogy is to lead to empowerment, in the sense of a student's gaining control over the forces shaping his or her life, one must develop courses that allow students who choose to do so to reassess the superficial and misleading paradigms brought into the classroom as a consequence of "the hidden curriculum." One must also try to empower students so that they can go forward with the knowledge and perspective to prevent new paradigms from arising in the classroom that rigidly block out such complicating perceptions that additional education and life experience ought to bring. But so long as one is teaching a particular subject (in my case, literature and culture), one's pedagogy cannot translate into chaos or operate without focus. To the contrary, I found out early on that the effort to cover too much ground from too many angles was self-defeating; it was necessary for me to demarcate rough areas of specialization where, in the context of the available resources of my own department, I could make a unique contribution. These contributions became, primarily at the undergraduate level, the teaching of cultures of people of color (at that time, the mid-1970s, still called "minority literatures"), and, at the more advanced and graduate level, Marxist literary theory (which I was first allowed to teach under the euphemism "Social Theory and the Arts"). The two areas intersected neatly, of course; I found the Marxist method central to teaching non-European cultures in the United States, and I found the issues of race, cultural difference, and all the attendant problems of canonicity and literary value central to the development of a Marxist theory appropriate to mid-twentieth-century cultural realities.

However, the choice of teaching U.S. Marxism in the 1970s turned out to be one that had to go forward with few precedents in the sense of models for syllabi, text selection, and classroom strategy. This is because, for many decades, the subject of the formative years of the U.S. Marxist cultural tradition, from the 1930s until the 1960s, had been treated harshly not only by the Right but by the Left as well. The founding text of contemporary Marxist literary studies, Fredric Jameson's *Marxism and Form* (1971), declares,

> When the American reader thinks of Marxist literary criticism, I imagine that it is still the atmosphere of the 1930s which comes to mind. . . . The criticism practiced then was of a relatively untheoretical, essentially didactic nature, destined more for use in the night school than in the graduate seminar, if I may put it that way; and it has been relegated to the status of an intellectual and historical curiosity. (Jameson ix)[2]

Of the twenty-five contributors to the newest collection, *Marxist Literary Theory: A Reader* (1996), edited by Terry Eagleton and Drew Milne, only one, Fredric

Jameson, is from the United States. Not a single essay, including Jameson's, refers to the work of a Marxist literary critic from the United States, from either the earlier or later generations. Ironically, the history of Marxist culture in the greatest imperialist power of the mid-twentieth century is held in the lowest possible repute. For once, then, the call for a greater focus on the United States is not an expression of "American chauvinism" but a demand to give voice to its unfairly trivialized tradition of Marxist cultural resistance.

Without doubt, the historic U.S. Marxist tradition (often called "the Old Left") has major limitations, due partly to factors such as an indigenous anti-intellectual tendency on the far Left, the heavily Stalinized U.S. Communist Party, and the virulence of a native U.S. racism that has deformed virtually every arena of cultural work, including that of radicals. Nevertheless, what exists is far richer and more complex than what has been acknowledged; what is required is that the teacher of U.S. Marxism grasp and explain the determining features of its specificity. It has become my view that an awareness of the full scope of the U.S. Marxist cultural tradition is an urgent necessity in the present political and social climate. In the face of so many allegedly "new" developments (postmodernism, "the collapse of communism," post-apartheid South Africa), it is crucial not to repeat mistakes of predecessors, and it is mandatory that we learn about models worthy of emulation.

The most important specific feature is the multi-decade dimension of the cultural legacy. The Marxist tradition is drastically misunderstood when limited only to its 1930s manifestation, which is a temptation for teachers because the economic crisis of the Great Depression momentarily thrust Marxism into a more central location in U.S. intellectual life than it obtained before or since. In regard to Marxist literary criticism in the academy, for example, the 1940s, not the 1930s, was the central decade, at least until the McCarthyite witch-hunt when scholars such as Edwin Berry Burgum, Harry Slochower, Margaret Schlauch, and Barrows Dunham were purged from their universities.

In addition, the U.S. Marxist cultural tradition prior to the New Left was primarily expressed in imaginative literature, not simply literary criticism. Many authors of critical works also wrote fiction and poetry (for example, Granville Hicks, V. F. Calverton, and Genevieve Taggard), and the leading Marxist reviewers in Left publications were themselves creative writers (such as Joseph Freeman, Isidor Schneider, John Howard Lawson, and Mike Gold).

A third consideration is the fact that, while the U.S. Marxist tradition is primarily identified with the Communist Party, there were smaller but indispensable contributions from Marxists associated with Trotskyism and other heterodox trends. The cultural criticism of Irish American revolutionary novelist James T. Farrell, the Caribbean-born C. L. R. James, and the largely Jewish American modernist circle around the *Partisan Review* certainly defies the characterization offered in *Marxism and Form*. Two important African American left-wing novelists, William Gardner Smith and Willard Motley, were independent of the Communist Party, and, of course, Richard Wright and Chester Himes evolved in more heterodox directions as well.

Perhaps the most crucial specific feature is the fourth: The U.S. Marxist tradition devoted major attention to issues of race—especially in relation to African American culture, although important efforts were devoted to Mexican Americans, Jewish Americans, and other groups. In this regard a substantial body of impressive African American cultural criticism—consistent with, but also going far beyond, Richard Wright's famous 1937 "Blueprint for Negro Writing"—remains dispersed throughout the pages of *Negro Quarterly*, *Harlem Quarterly*, *New Masses*, *Daily Worker*, *Mainstream*, *Masses and Mainstream*, *Political Affairs*, *Freedom*, and other publications. Many debates occurring in contemporary critical race theory are anticipated by these writings. Black music, widely discussed in the 1990s, is also a prime consideration of earlier discussions.

UNLEARNING RACISM

If the most significant feature of U.S. Marxist culture is its attention to white supremacism, then the radical teacher may be especially equipped to treat racism, which I regard as the most difficult and dangerous element in our social formation at present. At the same time, the effort to collaborate with students in a classroom community to "unlearn racism" is not merely the process of importing "enlightenment" from a text. Strategies are needed that will allow students to find the emotional and intellectual benefits of freeing themselves from racist culture and institutional practices.

Of course, such self-liberating strategies must be achieved within the confines of the courses that are assigned to a teacher. In the mid-1970s, when I began my first real teaching job, few beginning assistant professors could escape the obligation of teaching standard courses with titles like "Introduction to American Literature," "Introduction to the Short Story and the Novel," "Great Books, Part 3," not to mention occasional composition courses. Given inherited structures, conventions, and student expectations, it was frequently difficult to do much more than spice up the reading lists of such courses with additional women and people of color. Moreover, I quickly learned the inadequacy of the popular formulation of radical teachers of the day, which was that we aimed to see "that the work of Frederick Douglass, Mary Wilkins Freeman, Agnes Smedley, Zora Neale Hurston and others is read along with the work of Nathaniel Hawthorne, Henry James, William Faulkner, Ernest Hemingway, and others."[3] In fact, such an all-inclusive program was chimerical from the perspective of the time constraints of a single course. At one point I had a conventional course taken away from me by the undergraduate chair because I had achieved a multicultural and feminist expansion at the expense of a number of canonical white male British authors. In contrast, I never heard of a conservative faculty member at my institution being relieved of a course due to its complete exclusion of female writers or writers of color, despite the widespread hue and cry in the media about "left-wing thought police" having taken over English departments. Specialized courses offered far more opportunities to promote strategies of unlearning. Thus I passed the late 1970s and early 1980s experimenting with a sequence of undergraduate courses that used titles such as "Politics and the Novel," "The Urban Novel of Social Protest," "Literature and Revolution," "Literature of America's Great Depression," "The Radical Novel in the United States," "Rebels, Poets and Dissenters in the New England Rebel Tradition," "The New York Intellectuals," "New Left Thought," "Race and Ethnicity in Twentieth-Century United States Literature," and "Marxism and American Writers."

By and large these were "negotiated" efforts, a mixing of a certain percentage of canonical writers—even among those with radical politics—with women and writers of color. Still, time constraints hardly allowed one to include a range of different racial and ethnic groups, not to mention writers of both genders and a range of political and literary orientations per group. Thus I reluctantly began to phase out the canonical writers in the highly specialized courses, and decided to design a more regularly offered upper-level course called, at first, "Literature of Oppressed Minorities in the United States." Such a course without Euro-American writers, male or female, but including many diverse writers of color, opened up considerable space for strategies of unlearning the hierarchies that had hitherto obliterated so much extraordinary cultural practice. Within a few years I became conscious of the possibility that the phrase "Oppressed Minorities" might give off a negative signal, as if the readings were focused on victims and tales of misery. Thus I switched to the more neutral rubric of "Literatures of People of Color in the United States" with the subtitle "Black, Chicano, Native American Indian, Asian American and Puerto Rican."

The psychological stress of teaching such a course to undergraduates in a collective manner—with efforts to decenter authority and promote complex views of race—was unrelenting. Often it was difficult to avoid a situation in which the small number of students of color in the class felt as if they were on display, willy-nilly the arbiters of the "authenticity" of the literatures to be discussed. There was also the problem of my own role, as the dispenser of grades. How could I avoid the implication of my already given status as "teacher," which seemed to broadcast that, no matter what I claimed, I "really" was going to judge everyone's degree of racism? How does one create a climate of trust in a classroom probing racial oppression and resistance to it, while the news media outside are promoting stories about left-wing storm trooper professors who are persecuting white males and destroying Western Civilization? There were not at this time, in the early 1980s, many samples of syllabi for the courses I sought to teach, nor was I in the situation of teachers of "The American Renaissance" and other conventional courses who could at least model their own efforts on classes they themselves had taken in graduate school. (Later, in 1983, Paul Lauter would edit the excellent collection *Reconstructing American Literature: Courses, Syllabi, Issues.*) Term after term I experimented, perpetually on an emotional roller coaster as I sought to be responsive to all constituencies among the students while remaining true to my pedagogical beliefs. The basic structure of "Literature of People of Color in the United States" was a series of background presentations on the history of the different populations and literary traditions, which I based on a reading of influential texts by scholars in the field. Frequently I brought in guests—African American, Chicano, Native American, and Asian American writers, teachers, even graduate students carrying out special research—to displace myself as spokesperson and authority. In the framework of lectures by myself and rigorous reading, I turned some classes over to groups of students, making it clear that I was available as a consultant but that the students had free rein for certain sessions to organize the agenda so as to meet their needs and concerns. Occasionally I used films and videos of the writers we were studying in which they expressed their literary and social views in their own words. At various times I gave a great emphasis to breaking the class down into small group discussions, sometimes with suggested discussion questions, and with rotating student facilitators. Other times I began sessions by having students write for ten minutes on a particular topic, so as to give each one time to formulate their thoughts on a subject. In order to avoid establishing a canon of texts for each population under discussion, I instituted a policy of rotation of books every term, which also helped me keep up with scholarship in fields I had never been able to study in my own graduate or undergraduate education. But in many cases no literary criticism was available to help me out.

One might surmise that, after years of teaching such a course, I could, by 1996, describe the form and content of the "perfect" version resulting from such ceaseless experimentation. In truth, it seemed as if strategies worked and didn't work depending on the unpredictable factors such as the chemistry of the mix of students that term (especially the presence of a particular student, charismatic for one reason or another, who was especially enthusiastic, or hostile); the political situation on campus; and even developments in my own career and personal life. When I examined student evaluation forms, I discovered that the same lectures might be cited by different students as scintillating or boring; the same classroom format might be praised as liberating or excoriated as repressive; the same guest speaker would be judged an extraordinary addition or a waste of time; and the same book was "too obvious" or "too difficult."

Ultimately, the class that began as "Literature of Oppressed Minorities" evolved in a drastically new direction. But this was caused more by changes in "objective conditions" on our campus than conscious decisions based on clear proof of strategies that reliably "worked." The context was the late 1980s, when, as a consequence of massive student demonstrations against racism that garnered national attention, the university began an aggressive search for faculty of color, even introducing a loose "race or ethnicity" course requirement for undergraduates. The subsequent appearance of just a small number of African American, Asian American, Chicano, and Native American scholars on the faculty created a new and far more positive situation. Suddenly I had colleagues with whom to consult on scholarly matters, and it was no longer the case that if my survey were not taught, such literatures would be entirely absent from the curriculum. The obligation I felt so strongly to represent, even minimally, each and every group no longer weighed so heavily on me. The chance to try to develop innovative and more challenging strategies for grasping aspects of racism in greater depth and from new angles was available. Dropping the obligatory survey dimension allowed for more intensive interrogations of the interaction of race with the categories of ethnicity and gender, and in a wider range of literary forms.

Thus I reformulated "Literature of People of Color in the United States" into "Resistance to Racism in Twentieth Century United States Literature." Two new features were introduced. First, a sequence of texts on the evolution of racism allowed students to explore the ideology originally used to rationalize slavery and to probe more modern forms of the reproduction of racist social structures and thought. Second, the course now included a range of texts that treated racism by authors who were Euro-American and of various political outlooks. These latter works allowed Euro-American students (still the majority of enrollees) to see themselves more positively, if they so wished, as participants in the antiracist struggle. In addition, the new format freed me from the necessity of trying to give equal representation to all the major groups of people of color; it was now possible to devote greater attention to issues of gender and sexual orientation, as well as new varieties of literary representations of racism and resistance. The films and readings of "Resistance to Racism" were loosely organized under four general topics. In one version, these were "Resistance to Slavery," "Varieties of Racism and Resistance," "Resistance to Racism in the 1950s," and "Into the Mainstream." Nearly half the authors of a typical syllabus were women, and the list always included several writers who were African American; in addition, the different versions rotated among writers from Asian American, Latino, and Native American communities, as well as from antiracist Jewish American and other Euro-American perspectives.

"Resistance to Racism" drew twice as many students (seventy to eighty) as the earlier "Literatures of People of Color in the United States" (thirty to forty). At first, this was because the course reflected the climate of concern during the antiracist struggles. Later, enrollment remained large, probably because the course fulfilled the new "race or ethnicity" requirement. Still, not only did many of the old problems remain, but a new one entered the picture: increased size meant teaching assistants, which introduced yet another unpredictable factor into the equation. Moreover, I had aged fifteen years by the time of this switch. I was no longer a young professor of twenty-eight, often mistaken for a graduate student. Now I found that fewer students were comfortable calling me by my first name, and it seemed that my efforts to create an egalitarian classroom environment were sometimes seen as strained and even artificial.

UNLEARNING MARXISM

Strategies for introducing Marxism into the curriculum followed a pattern parallel to the teaching of race issues, partly because the explosive concerns of race remained central there as well. Moreover, if one were to make a sophisticated and up-to-date Marxism available to students, the pedagogical practice required one to "unlearn"—progressively, not by shock therapy—simplistic and truncated versions of Marxism that many had picked up from conventional textbooks, the popular media, and even left-wing authoritarian political groups and countries that exploited Marxist ideas to legitimate their own power or goals. The pedagogical task was, How to problematize Marxism by letting it emerge as a self-empowering tool for understanding matters such as racism and culture?

At first I experimented with courses on "Politics and the Novel," "Literature and Revolution," "Literature of America's Great Depression," and "Marxism and American Writers." As before, I was starting from scratch with few models, and the survey course, which of necessity had to be my initial approach, eventually became a liability. To teach the literature of several revolutions—the Russian, Chinese, and Mexican, and the Spanish Civil War—required a substantial amount of background material, and one could have time for only a very small number of literary texts to "represent" complex history. Likewise, "Politics and the Novel" seemed to require the inclusion of the "classics" that defined the field (by Malraux, Silone, Dostoevski, and Orwell), leaving too little room for women, writers of color, and, in some cases, artists with longer-term commitments to social transformation. Moreover, a survey of Marxist criticism had to include the "greats"—not only Marx and Engels, but Lukács, Gramsci, Williams, Benjamin, Althusser, Jameson, and so forth—which, again, left minimal time for Marxists who were female and of color.

What began basically as a thoroughly international approach to Left writers and Marxist criticism eventually became rerouted to a U.S. focus. Once more, certain objective changes in the academy played a role. The explosion of interest in theory that became institutionalized around 1980 meant that other faculty members besides myself were teaching Benjamin, Althusser, Williams, and so forth, although they less frequently included Marx and Engels. The development of postcolonial studies and the recruitment of women faculty meant that texts by people of color and women were being taught by others, too. Thus I newly designed an undergraduate U.S. literature course called, simply, "Writers on the Left," which had the advantage of allowing me to introduce students to my view that the preponderance of the Marxist cultural critique before the 1960s came through creative writing. The fluid chronological boundaries of such a course allowed me to engage problems in the tradition as they unfolded under different circumstances. By this point, too, I had "unlearned" my Frankfurt

School bias against popular culture, and the flexibility of the course allowed me to treat Hollywood films, detective fiction, and so forth.

"Writers on the Left" began with texts from the early 1930s, when a new generation of radical writers set out to revolutionize the U.S. literary landscape by directly confronting the issues of racism, class oppression, sexism, war, and exploitation in their fiction, poetry, drama, reportage, and criticism. In works such as *Jews without Money* (1930) and *Uncle Tom's Children* (1938), authors such as the ghetto-born Jewish American Michael Gold and the Mississippi-born African American Richard Wright expanded the boundaries of the content and form of art in ways that left an indelible mark on our culture and national consciousness. Pioneering socialist-feminist writers such as Tillie Olsen and Meridel Le Sueur published chapters of works that would later achieve acclaim as *Yonnondio* (1974) and *The Girl* (1978). Already established writers responded to major political events of the 1930s, exemplified by Ernest Hemingway's treatment of the Spanish Civil War in his novel *For Whom the Bell Tolls* (1940).

Next, the course traced how, by the post–World War II era, many of these writers and their associates were under direct attack by the state and federal governments, the news media, the churches, and demagogic politicians. Some were sent to prison, others went into exile, and still more repudiated their pasts or simply disappeared. Culturally, traditions such as the proletarian novel diminished (although they didn't vanish) and mass culture increased as the site of much radical cultural critique.

My course on literary criticism, while it retained the broad title "Marxism and Cultural Studies," explained in the syllabus description that there would be a special U.S. focus. Thus Marx, Engels, and a few select European luminaries were always included, but a major portion would concentrate on Marxist treatments of race and culture in the United States, popular culture, neglected texts, and so forth. That course, too, usually met twice a week to introduce students to some of the classics as well as the latest thinking in Marxism and cultural studies. Some of the conceptual categories we explored in relation to culture were gender, race, mass culture, postcolonialism, internal colonialism, New Historicism, resistance literature, Modernism, and commitment. Throughout the term we applied our theory to a variety of works of fiction, poetry, drama, and documentary film. A special focus was Marxist interpretations of the novel, especially in relation to racial representation of subaltern groups in the U.S. context.

MARXIST SCHOLARS IN THE PUBLIC SPHERE

Here I will provide some summary remarks that depart from classroom teaching and university-specific responsibilities to suggest possibilities for activism among socialist teacher-scholars in the Public Sphere of the 1990s. Unfortunately, we are still in a cultural situation where, for more than a decade, there has existed a concerted campaign by the national media, ultimately fueled by right-wing foundations, to witch-hunt faculty with left-wing views and stigmatize them for attempting to "indoctrinate" students with allegedly "politically correct" attitudes. Most recently, the fruits of this campaign in a reactionary backlash against women and people of color can be seen in the assaults on affirmative action in California and Texas. A further danger is the economic polarization in our society that has meant a continuous "downsizing" that is now spreading to an increasing number of universities where new attacks on the tenure system are under way. In such a situation, no radical professor can operate without awareness of the history of the massive anti-radical campaign of the McCarthy years, a purging of dissidents that has never comparably struck professors of any political persuasion other than the Marxist Left.

However, rather than trying to concoct defensive measures for individual survival on the campus, the radical teacher would be wiser to maintain his or her connection to the egalitarian social movements that first opened up the doors of the university in the 1960s for the democratization of cultural study and pedagogy that we now enjoy. It is true that some of the earlier social movements have disappeared or are temporarily in decline, but many are far from deceased. To the extent that radical teachers turn inward, substituting their individual careers for their much-needed participation as organic intellectuals of an emerging new society, they will weaken the fragile conditions that allow socialist culture to exist in the universities; they may even compromise the quality of their scholarship, which, after all, is dependent to some degree on "practice" for self-correction.

Radical scholars are well situated to take the egalitarian values championed in their classrooms into the broader arenas of the Public Sphere. As Marxists, we might seek opportunities to create a new, nonsectarian organized socialist movement that combines the efforts of several generations of Left activists; of trade unionists as well as students and committed scholars; and of individuals of historically differing socialist traditions who now might collaborate, for a change, to take advantage of each other's strengths.

Such a venture, however, is not merely a one-sided effort to bring some fresh air into the stagnating atmosphere of the U.S. socialist Left. Marxist activist-scholars of today must be equally motivated by a conviction not to repeat mistakes made by socialists in the past. The historic revolutionary-socialist tradition, critically assessed, could be the basis for creative advances that might be meaningful to the younger generations of activists. University-based scholars, with their knowledge of history and theory, are a crucial element in this new mix.

In contributing to a new socialist movement, Marxists of the 1990s must be free of the hidebound orthodoxies that failed to build a large and lasting movement out of the promising radical ferment of the 1960s and early 1970s. Already there have been positive moves away from "vanguardism" and fetishism over "correct program." But there must simultaneously exist an agreement that one must not "throw out the baby with the bath water." Many of the failings of the U.S. Left were caused not only by errors of theory and practice, but also by "objective" difficulties—for which no particular school of socialism has yet found a solution. Thus, not everything in the legacy need be jettisoned, especially in the absence of convincing alternatives.

Socialist educators must be part of a militant resistance against the rightward trends that are overtaking the Left domestically and internationally. In the face of such pressure, socialist scholars are uniquely situated to offer intellectual leadership by personal example that will enable radicals to resist the temptation of the two trajectories that have most often derailed socialist movements of the past when confronted by difficult and unanticipated events.

One familiar paradigm is that, in the name of "newness," radical teachers, scholars, and intellectuals have done little more than orchestrate the progressive abandonment of almost all the distinguishing features of the revolutionary socialist project—working-class independence, a proletarian orientation, classical Marxist theory, internationalist anti-imperialism, and a commitment to organization building. This is most often carried out under the banner of going "beyond" Marxism. The other pattern is to use a Marxist platform or organization to create a religious fervor of belief around a "true program," or to idealize some far-off country that supposedly represents the vanguard of humanity. Publications of such political tendencies are usually characterized by a heresy-hunting atmosphere, with the focus especially on exposing everyone else's alleged opportunism. In the case of the Maoist phenomenon, which had a surprising influence on many intelligent and committed U.S. students and scholars in the

1960s and 1970s, the hallmark was crude and simplistic political coding of culture and rival political policies as "racist," "reactionary," and "fascist."

The first orientation, one of endless "discussion," leads, at best, back to discredited liberalism, if not complete collapse. The second, a kind of two-dimensional militancy, guarantees short-term survival, but political life in a sterile, mind-deadening world, usually characterized by practical impotence. Socialist intellectuals in the 1990s need to develop ways to defend the necessity of militant socialist activism and the relevance of revolutionary socialist politics, without falling into pat formulae about "the correct line" or pointing to a particular group as the "only" revolutionary "party." To the contrary, socialist intellectuals should build forums of debate and discussion with an institutionalized policy of including a range of voices from the nonsectarian Left. In my view, it is the commitment to building a revolutionary, feminist, and multinational organized socialist movement, combined with institutionalized political pluralism, that is the most urgent need of socialist scholars in the public sphere.

What about the legacy of classical Marxism? Once again, university-based scholars are indispensable in helping to achieve theoretical clarification for the broader Left. Of course, self-critical socialist intellectuals should have no "line" on history or theory, but we gain nothing by obscuring the fact that modern socialist thought is substantially influenced by the tradition of classic thinkers such as Marx, Engels, Luxemburg, Lenin, and Trotsky. All of these are today being traduced and caricatured in books and articles produced by individuals funded by right-wing think tanks; and some postmodernists and post-Marxists are also presenting distorted interpretations of the classics to justify their own new political positions. Socialist intellectuals can enter the Public Sphere to provide accurate and sophisticated responses to both of these phenomena. At the same time, the classical tradition has been crucially enriched by thinkers such as Du Bois, Malcolm X, Che Guevara, Gramsci, Lukács, and Fanon, as well as dozens of younger theorists, female and male, from many countries. By critically teaching, discussing, and writing about such thinkers, we keep them alive as resources for future liberatory social movements.

Finally, there is the responsibility of Marxist intellectuals to remain up-to-date in terms of the most recent trends in intellectual and cultural thought. In this respect, university-based socialists in the Public Sphere should respond to the variety of new ideas clustered under the rubric of "postmodernism" with friendliness toward those of this trend who seek to join socialist activists in creating a more enriched liberating theory. On the other hand, socialists should remain ready to challenge those who seek to put old wine in new bottles or sell snake oil to cure our Marxist blues.

While socialist intellectuals may have different opinions as to precise changes taking place in the working class and the economy, to be a socialist in the 1990s means that one is still convinced that working people, expressing their aims through unions and workers' parties, remain central to the process of social transformation. Whatever the recent setbacks, especially the defeated strikes of the Staley and Caterpillar workers in the United States, the power of organized workers is repeatedly confirmed, most recently in the magnificent French strikes of early 1996.

Still, the reaffirmation of the working class as agency does not mean adherence to simplistic class reductionism. With our historical consciousness and access to resources, Marxist scholars and teachers should know better than anyone else that working people are not simply defined by their class. Workers are also of different sexes and sexual orientations, ethnic and regional groups, nationalities and socially constructed "races." Historical materialism today is dead without the vital infusion of feminism, antiracist theory, ecology, gay and lesbian theory, advanced cultural theory, and many other fertile perspectives. Once again, it is socialist teachers and intellectuals who can bring socialist policy on such issues aggressively into the Public Sphere in our extra-university writing, speaking, and activism.

Notes

1. In this passage Giroux defines the "hidden curriculum" as "the unstated norms, values and beliefs that are transmitted to students through the underlying structure of meaning and in both the formal content and the social relations of school and classroom life."

2. Harvey Teres first drew my attention to this passage when we presented papers together on U.S. literary radicalism at the June 1986 session of the Institute on Culture and Society of the Marxist Literary Group, Carnegie-Mellon University, Pittsburgh.

3. This appears on the cover of Paul Lauter, ed., *Reconstructing American Literature* (New York: Feminist Press, 1983).

WORKS CITED

Eagleton, Terry, and Drew Milne, eds. *Marxist Literary Theory: A Reader*. Oxford: Blackwell, 1996.

Franklin, Bruce. "The Teaching of Literature in the Highest Academies of the Empire." In *The Politics of Literature: Dissenting Essays on the Teaching of English*, ed. Louis Kampf and Paul Lauter. New York: Vintage, 1973.

Freire, Paolo. *The Politics of Education*. Amherst, MA: Bergin and Garvey, 1985.

Giroux, Henry A. *Teachers as Intellectuals: Toward a Critical Pedagogy of Learning*. Amherst, MA: Bergin and Garvey, 1988.

Gitlin, Todd. *The Sixties: Years of Hope, Days of Rage*. New York: Bantam, 1993.

hooks, bell. *Teaching to Transgress*. New York: Routledge, 1994.

Jameson, Fredric. *Marxism and Form*. Princeton: Princeton University Press, 1971.

Kampf, Louis. "The Scandal of Literary Scholarship." In *The Dissenting Academy*, ed. Theodore Roszak. New York: Vintage, 1968.

Lauter, Paul, ed. *Reconstructing American Literature*. New York: Feminist Press, 1983.

Wright, Richard. "Blueprint for Negro Writing." *New Challenge 2* 2 (Fall 1937): 53–75.

Cultural Studies by Default

A History of the Present

Mike Hill

10

As of 1993, ten thousand researched articles, collections, and books can be found on Madonna (and these just in English).[1] Such numbers beckon various conclusions about the current status of Cultural Studies, its interest in popular, mass, and/or commercial culture, its ability to find political nuance in unlikely places, its hipness, and perhaps its inherent banality. Whatever conclusions one wants to draw on the spate of work inspired by the material girl, let it be said to begin with that Cultural Studies (hereafter CS) has arrived. It has been less easy to say, however, now that CS is so abundantly here, just exactly what it is. Ross Chambers suggests that CS is a way of seeking the "occulted context[s]" within which otherwise mystifying processes (the determination of cultural value, the formation of human relationships) operate.[2] Mediated within language, by history, and according to place, values and identities thus stand a chance of changing. But if CS is about context finding (and the changes attendant to that practice), then the serious difficulty in defining CS itself should be no small wonder.

Indeed, the kind of seeking that tends to occur by way of CS has left "occulted" the very contexts within which the identity of CS might itself eventually be scooped (the alternative being to account for multiple contexts simultaneously, which would lead to contradiction. You have to suppress certain contexts, in order to name others). Thus, CS in this country is a practice of scholarly research both very conscious about the conditional realities of meaning and unsure what CS itself means, if it means anything at all. Like a casual stroll going nowhere in particular, doing CS is, of course, a privilege, and one increasingly difficult to sustain. It has led some to suggest that CS, for its lack of disciplinary accountability, has become either politically anesthetized or intellectually bankrupt. And with that charge comes typically the prescription to rediscover the truer origins of CS, its claims on teaching and activism. This tends to mean, by extension, leaving all that theoretical attention to "occulted contexts" alone for a while.

In coming to terms with the charge to (re)claim CS's lost pedagogic and activist past, this essay addresses a certain convergence within the current "culture" of, shall we say, studying Culture, the fiction of their separability being precisely at the center of what CS may or may not be. This convergence involves (1) perceptions about the history of CS; (2) what those perceptions reveal about the present stakes of CS; and (3) how those "present" stakes are determined within the context of a profession that seems itself to be going the way of "history." More specifically, I want to discuss, first, what I'm inclined to recall with a sense of seriousness its founders may have never intended, that is, the Birmingham "legacy."[3] My concern here is with stories of CS's immigration, its crossing troubled waters and reaching the destination of, until recently, more or less privileged neighborhoods in the United States, as high-end, lowbrow, institutional qua political work. Second, as part of this "legacy," I want to revisit a certain impasse that began to develop around the British New Left over theory and political commitment, and that continues in multifarious guises to shape and be shaped by the mounting problems of current U.S. academic life.

These problems have fundamentally to do with the third, and quite differently volatile element, which I think of some consequence in examining the U.S. CS mix: academic training and employment. I follow here a recent MLA Graduate Student Caucus president who—in following lots of other concerned members of the profession[4]—wants to make central to our loftier concerns what he calls the "academic Great Depression."[5] How to measure the job crisis? Are there simply too many Ph.D.'s proportionate to the numbers of jobs, as some allege, and have these troubled multitudes (my cohort, in fact) been mistrained in the weary ways of theory; are they cerebral overachievers, given where and what they (we) are likely to teach, if they teach at all? In a manner of speaking that betrays my larger purpose here, has the Ph.D. become too "popular"? And how does the strained combination of producing would-be theory czars and an academic underclass relate to the hailing of teaching and political activism as the primary features that distinguish real CS from theory's ambivalent infatuation with contemporary popular culture?

I should like to keep my comments hypothetical in this section of the essay on academic employment for more or less obvious reasons, but I wonder whether the job depression signals—in the "occulted context[s]" within which CS tends to work—an unwelcome revenge of the popular. This term, "the popular," in the specific sense that I mean it, will take some explaining, in terms of both how it relates to the Birmingham "legacy" of CS and the way CS has been evidently transformed. But what I want to argue, in sum, is that the ambivalent political desires once located within popular culture (and concomitantly "outside" academe) remain, in a backdoor kind of way, a more pronounced feature of the slippery critical practice of CS than the calls for teaching and political commitment tend to imply. I would like to suggest, further, that the relationship between the "popular" and a politics for which CS has developed a certain nostalgia has come to bear on us in other than institutionally friendly ways. Rather than this late arrival of politics to CS being seen as solely an aberration (and it is that), I think the protean value of studying popular culture is a condition CS has ushered in precisely by its relative "popularity" in academe. This "popularity" in the context of the job crash takes on an unlikely material association having to do quite simply with economics. Such an association by default, between CS's theoretical leanings and the economic matters that have come up, as it were, from "below," is one CS has seemed historically both to want (in the form of working class relevance) and not want (in the form of a certain distance from unreliable pleasures of mass culture). In short, it is an ironic feature of CS that it is ill prepared to recognize what turns out to be one of its most salient features: the mark of a labor crisis.

THE DEATH OF CULTURAL STUDIES?

> I wish I'd never heard of that damned word [culture]. I have become more aware of its difficulties, not less, as I have gone on.
>
> —Raymond Williams, *Politics and Letters*

The critical return of the ordinary . . . must destroy all varieties of rhetorical brilliance associated with powers that hierarchize.

—Michel de Certeau, *The Practice of Everyday Life*

Everyone seems to know the boilerplate story of CS, how it originated in Britain sometime around the late 1950s; and everyone seems to know that it was a practice primarily concerned with political activism and the teaching of (nonacademic) workers. Even though British CS is associated with important books by the likes of Richard Hoggart, Raymond Williams, and E. P. Thompson,[6] its roots are in broader, extracurricular social movements. Sometimes with excitement, and sometimes as a stern reminder of our own apparent detachment, we hear tell, for example, of the thriving numbers of New Left clubs and centers that existed across Great Britain by 1961.[7] For U.S. Leftist intellectuals in the age of Buchanan populism, such organizational centers, combined with the proliferation and conversion of the British polytechs, intimate a rare vision. One sees legions of ready and willing workers, the real makers of history, cooperating toward a future made available, in part, through the kindly stewardship of an attentive and sympathetic intellectual vanguard. Indeed, a dozen issues before the journal's editorial reorientation in the 1960s under Perry Anderson, the first issue of the *New Left Review* declared with a sense of optimism unimaginable today that "we are in our missionary phase."[8]

If this account of British CS is pat and betrays a certain longing for academe's lost political soul, for all of that, I think there is a point. It is indeed tempting to cite British CS as an example of golden age solidarity between academics and the masses, a way of explaining away the complexities, contradictions, and ambivalences that derail CS from its would-be political missions. British CS is made sometimes to function as an index of stony activism, of philosophical certainty, political purity, a kind of wonder years version of the radical life of the mind.[9] This scenario, while no doubt mythical, subtends today's conscience-sensitive hunt for the ways and places in which U.S. CS works and doesn't.

The Birmingham model of Center for Contemporary Cultural Studies (CCCS) is at best a troubled fit within the conditional mandates of U.S. academe. For starters, its institutional marginality and the low-profile objectives seem decidedly more pronounced. Until it was established as an independent unit in 1974, the only full-time faculty at the Center were Hoggart and Hall. There were two half-timers, Richard Johnson in history (who eventually succeeded Hall as the CCCS director), and Michael Green in English. Most folks who were associated with the center, as I read its history, could hardly have hoped for (nor indeed may have wanted) academic careers. British CS was hardly a fast track toward professional security, nor was it a tollbooth or gatekeeping device separating graduate students from the jobs they worked so hard to secure. But neither should British CS's institutional marginality be too easily elided with a romantic polarization between, on the one hand, the impoverished but engaged life of activism and teaching, and on the other, the stoic denial of a life of scholarly writing and research where one is somewhat more removed from material manifestations of oppression. Though he started in adult education and was active in the CND, by 1965 E. P. Thompson (he was just forty-one) had published two major books, edited three collections, written a number of pamphlets, and authored seventeen articles, all from a farmhouse retreat or bishop's palace in Halifax, Leamington Spa, or Warwick.[10]

Indeed, in a less niggling way, Thompson is the right player to recall for complicating the myth that makes British CS the keeper of our political conscience. In particular, around the issue of working-class authenticity that he and other members of the CCCS front line attempted to find and preserve, there rumbles an impending theoretical imbroglio that still shakes and shapes debates over the masses ("popular culture," "the public," "the people") and the production of knowledge. The rift within the British New Left over "theory" has, like so much other CSiana, taken on legendary status (and I won't take a lot of space rehearsing it here); but unlike the earlier, easier legend of CS's "missionary phase," this legend is more useful for producing an account of CS that eventually goes beyond what we tell each other it used to be. Consider, for example, the telling anguish implicit in Raymond Williams's remarks over his split allegiances to working-class culture and what he wants to hold forth intellectually as their resistance to oppression:

> When you recognize in yourself the ties that still bind, you cannot be satisfied with the old formula: Enlightened minority, degraded mass. You know how bad most "popular culture" is, but you also know that the irruption of the "swinish multitude" . . . is the coming to relative power of your own people.[11]

The "old formula" is measured for Williams as much by cultural conservatives like Edmund Burke, Matthew Arnold, and F. R. Leavis as it is by the British Communist Party,[12] and this original instance of a de facto intellectual elitism colliding with a radical politics in theory is, in fact, the current "legacy" of British CS.

Here and now, the most distinctly operative feature of that discipline-which-is-not-one is the very ambivalence over the political status of mass culture that Williams tries, in all good intention, to strain out of the mix. This ambivalence is manifest, originally, through the "old formula" of cultural elitism that makes Edmund Burke the unlikely bedfellow of the CPGB; and it is manifest in quite a different and more recent way in the current brand of cultural populism being served up as decoded resistance in the CS section of a Barnes and Noble superstore near you.

A locus classicus for CS's interminable political ambivalence is Raymond Williams's article "Base and Superstructure in Marxist Cultural Theory," which appeared originally in the *New Left Review* in 1973.[13] No longer is culture, according to Williams, the mere epiphenomenon of an economic base that determines it. Culture is neither seamlessly oppressive nor authentically radical. It is reducible neither to the pronouncements of a talented minority/intellectual vanguard, nor to the trump card of absolute ideological offense in the capable hands of organic revolutionaries. Culture, as the slogan from *The Long Revolution* goes, is a "whole way of life."[14] It retains features of as much mass delusion as it does "residual," or even "emergent," forms of resistance. Thus, culture is summed up as "the general process which creates conventions and institutions, through which meanings that are valued by the community are shared and made active."[15]

The difficulties evident in Williams's attempts to make culture include both the stuff of Enlightened as well as mass consciousness—those "ties that still bind" both to neither's liking—surfaces again in the collision between "theory" and what E. P. Thompson hoped beyond hope would remain "the people's" allegedly less complicated "initiative" for making better their own lives.[16] The imminent condemnation of "theory" (Thompson claims it obscures the more or less self-evident processes of "people" power) occurs just about the time of CS's forced immigration to the United States under Thatcher. Subsequently, even if now in more explicitly "theoretical" guises, what Thompson and others saw as a developing detachment between intellectual work and political desire balances on CS's remaining uncracked nut: ideology and agency. A proper history of the tangled influences that saw this problem emerge in the British context would require a great deal more detail than I can deliver here. One would need to focus on, for example, moves between the skeptical (Althusserian) and hopeful (Gramscian) turns to continental Marxism, the (further) severing of an instrumental connection between economic initiative and culture as evident in the "Nairn-Anderson thesis" and, perhaps most important, the early influences of feminism

and psychoanalysis associated with, among others, Juliet Mitchell,[17] and the for-
midable presence of *Screen*.

However, for my purposes the ideology question can be addressed in more or
less general conceptual terms. This will not be earth-shattering material for those
familiar with recent debates over post-structuralism and political commitment,
but because the issue of ideology and its relation to knowledge is something that
still is largely unresolved for what counts as CS, I think it bears a certain amount
of repetition. Consider: ideology is traditionally defined as a set of imaginary
relations that interpellate the masses as individual subjects and therefore mystify
the masses' actual relation to the material conditions of their lives. A properly
materialist critique of subjectivity, by extension, means the collectivization of
the individual will.[18] Granting this, then at what point, in what manner, and
where does the transformation of that subject from an ideologically interpellated
one to a "materialized" or "massified" subject become possible? Marxist philosophy insists, rightly I think, that ideology produces how and what we think we
experience, our known desires, and as such, our identities and relational rights.
But to bring that subject out of ideology (or in a critical relation to it), to make
the subject an agent of "mass" processes that both situate and (one hopes) dislo-
cate it, launches some nettlesome questions regarding CS as "missionary" work.

The problem Williams identified long ago for CS is that the masses themselves
must be kept at arm's length. When the relation is construed otherwise, the work
of CS starts to take on certain features of the mass culture CS is supposed by some
to be working very differently upon. The totality of "culture"—its becoming a
"whole way of life"—takes on something of a ruthless quality at this point. CS is
now made barely distinct from what it allegedly singles out as examinable. As
Meaghan Morris put it with characteristic savvy, the very moment it is supposed
to have arrived CS comes to look banal, disposable, and ineffective, inadvertently
complicitous with the power plays of the world of commerce and coercion it
wants to locate "outside."[19] What such an impasse seems to signify, in fact, is an
overavailability of resistance within popular culture and, further, a resistance
that refuses to meet the institutional expectations placed on CS to make the
masses properly accountable in writing. On my survey, as we stumble along the
dotted line between Madonna studies and "missionary" work, the difference
between using CS to sift opposition from the immanent messiness of popular culture and the current tendency to dismiss serious attention to the popular as sell-
ing the revolution down the river of capital is a difference that has never been
less distinct, nor more cooperative in its political irrelevance.

TEACHING IN TRAFFIC

> I never have the impression that my experience is entirely my own, and
> it often seems that it has preceded me.
>
> —John Berger, *The Sense of Sight*

> *Master*: This is the day you've been working toward, when diligence
> and determination have at last conferred upon you the right to pro-
> ceed. But it is merely the first step in a precarious journey.
>
> *Grasshopper*: Will you then take me no further, Master? Am I to struggle
> hereafter alone, without your wise counsel?
>
> —from *Kung Fu* (the television show)

Of the eight or more courses I teach each year, most are Introduction to Literature or basic writing courses. In the room I usually teach in, the window is broken (staying either all the way open or closed tight) and it overlooks a busy
street, filled every weekday with the noises of traffic. Monday is *Sir Gawain and
the Green Knight* to the tune of jackhammers; Wednesday is Ishmael Reed to the
halting screech of an accident and sirens; Friday, *Hamlet* or Baraka over an auto
alarm to which no one responds. There are, of course, constant horns. When we
talk about the material world and its connection (or not) to what the discipline of
English has singled out for us as "culture," in this particular classroom we expect
the world sometimes to talk back. We joke that what's outside is rudely intru-
sive, that the moment we try and say something intelligent (or even critical)
about it, the world takes us on and reminds us how reluctant it is to be put into
academically appropriate terms.

   I offer this little anecdote because teaching in traffic has lately got me thinking
about the material conditions for, as it were, producing materialist work. It has
got me thinking, specifically, about the waning possibilities of sustaining that
work, of doing CS, while having the access to the opportunities and resources, the
privileges really, that are required for such a thing. In what follows, I want as gin-
gerly as I can to discuss the collapse of the academic job market as a "material"
condition not incidental to the purported institutionalization of CS in this country, and I want to draw some tentative conclusions about what the practice of CS
and its persistently strained relation to popular or mass culture might be in this
light. I think there are political lessons to be drawn from the academic job crisis,
ones that have to do with CS's being an engaged critical practice, even if that

engagement doesn't come round in terms that the (or this) organic intellectual might desire, having read the right books.

If scholarly research in the United States has seen a relative boom in CS over the last ten years, it seems likely that this is due at some level to an institutional demand for it. An English professor at a major U.S. research university writes of the reconfiguration of his department, "our revisions [to a CS graduate curriculum] seemed attractive: in 1991 applications . . . increased by 288 percent over the previous five years, while the increase in applications to the Ph.D. was 547 percent. . . . Our department," he continues, "has received some recognition in news stories, journal articles, and institutional histories as one of several pioneering the development of CS curricula and programs."[20] That the rise in graduate applications bears a causal correlation to making CS an official part of graduate training is, of course, questionable. But these remarks are telling in other ways. CS in this country, with ironies and contradictions I think very close to its anguished heart, has taken on a certain entrepreneurial bend. The arrival of CS to this country has been more an "inside" job and a top-down affair than a thing brought about by political exchanges we might locate "outside" academe (where workers, economics, and progressive social movements are supposed to reside).

The curious thing is that the development of CS, having occurred primarily at research institutions as part of the latest turn in professional training, has conceivably produced a cohort of theoretically minded new Ph.D.'s who are destined for rather different kinds of jobs, if jobs at all. Michael Bérubé has it right, no doubt: "the discipline [of English] thinks it's going from literature to culture, and the market tells us we're going from literature to technical writing."[21] I would add that in going from "literature" to "technical writing"—and in going to a less insulated, less secure, less privileged workaday existence (our own and increasing numbers of our students)—CS is coming, alas, to a kind of materialist engagement in spite of its overt materialist pretensions, and this engagement is dictated according to the appropriately vulgar realities of labor exploitation, un- and under-employment.

The *ADE Bulletin*, the *MLA Newsletter*, the *Chronicle of Higher Education*, and other official publications bring the message of a disintegrating profession with masochistic (or is it sadistic?) regularity. The numbers are undeniable: in the fifteen years between 1976–77 and 1991–92, not once did more than half the new Ph.D.'s in foreign languages receive tenure-track jobs.[22] The statistics in English are really no better: in 1993–94, 41.6 percent of new Ph.D.'s found tenure-track employment. The recent low was in 1983–84 at 36 percent; the recent high, 1991–92 at 45.4 percent.[23] These numbers are, of course, compounded by an increase in the numbers of new Ph.D.'s on the market during the years corresponding to the decrease in jobs available, from a low in 1987 of about 650, to 850 in 1991.[24] (The U.S. Department of Education reports a 32 percent increase in Ph.D.'s in English, and a rise of 40 percent in foreign languages over the five years leading up to 1993–94.)[25] In terms of general funding for higher education, 1993 reports from state governments claim that appropriations have risen by a paltry 2 percent over a two-year period. In fact, there was an actual drop by 4 percent when the figures are adjusted for inflation.[26]

It is significant that the institutions most affected by the changes in funding and employment are the large, publicly funded Division I research institutions. The number of jobs offered at those kinds of schools, as of October 1993, has either remained the same or declined since October 1982. On the other hand, the number of jobs advertised at smaller, Division II nonresearch liberal arts colleges was up (in 1993) by 9 to 20 percent.[27] Between 1990 and 1994, the number of full-time faculty decreased at 28 percent of the English departments at research institutions. Two-thirds of them increased the number of TAs, and 25 percent increased their numbers of part-timers.[28] And one more statistic, just for good measure: of all the jobs in English advertised for 1993, 19.4 percent were in British literature, and 28.2 percent were in writing. The percentage of CS positions advertised was all of .5 percent.[29]

What kinds of conclusions might be drawn from these numbers, especially insofar as they reach into the tough issue of political struggle and, implicitly, CS's alleged abandonment of teaching and political activism? For one and most obviously, post-Fordist economic restructuring has not spared its magic on higher education, where the vast majority of teachers are themselves going to be exploited and marginalized in exceedingly material ways. For another, while Madonna studies may very well go far for those numbers left in a shrinking professional-managerial class, the lot for most other folks will be working closer to the bone in lower-level courses, and with burdensome teaching loads that will make research next to impossible. Indeed, with many of their students whose prospects for middle-class status are similarly on the sharp decline, the majority of would-be academics will share decreasing hopes for earning a living wage themselves.[30] Perhaps, in one sense, the "popular" has replaced the "canonical" as the inverted cultural capital with which graduate faculty in U.S. CS proceed to trade, but there are increasing numbers of new

Ph.D.'s being rather differently "popularized"—that is, pushed up against a material problem that, for all that materialist training or lack of it, a seven-year graduate apprenticeship only momentarily keeps at bay. The "popular" struggle against an undeniably ruthless economic system becomes less something found by dividing mass culture from our ability to account for it prescriptively in the books we write (or might have written), and more a point at which one finds oneself beginning.

Given the changes I have brought forth statistically concerning what life means for the vast majority of new Ph.D.'s, I am not about to argue for the dumbing down of graduate programs to incorporate less theory, less struggling with the ins and outs of CS, and more concern with institutional micro-politics. Nor will I suggest, as some have, that returning to the halcyon days of Lit. Crit. will somehow spawn jobs.[31] But the fact that the "real world" is creeping in on CS and changing the rules of the game, at precisely the moment many of us are being turned loose to determine what real CS is, is an irony too close to the cloaked ambivalence of CS's "legacy" to pass commenting on.[32] To ask where CS is in relation to the masses, to propose that we must choose exclusively to either sift through pop-culture, through all the ideology to the sterner stuff, or sit back and pronounce pop-culture's ceaseless capacity for opposition, is, I think, to miss an important feature of CS both now and originally.

Recall the CS "legacy," the impasse between theory and political commitment, between a "culturalist" or experiential notion of granting the masses some autonomy and a "structuralist" or ideology-minded notion that insists that mass experience is delusional and in need of the properly distanced intellectual to translate ideology into politics. There is palpable irony in that the popular ambivalence between (1) how the mass subject experiences itself ideologically and (2) how it might rethink itself materially with that essential act of interpellative misrecognition is precisely the ambivalence attached to the unsuspecting CS practitioner with the current defunding of academe (as symptomatic, of course, of the overall upward redistribution of wealth). This ambivalence, I shall say again, is the return of the ordinary to contemporary CS, in spite of its concomitant state of rarification as high-end academic research. In *The Practice of Everyday Life*, Michel de Certeau writes, "by being caught within ordinary language, the philosopher no longer has his [and her] own (proper) place. Any position of mastery is denied. . . . Philosophic or scientific privilege disappears into the ordinary."[33] An enterprise informed by a "legacy" of ambivalence, radical, entrepreneurial, both attendant upon the masses and aloof, CS wants to study the ordinary but is reluctant to become that way. CS has at the moment been denied the "mastery" of "philosophic privilege," and it is a denial that marks both its arrival and its ineffectiveness. That materiality has provided for both the death and, one hopes, an accidental politics for CS is an irony immanent to CS from its inception. Still it is an irony that brings about some alternative, if "ordinary," possibilities.

Indeed, a generation of would-be academics are being referred to in official places today as "itinerant . . . migrant workers."[34] Our self-redefinition is being made a symptom of "the down-sizing of America,"[35] which comes to us experientially as the reluctant admission that teaching and learning, like living well, eventually quarrels with "capitalism's inexorable logic of accumulation."[36] Of course, it would be pushing things to say that the late arrival of class consciousness to U.S. academe is a sure bet now that our lives are at stake. Nor would I want to put forth that the right context for CS is the defunding of higher education in this country. However, I would go as far as suggesting that the materialist-oriented interpellative misfires we like to write about going on "out there" in the foggy collective of the "popular" are something that ultimately refuses to be addressed secondhand. With all the risk and immodesty associated with political hopefulness, I would venture to characterize the new Ph.D. as a political hybrid, where the politics comes in ways for which we're not totally trained: one part lumpenpostmodernist, another part nouveau proletariat and, on the whole, engaged with economic conditions more easily written about than lived through.

CODA

If CS's politics has arrived, it has done so after the fact, and with precisely the ambivalences and disruptive banalities CS thought for a moment it could merely study. The split condition of the popular subject, where identity teeters between ideology and the material desires it doesn't yet know it has is no longer the masses' business to experience, and the job of Enlightened CSers to write up. I suggest that, at present, U.S. CS brings to its practitioners—and, in fact, quite by accident—the probability of having to entertain other than academic desires, and entertain as well something other again than the academic identities that once seemed possible. Mass culture in this very practical sense is distinct no more from the solid ground on which we do our work in political good conscience. Little separates the study of everyday life from the scholar's burden of living within it. Coming to terms with antagonistic social relations—let's just

call them labor—which the official "legacy" of CS says we must record as the collective agency of working people, turns out to be a process having as much to
with labor's forcing its more awkward presence upon us. If CS is here, I submit, it
is here by default.

NOTES

I would like to thank Amitava Kumar, Jeffrey Williams, and Carina Yervasi for reading an
early draft of this essay and for kind comments toward revision.

1. Cited in Ioan Davies, *Cultural Studies and Beyond: Fragments of Empire* (New York:
   Routledge, 1995), 138.
2. Ross Chambers, "Reading and Being Read: Irony and Critical Practice in Cultural
   Studies," *minnesota review* 43–44 (1995): 113–30.
3. I'm of course referring to Stuart Hall, "Cultural Studies and Its Theoretical Legacies,"
   in *Cultural Studies*, ed. Lawrence Grossberg et al. (New York: Routledge, 1992),
   277–94.
4. See Michael Bérubé and Cary Nelson, "Graduate Education Is Losing Its Moral Base,"
   Chronicle of Higher Education, 23 March 1994, B1–3. See also idem, eds., *Higher Education under Fire: Politics, Economics, and the Crisis of the Humanities* (New York:
   Routledge, 1995).
5. Erik D. Curren, "No Openings at This Time: Job Market Collapse and Graduate Education," *Profession* (1994): 57–61.
6. These books are Richard Hoggart, *The Uses of Literacy* (New York: Oxford University
   Press, 1970 [1958]); Raymond Williams, *Culture and Society* (London: Chatto and Windus, 1958); and E. P. Thompson, *The Making of the English Working Class* (New York:
   Vintage, 1963).
7. These include organizational centers such as the Campaign for Nuclear Disarmament
   (CND), the Workers Educational Association (WEA), and the National Council of
   Labor Colleges (NCLC).
8. Cited in Davies (n. 1), 12.
9. This is a point made first by Stuart Hall, reluctant spokesperson for the Birmingham
   "legacy" (and, of course, the director of CCCS by 1970). Hall wants to be neither the
   "tableau vivant," CS's "spirit of the past resurrected," nor "the keeper of the conscience of Cultural Studies." See Hall (n. 3), 277.
10. Ioan Davies calls Thompson "the ideal example of the 'free-born Englishman's' (or
    aristocratic) radicalism" (n. 1), 50.

11. Cited in Patrick Bratlinger, *Crusoe's Footprints: Cultural Studies in Britain and America* (New York: Routledge, 1990), 45.

12. Hall speaks eloquently of coming to CS through the problem of Marxism: "backwards: against the Soviet tanks in Budapest." Hall (n. 3), 279.

13. The reprint is found in Raymond Williams, *Problems in Materialism and Culture* (London: Verso, 1980), 31–49.

14. Raymond Williams, *The Long Revolution* (London: Chatto and Windus, 1961).

15. Ibid., 55.

16. I'm referring to the publication of *The Poverty of Theory* (London: Merlin Press, 1978). For Thompson, theory "destroys every space for the initiative or creativity of the mass of the people" (185). On the other hand, and still within the changing perimeters of British CS, just a year later Dick Hebdige took rather a different route with a decidedly theoretical (semiotic), resistance-within-pop-culture pitch, in *Subculture: The Meaning of Style* (New York: Routledge, 1979).

17. See Mitchell's 1966 *New Left Review* article, the title of which is a play off of Williams: "Women: The Longest Revolution." Cited in Davies (n. 1), 25.

18. The best essay I know of on mass agency and materialist critique is Etienne Balibar, "Spinoza, the Anti-Orwell: The Fear of the Masses." The essay is in his collection of essays, *Masses, Classes, Ideas* (New York: Routledge, 1994), 3–38.

19. See Meaghan Morris, "Banality in Cultural Studies," in *The Logics of Television*, ed. Patricia Mellencamp (Bloomington: University of Indiana Press, 1990), 14–43.

20. Philip E. Smith II, "Composing a Cultural Studies Curriculum at Pitt," in *Cultural Studies in the English Classroom*, ed. James Berlin and Michael J. Vivon (Portsmouth, England: Boynton/Cook/Heinemann, 1992), 47, 63.

21. Michael Bérubé, "Peer Pressure: Literary and Cultural Studies in the Bear Market," *minnesota review* 43–44 (1995): 139.

22. Richard Holub, "Professional Responsibility: On Undergraduate Education and Hiring Practices," *Profession* (1994): 81.

23. Betina Huber, "The MLA's 1993–94 Survey of Ph.D. Placement: The Latest English Findings and Trends through Time," *ADE Bulletin* 112 (winter 1995): 50.

24. "Facts and Figures," *ADE Bulletin* 106 (winter 1993): 62.

25. See "Earned Degrees Conferred by U.S. Institutions, 1993–94," *Chronicle of Higher Education*, 28 June 1996, A30.

26. Kit Lively, "State Support for Public Colleges Up 2% This Year," *Chronicle of Higher Education*, 27 October 1993, A29.

27. Betina Huber, "Recent Trends in the Modern Language Job Market," *Profession* (1994): 94.

28. "Highlights of the MLA's Survey of Ph.D. Granting Modern Language Departments: Changes in Faculty Size from 1990–94," *ADE Bulletin* 109 (winter 1994): 47.

29. Huber (n. 27), 100.

30. A longer essay might explore this point in terms of coalition building based in common economic struggle. One thinks, for example, of the Yale TA strike and the association that occurred there with the custodial workers. For a substantial article on the increasing burden low-income and immigrant students are bearing to attend college, see "The Widening Gap in Higher Education: A Special Report," *Chronicle of Higher Education*, 14 June 1996, A10–A17.

31. I don't wish to subscribe to the odd message put forth recently by George Levine that "the credentials we as professionals provide should not depend primarily and perhaps not at all on student's ability to negotiate complicated arguments about race, class, and gender" (14). I would suggest, rather, that these things are becoming increasingly the "primary" if occulted context of what we do, by default, whether we persist in entertaining fantasies of academic insularity or not. See Levine, "Putting the 'Literature' Back into Literature Departments," *ADE Bulletin* 113 (spring 1996): 13–20.

32. My thinking on CS as a fundamentally ironic enterprise has been greatly influenced by Ross Chambers's essay, "Reading and Being Read" (n. 2).

33. Michel de Certeau, *The Practice of Everyday Life* (Berkeley: University of California Press, 1984), 13.

34. Holub (n. 22), 80.

35. Sandra M. Gilbert, "President's Column," *MLA Newsletter*, summer 1996, 5.

36. John Guillory, "Professionalism: What Graduate Students Want," *ADE Bulletin* 113, spring 1996: 6.

Pedagogy and Public Accountability

Ronald Strickland

11

It is possible to see all the various postindustrial developments in the academy—such as the downsizing of faculties and other resources, initiatives to increase productivity, and the growth of more or less vocationally oriented areas such as composition, technical writing, and English as a second language—as moments in a struggle to determine whether, how, and to whom the academy is going to be held accountable. The concept of "accountability" has distasteful connotations for many academics—it is associated with reductive "bottom line" thinking that would limit academic freedom in research and teaching. But the terms of accountability wouldn't have to be conceded to the likes of academic administrators, state legislators, and neoconservative critics of the academy. Progressive teachers need to be engaged in this struggle, and we can begin by reconceptualizing pedagogy. In order to do so, we will need to move beyond the limited understanding of pedagogy and the public accountability of higher education that we have inherited from the modernist and civic humanist traditions.

Modernist English Studies

During the past fifty years of rapid expansion in the American university system, English studies has functioned as a sort of mechanism—an ideological state apparatus—to produce two variant modes of individual-as-subject for the late capitalist social order. One of these modes of individualism was that of the quietist and escapist reader of literature, aptly described by Terry Eagleton as "an historically peculiar form of human subject who is sensitive, receptive, imaginative, and so on . . . *about nothing in particular*" (emphasis in original).[1] A pedagogy focused on the cultivation of abstract aesthetic and emotional sensibility in the individual student correlated with the New Critics' "fugitive" rejection of modern industrial society. The other facet of individualism informing English studies, especially composition studies, has been the humanist ideal of the citizen prepared to participate, as an individual, in public deliberations on social policy. On first glance, it may seem that these two aspects of individualism are radically opposed to each other—the first teaching students to be passive and the second teaching students to be active participants in a democratic society. In practice, however, the pedagogical goal of civic humanist agency offers students little more hope for political empowerment than does the New Critical rejection of social engagement, since it is focused exclusively on *individual* agency.

Pedagogy and the Theory Revolution

By the early 1980s, with New Criticism under attack from various postmodern critiques, many teachers had turned to antifoundationalist discourses—poststructuralism, feminism, Marxism, antiracist and postcolonial critique, cultural studies, and queer theories—to make English studies more democratic and more responsive to the needs of teachers and students.[2] It is possible, in this context, to trace a "pedagogical turn" resulting from poststructuralism's problematizations of textuality and subjectivity. In literary studies, poststructuralism's rejection of New Criticism's focus on texts as units of self-determined meaning led to a rethinking of the ways textual meanings and cultural values are produced, and among the obvious targets for a broader analysis of this cultural production were pedagogical practices themselves. Similarly, in composition studies, the postmodern critique of textual integrity and autonomy raised questions about the production of student texts and the contexts in which writing is generated, leading to increased attention to the historical and social construction of discourse communities.

These insights should lead us not to seek the development of students as individuals but to see students as participants in the production of multiple, heterogeneous knowledges. The teaching project should not be oriented toward the transmission of authoritative "knowledge" but should be relocated in praxis—practice developed in a dialectical process of theorization and critique. I have theorized a radically antihumanist and anti-individualist "confrontational pedagogy" elsewhere.[3] Here I want to focus on the ways understanding "knowledge" and the relationships between teachers and students in these terms entails a reunderstanding of the public responsibilities of teachers and students and also of the public sphere as a potential site for pedagogical interventions.

RETHINKING THE PUBLIC SPHERE

It is useful to begin by reconsidering the term "public sphere." This term is often used to mean the bourgeois public sphere—the realm of discourse in which, it is commonly assumed, public opinion is formed and policy decisions are made. Postmodern theory has challenged the viability of this conceptualization, but its continued currency makes it useful as a point of departure for rethinking the boundaries of the classroom. In the context of this definition, it might be questioned whether the college classroom counts as part of the public sphere. It is generally true, for example, that teachers are expected to treat their classrooms as their own private domains. Various institutional traditions contribute to this understanding of the classroom as private space. The relationship between teacher and student is commonly seen as analogous to that between parent and child; academic freedom policies are designed to protect the privacy of individual teachers.

On the other hand, there are obvious reasons to think of the classroom as public space. The classroom might be considered part of the public sphere at least in that it is often seen as a training ground for students who will eventually enter the public sphere "proper," after preparation both vocational and civic. This understanding of the classroom as a public sphere informs the many activist pedagogies (adaptations of Paulo Freire's strategies, Henry Giroux's class-based resistance pedagogy, feminist and antiracist pedagogies, etc.) in which the classroom is seen as what Nancy Fraser has called a "counter-public sphere"—a local and

oppositional space in which subaltern subjects may prepare to contest the hegemony of a dominant social order.[4]

To some degree, at least since the 1960s, many progressives have seen the entire
academy as a potential counter-public sphere. Yet universities and even humanities departments are overwhelmingly dedicated to serving the interests of postnational capitalism. Postmodern theory doesn't seem likely to change this state of
affairs, though, I think, it can be made to support a general deprivatization of
knowledge and pedagogy; a rethinking of pedagogy such that the individual student or even the "classroom" need not be the focal point of the production of
knowledge. For postmodern pedagogies, the "knowledge" of a course must be
viewed as contingent, subject to dialectical contestation, and continually
involved in the process of production and reproduction. The knowledge of a
course will not be a hypostatized and homogenized disciplinary canonical tradition filtered through the teacher as master and text as master-resource. We must
break down the walls of the classroom in order to make it possible for knowledges
from other discourses to intervene, and to make the knowledges, rhetorics, and
literacies produced in a particular course available to engage other discourses.

READING THE INSTITUTION

One move in the direction of deprivatization would be to bring our students in on
the attempt to get a larger perspective on our work as teachers and intellectuals.
This must begin with theory, with the process of critique and auto-critique,
always identifying the enabling conditions, the regimes of truth that support our
taken-for-granted institutional structures and practices. In the wake of the theory
revolution we've had some success in providing students with the resources and
opportunities necessary to historicize and theorize the place of English studies.
But we need also to develop frameworks for specific local institutional critique.
We need, for example, to examine with our students the material conditions of
our work in the university. We need to locate our particular institutions in the
national academic prestige hierarchy. We need to locate our particular departments in relation to other departments in our own institutions. By identifying the
terms, limits, and conditions of knowledge production at various levels of the academic prestige hierarchy, we can make the ideological functions of knowledge
production available for critique, and we can make it possible to articulate local
goals and local agendas. In the absence of such a critique, academic standards,

canons, and orientations toward knowledge production set at elite institutions become the default conditions for English and cultural studies at all institutions. This prevents us from developing more productive agendas in the more numerous but less prestigious institutions.

Proceeding from a specific identification of the conditions of our work, we can begin to raise issues of accountability in collective rather than individualistic terms. For instance, in some of my courses I include a brief section on the economics of English studies. I ask students to read texts such as Evan Watkins's *Work Time*, which gives a detailed analysis of the work that gets done in a typical English department.[5] I provide data on student enrollments, tuition costs, fees, faculty teaching loads, and so forth. I want each student to be accountable, and I want to make the course and my work in general accountable, to a public that—to borrow a phrase Bill Clinton used in describing his cabinet selections—"looks like America." How much is it costing the taxpayers of Illinois to provide this course in seventeenth-century English literature? What is the demographic makeup of the class? Should we invest our resources in this course? How can we proceed in a way that will be most accountable to the interests of the public?

At the state university where I teach, students pay around 40 percent of the costs of their education in tuition and fees; most of the rest of their costs are paid by tax revenues. This is too large a share for the student (the student's share has been rising steadily since the Reagan-era effort to privatize higher education was inaugurated), and the high cost of tuition makes it impossible for many Illinois citizens to attend the university.[6] But many students are oblivious to how the remaining 60 percent of the cost of their education—appropriated tax revenues—is raised and distributed. They don't think about the subsidies they are getting, or about the uneven distribution of those subsidies. Therefore, when I assert that students have some responsibility to the society at large, some students inevitably reject my claim by saying something like, "my parents worked hard, earned money, and have paid for my college education—I can do what I want to do in college, I'm paying for it." I began providing the enrollment and tuition data as a way of engaging such students in the project of identifying the specific dimensions and limits of their privilege. Since they are only paying for less than half of their education, I ask, don't they think we should consider the interests of those who are paying most of the bill?

Demographically, our student body is whiter and somewhat more affluent than the population of the state as a whole. So some people—many people of color, many working-class people—are working and paying taxes in Illinois, supporting our endeavors, and yet not being represented sufficiently, as demographic groups, in our classrooms. Don't we need to be accountable to them? In Illinois, heavy reliance on local property taxes for general education means that schools in poor neighborhoods struggle with chronically inadequate resources while those in affluent neighborhoods enjoy the best facilities, faculty, and technology that money can buy. Perhaps we can't easily undo the effects of this inequitable system of primary and secondary education on our university admissions. But the very least we could do would be to consider issues of class and race, for example, in our seventeenth-century literature course. As it turns out, these issues are crucially important in English culture of the early modern era, and it now seems fairly self-evident that the New Critics' focus on metaphysical poetry constituted an extremely reductive way of defining the seventeenth century in England. But even if we didn't find readily corresponding issues of concern between the existing traditional course and contemporary constituencies of accountability, that wouldn't absolve us of the responsibility to engage the public. It might mean instead that the course needs to be dropped.

Teaching beyond the Classroom

Mas'ud Zavarzadeh and Donald Morton have argued that pedagogy should be understood

> not commonsensically, as classroom practices or instructional methods as such, but as the act of producing and disseminating knowledges in culture, a process of which classroom practices are only one instance. From this position, all discursive practices are pedagogical, in the sense that they propose a theory of reality—a world in which those discourses are "true."[7]

If it seems overly ambitious to claim all discursive practices as the purview of one's pedagogy, I can suggest a more modest realm of discourse to begin with: the curriculum. As Gerald Graff has demonstrated, the well-entrenched "field coverage" English curriculum has produced a situation in which specialists in ostensibly discrete literary-historical periods do narrowly focused research and teaching, with only a very limited obligation to justify their work to colleagues outside their literary-historical period, and with no obligation to question the larger assumptions about literature that set the boundaries of the profession.[8] The field coverage model thus functions as an administrative convenience achieved at the cost of sacrificing accountability.

In an earlier essay, entitled "Curriculum Mortis," I proposed an alternative curricular structure designed to institutionalize the engagement and conflict of competing discourses within the discipline of English studies.[9] Drawing on the theory-driven curricular reforms at Carnegie-Mellon and Syracuse during the late 1980s, I suggested a plan in which, after taking introductory courses in "Strategies of Representation" and "Strategies of Interpretation," students would encounter a curriculum mapped as a triangle with disciplinary discourses forming three corners: history, rhetoric, and poetics. Each student would take eighteen hours on one corner and six hours each on the other two corners. Finally, the student would take a senior seminar, for a total of forty hours. Courses that combined two or more disciplinary discourses would be mapped accordingly on the triangle, and such courses would be allowed to count toward the major requirement in any one of the discursive areas the course addressed. In this way transdisciplinary courses would be given a slight advantage over courses that addressed only one disciplinary discourse. The broad categories of history, rhetoric, and poetics were intended to correspond to the traditional subdisciplinary divisions of the department, but it matters less what the categories might be — or whether there are two, three, or more categories — than that various different disciplinary and discursive paradigms be articulated and situated in interactive relationships to each other.

My hope was that the triangle curriculum would institutionalize a constant process of rearticulation and negotiation among the various discursive paradigms that contribute to the production of knowledge in my department. However, after a lengthy process of consideration, the department adopted a compromise curriculum that incorporates a theory-focused introductory course and a senior seminar similar to those in my proposal, but the triangle was rejected. Instead, the department instituted a multi-track requirement based on genre categories — poetry, fiction, drama, and rhetoric. On the whole, I see this as a progressive development. The literary period courses are declining in importance and the new genre-focused courses are likely to be more theoretically self-conscious than the traditional courses; at the current historical-institutional moment it is more difficult to take as unproblematic that a particular kind of a text is a "poem" than it is to assume that the date of composition is the most salient defining characteristic of a text. But I regret having lost an opportunity to make accountability for one's theoretical assumptions an integral part of a curricular process closely involving each faculty member.

ENGAGING "VOCATIONALIST" PUBLICS WITHIN
THE ACADEMY

Progressive teachers of literature and cultural studies need to redefine and
reappropriate existing academic structures and resources in ways that will
enable us to reach out to broader constituencies within the academy. As I
argued in "Curriculum Mortis," we need to interact more with faculty and students in quasi-professional and vocationally oriented programs in our own
departments in order to hold vocationalists accountable to the democratic and
intellectual ideals of the university and the society at large, and in order to
hold academic humanists accountable to existing sociopolitical conditions. The
traditional hierarchy of prestige in which humanists smugly tolerate but ignore
vocationalists seals us off from these "publics" within the academy and their
constituencies without. There are issues of accountability and elitism here. But
our resistance to taking vocationalists seriously also inhibits our theoretical
self-consciousness. This affects our scholarship as well as our teaching. For
instance, among all of the excellent work in postcolonial criticism and theory
from literary and cultural studies scholars in the past ten years or so, one seldom encounters any mention of the ongoing effects of cultural imperialism
reproduced in our TESOL programs. I have read many brilliant critiques of
colonialist ideology focusing on canonical works, nonliterary documents, and
popular culture, but none of the postcolonial critics is thinking about the issue
of cultural imperialism in TESOL. The work published in leading TESOL journals such as *TESOL Quarterly*, meanwhile, tends to be positivistic and apolitical. Even in terms of the goals of liberal humanism, the strict separation of
vocational from academic courses is counterproductive, as Edward Said
demonstrates in his observations on English language teaching in the Persian
Gulf:

> In sheer numerical terms English attracted the largest number of
> young people . . . the reason: many students proposed to end up
> working for airlines, or banks in which English was the world lingua
> franca. This all but terminally consigned English to the level of a
> technical language stripped of expressive and aesthetic characteris-
> tics and denuded of any critical or self-conscious dimension. You
> learned English to use computers, respond to orders, transmit telexes,
> decipher manifests, and so forth. That was all.[10]

DEPRIVATIZING THE CLASSROOM AND VIOLATING COLLEGIALITY

Strategies to make our professional practices more directly accountable often meet resistance because they violate the unspoken codes of collegiality that prevent teachers from engaging each other, and their students, in public dialogue and debate. For example, I regularly teach a doctoral seminar in literary theory and pedagogy in which I assign students to write an essay on the pedagogy of a particular literature course they have taken or observed, developing a critique of the relationship between the teacher's theoretical orientation and his or her classroom practices. A few weeks in advance I send a note around to my colleagues saying that I will be making the assignment and that some students may be contacting them for interviews or asking for materials from their courses, and thanking them in advance for their cooperation. When I introduce the assignment to students, I describe it as an opportunity for them to closely analyze the work of a veteran teacher, and I suggest that they use the assignment as an occasion to talk about pedagogy and theory with someone whose teaching they've particularly admired.

Inevitably, however, some students and some of my colleagues are made very uncomfortable by this assignment. Some students say they feel uncomfortable because they are being put in the position of judging their teachers publicly (all of the students' papers in my courses are "published" on a listserv list and archived on a web page, and the students discuss the papers in the seminar). I see the assignment as an opportunity for teachers to have a careful and thorough critique of their teaching—a process from which it might be possible to identify areas of particular strengths to build on as well as weaknesses to focus on for improvement. But some colleagues react with suspicion, and, occasionally, with hostility when approached by the students. Some teachers haven't thought much about the theoretical underpinnings of their teaching practices, and don't like to be held accountable in this way. The assumption that the classroom is each teacher's private space is so strong that my assignment is sometimes seen as an invasion of privacy. Though I suppose this shouldn't be surprising, I think it is really quite remarkable.

EXTRACURRICULAR INTERVENTIONS

Progressive teachers should be alert to possibilities for intervention in extracurricular spaces that are often occupied by traditionalist and reactionary interests.

As an example, I'd like to describe one of my projects of this sort. In my department there are several annual student scholarships and awards, mostly named after former faculty members and funded by bequests from their families or their estates. These awards recognize the winners of various contests—the best essay in a literature course, the best work of fiction by an undergraduate, and so forth—and they are presented to students at the annual department banquet each spring. A few years ago I developed an alternative award, the C. L. R. James/Malcolm X Award, which offers a $300 prize for the best essay on a sociopolitical issue in English studies by an undergraduate student. The C. L. R. James/Malcolm X Award represents a pedagogical intervention and an implicit critique of the traditional department culture in several ways that may not be immediately apparent. First, the name of the award promotes a tradition of left and antiracist critique in opposition to the mainstream aestheticist aura of the other awards. And the name of the award implies a rejection of the petty individualistic vanity of the other awards. Unlike the namesakes of the other awards, neither C. L. R. James nor Malcolm X ever taught in my department. But students who consider submitting their work for this contest have before them a model of intellectual recognition that stands for something more than the recognition of an individual—the C. L. R. James/Malcolm X Award, as the award announcement states, is named instead for two important radical critics of Western culture. The award has the effect of encouraging faculty to include sociopolitical critique as a category when they are assigning paper topics in their courses, and it signals to students that sociopolitical critique is welcome in the English department. The award attracts students who are interested in radical cultural critique into our programs, and recognizes the work of students with these interests. Nonmajors who have submitted essays for this contest have subsequently switched their majors to English, and several of the contestants have pursued graduate studies in English. Several students have commented that the existence of an award that recognizes sociopolitical critique was a factor in their decisions; it helped make them aware of the possibility of doing radical cultural critique in English studies.

COMPUTER NETWORK-ENHANCED PEDAGOGIES

Some theorists have advanced the claim that Internet and hypertext technologies offer ready ways to realize the liberatory possibilities of postmodernism in the literature classroom. Yet technological innovations such as computer networks by no means represent a cure-all; their implementation will not necessarily foster the kinds of postmodern pedagogies I have been discussing. Indeed, this technology is all too easily co-opted by both vocationalist and liberal humanist pedagogies. Unless we wish to fall into the vocationalist trap of promoting the use of computer networks as yet another technological skill to be "mastered" and later converted into cold hard cash, or the liberal humanist one of assuming that computer networks will simultaneously allow for the expression of everyone's unique, individual voice and promote consensus through the suppression of difference, we will need to carefully and rigorously critique and theorize the pedagogical practices facilitated by computer networks. Furthermore, we will need to temper our characteristically optimistic faith in the progressive nature of technology in the face of the very real material conditions that limit access to these technologies for many people.

The possibility that students could have access to a broad intertext with a high degree of control over the possible connections that may arise in reading a complex text sounds appealing. But hopes for student empowerment through technology are generally conceived within a consumerist framework of prefabricated choices. While I reject these terms, I have experimented with the use of electronic texts as one of several means to reconfigure the local academic course as a public site of interaction and intervention. My experiments have used fairly low-tech and widely accessible Internet technologies such as e-mail, gopher archives, and the World Wide Web. In all my courses participants write weekly micro-essays taking positions on class discussion topics, and these are posted to an e-mail listserv list. Participants can access the list from any computer with a Telnet hookup or a modem. The list can include other students and faculty not in the class, and students and faculty at other institutions. The micro-essays can be cross-posted among different classes, different institutions, and from one semester to another. With the e-mail listserv list, the discursive space of the classroom can be expanded, and this in turn can facilitate the formation of a wider variety of articulated political positions among participants in the course. Over the past several years the texts written by me and by the students in my courses have been "published" on the university's gopher server and on the World Wide Web, making the texts available for public viewing. In this way the intellectual work of the course becomes more publicly accountable, and participants in the course can become involved in critical discussions with other students and faculty beyond the local department or institution.

Computer networks, whether classroom-based or worldwide, offer an opportune site for inaugurating a deprivatized, collective production of knowledge.

The virtual spaces created by computer networks constitute a landscape in which the traditional power relations between student and teacher can be significantly altered, in which students and teachers alike can speak from, critique, and explore various subject positions. In this discursive landscape the knowledges generated in the classroom can be (literally) linked to other knowledges, other voices, thereby creating a participatory "public sphere" radically different from the one nostalgically referenced by civic humanism—in which the private citizen speaks eloquently as "the common man" in a universal public forum; or, as Hollywood would have it, "Mr. Smith goes to Washington."

UNDERSTANDING OUR SITUATION

In accordance with Illinois state law, my university library keeps a printout showing the salaries of all university employees above a certain salary grade level. It's an interesting document. It indicates, among other things, that assistant professors in English earn around $35,000 per year, while assistant professors in marketing earn around $55,000 per year. This, for me, raises further issues of accountability. How does the university justify paying marketing faculty more than English faculty? Market demand, of course. But is market demand a legitimate criterion for determining the way resources are allocated in an institution of higher education? Does this mean that the academy values the teaching of English less than it values the teaching of marketing? Should English majors demand a rebate on their tuition, since they are being shortchanged in terms of faculty dollars expended? Or, if we're going to operate according to marketplace dynamics, can the English department compete by offering some marketing courses? I've read interesting cultural studies scholarship on the marketing campaigns and management strategies of companies such as Benetton, the Banana Republic, the Body Shop, and Baxter Health Care.[11] Maybe we practitioners of cultural studies could train marketing majors more cheaply than the marketing department. Or, if we can't compete with them, maybe we can join them. I've considered the possibility of trying to publish a few pieces in the journals where marketing professors publish, and then applying for one of their positions the next time they run an ad in the *Chronicle of Higher Education*. As an assistant professor in marketing, I could make more than some full professors in English! Oh, I know, they wouldn't take a leftist seriously in marketing.

This reminds me of another issue of accountability. Is it possible that, to whatever extent English departments really are hotbeds of radicalism—as some conservative journalists have insisted (though I don't believe it)—this tendency is a consequence of our underpaid conditions of employment? Twenty thousand more per year, for starters, could probably buy a lot of political correctness among English faculty. In the meantime, we need to remember how we're being valued by our institutions, and we must not forget that for a savings of twenty thousand per year, the academy should be willing to swallow some radical critique with its Shakespeare and company.

Liberal humanist orthodoxy has assumed that the humanities in general, and literary studies in particular, have a sort of antiauthoritarian quality that automatically counteracts the general tendency of educational systems to reproduce existing relations of power. In composition studies it has been assumed that the teaching of writing will automatically enable students to successfully function in a participatory democracy. Yet however broad the range of cultural experience represented in the texts, the goal of liberal humanist pedagogy is always to transform the student into an autonomous participant in the bourgeois public sphere, as the free-standing citizen of a mythical democracy that never was.

As a result, any political implications of the course and its texts or any political investments on the part of the student are always considered secondary to the "fundamentally human" experience of learning, which is assumed to transcend politics. Our students' general indoctrination in the ideology of individualism often prevents them from identifying structural causes of problems and larger social forces of oppression. If, for example, a disgruntled man bursts into a McGill University classroom and kills several female engineering students (we trust readers will recall this horrible incident from the fall of 1989), the ideology of individualism can only account for the action by describing the assailant as a perverse or insane individual. Students indoctrinated in the ideology of individualism have no language or intellectual framework for understanding the extent to which even the particular directions that such shockingly "perverse" or "antisocial" behaviors take are sanctioned and overdetermined by a long history of misogyny and a continuing devaluation of women in our culture. On the other hand, the overwhelming hegemony of individualism blocks students' access to the social power of collective action, limiting students' awareness of the possibilities and procedures for political action based on the shared experience of social groups and shared interests among groups. However useful the pedagogy of individualism may have been at a particular historical juncture, then, it is inadequate for the current historical moment. It is time to hold ourselves, our colleagues, and our students accountable to constituencies beyond the universal human individual conceived as the subject of the liberal humanist academy.

Notes

Some of the arguments and strategies presented here have been developed in collaboration with the Normal Research Collective, a group of graduate students at Illinois State University working on problems in theory, pedagogy, and cultural studies.

1. Terry Eagleton, "The Subject of Literature," *Cultural Critique* 2 (1985–86): 98.
2. For a detailed account of the effects of theory on literary studies, see James Cahalan and David Downing, "Selected Further Resources for Theory and Pedagogy: A Bibliographic Essay," in their collection entitled *Practicing Theory in Introductory Literature Classes* (Urbana: NCTE, 1991), 293–335. On the effects of theory in composition studies, see chapter 1 ("In the Turbulence of Theory") and chapter 2 ("The Changing Political Landscape of Composition Studies") in Lester Faigley, *Fragments of Rationality* (Pittsburgh: University of Pittsburgh Press, 1992).
3. See Ronald Strickland, "Confrontational Pedagogy and Traditional Literary Studies," *College English* 52 (1990): 291–300.
4. See Nancy Fraser, "Rethinking the Public Sphere: A Contribution to the Critique of Actually Existing Democracy," in *The Phantom Public Sphere*, ed. Bruce Robbins (Minneapolis: University of Minnesota Press, 1993), 1–32.
5. Evan Watkins, *Work Time: English Departments and the Circulation of Cultural Value* (Stanford: Stanford University Press, 1990).
6. For a detailed account of the Reagan-Bush attack on public funding for higher education, see Paul Lauter, "Political Correctness and the Attack on American Colleges," in *After Political Correctness: The Humanities and Society in the 1990s*, ed. Christopher Newfield and Ronald Strickland (Boulder: Westview Press, 1995), 212–25.
7. Donald Morton and Mas'ud Zavarzadeh, introduction to *Theory/Pedagogy/Politics*, ed. Morton and Zavarzadeh (Urbana: University of Illinois Press, 1991), vii.
8. Gerald Graff, *Professing Literature* (Chicago: University of Chicago Press, 1988).
9. See *College Literature* 21.1 (February 1994): 1–14.
10. Edward Said, *Culture and Imperialism* (New York: Columbia University Press, 1993), 305. For a detailed analysis of the institutional/intellectual hypocrisy of TESOL programs, see Beatrice Quarshie Smith, "Reading Culture and Society: A Multidisciplinary Study of Subjectivity in an EFL Setting" (Ph.D. diss., Illinois State University, 1995), especially chapter 5, "Postcolonial Subjects and EFL Reading Pedagogy."
11. See, for example, Paul Smith, "Visiting the Banana Republic," in *Universal Abandon?* ed. Andrew Ross (New York: Routledge, 1992), 128–48; Henry Giroux, "The United Colors of Benetton," in *Disturbing Pleasures* (Minneapolis: University of Minnesota Press, 1994), 3–24; Evan Watkins and Lisa Shubert, "The Entrepreneurship of the New," in *After Political Correctness*, ed. Newfield and Strickland, 90–108; and Shekhar Deshpande and Andy Kurtz, "Trade Tales," *Mediations* 18 (spring 1994): 33–52.

Part III

Intellectuals and Their Publics

Black, Bruised, and Read All Over

Public Intellectuals and the Politics of Race

12

Henry A. Giroux

> And where do intellectuals stand in relation to politics? . . .
> [T]hose who are mindful of the ties that link everything in
> this world together, who approach the world with humility,
> but also with an increased sense of responsibility, who wage
> a struggle for every good thing — such intellectuals should
> be listened to with the greatest attention, regardless of
> whether they work as independent critics, holding up a
> much-needed mirror to politics and power, or are directly
> involved in politics. . . . it does not follow that we should
> bar such intellectuals from the realm of politics on the pre-
> text that their only place is in universities or the media. On
> the contrary: I am deeply convinced that the more such
> people engage directly in practical politics, the better our
> world will be.[1]

In the last decade a multitude of books and articles have lamented the demise of public intellectuals in the United States. While the history of this discourse is too extensive to repeat, I plan to highlight two theoretical interventions into the debate over the current status of public intellectuals that raise important issues about the role and responsibility of intellectuals in American society on the one hand and, in light of the controversy surrounding academics as intellectuals, the relevance of defining higher education as an essential democratic public sphere on the other.

Russell Jacoby's widely read book, *The Last Intellectuals*, argued that the conditions that produced an older generation of public intellectuals in the post–World War II era had been undermined and displaced in the 1980s.[2] The unaffiliated intellectual functioning as a social critic writing accessible prose for

79

such journals as the *Partisan Review* offers for Jacoby an ideal of what it means
to mobilize a popular audience and a model for the role of a public intellectual.
Inhabiting the bohemian enclaves of Greenwich Village, these intellectuals and
the public spheres that support them have become an endangered species. In
Jacoby's narrative of decline, such public intellectuals as Jane Jacobs, Edmund
Wilson, Dwight Macdonald, Philip Rahv, C. Wright Mills, and Irving Howe have
been replaced by 1960s radicals who have forsaken the role of the independent
intellectual for the safe and specialized confines of the university.

But the university, according to Jacoby, neither represents a viable public
sphere nor provides the conditions for intellectuals to speak to a broader public
audience. More specifically, by sanctioning the privileges of professionalism,
promoting overly technical jargon, and cultivating new forms of specialization,
academics have been reduced to sterile technocrats, unable, if not unwilling, to
address the responsibilities of public service.[3] If we believe Jacoby, the public
intellectual has been replaced by the so-called radical academic who is interested
more in pursuing career advancement and the cushy rewards of tenure than acting as a proponent of social change.[4]

In a now famous essay in *Cultural Critique*, Cornel West focused less on the
demise of the public intellectual than on the emergence of a hostile climate for
black intellectuals.[5] For West, the recent shift in the broader political orientation
toward the right, the widening of the gap between middle-class blacks and an
ever growing black underclass, and the increasingly managerial logic of the university often intolerant of critical scholars—especially black scholars—have all
hindered the development and support of black intellectuals in this country.

Retrospectively, Jacoby and West anticipated a significant set of issues that
emerged late in the 1980s as part of a larger debate over the role of intellectuals
in the struggle for social change. Jacoby's argument that the university cannot
nourish public discourse resonates strongly with the current right-wing charge
that the university is too political—the unhappy result of an influx of "tenured
radicals."[6] For different reasons, both set of critics posit the university as a
depoliticized site and limit pedagogy to the arid imperatives of discipline-bound
professionalization and specialization.

On the one hand, Jacoby saw the university, with all of its complicity with
dominant ideologies and practices, as a conservative sphere that buys off even its
most critical intellectuals.[7] On the other hand, conservatives like Roger Kimball,
Charles Sykes, Lynne Cheney, and William Bennett translate a contempt for critical thinking and social criticism into appropriate educational behavior and see

the ideal university as an apolitical public sphere inhabited largely by a disinterested faculty engaged in an ahistorical conversation among great minds and pedagogically bound to hand down the ideas and values of the classics to a new generation of would-be thinkers.[8] The university of this latter scenario becomes in instrumental terms largely a mechanism for social and cultural reproduction and a repository of both the timeless knowledge and skills of the culture of business and the high cultural values and ideals of the dominant society.[9]

In contrast, Cornel West's essay provided a theoretical service by injecting race into the debate over the meaning and role of public intellectuals in the United States. Expanding on John Dewey's claim that "To form itself, the public must break existing public forms,"[10] West highlighted the ways racism operates as a structuring principle of dominant public spheres and a defining force in shaping the discourse on public intellectuals. West's argument provides a theoretical referent for challenging the context and content of much of the liberal discourse that has followed the recent discovery of black intellectuals. Accordingly, a decade later, West has become symbolic of what it means to assume the role of a black public intellectual, and he has labored to define a broader conception of the public intellectual, one that expands and deepens the responsibility of cultural workers engaged in the world of public politics. For example, he has observed that

> The fundamental role of the public intellectual—distinct from, yet building on, the indispensable work of academics, experts, analysts, and pundits—is to create and sustain high-quality public discourse addressing urgent public problems which enlightens and energizes fellow citizens, prompting them to take public action. This role requires a deep commitment to the life of the mind—a perennial attempt to clear our minds of cant—which serves to shape the public destiny of a people. Intellectual and political leadership is neither elitist nor populist; rather it is democratic, in that each of us stands in public space, without humiliation, to put forward our best visions and views for the sake of the public interest. And these arguments are present in an atmosphere of mutual respect and civic trust.[11]

Implicit in West's insight is the assumption that the disappearance of political intellectuals in higher education corresponds to the passing of critical politics in public life. The effacement of progressive politics from public life is forcefully demonstrated in the response of many liberals and conservatives to the rise of a group of black public intellectuals who have challenged the notion that such dominant public spheres as the university can be called race-neutral or race-transcendent.[12] Many black academics have raised the volume of the debate on the public intellectual by reinserting the notion of racial justice into public discourse while simultaneously redefining notions of social commitment, politics, and equality.

> "Public intellectual" is by and large an excuse, the marker of a sterile, hybrid variant of "bearing witness" that, when all is said and done, is a justification for an aversion to intellectual or political heavy lifting — a pretentious name for highfalutin babble about the movie you just saw or the rhyme you just heard on the radio.[13]

When one reads Jacoby's earlier attack on academics in higher education, it is clear that the lament over the decline of public intellectuals excluded black intellectuals, who appeared at the time to occupy the margins of scholarly and popular discourse. While specific individuals like Toni Morrison, Alice Walker, and Maya Angelou received attention in the national media (as artists and not intellectuals), the scholarly and popular press focused primarily on whites when it addressed the general malaise in intellectual life in America. Such writers as Robert Bellah and Benjamin Barber bemoaned the university's fall from public grace into "the quintessential institution of bureaucratic individualism,"[14] and urged various public foundations to support a new generation of public intellectuals. Yet they virtually ignored race as a crucial category within the larger context. In recent years, observations on race and democracy among a number of relatively young black intellectuals have helped to fill the lacunae, though not without prompting a great deal of criticism among both conservative and liberal intellectuals.

The discovery of the black public intellectual has nevertheless become the new American fashion — a hot topic in both scholarly publications and the popular press.[15] Expressing a historically conditioned anxiety and near manic fascination, journalists and academics seem obsessed with probing the mystique of the "new" black public intellectual with particular attention on such African American writers as Michael Dyson, Cornel West, Henry Gates, Gloria Watkins (bell hooks), Patricia Williams, Robin Kelley, Toni Morrison, Michele Wallace, Stanley Crouch, and Glen Loury.

But what began as a series of press releases heralding the ascendancy of black intellectuals has turned into a tirade of damning indictments, as indicated in the above "insights" by Adolph Reed. Heartening gestures toward the revitalization of a black public discourse now appear to be marked by cautious, grudging, and sometimes indiscriminate criticism, mostly from white intellectuals, suggesting that African American intellectuals are unqualified to assume the role of public intellectuals by virtue of their shoddy scholarship, their narrow focus on racial issues, and their willingness to pander to mainstream audiences. The rest of this essay analyzes some of these criticisms and their applicability to a thoughtful discussion of the role black intellectuals might play in keeping alive the spirit of public criticism while reviving both the moral and the pedagogical traditions of inquiry within and beyond the university.

In 1995 a series of articles appeared in the American popular press that framed the reception of the work produced by "new" black intellectuals. These articles legitimated a particular theoretical intervention in the debate about black public intellectuals that set the stage for the counterattack to follow. In the first instance, Michael Bérubé argued in the New Yorker that the advent of a group of black intellectuals commanding significant media attention was an appropriate and welcome phenomenon given the central place of racial issues in American politics and the eruption of creative work by blacks in the realm of culture.[16] Bérubé saw the unexpected prominence of such a group of intellectuals particularly welcome "at a time when the idea of 'the public' has become nearly unthinkable in national politics."[17] For Bérubé, the new black intellectuals not only disprove the claim that "the academy has been the death of the public intellectuals . . . [but also] have the ability and the resources to represent themselves in public on their own terms."[18]

Claiming that the arrival of the black intellectual was as important as the emergence of the New York intellectuals after the Second World War, Bérubé compared these groups less in terms of political and ideological considerations and more in terms of personalities. ("Whereas Daniel Bell was criticized for buying nice furniture in his forties, bell hooks now draws stares for driving a BMW.")[19] In the end, Bérubé said little about the substantive issues that inform the work of the black intellectuals he addressed, and especially notable was his refusal to engage bell hooks's feminist politics.

But Bérubé did echo a series of criticisms that would be taken up more stridently by others in the popular press. For instance, he argued that the rising chorus of enthusiasm from young admirers who are taken with the black intellectuals' fluency with popular culture may divert such intellectuals as Michael Dyson from listening more attentively to "the deliberations of Senate subcommittees."[20] Implicit in this criticism is the assumption that theoretical work that critically addresses popular culture is too far removed from the "real world" of politics. This is not simply a facile attack on black intellectuals who choose to write about popular culture; Bérubé's criticism can be read as a reductive dismissal of cultural politics as a politics of bad faith serving mainly as a "compensation for practical politics."[21]

Appearing in the *Atlantic Monthly* shortly thereafter, an article by Robert Boynton addressed a number of similar issues. Mingling his discussion of the new black intellectuals with a celebration of such earlier public intellectuals as Philip Rahv, Edmund Wilson, and Lionel Trilling, Boynton highlighted the theoretical and ideological differences between the two groups. Eulogizing the New York intellectuals, Boynton paid homage to their belief in the transformative power of high culture, their retreat from the mainstream, and their stalwart anticommunism. Measured against the history of these renowned white intellectuals, Boynton found, the new black intellectuals offered little to suggest that the two groups had much in common.

Damning with faint praise, Boynton granted the new black intellectuals importance because "they provide a viable, if radically different, image of what a public intellectual can be."[22] But Boynton's sustained criticisms of the new black intellectuals more than canceled any enthusiasm for their public role. Moreover, Boynton strongly implied that the stature of the new public intellectuals shrinks considerably seen next to the likes of Edmund Wilson and Alfred Kazin and those who hung around the *Partisan Review* and the New York City bohemia after the world war. For instance, Boynton's highbrow modernism caused him some discomfort when he addressed the writing styles of the new black intellectuals. The admixture of autobiography with social criticism and the amalgamation of black speech, history, and experience with academic discourse found in the work (for example) of Derrick Bell and Patricia Williams signaled for Boynton the centrality of racial identity in the work of such writers, a feature that Boynton concluded "would have made the young Jewish New Yorkers squirm."[23] Such writing represents, for Boynton, an aesthetic limited by a fixation on racial identities and experiences and is "more admirable in a belleslettrist than in a wide-ranging public intellectual."[24]

But more than race fixation haunts the credibility of the new black intellectuals. For Boynton, the new black intellectuals who slide easily between academia and the op-ed pages risk substituting theoretically rigorous social criticism for celebrity punditry. Barely veiled in this criticism is Boynton's displeasure with the forms of border crossing and social negotiations that mark the discourse of many black public intellectuals. It seems inconceivable to critics like Boynton that popular cultural forms can become serious objects of social analysis.[25]

Both of these essays omit the history of black intellectuals as well as the complicated historical narratives through which emergent black public spheres arose in this century.[26] For both Bérubé and Boynton, white intellectuals provide the legitimating trope for understanding the strengths and weaknesses of black intellectuals. This is not to suggest that either author indulges in a form of racism. But it does imply that the politics of whiteness provides a fundamental context for understanding how the discourse on black intellectuals is framed and addressed in the popular press. In this case, whiteness, as Toni Morrison reminds us, becomes invisible to itself and hence the all-pervasive referent for judging public intellectuals who speak and write in an effort to engage a broader public.[27]

The politics of whiteness provides an often ignored theoretical framework for understanding why black intellectuals receive routine condemnation for speaking in a language labeled either simplistic or "too public." One cannot but wonder why white public intellectuals like Jonathan Kozol or Barbara Ehrenreich, who write in accessible prose and speak plainly, are not subjected to the same criticism that Michael Dyson or bell hooks receives. Eric Lott, for example, refers to Dyson's more general writings as a "troglodyte's delight." When not drawing overt parallels to cavemen, he charges Dyson with "a leftism of good manners" designed to "furnish cautious analyses of the Other half for the unknowing."[28]

Lott's commentary represents more than a mean-spirited misrepresentation of the complexity of Dyson's work; more often than not, it appears to be symptomatic of the elitist posturing of a white academic unaware of (or unconcerned about) his own racial privileges, who exhibits a disdain for minority intellectuals who gain public recognition as they address a variety of public cultures. For Lott, Michael Dyson's diasporic writings and public recognition suggest that he has sold out, but for lesser known black intellectuals like cultural critic Armand White, similar forms of border crossings become oppositional.

Fame often breeds jealousy among academics, and Lott appears to have succumbed to petty sniping. But his analysis also suggests a one-dimensional response to black public intellectuals whose diasporic politics serves as a powerful critique of the white academic's often romanticized celebration of resistance as a practice confined to the margins of social and political life.[29]

One also finds a strong tendency, especially in the work of such writers as Robert Boynton and Sean Wilentz, to argue that the racialist story line of the black intellectuals represents a form of ghettoization, an overemphasis on the connectedness of black history, experience, and culture to their discourse. The notion that the history, intellectual legacies, and struggles of African Americans—along with their damning indictment of white supremacy and racial oppression—are more than mere flotsam "on capitalism's undulating surface" seems lost on many white intellectuals.[30]

More appears in this critique of black intellectuals than just an impoverished version of political and social history. One also finds a notion of the public intellectual that disregards the enduring formation and influence of racial injustice in national public discourse.[31] In addition, those scholars who reject the constitutive role that black intellectuals play in grounding their scholarship in African American history and discourse arrogantly assume that the moral, aesthetic, political, and social lessons of such work apply only to the interests of the black community, hence the charge that such work constitutes a "veritable ghettoization."[32]

Moreover, theorists such as Robert Boynton, Sean Wilentz, and Leon Wieseltier assume that when black intellectuals focus on race they ignore not only broader issues but also a range of questions relevant to democracy. This appears to be a catch-22 argument. If black intellectuals move beyond race as a central discourse in their work, they both lose their "authenticity," as some of their critics claim, and invalidate the very notion of the black public intellectual. But if black intellectuals focus on racial issues, they risk accusations of either pandering to the perils of celebrity writing or ghettoizing themselves along the borders of racial politics. Each position cancels out the other and conveniently disavows the complexities, struggles, and value of the hybridized discourses black intellectuals contribute to the national debate about racism, education, politics, and popular culture.

Equally important, neither position addresses the difficulties black intellectuals face engaging in social criticism within dominant cultural formations. The main casualty of such reasoning, however, appears to be a notion of democracy attentive to the legacy and contributions of black intellectuals and the vital role they play in their struggles to deepen the critical faculties of public memory and expand the imperatives of freedom and racial justice.[33]

Toni Morrison forcefully challenges the claim that black intellectuals are fixated on racial reasoning, defending racial politics as a pedagogy and practice for democracy and social responsibility rather than a position limited to the narrow confines of identity politics:

[T]he questions black intellectuals put to themselves, and to African American students, are not limited and confined to our own community. For the major crises in politics, in government, in practically any social issue in this country, the axis turns on the issue of race. Is this country willing to sabotage its cities and school systems if they're occupied mostly by black people? It seems so. When we take on these issues and problems as black intellectuals, what we are doing is not merely the primary work of enlightening and producing a generation of young black intellectuals. Whatever the flash points are, they frequently have to do with amelioration, enhancement or identification of the problems of the entire country. So this is not parochial; it is not marginal; it is not even primarily self-interest.[34]

Morrison's comments unmask the racist logic that often invokes "the racial story line" as a critique of black intellectuals, and she also affirms the critical capacities of black public intellectuals who as border crossers address diverse and multiple audiences, publics, racial formations, and discourses.

The assumption that intellectuals who speak to multiple audiences become ipso facto sellouts has gained considerable currency in the broader discussion of public intellectuals and black intellectuals in particular. While the dangers of celebrity are real, cautious voices like David Theo Goldberg's argue that when intellectuals intervene at the level of civic debate and speak to large audiences, they face enormous constraints regarding what they can say and how they represent themselves. Paraded as media stars, such intellectuals risk speaking in sound bites, substituting glibness for analysis, and compromising their role as critical intellectuals. Of course, black intellectuals are no less immune to aligning themselves with the ideology of professionalization or the cult of expertise than are their white counterparts in the academy. For instance, Henry Gates's emergence as a preeminent black public intellectual dispensing his expertise on rap music, black literature, and famous personalities suggests less the demise of what Edward Said calls the dominant discourse of professionalism than new indices to measure the shifting breadth and scope of academic professionalization.

Goldberg's position also implies that black intellectuals need to be vigorously engaged rather than simply dismissed or uncritically celebrated as Cornel West demanded in the early 1980s. For West, black public intellectuals must exercise a critical "self-inventory," manifest as a "sense of critique and resistance applicable to the black community, American society and Western civilization as a whole,"[35] a sentiment that resonates with Karl Marx's call for a practical politics that he described enigmatically as the "poetry of the future."[36]

Given the recognition of Henry Gates and Cornel West in the popular press as the most prominent black public intellectuals in the United States, it becomes all the more imperative to measure their role as intellectuals against their own critical standards. Both exemplify the dangers that public intellectuals face when they take on the responsibility of speaking for an entire generation of black intellectuals. In the current work of both West and Gates there are indications that the spirit of oppositional discourse that keeps alive the radical thrust of being a public intellectual is being compromised. For example, while it might be too much to expect Henry Gates to act like a democratic socialist, it is disheartening to witness his increasing allegiance to a centrist politics made manifest in numerous media appearances, hastily written publications, and op-ed commentaries in which he seems less concerned with social justice and the dwindling state of democracy in this country than he does in recruiting a number of high-profile African American intellectuals to Harvard University. Equally disturbing is the role he played as a coeditor in a recent publication of the *New Yorker* that featured black writers. Instead of using this forum as an opportunity to challenge the current right-wing assault on black youth, women, and the poor, Gates featured a series of stories defending Clarence Thomas, a piece on Dennis Rodman, a plug for the work of William Julius Wilson, who will soon join Gates at Harvard University, and a human interest profile on Buddy Fletcher, a successful black trader on the New York Stock Exchange. Of course, Gates does not altogether ignore the spirit of oppositional discourse; he includes a piece by Patricia Williams along with a brief three-page article highlighting a hodgepodge of "eight legends" who in three hundred words or less provide commentaries comparing the sixties and nineties and engaging the questions, "what went wrong, what went right, and what is to be done."[37]

If Gates's recent work appears to be moving dangerously close to the type of clever, safe prose typical of the Harvard Club, Cornel West's newest work does little to provide a more oppositional discourse. West's recent *Race Matters* appears smug and insensitive. While claiming that black public intellectuals need to pay attention to the younger generation, West barely acknowledges the struggles of young people in the urban centers (except, of course, through the pejorative claim that they embody a culture of nihilism). Withholding strong support for a younger generation of black public intellectuals, West berates them for wearing sloppy attire. Unlike Du Bois, whom he models himself after, West ignores the centrality of public education as a site of political struggle, and harshly dismisses the important work waged by black cultural critics "independent of the academy—journalists, artists, writers, feminist groups—as 'mediocre,' thereby offering no independent support to sustain black intellectual culture."[38]

What appears missing in the current work of both Gates and West is a model of leadership embraced by Du Bois later in his life. Positing a principle of self-critique and strategy for practical politics, Du Bois recognized that the best educated people are not necessarily those who are most enlightened ethically or politically. We can draw two conclusions from Du Bois's insight. First, public intellectuals, especially those whose pedagogical journeys are largely fashioned in elite Ivy League institutions, must use their scholarship as tools to address the most pressing social issues of the time; but they also must be attentive to those ideas, values, and practices that they need to unlearn, given their formative sojourns among the rich and the powerful. Second, intellectuals must do more than cross those borders that separate the university from the commanding heights of the dominant media, they must also cross those boundaries that separate academically based public intellectuals from the politics of "hopeful hope"[39] often exhibited among cultural workers struggling in the public schools, community arts programs, social service centers, shelters for battered women, and other spheres where such intellectuals toil without the fanfare of media hype or celebrity status.

Pedagogies of self-formation are always at work in presenting and representing ourselves as public intellectuals engaged in the struggle for social justice. Public intellectuals such as Gates and West need to be attentive to both what they have learned and what they need to unlearn in light of their close association with centers of power and authority. Clearly, West and Gates are decent human beings who see themselves as grandchildren of Du Bois's Talented Tenth and have taken on the burden of pedagogical sages and political activists. This is a difficult task. While both of these figures have exhibited how challenging and potentially transformative the role is, they have also, in part, indicated how slippery success and public celebrity can be when one attempts to hold on to an oppositional politics or egalitarian vision.

The contradictions that attend various appearances of both white and black intellectuals do not automatically suggest that public intellectuals are sellouts. On the contrary, such contradictions register the challenges that public intellectuals must face to avoid co-option either within or outside the university while assuming the challenge of addressing multiple and often broad audiences. It means that public intellectuals, especially those in higher education, must avoid an uncritical romance with American culture. For public intellectuals, critical independence and strategic autonomy must include a willingness to contest the cult of professional expertise and specialization with its emphases on hierarchy, competitiveness, and objective, dispassionate research. This suggests demystifying the dominant politics of professionalism while simultaneously creating institutional spaces for hybridized zones of intellectual work in which faculty can create the conditions for new forms of solidarity consistent with defending the university as a "public sphere, one of the few to remain in the post-Fordist moment, in which many citizens can address and debate public issues."[40]

This position, along with Goldberg's, may be far too dialectical for many theorists who air their views on black public intellectuals in the popular media. For example, Adolph Reed argues that the black public intellectual who speaks to diverse white and black audiences is little more than a modern-day version of Booker T. Washington, rewriting or explaining the mysteries of black America to please white audiences. According to Reed, such intellectuals turn their backs on a black constituency by refusing to address the collective capabilities of African Americans. Moreover, they gush over each other's fame and produce second-rate scholarly work. In the end, Reed dismisses black public intellectuals because they "are able to skirt the practical requirements of . . . avoiding both rigorous, careful intellectual work and protracted committed political action."[41]

Whereas David Goldberg supports the notion of the black public intellectual but rightly notes the dangers attendant upon any role that requires one to engage a massive public audience, Adolph Reed simply dismisses intellectuals as sellouts. Reed echoes the sentiments of many liberal critics who fail to grasp the political and pedagogical value of black and white intellectuals who locate themselves in the border zones that connect diverse groups, contexts, and public spheres. Cut loose from the ideological moorings of separatism and assimilation, black critical intellectuals, in particular, must renegotiate their place from the experience of "uprooting, disjuncture, and metamorphosis . . . that is, a migrant condition, . . . from which can be derived a metaphor for all humanity."[42]

As a dynamic discourse between scattered hegemonies and diverse social struggles, the hybrid rhetoric of the new black public intellectual is one that opens up new forms of enunciation, asks new questions, and incites new forms of shared antagonisms on either side of the racial divide. Homi Bhabha correctly argues that writers like Boynton, Reed, and Wieseltier fail to grasp the provocation of cultural hybridity, rhetorical and political. Boynton's account doesn't quite get a hold of the scandal generated when one occupies the hybrid position as a form of engaged intellectual and political address—a space of identity that Reed describes as "flimflam" and Wieseltier dismisses as, in Cornel West's case, artful dodging.[43]

For Bhabha, living on the boundary promises more than self-serving, celebratory posturing. Far more important, it offers a rhetorical and political borderline space from which to refuse the inside/outside duality, the binaristic reductionism of pure or contaminated, and the static divide between margin and center. Bhabha captures the progressive political and pedagogical possibilities of the black intellectual as a border subject critically negotiating overlapping, contradictory, and diverse public spaces while opening possibilities for new forms of solidarity:

> Communities negotiate "difference" through a borderline process that reveals the hybridity of cultural identity: they create a sense of themselves to and through an other. Reed's metaphoric boundary between black and white communities, cannot then be assumed as a binary division. And black or minority intellectuals committed to an antiseparatist politics of community have no option but to place themselves in that dangerous and incomplete position where the racial divide is forced to recognize—on either side of the color line—a shared antagonistic or abject terrain. It has become a common ground, not because it is consensual or "just," but because it is infused and inscribed with the sheer contingency of everyday coming and going, struggle and survival.[44]

Bhabha offers his challenge to minority intellectuals, but its larger significance expands the very meaning of the public intellectual whose work cuts across the divide of race, gender, and class. In this hybridized border area the processes of negotiation, indeterminacy, struggle, and politics provide a new set of registers for developing the conditions for transformative social engagement.

The debate over the public intellectual cannot be abstracted from a broader discourse regarding the centrality of racial justice within democratic public life. Nor can such a debate ignore how public intellectuals address the primacy of the pedagogical in providing the conditions for audiences to reconceptualize their role as active and critical citizens in shaping history and mapping the political dimensions of their economic, social, and cultural lives. The role of the public intellectual is inextricably related to mechanisms of power, politics, and ethics. Recognizing this connection offers no relief for those who deny the relevance of politics in the university just as it demands more from those academics who reduce their role to that of the apolitical technician or neutral guardian of Western high culture. The importance of the concept of the public intellectual is that it provides a referent for rethinking the university as one of a number of crucial public spheres that both offer the promise of lending "reality to what were fundamentally moral visions"[45] and articulate a new vision of what education might be, who has access to it, and what opportunities might be produced by those individuals and groups who recognize and try to shape themselves in the dynamic of citizenship and public accountability.

Notes

1. Vaclav Havel, "The Responsibility of Intellectuals," *New York Review of Books*, June 22, 1995, 37.

2. Russell Jacoby, *The Last Intellectuals: American Culture in the Age of Academe* (New York: Basic Books, 1987).

3. I think Michael Denning is right to argue that "the demand that all leftist intellectuals be literary journalists, writing plain English for plain people, is no less objectionable than the Old Left demand that playwrights write agitprop and novelists stick to a comprehensible social realism." Michael Denning, "The Academic Left and the Rise of Cultural Studies," *Radical History Review*, no. 54 (1992): 36. For sustained critical commentary on the politics of clarity, see Henry A. Giroux, "Language, Difference, and Curriculum Theory: Beyond the Politics of Clarity," *Theory into Practice* 31, 3 (summer 1992): 219–27.

4. According to Jacoby, the academy undermines the oppositional role that academics might play as public intellectuals. This is especially important in light of Jacoby's belief that "Today's nonacademic intellectuals are an endangered species" coupled with his claim that "universities virtually monopolize . . . intellectual work." Jacoby, *The Last Intellectuals*, 7, 8.

5. Cornel West, "The Dilemma of the Black Intellectual," *Cultural Critique*, no. 1 (fall 1985): 109–24. Reprinted in *Keeping Faith* (New York: Routledge, 1993).

6. This charge can be found in Roger Kimball, *Tenured Radicals: How Politics Has Corrupted Our Higher Education* (New York: Harper Perennial, 1991).

7. A number of books provide a far more thoughtful and optimistic view of both intellectuals and the academy as a viable public sphere. Some important examples include Bruce Robbins, ed., *Intellectuals: Aesthetics, Politics, Academics* (Minneapolis: Uni-

versity of Minnesota Press, 1990); Andrew Ross, *No Respect: Intellectuals and Popular Culture* (New York: Routledge, 1989); Stanley Aronowitz and Henry A. Giroux, *Education Still under Siege* (Westport, CT: Bergin and Garvey, 1993); Bruce Robbins, *Secular Vocations: Intellectuals, Professionalism, Culture* (London: Verso, 1993); and Michael Bérubé, *Public Access: Literary Theory and American Cultural Politics* (London: Verso, 1994).

8. Conservative books on this issue are too numerous to mention, but representative examples include Allan Bloom, *The Closing of the American Mind* (New York: Simon and Schuster, 1987); Charles J. Sykes, *Profscam: Professors and the Demise of Higher Education* (Washington, DC: Regnery Gateway, 1988); Kimball, *Tenured Radicals*; Dinesh D'Souza, *Illiberal Education: The Politics of Race and Sex on Campus* (New York: Free Press, 1991).

9. This issue is examined in great detail in Aronowitz and Giroux, *Education Still under Siege*; and idem, *Postmodern Education* (Minneapolis: University of Minnesota Press, 1991).

10. John Dewey, *The Public and Its Problems* (New York: Holt, 127), 31–32.

11. Cornel West, cited in Henry Louis Gates, Jr. and Cornel West, *The Future of the Race* (New York: Knopf, 1996), 71.

12. For a critique of this issue, see Patricia Williams, *The Alchemy of Race and Rights* (Cambridge: Harvard University Press, 1991), especially "The Death of the Profane," 44–51.

13. Adolph Reed, "What Are the Drums Saying, Booker? The Current Crisis of the Black Intellectual," *Village Voice*, April 11, 1995, 35.

14. Paul Desruisseaux, "Foundations Are Asked to Help Train and Encourage New Leaders," *Chronicle of Higher Education*, April 30, 1996, 19.

15. The "discovery" corresponds with a reality more complex than the media suggest. The category black public intellectual should not suggest an ideologically specific group of black intellectuals, as is generally the case in media coverage. In fact, those black intellectuals who have received the most recognition are characterized by a wide range of ideological and political positions extending from left-progressive and liberal to conservative and nationalist. Moreover, the distinctiveness of the group is taken up around the signifiers of class, race, and numbers. As Gerald Early points out, "Indeed, for the first time in African-American history there is a powerful, thoroughly credentialed and completely professionalized black intellectual class. . . . [Moreover] today's generation of black intellectuals has been well publicized; in fact, it has access to the entire machinery of intellectual self-promotion." Gerald Early, "Black Like Them," *New York Times Book Review*, April 24, 1996, 7.

16. See, for example, Gina Dent, ed., *Black Popular Culture* (Seattle: Bay Press, 1992).

17. Michael Bérubé, "Public Academy," *New Yorker*, January 9, 1995, 80.

18. Ibid., 75.

19. Ibid.

20. Ibid., 79.

21. Ibid.

22. Robert S. Boynton, "The New Intellectuals," *Atlantic Monthly*, March 1995, 56.

23. Ibid., 70.

24. Ibid.

25. Boynton's modernist hangover and dislike of critical work that addresses "popular" issues are made more visible in a theoretically incompetent and politically conservative critique of cultural studies that soon followed his piece on black intellectuals. See Robert S. Boynton, "The Routledge Revolution," *Lingua Franca* 5, 3 (April 1995): 24–32.

26. On the black public sphere, see the wide-ranging essays in "The Black Public Sphere Collective," *The Black Public Sphere* (Chicago: University of Chicago Press, 1995).

27. Toni Morrison, *Playing in the Dark: Whiteness and the Literary Imagination* (Cambridge: Harvard University Press, 1992).

28. Eric Lott, "Public Image Limited," *Transition*, 5, 4 (winter 1996): 68, 54, 53.

29. One of the worst examples of this type of critique can be found in Leon Wieseltier, "All and Nothing at All," *New Republic*, March 6, 1995, 31–36. In a highly selective and grossly simplified reading, Wieseltier concludes that after reading all of Cornel West's works, he finds that "They are almost completely worthless" (31). One can only assume that West's popularity rests solely on the hype of the media culture and the cult of celebrity.

30. Cited in Michael Hanchard, "Intellectual Pursuit," *Nation*, February 19, 1996, 22.

31. For an excellent analysis of this issue, see John Brenkman, "Race Publics: Civic Illiberalism, or Race after Reagan," *Transition* 5, 2 (summer 1995): 4–36.

32. This position is addressed and criticized in Michael Kilson, "Wilentz, West, and the Black Intellectuals," *Dissent*, winter 1996, 93–94. Two of the most famous critiques of this position can be found in Harold Cruse, *The Crisis of the Negro Intellectual* (New York: Morrow, 1967); and Richard Wright, *Native Son* (New York: Grossett and Dunlap, 1940).

33. On the issue of the black public sphere, see Houston A. Baker, "Critical Memory and the Black Public Sphere," *Public Culture* 7, 1 (1994): 3–33.

34. Toni Morrison, cited in Joy James, "Politicizing the Spirit," *Cultural Studies* 9, 2 (1995): 220.

35. West, "Dilemma of the Black Intellectual," 12.

36. Karl Marx, *The Eighteenth Brumaire of Louis Bonaparte* (New York: International Publishers, 1963), 18.

37. See *New Yorker*, April 29 and May 6, 1996.

38. David Theo Goldberg, "Whither West? The Making of a Public Intellectual," *Review of Education/Pedagogy/Cultural Studies* 16, 1 (1994): 5.

39. I take the phrase "hopeful hope" from the insightful article by Nell Irvin Painter, "A Different Sense of Time," *Nation*, May 6, 1996, 38–43.

40. Jeffrey Williams, "Edward Said's Romance of the Amateur Intellectual," *Review of Education/Pedagogy/Cultural Studies* 17, 4 (1995): 397–410.

41. Reed, "What Are the Drums Saying, Booker?" 35. Reed attempts to backtrack on this attack in a more recent response to criticisms of his piece on black intellectuals. The latter commentary simply dismisses a number of black intellectuals for not taking a critical stand on Louis Farrakhan's role in the Million Man March and his recent global tour to a number of dictatorships in Africa. Reed says little about his role as a public intellectual speaking for a newspaper and readership that are largely white. He simply assumes that because other black scholars differ with him on the significance of Farrakhan's role in national politics, they do not hold themselves accountable for the positions they take as public intellectuals. Hence, Reed implicitly proclaims himself the only black public intellectual with integrity. See Adolph Reed, "Defending the Indefensible," *Village Voice*, April 23, 1996, 26.

42. Salman Rushdie, "In Good Faith," in *Imaginary Homelands: Essays and Criticism, 1981–1991* (London: Penguin Books, 1991), 394.

43. Homi Bhabha, "Black and White and Read All Over," *Artforum*, October 1995, 17.

44. Ibid., 14.

45. Brenkman, "Race Publics," 8.

"The Inescapable Public"
Teaching (during) the Backlash

Rachel Buff and Jason Loviglio

13

This collaborative essay explores the politics of difference in and accessibility to the classroom. It contrasts the experiences of Jason Loviglio and Rachel Buff in different classroom settings. Loviglio teaches American studies at Private College in rural Maine. Buff teaches American history at State College, a small public college in a deindustrialized city in New England.

The impact of the current retrenchment takes different forms at the two institutions where we teach. In Buff's U.S. history survey, 1877 to the present, the predominantly working-class students at State College divide most profoundly by race and their concepts of who an American is and can be. Student conceptions of a unified public sphere are crucially splintered by in-class fractures over claims to a proud national past. In a course entitled "Mediated Voices, Grotesque Desires, and the Disembodied Politic: The Crisis of the Public Sphere in Postmodern America," Loviglio encounters mostly white affluent students who understand "the public" to mean all those things that cannot be embraced by the reassuring concept of "the private." "The inescapable public," in one student's telling phrase, is experienced as a frightful and chaotic landscape lurking just outside available strategies of understanding.

The essay takes the form of two brief anecdotes from our experiences in the classroom, and a dialogue between the two of us as we compare notes on a semester of teaching. We both teach courses that historicize the relationship between politics and everyday life.

In the course of the semester, both of us find the task of teaching the historical importance of public life daunting, in light of the present climate of conservative retrenchment. We are struck by the powerful ways the prevailing political and cultural backlash against "the public" inscribes itself into our classrooms, our lives, and the lives of our students. Understanding these dynamics, we argue, is a necessary task of both Cultural Studies scholarship and a successful Cultural Studies pedagogy.

The contexts in which we teach differ, as do our institutional and disciplinary limitations. In this essay, however, we consider how the problem of "the inescapable public" grounds both of our in-class struggles. We argue that it is precisely at this moment of contestation over a local public that our pedagogy can be most effective.

We don't intend this collaborative essay to be prescriptive. Rather, we mean to open up a dialogue about reclaiming the classroom as a site of struggle, as a ground zero for the theory and practice of Cultural Studies. Comparing notes with other teachers, we argue, is vital to making sense of the often lonely and exciting work we do in the classroom.

VOTING WITH OUR FEET: PRIVACY AND POWER IN A LIBERAL ARTS COLLEGE

Small College inhabits a picturesque campus of red brick buildings perched atop The Hill in an old mill town, which is organized around a sprawling parking lot known as "the concourse" in its downtown and an even more sprawling Wal-Mart hunkered down ominously at its periphery, near the interstate. From almost anywhere in town, you can see the College's library tower, illuminated at night with a dreamy indigo glow; the light is ostensibly there to warn small aircraft using the airfield near the Wal-Mart, but from the ramshackle neighborhoods by the train tracks where I lived when I taught at College, the light seemed to signal less a warning than an ambivalent come-on, like the green one at the end of Daisy Buchanan's dock.

From The Hill, the view of town is obscured by the ubiquitous pines and the cultural self-sufficiency of the campus. Like many colleges, Small College talks endlessly about its own diversity, to prospective students as an admissions strategy, and, more profoundly, to itself as a way of imagining the campus as a vital and vibrant community. For all this talk of diversity, the student body (91 percent white, 40 percent from private schools) is remarkably homogeneous.

For the first meeting of my seminar on "the crisis of public discourse," I plan an exercise to get students thinking about the everyday meanings we attach to the terms "public" and "private." I have in mind the notorious fuzziness of these terms, their multiple overlapping and contradictory definitions, and the shifty, unreliable borders that separate the two at any given moment. I ask the students to divide up the spaces in their lives into two columns on a sheet of paper, under the headings "public" and "private." The idea is to begin with our own definitions of these terms before diving into the difficult readings that theorize and historicize them. I expect that, taken together, the unruly collection of public and private spaces we generate will be a compelling artifact pointing to the instability of these terms.

However, the eighteen students in the seminar come up with a catalogue of "public" and "private" life that is not at all unruly. "The Public" emerges as an eerily null set for almost everyone, an ominously vague world of shadows: the streets, cities, and "anywhere I can't control." Under "The Private" heading, students compile a fairly uniform list of highly evocative spaces: bedrooms, beds, phones, friendships, church pews, vacation homes, e-mail correspondences, minds, bodies, cars, basements, and dormitories.

As I write the master list for each category on the blackboard, we begin to talk about how we experience "public" and "private" in greater detail. Students' understanding of public space is almost uniformly negative in both senses of the word. They define "the public" as all those things that fall outside the reassuring embrace of "privacy."

For many of these students, privacy is primarily about property and control. "My car is the one place where I can control who can be there and who can't," one student offers. Several other students define privacy as freedom from surveillance.

I am surprised by the importance of privacy for many of these young, affluent, white, and academically talented students. As they describe the social and political maps of their everyday lives, it becomes clear that many of these young people seem to be already exhausted by the prospect of a life spent dodg-ing the slings and arrows of an inescapable public sphere. And when I press them about the public parts of their days, they grow silent, almost sullen. Sev-eral times, discussion grinds to a halt, until I relent and steer the class back to a discussion of the pleasures of "private space." Remarkably fluent in tracing the contours of their daily movements between the social enclaves that mark one side of campus from the other, these students seem to regard the world beyond these enclaves as uncharted territory.

The more we talk about it, the more I understand that the fundamental premise of my course, diagnosing the erosion of public life, the crisis of public discourse, begs a very important question as far as my students are concerned: who cares? Among the young, affluent students of this college, there is no nos-talgic longing for some phantom public: the private is the reservoir for all their hopes and dreams. Worse than a phantom, the public has ceased to resonate even as an imaginary space.

One of my objectives for the course is to test the idea of the classroom public sphere, a local interpretive community in which students and teacher try to make sense of the multiple border crossings between public and private spheres that crisscross our social, intellectual, and economic lives. But in this particular classroom, and perhaps in many others too, these borders offer a kind of political asylum, that is, an asylum from politics. After years of teaching undergraduates in a large, public commuter university, I was not prepared for the powerful ways that residential campus life inscribes itself on the academic and political lives of the students.

The following week, I bring up the idea that the classroom can be thought of as a site for a kind of public discourse, and I ask them to consider what sort of definition of public would be most "useful" in imagining this. I ask them to imagine what sort of changes we would have to make in order to create an inter-pretive community.

This line of inquiry turns out to be lively and fairly productive. But our dis-cussion of the possibility of public discourse in the classroom quickly turns to the real scourge of all campus speech: P.C. The overwhelming group consensus is that the pressure to "be P.C." has a chilling effect on political expression and even casual conversation in and out of the classroom. Interestingly, the origins of this pressure are not the administration or faculty, but fellow students. It is social rather than police pressure that scares them. Indeed, except for one stu-dent government representative, none of the students are even aware of the school's "verbal harassment code." Although a chorus of anti-P.C. testimonials may not sound like a promising start, it proved to be the turning point in our ability to talk about the politics of public and private speech.

As the schedule of student-led discussions kicks in, we become more self-conscious about what kinds of conversations are possible in our classroom. This process inevitably leads us to consider issues outside the classroom and the ways they pull us in different directions and threaten to fracture the "common ground" we share as co-conversants. Pushing the limits of this common ground becomes a theme in the weekly student-led facilitations, which begin to take up more and more of our three-hour class time. The process reaches its most powerful point on our November 7 meeting, which is also the day state voters go to the polls to decide on Ballot Question 1, a referendum that would change the state constitution to ban all civil rights protections to gays and lesbians (as well as other groups not already protected).

On this day, three students facilitating our discussion of political expression on campus try an exercise that I would never have dared to try. They have the class—me included—stand up in the middle of the room and designate one side of the room the "yes" side and the other side the "no" side. Then they tell us we will be asked questions and we will have to vote with our feet. The first question asks us how we plan to vote on Maine Ballot Question 1. After that, we are asked to pass judgment on a host of other local questions. After each vote, the facilitators encourage people on each side of the room to explain their positions. By several different measures, it is the best day of the course: each student speaks, including several who have done so infrequently or not at all up to that point. More important, in our crisscrossing of the classroom floor, we physically enact the unruly, shifting, and vital work of public discourse in a way that my "public-private" exercise had failed to do.

We move as a group—all of us—to the "no" side of the room when asked how we would vote on Question 1. Thereafter, we split into countless temporary blocs; if there are any hard and fast alliances, they are difficult to discern in the room. I am struck by the way we all talk about where we stand. Several students express frustration that there is no "middle ground" where they can stand to reflect their ambivalence about a particular question, its wording or its implications. Again and again, students move from one side of the room to another after being persuaded by a particularly compelling argument.

The facilitators, who had asked us to vote on Question 1 on secret ballots at the beginning of class, interrupt our discussion to alert us that two people had voted "yes," that is, voted to make illegal all civil rights protection for gays and lesbians.

Still standing, only now more or less standing around, we begin to process this information. One student says it proved we still haven't made the class a place for free public discourse; one of the facilitators says she is disappointed that two people had chickened out. Another argues that a public "yes" vote would mean social ostracism on campus and says she sympathizes with holders of unpopular views. Several students murmur their assent. Another woman, visibly angry, asks her—and the rest of us—why she should feel bad for people who want to keep private their desire to use their vote to deprive other people of full citizen status. "Why should they be protected from me telling them to their face that they are wrong and that their wrongness has a human cost?"

It is hard to respond to this and so none of us do. It is about time for class to end anyway. A handful of students linger after class talking about the anger and awkwardness still ringing in the air, and perhaps trying to take stock of the way we have changed the stakes in our classroom public. We have all felt the common ground moving underneath our feet, even as we moved back and forth across the room, rearranging ourselves in response to the specific and local problems we all care about.

The class is different after this meeting. The classroom becomes the site for often heated debates about the public cost of choices made in private and about the intimate effects of public initiatives. These American studies seniors found that their social enclaves are sturdier and at the same time more porous than they have imagined, and can survive these weekly forays into the inescapable arguments calling to them from beyond Winthrop Hill.

GROWING UP IN PUBLIC: THE VIEW FROM STATE COLLEGE

The State College student body is predominantly made up of white, working-class students. When I ask colleagues about how this classroom makeup is possible in a city that has always been shaped by trends in immigration, where 50 percent of current public school enrollment is minority students, including growing Latino and Asian populations, I am almost always told that the one community college in town is "taking care of that population." Although there are many students for whom English is a second language, there is no ESL program.

My project in my U.S. history survey course is to create a classroom public that will allow students to explore the issues that shape, among other things, this variable access to education. This project is not without its challenges. At the same time that it is the most affordable four-year rung of the public system, State College is extremely educationally conservative. Students are unused to discussion sessions, unused to interpreting the facts independently of other authorities. So there are obstacles created both by the College's admissions and financial aid policies and by the dominant pedagogy of the institution. But these obstacles, ultimately, do not stop the students—single mothers, young people working their way through school, ROTC recruits—from vehemently debating the same issues of equal access, citizenship, and rights that have already, in part, defined their experiences of public education.

Class discussions, for some reason, become very intense in one out of my four survey sections. It starts almost immediately, when we discuss the role of black women during slavery. The class splits, a group of white women arguing that female strength was necessary among slave women, that this was desirable and did not cancel out or rival male power. The one African American student, a single mother herself, replies that these women cannot understand what it means to be forced to be strong. A group of young white men sit in the back together. They snicker when issues about gender or sexuality come up, often, it seems to me, silencing people who might otherwise speak. But in this case, they agree with the perspective articulated by the African American woman; their small ground for coalition with her concerns the prerogatives and perpetuation of male power.

The vehemence of this debate, which brings two women to the brink of name calling and yelling, sets the tone for class discussions for the remainder of the semester. The configurations of the debate also polarize the class along the lines of both race and gender, obscuring alliances that might bring these students to assert a common interest. As a social space, the classroom becomes fragmented and volatile.

In the wake of this first conflict, it seems to me that the vocal group of young white men will silence opposition from white women, as well as from some of the few Latino and Asian students there are in the class, all of whom happen to be male. Masculine prerogative is a reassuring banner that unites these unlikely allies, as we consider the Great Wave of Immigration, labor unrest, and the feminization of immigrant labor around the turn of the century.

I have a feeling that some of the white women and some of the men of color in the class are now afraid to speak, afraid of allying themselves with the lone

African American woman, who continues to dauntlessly articulate her point of view, sometimes with the help of a sparsely attending, very articulate African woman. The social geography of the room arcs away from these two, so that their chairs get closer to my desk and further away from everyone else.

For a while this class helps me understand some of the powerful functions of whiteness, the ways this soothing and vacuous identity inhibits progressive coalitions. In my class, there is a temporary silencing of gender differences. Many of the white women hesitate to comment about gender inequities that unite working-class immigrant and African American women at the turn of the century.

This situation breaks down dramatically when we get to the post–World War I period: the Palmer Raids, immigration restriction, the execution of Sacco and Vanzetti. The two women at the front of the class argue that Palmer was contradicting the Constitution, and that immigrants had a right to free speech and due process. Being an American, for them, means being able to debate, to disagree with the authority of the ruling class.

Such public defiance, though, is untenable to some of the young men at the back of the class. The comments of one young man encapsulate the racial tension that has, quite literally, reconstructed the social geography of this classroom. "If you don't like it here," he says, directing his comment to the front of the class, "why don't you go back to Africa?"

The class shatters around this: others who sit in the back of the class try to rephrase the words of their comrade; a white woman who has gradually moved her chair away from the bloc at the back of the class resists this notion of "going back." Another woman points out that everyone in the room could "go back" to somewhere. A quieter Italian American man takes on the men at the back and tells them the same thing.

A lone Vietnamese man, who has been quietly moving his chair closer to the men at the back, speaks about the disappointment of immigrants, about his high hopes for America and the discrimination he faces here every day. The leader of the bloc at the back, an ROTC recruit who has often spoken against affirmative action based on the struggles of the men in his family, responds with an impassioned plea for loyalty to the nation: "I'd kill my own mother if it was in the line of duty!" People begin to yell at each other; I stand in the front of the room, which has now become the back, away from the action, trying to get enough order for people to be heard. It is now time to go.

After this class session, the easy alliance, the coalition around whiteness and hopes of upward mobility, shatters. Many of the men and women who were silent before we got to the 1920s speak in much more independent voices after this point. A couple of the members of the hard-core group of white men come to class much more sporadically, while others, still sitting in the back, refer back to earlier arguments to articulate their discontent with the changes in the room. Some of the quieter men begin to speak in independently conservative voices, as does a young white woman who has frequently argued with the more progressive elements in class. Many other women speak much more freely now, and alliances between single mothers and younger students, between the one or two openly lesbian women and the outspoken but very straight-identified women in the class become possible. I notice that the Vietnamese man speaks more, and brings up the stories of his family's emigration from Vietnam when we get to the war. The class moves on, dealing with national mobilization for World War II, the construction of suburbia in the postwar period, the 1960s, the 1970s. I stand talking with one of my students in the smoking section between buildings after class one day, and a friend of hers says, "Oh, is that the class with all the arguments? I want to take that one!"

All of this makes me think about the kind of debate I have encouraged, the pedagogy I have employed in my attempt to make the classroom function as a public sphere where history and its contemporary discontents are reviewed. When I first introduce the discussion section of the class, students are deeply uncomfortable talking to each other. The class proceeds, its topography developing along the lines prescribed by the politics of admissions and recruitment. But in this institutional context, as in any other one, other imaginative possibilities are available.

These debates, which allow students to see the past as directly related to their experiences, also result in the shattering of a temporarily unified public. Some students become much quieter as the issues heat up. At the same time, this fragmentation permits the emergence of another public, one that existed just beneath this makeshift coalition around masculinity and whiteness. Temporary and unstable, the post–Palmer Raid alliances nonetheless bring students into a radically different relationship with one another.

Dialogue: Toward a Pedagogy of Access

JL: In different ways, we're both talking about the problems of access in our classrooms and more broadly, at the institutions we teach in. As you put it, Rachel, when we first started working on this article, a Cultural Studies pedagogy points beyond simply teaching our students about the operations of power and knowledge in society and helps shed light on how power operates in the class-room, too. What are the biggest challenges facing students at State College in terms of access?

RB: It's an interesting problem. Access to education at State is mediated in cru-cial ways, both in terms of what can go on in the classroom and who gets to be there in the first place. For example, the African woman who I refer to as the only ally for that African American woman in my class disappeared for three weeks during the semester. She was an A student. When she returned she told me that the financial aid office had advised her not to come to class until her accounts were square. So the institution kept her out of class intermittently, and that wound up changing the social and political geography of our classroom.

JL: Your anecdote really conveys a powerful sense of how the students shape the way history gets talked about and understood in your classroom. How can a Cul-tural Studies pedagogy respond to the effects of policies like financial aid and affirmative action and how they affect what goes on in the classroom?

RB: This is tough. I told that one woman to spread the word among students that I'd rather have you in class no matter what your financial aid situation is. But obviously there are plenty of other people who aren't on campus at all because of such policies. Very mundane things like classroom discussions are constantly being transformed by larger policy issues: who gets into college, who is able to attend once they get there. We missed her input when she wasn't there, and that's just one person.

Part of the radical impulse of a Cultural Studies pedagogy, it seems to me, is to make the issues that transform our classrooms part of what we discuss inside them. The classroom is the place where students learn the history of how we got to this place and time in terms of democracy and access. And at the same time they are practicing skills that I think have been systematically underdeveloped in public education: discussion, argument, interaction.

These issues are really stark at State; but in your classroom at Small College, the anxieties around issues of access are different.

JL: Right. Obviously, the question of access is more sharply delimited at a pri-vate college than at a public one. What's striking is that despite the privileges and the fact that Small College does ensure some class mobility and security, my students still fear the public and assume that any venture into a civic sphere may cost them access to private privilege. In one sense, their academic experiences have taken them away from the public and insulated them.

RB: Your students fear the "inescapable public," but at the same time they make such great use of the classroom as a public arena. What's the project of a Cultural Studies pedagogy in this setting?

JL: A lot of it involves asking them to pay attention to the public, not just as inescapable but also as a powerful concept for thinking critically about the relationship between discourse and community. It turns out that there were fault lines undermining the campus aura of privacy and homogeneity. They just needed a forum to be expressed.

RB: What moves them to leave the comfort of that privacy for the uncertainty of the public?

JL: Well, that's really tricky. And it gets us to questions about how we define the one and the other. What is public about the speech that gets spoken in a seminar at a small private college? What is private about it? It's not always clear.

It is clear that American studies seniors at Small College can trade on their "good communication skills," which enable the kind of fluency and mobility that emerged in our class discussions and which also promise to help them land lucrative jobs in the ranks of the professional managerial class.

They know how to traffic in personal anecdotes and opinions. But often this style of discourse is predicated on a certain idea about opinions: everybody is entitled to their own. Speech and, by extension, opinion are the ultimate private.

In some ways, however, my students took the class over in ways that drew on but also contradicted their remarkable social fluencies. In both of our classrooms, getting out of the way seems like an important pedagogical tool.

RB: Issues of voice and power are slightly different at State College. Since my students don't imagine themselves necessarily as important historical actors, when they do speak out, there isn't the same patina of carefulness that you describe. I think that their models for saying what they think come more directly out of television talk shows and radio call-ins than what they have learned so far in educational or civic institutions. Since State students don't imagine that what they say will have power, they are, in a certain way, free to speak.

When it became clear to students last semester that my classroom was open to discussion, and things came up that they wanted to talk about, there was an open field. State students were able to deal with a pretty highly fragmented and contested public. I think the trick at a place like State is to validate the importance of the kind of work that they are already pretty skilled at.

JL: I think that's the trick for a Cultural Studies pedagogy in general. You're talking about the classroom as a site where we can support what happens without us in addition to helping students gain access to the more academic forms of expression.

RB: Exactly. That's why it's important to allow debates that touch on contemporary topics to go on in a history class; why our knowledge of the past should always be mixed with our experience of the present. We've talked before about how much pressures from the backlash on our own campuses would standardize curricular development, impose set standards on student progress.

JL: A Cultural Studies pedagogy enables us to take on the effects of that backlash on our students, and in some ways on the classrooms and campuses where we work. Our anecdotes and discussions point out ways that opening up the classrooms cleared a space for students to transform them.

Pedagogues, Pedagogy, and Political Struggle

14

Carol Stabile

> Caught off guard by the increasingly brutal intrusion of the profit motive into the cultural sphere, obsessed with their internal divisions and squabbles (disciplinary, ethnic, sexual, etc.), cut off from society to such an extent that they no longer even realize their extreme degree of isolation, American intellectuals have never seemed so impotent as today. And never has their progressive wing been so unaware of this impotence and its causes—at the front rank of which stands this very lack of awareness or, worse, the illusory belief that acts of language in the classroom are "interventions" into the political struggles of the day.
>
> —*Loic J. D. Wacquant,*
> "The Self-Inflicted Irrelevance of American Academics"

When I was a graduate student, one of my professors suggested that our pedagogical mission as academics was to produce workers who got to work on time, listened to instructions, produced on demand, and were a disciplined capitalist workforce.[1] At the time, dewy-eyed from a seminar on teaching composition that foregrounded the liberatory potential of writing, I dismissed this claim as being unnecessarily pessimistic. Today, I think that this suggestion offers a useful corrective to the conflation of professional with political practice. The following essay explores the limits of the institutional context in which pedagogy takes place, with specific attention to the effects of a primarily institutionalized disjuncture between theory and political practice. This essay is not intended to be an indictment of what we do for a living, nor should it be construed as an attack on individuals. Rather, it is an attempt—in places tentative, processual, and polemical—to begin an urgently needed discussion about what Wacquant describes as our lack of awareness of "our impotence and its causes" and to move us in the direction of more effectively challenging the conditions that have produced this.

Central to the aims of this brief essay is a fairly simple, albeit controversial, premise: capitalist education is organized and has a purpose, which is held in place by a number of other institutions and their ideologies. In a word, the educational system in the United States reproduces and maintains divisions between capitalists and workers, thereby reproducing (as my professor suggested) capitalist relations of production. This organization and purpose are manifest in the historical link between educational institutions and industry, with the former being directed by the needs and interests of the latter. The current crisis in education is, in large part, a reflection of the changing structure and needs of the corporate world. The National Education Summit, held in March 1996 to discuss the future of "public" education, vividly illustrates this link. The list of planning committee members and participants reads like a "Who's Who" of capitalist luminaries: CEOs from IBM, AT&T, BellSouth Corporation, and the Boeing Company; Governors Pete Wilson of California, Tom Ridge of Pennsylvania, and George W. Bush of Texas; and representatives from conservative think tanks like the American Enterprise Institute, the Family Research Council, and the Heritage Foundation.

The nature of the link between corporations and education is becoming more obvious today as public schools, universities, and educators are being held accountable to private, as opposed to public, interests. The ongoing privatization of public institutions and its logic of obedience to the dictates of the market, however, signal an intensification of already existing features of U.S. education, rather than a radical rupture with the past. Because public schools at the primary and secondary levels are funded by property taxes, the school system itself has ensured that resources are not distributed equally. Wealthy communities continue to provide excellent resources for their children while, as Jonathan Kozol (1991) has movingly documented, the poorest communities are not equipped to educate their children. At its best, integration was meant to redistribute some of these resources. Current efforts to roll back some of the minimal gains of the sixties in the shape of "resegregation" bear witness to a process of intensification, rather than some dramatic departure. At the university level, it takes a great deal of work to ignore such fundamental inequalities in light of their material manifestations, which have been made more visible by an increasing division between rich and poor. Universities are frequently the largest property owners and employers in communities, and most of their employees are nonunionized. The current crisis in employment prospects for both undergraduates and graduate students, cuts to financial aid, the exclusivity of admissions policies, and the fact that many of our students must "balance" college with full-time employment all point to inconsistencies between higher education's avowed mission and its realities.

The organization of our educational system is reflected in the content and structure of curricula. From the age of five onward, the vast majority of students are taught to be obedient, to arrive on time, to produce on demand, and basically to do as they are told without question.[2] Those of us educated in the U.S. public school system may recall a section on report cards that listed areas where improvement was "deemed necessary" with categories such as "I have materials ready for work," "I listen attentively," "I use good manners," and, most revealingly, "I obey quickly and cheerfully." Students who rebel against this imposed docility are diagnosed, disciplined, and subjected to a variety of punitive mechanisms. Overworked teachers in overcrowded classrooms, moreover, seldom have the time or resources to deal with more challenged and challenging individual students. In addition to inculcating work habits that prepare children for wage labor, students are tracked into various positions during the educational process and are diagnosed in ways that determine their economic futures (i.e., "gifted and talented" programs, college preparation versus vocational training, and so forth).

Along with institutions like the media, the educational system in this country also teaches students from a very early age to be passive consumers of products, information, and politics. Democratic choices are reduced to consumer choices. Students are not encouraged to question the limited menu of choices available to them, but only to resist in the most individualized, institutionalized manner. Education in no way encourages students to think of organizations as something they make, but as something made for them. In fact, from the structure of the classroom itself to the content of the Cold War ideologies still being taught via textbooks published almost exclusively by multinational corporations, education actively discourages involvement in decision-making processes. Students, like consumers in general, can complain about institutions and organizations and, individually, they can boycott them, but the possibility of building oppositional organizations (not to mention the necessity for these) is denied. By and large, education manufactures consent and acquiescence to the status quo.

If this is to be done effectively, the content of curricula must deny even the possibility of alternatives (either past or present) to capitalism. Thus, the educational system promotes understandings of history and contemporary current events that make the capitalist mode of production appear natural and inevitable. Histories and information that might contradict such understandings are routinely suppressed or dismissed in textbooks, newspapers, and other capitalist media. John Patrick Diggins provides an example of this in a recent *New York Times* op-ed piece, where he objected to revised National History Standards that modestly claim that Africans and Native Americans played a historical role in the settling of the Americas. His objection to the revised standards was that they "have students begin the study of history immersed in past cultures whose people perpetuated undemocratic rites and other systems of submission." According to Diggins, "Freedom flowered in America because of two unique and possibly unrepeatable conditions: the absence of feudalism and the presence of a Calvinist-Lockeanism that bred the Protestant ethic and the 'spirit' of capitalism" (1996). Thus, responsibility for oppression is downloaded onto the oppressed and a history of overt repression (including slavery and the genocide of Native Americans) is subsumed beneath the flowering branches of capitalism.

At the university level, we are the trustees, inheritors, and, to a large extent, beneficiaries of such educational legacies and, as agents, we must operate within constraints established by and in the spirit of capitalism. I am not making an argument about complicity here, because the term and the debate suggest that noncomplicity is a possibility, as is a certain kind of political purity. Rather, I am arguing that such agency as we have must be contextualized and understood within the limits imposed by the institution. *Agency begins only at that point at which we recognize and think critically about these limits.*[3]

Our own training as academics mitigates against such critical thought. Teaching, especially within the humanities, is widely represented as a mission, or vocation, into which teachers are called. Professors are unlikely to recognize teaching as work they perform for an institution that is part of the corporate world and are even less likely to recognize themselves as wage laborers who must sell their labor power to survive. Yet like traditionally feminized labor, teaching is ideologically privileged and institutionally and economically devalued. At research institutions, for example, economic capital (or cultural capital that at some point can be converted into economic capital) is accumulated through research and publication and not, notably, through teaching. One may be professionally rewarded for research and publications through tenure at a prestigious research institution, reduced teaching loads, and general career advancement, but similarly material rewards for excellence in teaching are rare. The notion of teaching as a vocation works to mystify the relations of production in the university for both faculty and students, much as the ideology of motherhood serves to mystify relations of production in the household.

Of course, academics with tenure and tenure-stream jobs traditionally have enjoyed more privilege than other segments of the workforce. Our work lives are more flexible, we can pursue teaching and research interests that appeal to us, and we can take a certain amount of satisfaction in the work we perform. Such comparative privilege affords many the illusion of autonomy from economic determinants, although the increasing contingency of many academics, as well as a speedup in both publishing and teaching, presently threatens to undermine this illusion. As overt attacks on tenure intensify within the humanities, as tenure itself is circumvented covertly through the elimination of tenure-stream job lines (in other areas of the university, this has already happened), as the university increasingly relies on adjunct and part-time workers, we can expect this illusion to have increasingly less purchase, especially among graduate students, recent Ph.D.'s, and junior faculty.

The effects of "restructuring," "downsizing," and privatization, in short, are being experienced now in higher education, and although the objective conditions have changed as a result, the subjective conditions are changing more gradually. The ideological glue that permits us to live a number of contradictions is an investment in our own agency as individuals (an investment reinforced by the rhetoric of vocation and our graduate school training as "apprentices") and the related belief that the university is a democratic institution. Just over a year ago, for example, the University of Pittsburgh eliminated a health care option for its employees in favor of a Blue Cross/Blue Shield monopoly that was said to benefit the university's medical-industrial complex. A faculty vote had overwhelmingly supported maintaining the option, but the administration eliminated it anyway, thanking the faculty for their "input." During a subsequent, unsuccessful attempt to organize faculty, this event caused some faculty to rethink their belief in the democracy of the institution, but many faculty members maintained the belief that their individual voices were heard and privileged by the university, and that a union was therefore unnecessary.[4] We frequently reproduce a similar belief in individual, as opposed to collective, agency in our students. Indeed, given the mandates of university teaching, it is all but impossible not to do this. Students are graded as individuals, collaborative work is economically and institutionally discouraged within the humanities, and team-teaching of courses occurs infrequently.

In addition to certain illusions about institutional democracy, academics are further confronted with the intensification of anti-intellectual sentiment in U.S. society as a whole. The hegemony of corporate interests has insured that left academics have little access to so-called public debate, that most information used in such debates is supplied by reactionary think tanks, and that when we are represented, it is as elite "mind" workers. A case in point was a recent (and, as it turned out, successful) attempt to oppose the transfer of the only public television station in Pittsburgh that carries local and alternative programming from a noncommercial to a commercial license. When a coalition formed in protest of the transfer—a coalition that centrally included labor activists—our resident think tank (the Allegheny Institute for Public Policy, which is funded by the reactionary Scaife Foundation) sent a press release to all local media outlets, claiming that public television was valued only by "yuppie knowledge workers" who, "besandled by Birkenstock have shoe-horned into VW buses to come out in defense" of public television.

The size and strength of the forces arrayed against us should not be underestimated, since many academics have not only misunderstood this terrain, but, as Wacquant suggests, have resisted in ineffective ways. One left response to institutional constraints might be described as academic populism, in which we consider our role as educators as one of empowering our students as writers, readers, and thinkers. Reproducing the belief that the university is a democratic institution at the level of the classroom, students' individual voices are privileged and respected.

Although its intentions are sincere and frequently admirable, academic populism invariably encounters a number of contradictions. As Pierre Bourdieu observes, "Inspired by the need to rehabilitate, populism, which may also take the form of a certain relativism, tends, as one of its effects, to disguise the effects of domination," thereby forgetting that this is "a game in which the dominant determine at every moment the rules of the game" (1990, 153). The relativism that Bourdieu refers to relies on the concept of the marketplace of ideas, reinforcing a belief that students already bring with them: that everyone has a right to her own opinion. If we take as a rather modest pedagogical aim the attempt to engender critical thought, students must be disabused of their investment in such an illusion. Their "opinions" are frequently based on little information or critical analysis; consumerist practices aside, their opinions on politics and current events are strikingly homogeneous; and even if their opinions diverge from the norm, they need to realize that their individual opinions will not be valued in the wider sphere of U.S. society.[5] Rather than empowering students to express their opinions, it seems more important to give them information and skills that allow them to gather information from disparate sources, analyze it, and formulate informed evaluations, since critical thought involves understanding where "opinions" come from in the first place.[6]

Second, insofar as it cannot confront contradictions between the "democratic"
classroom and the undemocratic realities that surround that classroom, academic
populism disguises the effects of domination. Those who teach at more privileged
institutions might ask themselves what it means to legitimize the voices of students who already enjoy substantial privilege? Or to permit the textual "voices"
of certain African American, Latina, Native American, and working-class writers
to stand in for the actual presence of those groups in classrooms? The pluralism
and neutrality of the term "difference" leave untheorized issues of systematic
domination.

For less privileged students, the contradiction between the democratic classroom and a world in which they have never had any input into decision-making
processes can be immensely frustrating. Aside from the fact that most students
realize that their professors assign grades at the end of the semester, do we actually think that students who have direct experience of welfare bureaucracy,
unemployment, or incarceration in the United States actually buy into our illusions? Providing that our students actually get jobs that pay a living wage, what
kind of voice as individuals will they have in their workplaces? What kind of
voice, again as individuals, will they have in political processes? While the illusion of democracy and plurality in the classroom may be a comforting one, it
does not prepare students for understanding (much less fighting against) the less
than democratic realities of their futures. Furthermore, students who collectively
organize to promote democracy in universities are routinely subject to expulsion
(as in the case of a protest by Latino/a students at the University of Illinois five
years ago) and various other repressive measures (as in the case of the graduate
student strike at Yale in 1995).

Ultimately, the belief that we empower students as individual agents within
society evades the question as to why we educate students, and for what purpose
we educate them. The term "cultural worker," frequently used to describe the
telos of critical pedagogy, is symptomatic of this point. The notion of "cultural
workers" that proliferates in cultural studies implies an autonomy from the marketplace—a romanticized understanding of education that mystifies the relationship between "culture" and "society," and "cultural workers" versus wage
laborers, much as the rhetoric of the educational mission mystifies our own labor as
teachers. Frankly, I'm not sure what a cultural worker looks like. Does the term
refer to members of the ruling class, students such as those I taught as a graduate
student at Brown University, or students who learned ideological analyses and
semiotics so that they could go on to take up their positions as owners or managers

of the culture industry? Or does it refer to educating communications workers, who may go on to poorly paid, nonunionized jobs in the communications industry? The very phrase seems a strategy for avoiding these questions.

Despite its deep contradictions, academic populism expresses sympathy for students and often grapples with its own institutional privilege. In this respect, it is preferable to academic ultraleftism, which is characterized by its fashionable theoretical posturing, dense theoretical jargon, and a refusal to participate in building or organizing anything except a career. Wacquant notes that this position is endogenous to the intellectual milieu of the university itself: "it lies in the sickly self-absorption of the university microcosm, its closing onto itself, its palace wars (or muggings) and intestinal controversies whose sound and fury are matched only by their inconsequentiality—in all senses of the word" (21). Having taken note of the institutional context, declared its independence from that context, academic ultraleftism cultivates a sense of marginality—if not autonomy—from the institution, thereby seeking to deny the material conditions of production. The production of "cutting-edge" theory and critiques of cutting-edge theory is considered to be political intervention. Activism, on the part of either faculty or students, is routinely dismissed through a litany of the left's failures or a reification of theory and theoretical jargon, severed from any relationship to practice, not to mention historical context.

As a result of such practices, academic ultraleftism is extremely alienating. Insofar as it reinforces the already existing anti-organizational tendencies of the institution, it is also downright reactionary. Because academic ultraleftists seldom have contact with organized political struggles, they can maintain a level of ideological purity and dogmatic certainty whose very existence is based on its unaccountability. Rather than engaging with critiques and making persuasive arguments, academic ultraleftism merely reproduces pedagogical and academic authority, creating animosity and academic sectarianism.

The insularity and self-absorption of left academics also lead to a false inflation of the importance of our professional activities. Listening to some, one gets the sense that we are paid to "be political," and it is sadly true that academics often substitute professional for political activity—a substitution not very prevalent among other workers.[7] In part, academic ultraleftism is a response to the contemporary economic context of the U.S. academy and "is to be expected when the political space of academia's dissidents has shrunk to disputes over positions, grants, fellowships, journals, and other means of access to the cenacle that are diminishing as the rampant privatization of institutions of higher learning marches on" (Wacquant 1996, 21). For politically minded, ambitious academics, intensified competition for jobs and fellowships, and the quantity of publications that these both require have led to a speedup that may leave little time for political activism. Declaring that our work is activism allows us to maintain the illusion, at least, of political engagement.

This way of thinking about academic labor does not lead to the kind of politics it claims for itself. If one declares that academic labor—be it teaching, publishing, or some combination thereof—is in and of itself political, then there is no need for engaging in collective political struggle. The professional becomes the political, individualized practices and lifestyles become political practices (in the academy as well as U.S. society in general), and an often privileged group of workers can rest comfortably at night, well insulated from the painful, difficult realities of actual political struggle. In the case of postmodernism (which is a variation on academic ultraleftism), such conclusions also lead to the belief that we need not act in solidarity with oppressed peoples because they have taken matters into their own hands by engaging in acts of discursive resistance. Given postmodernism's moral prohibition against "representing" oppressed groups, such solidarity is itself represented as oppressive, or a ruse of authority.[8]

In part, the substitution of the professional for the political results from a confusion between ideology and politics. While knowledge and information are transmitted ideologically, knowledge is not in and of itself political, although its uses can be (how we act on the basis of the information we receive). This conflation leads us to grossly exaggerate the significance of what we do. As Ellen Meiksins Wood puts it, we have put "intellectual activity *in place of* class struggle" (1995, 10) and, as a result, misunderstand academics as world-historic agents, constructing universals from that flawed premise.

Nevertheless, as a student who was (and continues to be) inspired by those who taught me about what Angela Davis describes as "suppressed moments in history" (1992, 323), who taught me how to think critically and self-critically about the world around me, I do not want to overlook the fact that education can lead to political awakening. Some of these teachers were academics who acted in solidarity with workers at political organizations, picket lines, demonstrations, and rallies—whose political commitments were expressed modestly and materially through their actions, rather than through classroom monologues or through abstract theoretical arguments. I understand, in short, the ways we as educators can provide information, critical insight, and radical transformations at a micropolitical level.

But can we teach students to act on the information we give them within the context of the university classroom? Can the divide between theory and practice be bridged within the span of a three- or even four-month semester and in a single course? Let me pose this dilemma in another way. Last year, I taught a course on the rhetoric of agitation and control. It turned out to be one of those rare courses in which knowledge flowed out of and into the classroom. Students read about the Homestead Strike, the civil rights movement, the Black Panther Party, SDS, and the feminist movement, discussed what they had read with friends and family members, and brought their stories back into the classroom. Learning about the rich, problematic, often contradictory history of organized struggle against capitalism, racism, sexism, and homophobia, along with specific organizational strategies undertaken during these struggles, students began to think critically about the official histories and information they had received. They argued passionately, worked through conflicts, moved each other, and were deeply moved. At the same time, however, students felt as though they had nowhere to move, no movement to build or to join in building; thus they alternated between nostalgia and frustration. This sense, in large part, followed from the limits prescribed by the institutional setting itself. As individuals, teachers dare not lead their students into political struggles without incurring risks that might result in loss of employment. A classroom, moreover, is not a political organization and, given the uneven power relations inherent within it, cannot operate like one.

This point returns us to the premise with which this essay began: that capitalist education is organized and it has direction—it leads students toward their positions within the capitalist mode of production. One of the questions we as left academics must ask is, to what point are we leading students? For moving people without either organization (teaching them to act only as individuals) or direction (toward organized political struggle) leads nowhere. We can and should analyze the ideological elements of knowledge in the classroom, and students can and do become critical thinkers.[9] But for students to transform critical thinking into political action—to act on the information they receive—means moving beyond the immediate context of the institution and learning lessons that cannot be taught in a university classroom. We learn through collective struggle how best to fight against racism, sexism, and homophobia, and participating in such struggles leads to political transformation. The teacher/student division also becomes meaningless in the context of political struggle, for political education necessarily involves a continuous, collective process of learning, unlearning, and relearning certain lessons—a process in which we are all students operating with various levels of skills.

If our understanding of, and responses to, institutional constraints are inadequate, what can we do? In the first place, we can continue to organize to maintain what progressive policies remain on our campuses. We need to actively
defend and support affirmative action policies, support workers' rights to organize (including graduate students), and fight against the reactionary attack on
public institutions. But we cannot work effectively if we remain isolated on the
terrain of the university. If we speak out as "public intellectuals" only when our
own privileges, professional reputations, and workplaces are at stake, we should
expect little support from outside the academy. Our larger goal must be to dis-
mantle the very notion of an "academic" left and to break down the divide that
artificially separates us from other workers, to learn to speak not as individuals,
but as representatives of a broader struggle for a democratic society. This
requires that much of our training as academics be unlearned and that the anti-
intellectual bias so carefully cultivated by reactionaries must be demolished,
although not along the lines of the pro-intellectual bias of "public intellectuals."
For example, many of us must learn how to listen, to participate in meetings that
are counterintuitive to those trained to facilitate university classrooms, and to
understand the ways our education and our privilege often speak through us.

In the end, the overvaluation of academic work—or the notion that the professional and the political are somehow identical—may be nothing more than a
symptom of the current economic crisis as it plays out in the humanities and liberal arts. Previous, humanist understandings of what we do have been shattered;
what is emerging in their place is a form of functionalism that insists on "compe-
tence" and "professionalism," that emphasizes skills, job training, and retraining
for jobs that simply do not exist. This breakdown may provide unique opportunities for building solidarity, but unless we are rigorous in thinking about our
labor and its limits—unless we find collective ways of confronting the systematic, organized structures of oppression and acting on that knowledge—we will
be in no position to help build and participate in the struggles that are most certainly coming this way.

Notes

A number of people have contributed, both directly and indirectly, to my thinking about
this essay (although they will probably disagree with some of its points) and to my own,
continuing education. I am especially grateful to Anthony Arnove, Lisa Frank, Belden

Fields, Elisa Glick, Bill Keach, Deepa Kumar, Allen Larson, Dan McGee, Nagesh Rao, Matthew Reichek, Gretchen Soderlund, David Barry Rapkin, and Ashley Smith.

1. I use the term "academic" in the following essay to specify those intellectuals trained and employed by institutions of higher education.

2. Here I am describing the organization of public schooling in this country, not— notably—private schools catering to the ruling class.

3. It is important here to underline the fact that I am referring to left, or anticapitalist, political agency. As David Price's "Cold War Anthropology: Collaborators and Victims of the National Security State" (paper presented at the American Anthropological Association, November 1995) makes clear, reactionaries also possess—and can more powerfully deploy—political agency. See also Price's "Subtle Means and Enticing Carrots: The Role of Funding in Cold War Anthropology," in *The Cold War and the University*, vol. 2 (New York: New Press, forthcoming).

4. Anti-union sentiment was, of course, more complicated than this, although by and large it came down to issues of professionalism involving a qualitative distinction between our labor and that of "workers."

5. When confronted with the notion that "everyone has a right to her own opinion" (which is generally a way of opting out of an argument)—the belief that U.S. society is composed of a plurality of diverse perspectives—a friend of mine uses the following strategy. She lists a number of current issues or events, asks students to write down their opinions, collates the responses (generally received from the media), and then presents the strikingly homogeneous results to the class.

6. While students express a wide range of opinions on commodities, the range of opinions on political issues is strikingly homogeneous. Unless one's goal is to affirm their consumerist practices, this homogeneity needs to be considered.

7. Frequently, this substitution gives academics carte blanche to exploit and abuse other workers at their institutions (particularly, but not exclusively, secretaries). Because they are never required to practice their politics, some can hide behind a progressive veneer or ignore the contrast between what they teach or write and what they do. The ongoing labor struggles at Yale University are instructive here, since a number of academics who claimed progressive politics were forced to expose their actual class interests and collaboration with the administration when confronted with pickets.

8. For further critiques of this aspect of postmodernism, see the *Monthly Review*'s special issue on "The End of History" (July–August 1995), as well as Ellen Meiksins Wood, "Modernity, Postmodernity, or Capitalism?" *Monthly Review*, July–August 1996, 21–39.

9. I realize that the notion of "critical thinker" may be equally problematic, the problem being that students learn to think critically, but not to act on such criticism. Allen Larson perceptively describes this as "the pedagogy of the depressed."

WORKS CITED

Bourdieu, Pierre. 1990. *In Other Words: Essays towards a Reflexive Sociology*, trans. Matthew Adamson. Stanford: Stanford University Press.

Davis, Angela Y. 1992. "Black Nationalism: The Sixties and the Nineties." In *Black Popular Culture*, ed. Gina Dent. Seattle: Bay Press.

Diggins, John Patrick. 1996. "History Standards Get It Wrong Again." *New York Times*. 15 May, A15.

Kozol, Jonathan. 1991. *Savage Inequalities: Children in America's Schools*. New York: Harper Perennial.

Wacquant, Loic J. D. 1996. "The Self-Inflicted Irrelevance of American Academics." *Academe*, July–August, 18–23.

Wood, Ellen Meiksins. 1995. *Democracy against Capitalism*. London: Cambridge University Press.

Meanwhile, in the Hallways

15

Timothy Brennan

What is the chain of decision making — the "chain of command" if you will — between the academic department and the state legislature? It seems important to ask whether there are meaningful ways of seeing the department not as, metaphorically, a government but as its complement on a smaller scale. Can professors be said, for example, in some way to be performing the tasks first launched by university provosts, perhaps at the urging of a trustee who had been convinced at lunch of the merits of state assemblyman X's comments on the "need for accountability"? How do opinions in this arena metamorphose into policies, especially when there is so much prima facie evidence that those with the opinions in this case often distrust or fear the policy makers? Is the process one that deserves to be characterized by the somewhat self-congratulatory word "negotiation," which alludes to a layered series of exchanges of opinion through trade journals, intra-university memos, off-the-cuff talk in university hallways, and so on? Or is it only a matter of state legislatures choking off the flow of money, and thereby leaving those in the lower echelons to improvise their conformity after the fact? Is it, in other words, a reliving of the Westmoreland thesis: "grab them by the [throat] and the hearts and minds will follow"?

COLLEGIALITY

Let me begin with an actual quotation from a recent memo from my department's graduate committee: "Unfortunately, we cannot accept your proposal for a cultural studies core course in English. The course's relationship to literature is unclear. . . . In addition, the committee found an unusually strong ideological commitment to social constructionism, which is questionable in academic work."

This sort of response—one that blithely discards over three decades of debate over the honorable ambiguity of the term "literature," and ideologically outlaws ideology—is a fairly typical sign of the three-front war against cultural studies today.[1] What interests me is the conflictual, ideologically mixed nature of the assault, especially as it passes through the intangible acts of people whose conduct is perceived as unrelated, even hostile, to the policies of their extramural superiors whose subjects they often consider themselves to be. I am referring here not to actual organizations such as the National Association of Scholars or Teachers for a Democratic Culture that have sought to influence governmental policy through petitions or editorial campaigns, but rather to that sizable group of unaffiliated individuals who see their work as operating in the smaller and more interpersonal spaces of their own departments.

The various groups arrayed against cultural studies at present might be characterized, I am suggesting, by more than the "traditionalist" sentiments found in the above quotation. The first group is a vigorous (even hysterical) majority reasserting a 1950s and 1960s understanding of literature as though criticism from, say, Lukács or Barthes to Habermas or Deleuze had simply never been written or discussed. But the second group takes the exact opposite position; this group consists of cultural studies advocates seeking an easy cathexis of continental modernist and postmodernist theory onto the collective institutional critiques of an earlier era. Finally there is a smaller and sterner group of the disillusioned, who declare a plague on both their houses, deliberately allowing cultural studies to dissipate as a university-based option in recognition of its political soullessness. Notice, then, that what conspires against cultural studies as an academic practice is a vector of incompatible positions whose focused energies converge on their target for the simple reason that the *place* of their operations is an institution whose very reason for being defies the goals cultural studies sets for itself.

My interest, then, is to explain in what sense the American academy is such a place, and to do so by looking at some of the ways an academic department functions. I look at cultural studies as I have known it—as a professor still invested in traditional literary study who has acted as a consultant on the formation of cultural studies programs at Purdue University, the University of Michigan, Wesleyan, and more recently, as part of a working group at Stony Brook made up of representatives from eight departments in the humanities and social sciences. This experience, along with my research in non-Western literatures, has given me a different sense of cultural studies' origins than the one I am accustomed to reading, so I would like also to give a somewhat schematic account of that alternative genealogy in the essay's second section.

The story of my school, first of all, is an interesting one. Part research university and part community college, looking upwards and downwards in equal measure, exposed to the blasts of state budget cuts with no windbreak of alumni cash, and yet gauging itself by the standards of the nation's top schools with a faculty scrambling (and largely getting) the highbrow fellowships, honoraria, and big-name publishing contracts of the endowed institutions whose degrees decorate their names in the school bulletin. One of four "flagship" universities in the New York state system, a brainchild of the Republican governor Nelson Rockefeller during more opulent times, but for all that a state system of the East not the West Coast, and so a public system that could never be the first choice of the best students in a region where the Ivy League, the finishing schools, and the opulent private colleges are spread out across the land. It is, moreover, a deeply integrated school—about 40 percent minority—drawing its Caribbean, Latino, Asian, and white ethnic students from New York's outer boroughs as well as from non-shore Long Island.

In this world of schizophrenic longing and ressentiment, various internal memos and academic plans witness an exhausted return to the judgment that here we cannot afford to be "theoretical," but have to confine ourselves to basic training for the undereducated. There are naturally many currents counter to this view (which in any case is rarely stated so bluntly), but the common argument is that the study of media, music, and design in English classrooms gives little more than uncritical support to the unchecked advance of secondary orality. We are the pale; besides us, what line of defense lies between our students and commercial television? In the inside/outside dichotomy, curricular conservatives score the first points by identifying the "cultural studies" types as proponents of a cultural laissez-faire so beloved of Republican administrators and neoliberal champions of America's global cultural appeal. The cultural studies professors can only protest the brutal equation between their deviating from an exclusive focus on literature and the flight from studying literature altogether, which is not their point; rather, they must see their own work as an attempt to give students a chance of reading literature better armed. I recognize, of course, that attacks on cultural studies have probably been more decisive and influential outside the university than within it—attacks waged by media and think-tank intellectuals and later picked up by legislators who for a variety of reasons wish to limit (or even end) funding to higher education. But since that particular problem has been more thoroughly dealt with elsewhere, I am not going to return to it here except glancingly.[2]

The social function assigned to universities by government, in a necessarily distant understanding of the universities' role in the practical training and conditioning of a workforce, seems not to be consciously shared by local faculties who nevertheless carry these objectives out. And yet, by an inefficient series of mediations—a system of enticements, hints, punishments, and leads—individuals grope uncertainly toward the areas of approval that emanate at great remove from the distributors of funds. What one soon recognizes is that this area of approval—at least as it concerns the humanities—arrives as a negation. As such, we are positioned in what I will argue below is cultural studies' imperial link. "Culture" must be doubly circumscribed, first as an artifact of genius, second as the product of a European or American legacy. Although there are dozens of arguments used in the process of defunding and delegitimating the humanities, this is the one nonnegotiable demand. It is, moreover, a negative one in that it tells us what culture is not or must not be taken to be—popular, but also (in the inevitable racial coding of late twentieth-century America) non-Western or third world. Although mentioned by other analysts of the P.C. wars, for example, this credo, I would argue, is the one thing that links "mainstream" faculty members with the untrained, unspecialized, and largely philistine members of state legislatures. And it is perhaps the only thing.

The way these confluences function, at any rate, would seem to have little explicitly to do with government alliances. A familiar right-wing assault on the fiction of an overpoliticized classroom has nevertheless overlapped with a left populist critique of cultural studies. This remarkable alliance is due to a peculiar transposition that has taken place between customary ways of seeing the state and the market. Recent events (the Sokal affair, for example) suggest that this alliance has primarily been the result of a set of misconceptions about the stakes of "representation" as they have concerned scholars in the humanities and social sciences over the last few decades. The dismissal of those stakes has been made easier, of course, by the susceptibility to parody of the notoriously overrefined, demanding, at times intentionally ludic writing of French postwar philosophy, and the misconceptions bring right and left journalists and activists together in the inaccurate declaration that cultural studies simply is this theory. And here, then, is where I would like to give a different account of cultural studies' origins.

ETHNOGRAPHIC STUDIES OF METROPOLITAN LIFE

What Clifford Geertz very early called the "sudden vogue of a grande idee"—culture—had really been the concept "around which the whole discipline of anthropology arose." All the concretizations and claims to immense and previously underanalyzed relevance of what Clyde Kluckhohn referred to as "a way of thinking, feeling, and believing"—all the magical importance, in other words, associated with the concept in the work of Raymond Williams, Gramsci, and others in the cultural studies fold—had been centrally theorized as a matter of course within anthropology for at least a century.[3] In one sense, then, cultural studies is a guilty reflex of anthropology, or rather a response to changes within anthropology brought on by the two-way impact of Europe's intercourse with the rest of the world while setting up a global system of colonies, financial arrangements, product lines, and immigration bridges. Cultural studies is fundamentally a reaction to the consequences of modernity—but modernity seen specifically as an imperial creation. It inverts the ethnographic field of vision, turning its magnifying glass on metropolitan subjects. It does so, moreover, without irony and in a systematic, "scientific" way rather than as satire—which is what separates it, for example, from well-known early modern instances of cultural distancing and self-parody like Montesquieu's Persian Letters, Voltaire's *Candide*, or for that matter, Apuleius's *Golden Ass*. An imperfect but workable (and short) description of cultural studies might be simply ethnographic studies of metropolitan life.

If one were to chart the MLA job lists, conference agendas, and special issue topics of journals over the last decade, they would all point to the parallel rise of two fields—on the one hand, and originally, "race," "non-Western" literatures, "ethnic otherness," "postcoloniality," and so on as new objects of knowledge (which in its present phase can be traced most directly to the Black power and third-worldist writings of the 1960s); and then, with gathering assurance, and as a purportedly new methodology, cultural studies. Oddly, the dramatic links between the two trends have not been given much attention, in part because of the endemic paternalism that exists toward the potentials of non-Western theory (by which I do not mean the theoretically informed work of minority academics within the academy), and also by corollary, as a result of the misconceptions surrounding the real origins and visions of cultural studies' European forerunners (roughly between the 1880s and the 1960s). Whatever else, cultural studies — like the colonialism that prompted it — is about the meeting of alien forces. It arises when it does because of the social developments that forced together disparate traditions of thought among various national intelligentsias — first in Europe, but then increasingly as a result of the fertile exchanges and conferencings of the Third International and the explosive period of decolonization, as a two-way discussion among first and third world intellectuals. It was an intellectual act of factoring in the volatile juxtapositions of style and attitude that colonialism created — a factoring that explains the innovative, cross-disciplinary writing of Herbert Spencer, Oswald Spengler, and Freud as much as it does, say, Trotsky in his reflections on Soviet drinking habits and movie-going, or the romantically antibourgeois work of the European avant-gardes.

The systematic alienation of its innovators — from Paul LaFargue, Tristan Tzara, Alexandra Kollontai, and Freud through Du Bois, Gramsci, and Raymond Williams — could be expressed forcefully (if a bit peremptorily) as their being Jewish, Sardinian, African, socialist, Welsh, female, proletarian, gay, but always foreign. One thinks immediately of class as race, and of art as commercial ruse, in the colonial or imperial motifs of these European intellectuals and artists — Tzara's African nonsense poems; Freud's grand "unified field" theory of phylogeny as tribal dream and primitive childhood; Bolshevik cultural theory as outgrowth of the crucial Baku "meeting of the peoples" in Soviet Asia; Trotsky's third-worldist theory of permanent revolution; Gramsci's well-known comparisons of Italy's South with the greater global "South" under Europe's sway. One sought new ways of explaining culture's provenance and modes of replication precisely because it had become in a new way opaque and troublesome. "Culture" became a problem because Europe had begun to seem strange to itself.

At the same time, the "dialogue" between first and third world intellectuals contributed to cultural studies from the other side. The experience of global dependency provided many "marginal" intellectuals (living, at least partly, outside Europe) with the framework to create and develop what we now identify as new. It did this in at least two clear ways: first, in the incessant and practical manner in which the experience of dependency illustrates how all culture is, apart from being a "way of life," also a matter of public policy; and, second, in its ability to illustrate the consequences of the ethnographic paradigm. Amilcar Cabral, for example, had said that "culture is . . . a determinant of history." Perhaps the alien world this declaration emanates from—and more to the point, places us abruptly within—cannot be appreciated in so small and fleeting a sampling of his writing. For implicit in its terse phrasing was a set of corollaries: cultural value had to be gauged by its "resistance to foreign domination"; the cultural manifestations that arose in the course of wars of liberation were always "an act of denial of the culture of the oppressor"; the political and economic domination of a people required that imperialism destroy the cultural personality of those it would domesticate. Ethnography, as we are now accustomed to remarking, ambiguously sought to preserve what was being destroyed, even while domesticating it.

In a rather different sense, the question of cultural policy is a privileged one in third world societies simply because the states are often newly formed or relatively naked in the way they exercise power, or simply imported from outside—conditions that conspire to create very fragile hegemonies. In the case of popular regimes, the government often bared its strategies to the scrutiny of its own intelligentsias and by doing so allowed Western intellectuals to study and comment on them from afar. At the same time, these states, starting from scratch and having a much clearer conception of what they rejected than what they embraced, set out on a process of eclectic study of external cultural models, thereby posing generally and across the society as a whole questions that brought those without power into the problems of cultural debate. All of this was quite different from metropolitan Europe or the United States, and the glance cast by intellectuals within those regions toward the fragile polities elsewhere provided insights from which we now benefit. In spite of the justifiable shift more recently to postnational frameworks and globalization, which would seem to consign these problematics to the past, recovering these modes of commerce is vital to any historical reconstruction of cultural studies as a field that lives on.

It is almost never noticed, for instance, that Gramsci's cultural writings had been translated into Spanish and had become a part of standard Latin American intellectual discourse well before they had in the United States or Britain. For objective reasons, and as peoples caught "in between" a domestic sensibility on the one hand and the violence of ethnographic inquiry on the other, writers in the third world had understandably faced the call of cultural studies at an early date, nourished as they were also by first world theorizations. In this spirit the former president of Mozambique, the late Samora Machel, wrote,

> The coloniser recognised the patriotic, liberating and revolutionary force of popular culture. Its objective was to make popular culture folkloric and exotic, without intellectual value, the symbol of an inferior culture. . . . In the recent history of Africa, the itinerary of the Francophone community shows us how, behind the seductive image of an apparently inoffensive and even generous cultural instrument, French troops and mercenaries disembark.[4]

This admittedly polemical formulation, which would undoubtedly have to be qualified in important ways in the less rallying essays of the ethnographers, nevertheless hints at a possible transposition to metropolitan debates over the stakes of "mass culture" in evening out and communalizing disparate peoples on the national terrains of Europe and North America, kept in check, of course, by immigration legislation and the thin blue line. The problematic idea of "culture" with which we began this section—as an opaque rather than a transparent thing, as what Freud noticed in his writings on parapraxes contained all that was most important to our questionings, but which we did not question—continually faced a process of reinsertion into stable, European forms of meaning, here subsumed under the category "mass [that is, American mass] culture." As implied by the above, we should notice, then, that "culture" figures in the still emergent field not only in multivalent but also in self-contradictory ways:

1. In one sense, the concept signals a democratic urge to break out of the impasse of the "arts" in an older aristocratic or bourgeois sense by bringing study more in line with, on the one hand, social movements for the representation of marginal groups, and on the other (and this is the conundrum of the mass-culture debate), a popularity often targeted by aesthetic modernism—namely, the popularity of the market.
2. Next, it is a response to the leads provided by the objectification of foreign cultures (their sheer variability) in anthropology, itself a discipline bearing the fruits of capitalist expansion abroad.
3. Finally, given the very tensions between its conflicting bases in minority expression and the market, it signals the situatedness of the researchers

themselves within artistic intelligentsias—the desire to *be* politically and socially engaged without having to leave the realm of an albeit modified aesthetic and intellectual culture: to be political *in* the study.

The difficulty in accounting for the obstacles to an American cultural studies rests in the inability to sort out the massively conflicting interests represented by this transition, in which bohemian or modernist disgust with bourgeois art is confused with socialist strategies for a "new vision," and where populist educational strategies are jumbled together with utilitarian schemes of basic "training." One reason it is so difficult to see cultural studies' origins, then, is the mutual confusion of conflicting constituencies. The reasons cultural studies cannot be said to have started in the Frankfurt School or in the Center for Contemporary Cultural Studies at Birmingham (as others have pointed out) is not simply that prior cases can historically be found. It is rather that it cannot be based in any one institutional site. Cultural studies is not only a disciplinary invention of an institute or individual, but a recurring intellectual hunger, a deviant orientation, that becomes sensible in historically transformative moments. Like Ishmael Reed's "Jes Grew," it keeps arising at moments of hegemonic fissure.[5]

To understand what makes cultural studies worth doing, then, one has to locate those moments of hegemonic fissure—in the United States, those conjunctures that played the role here that adult education did in Britain, that media policy think tanks did in Allende's Chile, or that women's cultural groups did in the Soviet Union with their popularization of "*byt*" (everyday life) as a political category.[6] The lessons of Birmingham caught on over here for many of the same reasons that studies of imperialism (née postcoloniality) did: as a counter-counterreformation in the dreary days of Reaganism. Thus, as grad students in the early 1980s, many of us (perhaps typically) began working our way through the CCCS working papers. They struck us as exciting, but not new really. Utterly modern and malleable, but not localizable nor infinitely extendable, cultural studies is, or ought to be, the name applied to any inquiry freed from the radical division of intellectual labor as a protest against technocratic specialization. It was not, in other words, the organic intellectual grandeur of Goethe—art historian, botanist, architect, and playwright—but the urge, against the stream, to reassert totality in the face of political and economic pressures to view generalist knowledge with suspicion—to make this generalism an act of social critique available to all. In Europe and the United States, a variety of hegemonic fissures surrounding religious belief, world culture, militarism, sexuality, and citizenship—in the context of emergent nationhood and the bid of national cultures to play leading roles on the world stage—produced a variety of intellectual developments that logically fed cultural studies at a later date. Among these, one would look to neo-Hegelian "*Kritik*," *Geisteswissenschaften*, Spencerian biologism, Veblen's and others' "American character" studies, Dada, Freud's work on parapraxis, and the work of historians and sociologists like C. Wright Mills, Daniel Bell, Barbara Ehrenreich, William Appleman Williams, Christopher Lasch, and Jessica Mitford. These, on the other hand, did not just represent disciplinary innovations. As the above suggests, they were about race, about mutually strange lifestyles mashed together, about what Ortega y Gasset from his elite modernist perch called "the revolt of the masses"—that is, the bringing in to cultural debate and taste formation laborers and commoners, now wed to the middle classes in the role of consumers. Current cultural studies has a foreshortened understanding of its historical origins.

What, after all, *made* Birmingham? Much of the talk in the United States by British exiles about the famous jousting with *Screen* in 1960s and 1970s Britain gives a poor picture of what was at stake. Birmingham's most active years occurred during a period of epochal transition in the Labor Party, when a left faction saw the party's complicity in anti-immigrant legislation, and the Asian and Afro-Caribbean communities had become too populous to ignore. For the first time, they were beginning to have success in forging internal alliances, electing representatives to Parliament, and representing themselves positively in the media as British subjects. It is no coincidence in that sense that the most prominent, and surely the most successful, writing of the center dealt with race: *Resistance through Rituals*, *The Empire Strikes Back*, and above all, *Policing the Crisis*, which is to cultural studies in its Anglo-American form roughly what *Capital* is to organized Marxism. To shift to the case of Germany, one had the fertile groundwork of Weimar culture, whose communist and social democratic agencies at all levels of public art and popular journalism had fed upwards into traditional high-cultural venues, making an institute of the Frankfurt type seem natural and even overdue. The Frankfurt School would not have existed without the organized socialist infrastructure of Weimar Germany.

In the United States of the 1980s, by contrast, left intellectuals fled into the university as a last and weak refuge during a period of corporate resurgence and imperial self-affirmation. The current problem of cultural studies consequently is its articulation as a memory of better times in distinct locales, wielding a set of verbal and imagistic weapons that are quite incapable of performing the tasks it sets itself, and so understandably it ends up overestimating the power of those weapons while weakly imitating what it pretends to emulate. With no movement in the general culture, its practitioners cannot distinguish between the market sense of popularity outlined above and a rather different utopian longing for a new consciousness, collective, wholistic, and opposed to empire. Much of the commentary on cultural studies, however, is unable to distinguish between retreat and advance, between co-optation and assertion. The inability, one could say, is what postmodernism is all about.

Horkheimer and Adorno, after all, coined the term "culture industry" as two men escaped from Nazi Germany, who found replicated in the liberal West many of the same cultural strategies familiar to them abroad in more incipient forms. As an inversion of earlier alien reckonings with "America"—the combination of self-flattery and inferiority complex that placed the diagnoses of Alexis de Tocqueville, the Viscount Bryce, and later, other foreigners in such high regard (in our circles, the literary critics Sacvan Bercovitch and Werner Sollers, for example; or the long string of other commentators on America from Baudrillard to Andrei Codrescu)—Frankfurt's gestures of suspicion, its naked exposé of America outside its myth, was the sort of abrasive social critique originally found in the field now called "cultural studies." It took another layer of outsider reflections, from France and England particularly, to mute these cries, and to give back to cultural studies a modus operandi that stopped short of holding America up as a laboratory specimen. That is, the drift of horror and depression in Leo Lowenthal's studies of American religious radio demagogues, for example, or Adorno's bemused wanderings through the irrationalist media entertainments of the U.S. daily press, and so on—all of these became more or less predictable and comforting by later waves of Continental, and Continentally inspired English, commentators—who like the Frankfurt writers were residents on American soil. Only now they worked under conditions of celebration and relaxation at California institutes and Ivy League research facilities without the shock of mass protest to temper their gloom and give "materialism" its good name back.

The American road of cultural studies, one might say, has been a wending away from the sociological "hardness" of Frankfurt's accusatory nonconformism toward a reading of the cultural text—a subversion, as it were, of the scientistic intentions of literary theory. This incongruity that moves simultaneously toward and away from relevance is the conundrum of cultural studies in its American form. An eagerness to conflate literary theory as such with the cultural studies legacies of Third International Europe and Latin America, or the memorable postwar outbursts of the Bandung intellectuals, dovetailed too easily with the

comforting illusion of a 1980s substitute radicalism. Combined with the customary and embarrassing American diffidence toward Europe, this conflation was
given fuel by the central figure of the United States itself as imperial center, factory of a global mass culture (playing much the role that Machel identified in
France), and major employer for celebrated European and third world academics.
The leads of the interwar Third International and the creative outbursts of the
Bandung generation were swept away, and with them the history that explains
why Frankfurt and Birmingham were so vital, and why U.S. cultural studies is
for the most part so unsatisfying.

REVENGE OF THE NERDS

Given the three mutually antagonistic constituencies arrayed against cultural
studies as described above, we find again an unexpected confluence of positions.
The conservative complaint is not entirely wrong, after all. In the muscular
reassertion by wings of English faculty for a return to standards—often by precisely that wing that has ceased to be active professionally, or has stopped
attending conferences, and who publishes very little—we find echoed a charge
typically found in the popular press, namely, that cultural studies is the market,
and its representatives a fifth column for an offensive democracy of taste so
loathed by modernists from the time of Flaubert onwards. In other words (in this
view), it is they, not the traditionalists, who are the natural allies of state legislatures, in a more general trend toward the privatization of the public sector. In
that sense, the neotraditionalists see themselves as the no-nonsense workers in
the academic trenches teaching skills while the cultural studies advocates are a
frivolous bourgeoisie jet-setting aimlessly, leaving their colleagues behind to do
the thankless jobs. While accurate at the upper reaches of salary in the best
schools, the charge is also insincere—a transparency from *New York Times Magazine* features overlaid on the struggling and the underpaid either to silence the
vocal or to heroize inactivity.

English departments in this country are largely filled with hardworking, concerned, and poorly paid professionals, who at great cost to themselves—whatever their views on "tradition"—struggle to make a place for thinking about,
evaluating, and learning from the past. There is something heroic about their
work, regardless of the wars that separate their factions—wars amplified by a
public condescension toward intellectuals generally and the hysterical pressures

of shrinking job markets and legislative defunding maneuvers. But while giving that reality its due, we should acknowledge the culture wars have also produced their own morbid symptom, discussed forcefully in the hallways, but rarely set down in print. A colleague once called it the "revenge of the nerds"—the anger of once prominent professors resentful of the market-driven notoriety of cultural studies celebrities doubling as teachers and sought-after personalities at various humanities institutes.

From two political poles, and with very different motives they join voices (in another confusion of categories) with left journalists to insist that intellectuals speak to the public directly about their immediate needs: a worthy goal with immense populist appeal, but one without any space granted to debates about how needs are met, how apparently distant or abstract inquiries condition material life, or how the production of knowledge—although one cannot see or eat it—dictates outcomes. Leaving alone that "needs" are differently defined here, the charge too easily becomes a way of defending academic life as a rather grim and straightforward set of duties, trudging to class with one's Norton anthologies in the belief that one can explain literature's meanings as Muhammad recited God's word. It is all right to set one's students to interpreting, just not to ask what doing so means. Defending "traditions" becomes a strategy for laziness. They experience no fundamental disciplinary doubt, self-questioning, redefinition, or exploration, and mediocrity is dressed up in the costume of sober "judgments" about the limitations of their students, the reality of underfunded state universities, and the enduring value of "solid" canonical instruction. As others have pointed out, the canon is filled with men and women who, in their own times, stretched boundaries, challenged authorities, and expanded the realm of what it was possible to imagine. Swift, Perkins Gilman, Blake, Naylor, Whitman, Twain, Charlotte Mews, Du Bois—all stood for exactly the kind of skeptical, even hostile, position toward the pieties of "Western Civilization" now captured by the canonical reformers ridiculed in the name of the canon.

On the other hand, complaints against cultural studies by traditionalist professors who speak of ill-training and diletantism are pointing to a real fault—although they do not offer clear alternatives. Many of the graduate students most eager to pursue cultural studies are those who read their Freud through Lacan, read back from Eagleton to Marx after the fact in a time-saving operation, and discover Nietzsche by way of Foucault's writing on the body; who may not even have read the originals very well or very thoroughly, and whose knowledge of Weimar, of Bandung, of 1848, and of Suez is as thin as a footnote in Ernesto

Laclau; and whose sense of the sheer repetitiveness by pomo theory of the views
elaborated in Spengler, Worringer, Veblen, Kollontai, and C. Wright Mills is as
evanescent as the specters of Derrida. Among graduate students, what intimacy
is there, really, with the republic of letters as it once existed in every journal and
daily as late as the 1970s, elaborating so carefully as it did on Joycean punning,
Shakespearean biography, and the "avant-garde" it took to be John Updike's
novels of New England disenchantment? And if very little, then what kind of
revolt can there be against a bastion they suppose to be silly, ancient, and
already crumbling, rather than merely lying fallow behind a concealed bulwark
with a sense of its own powers of longevity? What helps to silence cultural studies is the simple ignorance of the very trainings cultural studies professors
sought to supersede—an ignorance of the very knowledge that gives the supers-
ession meaning—and to find in return a doubtful look of impatience before the
flight to faculty who will give them what they came already wanting. Along with
overwrought graduate committees suspicious of newfangled notions of dubious
provenance, a graduate consensus from below also forms curricula. By its actions
it votes, and the pressures of that voting can be tangible.

To know what cultural studies faces is to look not only at the level of the state
legislatures and high-profile purging, but the silencing anxieties, the deliberately
floated rumors, and the stealthy alliances of the hallways. One of the acts that faculties find it hardest to forgive is uncollegiality. If not for the code of silence
entailed by that decorum, we would all have a more candid set of analyses of the
warfare that drives the internal life of academic departments, harms careers, sours
the life of the mind, and intoxicates teachers for hours when speaking off the
record. Nothing is more striking, in fact, than the disparity between the sheer
number of hours dedicated to maneuvering behind the scenes (or sizing up the
maneuvers of others) and the relative absence of studies of the mechanics of such
warfare in published articles on pedagogy, curriculum, and high-sounding matters like "professionalism." Given their pestilential bigotries, colossal paranoias,
decades-long harboring of grudges, and the collapse of the inquisitive mind, perhaps only nursing homes are unhappier places than some English departments.
Cultural studies appears to be both a natural bone of contention within the battles
themselves and the subdiscipline best suited for conducting the candid analyses.

And yet one wants to ask whether the future of cultural studies should be
taken up with pressing that agenda. The signal failing of the academic is propor-
tion, and if cultural studies made analyses of the "lived but unlearned" possible—if it threw the words "ritual," "dogma," and "superstition" back in the

face of the denizens of shopping malls—it also gave the contemplative professions a believable lie called the politics of culture. I close, then, with a contrast.
Rose Sanders is a civil rights lawyer in Georgia who is trying hard to get people
to bear witness to the anti-Black campaign of torching Southern Black churches.
Her message is that a crisis like these lapping flames and night-riding memories
palls before the permanent crisis of the "atrocities in our schools" where children are taught to devalue Black life. The "violence against young Black
minds"—that is where she argues the focus should be. I think of this, and think
how much more needs to be said about it, and how much more it needs to be
said. And then I think of the schools I know where this atrocity is palely mimic-
ked by professors who call the inquiries of our affirmative action office "silly" in
open memos to the department, and who in departmental meetings humor the
assembled by referring to our students as being capable of little more than a
vocational training in "typing."

Intellectually, the question is to *alienate*—to make strange this culture so that
other cultures can be seen; to preserve the right to critique culture without aes-
theticizing it. These are the essential characteristics of the cultural studies lineage,
I have been arguing. But it is not at all clear that the setting up of cultural studies
programs aids this effort. We should be thinking instead, perhaps, of campaigns
for revising the curricula of high school textbooks; for defending those earlier
revisions now under brutal attack; for the concept of one big school system—a
national public system, free and compulsory through the college level—and for
which no private or vocational schools could substitute; for a national union of
professors that would put an end to conspiratorial salary caps, the weakening of
academic freedom, and the adjunct system. Involvement in those efforts would
clarify and enrich whatever more archival, aesthetic, or more modestly critical
research we did on film, music, or the republic of letters. And that is the sort of
thing cultural studies should not so much turn to, as come back to.

NOTES

1. The course in question (not my own, it should be said) was customary cultural studies
   fare, roving from film theory to semiotics, and including the more traditional literary
   criticism of figures like Bakhtin and Raymond Williams.
2. See, for example, Ellen Messer-Davidow, Paul Berman, and Michael Bérubé.

3. Clifford Geertz, "Thick Description: Toward an Interpretive Theory of Culture," in *The Interpretation of Cultures* (New York: Basic Books, 1973), 4–5.
4. Samora Machel, "E no processo da luta que forjamos a nossa ideologia," *Tempo* (Maputo), Sept. 1978. Reprinted in *Communication and Class Struggle*, ed. Armand Mattelart and Seth Siegelaub, vol. 2 (New York: International General, 1983), 25.
5. It is, for one thing, what I remember myself and others doing as undergraduates at Madison in the mid-1970s. In our English courses (or for feature articles in the *Daily Cardinal*), we participated in collective projects on the lyrics of country Western music, Firesign Theatre's L.A.-based radio art, and the cultural work of Blacks in the Communist Party. These efforts were not unusual.
6. See Wendy Goldman, "Women's Cultural Work in the Soviet Union" (talk delivered at the Institute for Culture and Society, Carnegie-Mellon University, June 1995); Katerina Clark, *Petersburg: Crucible of Cultural Revolution* (Cambridge: Harvard University Press, 1995), 21–23, 242–43.

Posttheory, Cultural Studies, and the Classroom

Fragments of a New Pedagogical Discourse

16

Jeffrey R. Di Leo and Christian Moraru

It seems to us that the emerging critical and pedagogical voices have reached an unprecedented state of professional self-awareness. One is witnessing, as we argue, the abrupt rise of the profession as an object of critical scrutiny in its own right: we read it as a literary or cultural phenomenon. Moreover, it is our privileged text. We read the way or ways we read and teach, seeking, much more specifically than in the past, to comprehend and take full advantage of the interplay of classroom and sociocultural practices. We are increasingly interested in how the teaching-learning complex hinges as much as bears on its context. At the same time, we have noticed that a similar interest has been played out in a variety of arenas in the wake of the cultural studies movement. They range from specialized publications such as *Profession* or *Lingua Franca* to individual works—either established but reread with a renewed passion, like Paulo Freire's, or more recent, like Spivak's and Giroux's—to exchanges in more popular and "accessible" publications. Granted, these interventions were staking out a timely critique of pedagogical structures in place; yet it is also clear to us that most of them were at the same time symptoms of a crisis of which they seemed to be less aware. Suggesting several possibilities of addressing the teaching spin-off of this critical moment, which is definitely part and parcel of the late "crisis in cultural studies," constitutes the main scope of the new pedagogical self-reflexivity we advocate. As Paul Smith insists in his "Questioning Cultural Studies" interview in the *minnesota review* a couple of years ago, one form cultural studies has taken lately has been the "critique of particular disciplinary productions of knowledge and therefore of the institutions which produce these knowledges, in such a way that some of the divisions between disciplines, between knowledge and politics, between professors and students, between the university and what people call the public sphere, could get reconvened or rethought." It strikes us that this critique and the cultural critique project in general must be retooled in view of the specific classroom accomplishments to date.

The mode of interrogation whose urgency we are pointing out actually deepens the social and political concern at work in the cultural studies project. Apparently, a new generation of critics and teachers is willing to take this job: Jeffrey Williams has called it the "posttheory" generation. It sets out to carry through a more in-depth analysis of the profession as *text* unfolding within specific contexts and locales in the hope of identifying the interpretive and educational means liable to link up credibly the textual and the contextual. In exploring the former, it aims at being an active part in the articulation of the latter. The stakes of this analysis are ostensibly high, as the direction of the academy is contingent on the outcome of this process of self-comprehension and self-criticism. This process is important as it should empower us, for example, to meet the attacks coming from less progressive quarters both inside and outside the academy.

Overall, we find it reassuring that the reflection about classroom practices and the university in general as a textual domain *sui generis* has not just haunted one particular grouping of critics, but rather seems to be a matter of larger concern. However, as of now, only a few critics and teachers have employed theory in an adequate way to read the current position of the university and their own positioning within pedagogical practices and discourses. We might identify this new way of "doing" theory as pragmatic or instrumental: the posttheory critics normally attempt at "doing things" with theory instead of doing theory per se. It would be probably fair to say that the "posttheory" generation's secret dream is to make theory work in traditionally nontheoretical spheres and on nontheoretical concerns. One might view Michael Bérubé's poignant anatomy of cultural politics in *Public Access* as an exemplary work in the area—a work also aiming at doing away with the theoretical self-sufficiency and jargon that have already alienated various audiences. In brief, the generation now in the process of gaining a distinctive voice works to open up a space of aesthetic transcendence and intervention, and to set up a dialogue between spheres that other critical and pedagogical discourses have tended to keep apart.

To be sure, this "metaprofessional" discourse emerges in the wake of the cultural studies model dominating the critical arena since the late eighties. One might view this newer discourse as a spin-off of the culture theories that challenged and ultimately displaced the formalist paradigms of the seventies and early eighties. What we are facing right now may mark a turn from cultural studies—whose "crisis," again, quite a few voices have already pronounced—to theories of the "academic condition." Of course, one could still argue that the increasing focus on, and exercise in, metaprofessional discourse includes a refashioning of the cultural studies agenda wherein the profession itself becomes a priority of critical attention. As we contend, though, we are facing a paradigm shift that will entail a substantial revision of most of the working assumptions of cultural studies. It is our job in the years to come, we think, to think through this change in direction for at least two reasons.

First, the impetus for this reconfiguration lies in the fact, in the wake of cultural studies, both academic and nonacademic institutions have in the last ten years or so increased the pressure on scholars and teachers to rejustify their work. Second, we found some of the less scrutinized assumptions of cultural studies problematic from a pedagogical point of view. While formalism-inspired pedagogies underemphasized the material identity of the learning subject, cultural teaching was not completely successful at setting the stage for an effective exchange among the plethora of subjects that have suddenly shown up in classrooms. This is why the latter still have to become an "intercultural epiphany," the site of a true "cross-cultural translation," to use James Clifford's words. Creating this site might very well be one of the posttheory generation's main challenges.

Generally speaking, the posttheorists appear to be more willing and ready to use theory than the cultural studies scholars. Posttheorists are seeking less to work out new theoretical models or to expand the ones already in place than to employ preexisting theory to position their work both "on" and "off" campus. More to the point, posttheorists strive to renegotiate the mutual articulation of the two domains. They may be moving toward a new eclecticism in that they often resort to anything that suits the purpose at hand. Again, theirs is a pragmatic approach to theory, which enables them to assess various theoretical models on the basis of the sociocultural and political insights that these models bring about.

Nevertheless, we want to emphasize that the posttheory option by no means involves an *antitheoretical* position. We believe that the traditional "resistance to theory" in classroom, departmental meetings, curricula, and elsewhere has been overcome. The "gap" between teaching and theory has been "bridged," to recall the title of a recent anthology of essays dealing with the painful issue of "literary theory in the classroom." Much remains to be done, though, at the undergraduate level. And even more remains to be done as to the formative impact of theory-teaching. As D. G. Myers has put it, theory is still presented primarily from a historical, informative perspective. Now, posttheorists stress and concretely rely on the formative dimension of theory rendered accessible in the undergraduate classroom. In other words, they both question extant theoretical sources and use them, interrogate their cultural-political effectiveness and employ the critical models they supply to further students' critical thinking in general—a thinking not necessarily limited to judging only literature. At this juncture their priority seems to be relating textual experience to life experience, training the student as a reader of the social space. As we have discovered in our own teaching, certain critical paradigms do not pass the test of the social extension of classroom practices—and should be revised in the light of this lack of effectiveness.

Posttheory critics complete the progression of postmodern skepticism about grand narratives. While they share with the cultural studies generation a healthy suspicion of all metanarratives, they nonetheless tend to part company with it insofar as the cultural studies project still evokes (1) an idea of novelty and epistemological progress, the notion that bringing about a "new" alternative to formalist approaches such as poetics, post-structuralism, and so forth is an end in itself for critics; and (2) a modernist metanarrative—the neo-Marxist paradigm, for example. Most important, posttheory critics and teachers of the mid-nineties are wary of adopting in toto theoretical models worked out in completely different historical and cultural-political contexts. Their skepticism regarding metanarratives is even more pronounced than that of their immediate predecessors.

Once again, they reject the self-sufficiency of theoretical novelty and endeavor to understand the institutional structures perpetuating it.

The critical foci of metaprofessional discourse spotlight five major areas: (1) the new integration of teaching and research; (2) the politics of tenure and placement; (3) the rhetoric and meaning of visibility; (4) the logistics of publication; and (5) public accountability. As we insisted, posttheorist critics and teachers define themselves not through adherence to a "new" theoretical model, but rather through investigations into and positions on these five areas of concern. Though these five zones do not exhaust what the posttheorist thinks the profession covers, they surely form a great part of what we call metaprofessional discourse.

Tenure and placement policy, to begin with, proves to have a strong impact on both the academic (public) and personal (private) identity of posttheorists. Most definitely, this new generation of academics view the professional world not as an oasis, but as a desert through which they are doomed to roam for years after receiving their Ph.D. Moving from one short-term appointment to another has become a commonplace rite of passage. Placement and job market conditions spawn a kind of nomadic identity that was the exception in the golden age when tenure-track positions were more readily available. Metaprofessional discourse problematizes this institutional nomadism and helps us understand its sociocultural and political ramifications in a field where academic and personal identities tend to be more and more constructed in transit.

It seems to us that new strategies of integrating teaching and research are very much needed and ought to be effected at a new, more basic level. While teaching graduate seminars, many posttheorists strive to turn the undergraduate classroom into a theory-friendly environment. They struggle to "humanize" theory, not to "overcome" or "forget" it. Their goal is, in this regard, to render theory accessible to students and convince them that its study can empower them, help them perform a deeper reading of the social text. They try to share their own research as much as possible with students of all levels — even if in doing so they risk "watering down" their own positions. First and foremost, they make an effort to convince their students that theory is something for them to use, and not just to be studied in itself. They hardly believe that theory is the crown jewel of the profession, something reserved only for graduates or, at best, advanced undergraduates. What might become sacrificed in rigor and completeness is overshadowed by the high level of respect students may acquire for a posttheory classroom that sheds new light on the students' relationship with literature, society, and ultimately themselves. Posttheorist teachers regard literature as one textual practice among many, and understand that they cannot afford to ignore an emerging type of literacy, namely, the primarily visual and auditory set of discursive practices that surround students and make up an important part of their background. Furthermore, the posttheoretical classroom cultivates the reading-writing complex as a social modus operandi learning subjects carry over into the public sphere, and are encouraged to use for formulating and eventually reformulating their sociocultural positioning regardless of their profession. Again, if identity turns out to be relational or conjunctural, as James Clifford insists, then the reading-writing complex could and should become a tool to read and rewrite the web of relations in which social subjects are woven.

Posttheorists lay a new type of emphasis on professional visibility in all its forms. Many of them indeed explore new ways of connecting up their work and the social horizon. They consistently search for new avenues of social effectiveness and transacademic communication such as electronic media and cyberspace in hopes of increasing the quality and quantity of the communal presence publicly associated with teaching and research. Much of their metaprofessional discourse is devoted to exploring the potential held by new forms of scholarly visibility.

In line with this, posttheorists show a strong interest in creating new arenas and instruments of expression as well as in using channels that have traditionally been ignored. Over the past few years they have founded new journals such as *Journal X*, *differences*, or *Symplokē*, which provide forums for critics sharing similar beliefs about the field. There is also a growing trend among posttheorists to publish in more popular and publicly accessible venues such as *Harper's* or the *Village Voice*.

Posttheorists are especially concerned with what we may call the reconstruction of the whole notion of academic accountability. First, they believe that what goes on in the profession must be accountable both inside and *outside* the profession. One of the ways they are achieving this goal is by moving away from theoretical parlance. They tend to replace obscure lingo with a lingua franca accessible to less specialized audiences. We believe that this lingua franca places the public in a better position to grasp the major stakes of an activity that has in the past hid behind terminological clouds. Second, the reconstruction of accountability entails an attempt to demonstrate that various models of critical reading and classroom practices can be successfully applied to "public discourse" at large, including political discourse, media representations of everyday life, advertisements, and assorted cultural environments. Posttheorists endeavor to show how various critical models or tools can enable nonacademic subjects to locate their own social and political position. They confront the current, mutual alienation of academic and nonacademic communities and hope to bridge the gap between these by identifying common grounds, interests, and languages.

Finally, reading and writing remain the main focus in a posttheoretical classroom. Moreover, unlike Peter Rabinowitz, for example, who has recently spoken "against close reading," we believe that the largely positive pedagogical implications of the New Critical notion should not be underestimated. When thoroughly effected, close reading should not shut the reader off from the context within which that reading is undertaken. As Derrida has argued in his essay on the university, it is critical reading—which cannot be but "close," insistent, even obstinate—that actually links up the academy and the "real" world. Textual intervention also renders possible what might be called the university's interpolation of the social-political text. While "talking" to and with their students about literary works, posttheorists also talk and write "back," as it were. The posttheoretical classroom is the locus of reading and writing per se, a locus that, most remarkably, does not merely "double" the articulation and hierarchy systems of the public space, but actively intervenes in them. As critics from Derrida to Jonathan Culler and Bill Readings have repeatedly insisted, the university and the reading and writing taking place within its permeable margins do carry "political performativity." Reading and writing do not simply "describe" texts; on the contrary, the act of interpretation wedges into the organization of the larger community to which the classroom's "interpretive communities" belong.

The posttheory teachers thus bring forth a twofold critique, both textual and social, as their work—again, reading and writing—ceaselessly challenges, adapts, revisits, interrupts, disrupts, or completely reworks the larger set of rules and principles (the "contractuality") undergirding any act of reading. Posttheory pedagogy takes up post-structuralist models of textuality and textual engagement to impact on nontextual zones of social life—in fact, the political performativity referred to above simply brings into question the existence of such zones. As we empower students (post)theoretically, the cultural-political articulation of the social institutions shaping their lives will become more transparent to them. As a result of the posttheoretical use of the classroom, the public space becomes a focus of critical and political reading, which opens up possibilities for active intervention, boundary renegotiations, and effective change.

Part IV

Cultural Studies Pedagogies

Other Worlds in a Fordist Classroom

17

Vijay Prashad

> Our educational service is not a public service, but an instrument of special privilege; its purpose is not to further the welfare of mankind but merely to keep America capitalist.
>
> —*Upton Sinclair*, The Goose-Step

> By the time we graduate, we have been painstakingly trained in separating facts from their meaning. . . . We wonder that our classes, with few exceptions, seem irrelevant to our lives. No wonder they're so boring. Boredom is the necessary condition of any education which teaches us to manipulate the facts and suppress their meaning.
>
> —*Steve Golin*, New Left Notes

From the early 1960s, American university students entered a long era of disenchantment. In an angry moment in the history of American education, Mario Savio on 2 December 1964 announced to a crowd of about six thousand at Berkeley that the university is a firm, the board of regents or trustees is a board of directors, the president is a manager, "the faculty are a bunch of employees and [the students are] the raw material" (quoted in Draper 98). Savio, a twenty-two-year-old veteran of the SNCC voter registration campaign in Mississippi, forced his fellow students to recognize that the academy was not immune from the dynamic of commodification that overwhelmed social life. Six years later, a nationwide strike on college campuses reminded the academy again that its purpose should not be corporate, but social; on May Day 1970, students put forth the slogan "On Strike, *Open It Up!*" to demand that the universities reconstitute themselves to "serve the people" and not to produce willing workers for corporate America. In the decades since

1964, student protest acted as a viable barometer of student frustration with the relentless commodification of pedagogy. In our own time, we need to acknowledge the struggles among the graduate students at Yale to unionize, the struggles among the students and faculty at CUNY/SUNY to protect quality educational institutions, and the struggles by students across the country to revitalize their curricula by including ethnic studies, Black studies, women's studies, Latino studies, and Asian American studies.

Political unrest to reconstitute education is only one face of the prevailing student disenchantment with the academy. Teachers commonly experience student disengagement from academic life in two contradictory reactions: unflinching certainty and cynical boredom. The former (certainty) takes the verities of common sense and treats the classroom as a place to either validate ideas or learn how to put the ideas into operation. The disillusionment of the latter (boredom) is profound, for it stems from a sense that the nexus of state-school-family is hypocritical and anachronistic. The deracinated slackers of America are not simply lazy; rather, their cultural icons demonstrate their lack of trust in the institutions of American life. This brief essay draws its legitimacy from the sense that this disenchantment is not simply a collective hallucination of the new generation, but reflects a contradiction between the goals of the corporate-university and the pedagogical urges of the vast mass of the youth who are excited to learn, but find they have neither the time nor the money to challenge themselves. Drawing from an analysis of the university's social role, this essay takes as its principal object of investigation the way other worlds enter the classroom: either as lesser forms (cultural absolutism) or as alien forms (cultural relativism). This essay will offer an educational principle, founded on multiculturalism, that embraces the decentralization of our institutions as well as the valorization of *contradictions* as the ideological basis of our pedagogy.

FORDISM OF EDUCATION

In an essay designed to make sense of the international student rebellion of 1968, Gareth Stedman Jones pointed to the directions in which the modern university guides its charges. Jones argues that the university trains students to play three roles in the marketplace: as technicians of *consumption* (market researchers, media planners, entertainment specialists, fashion designers, advertisement copywriters), as technicians of *consent* (journalists, editors, television personalities, film-makers, personnel managers, teachers), and as technicians of *production* (various types of engineers and chemists) (G. Jones 31). The last category of workers, the technicians of production, is a breed apart. Separated from other students from the inception of college, these "science majors" gravitate toward a hypervocational training. Between O-Chem, P-Chem, and calculus, they barely have any energy and enthusiasm for their "blow-off" courses (i.e., their breadth of study requirement in social studies and the humanities). Their minds are trained to respond to the Cartesian world of science whose conceptual empiricism drains an appreciation of social and political complexity from scientific consciousness (Latour; Bernal). For the future technicians of consumption and consent, the major they select in college is not significant for their careers (whether one selects history, English, or political science does not truly affect one's law school application). For these students, college has become a necessary but insufficient condition for entry into the middle class. Their vocational training begins in professional school. The liberal ideal, it seems, suits these students who, unlike their friends in the "hard sciences," have no immediate "facts" to master. The liberal ideal, however, has been rendered anachronistic by the pressures put upon students by the long-term crisis in advanced capitalist countries set in motion in 1973. That the liberal ideal is "anachronistic" in a systemic sense does not imply that teachers should accede to corporate pressure on the centers of learning; the acknowledgment that the liberal ideal is at odds with corporate pressures removes all illusions that the corporations will be able to "save" education by such devices as privatization. For teachers to put our hope on business for the salvation of education demonstrates a feeble capitulation to the eventual demise of the ideals of human consciousness.

The contemporary university is no longer a cloister to which the youth retire to "play" with ideas away from the cares of the world; these few postadolescent days cannot be spent without an eye to the prospects of each student in a world in which the gains of increased productivity (due to technology) have been monopolized by transnational corporations. The four years of college serve as an apprenticeship for the work life of corporate America rather than a crucible for the production of well-tempered citizens. In a book on prisons, Foucault pointed to the close congruence between modern punitive, industrial, commercial, medical, military, and educational institutions (Foucault 314). The classroom, like the jail-block, is organized to maximize surveillance. What sets the classroom off from the prison and the factory is that the academy takes as its special charter the dual task of producing docile bodies as well as enlightened individuals. From

Rousseau's *Emile*, European educational institutions stressed the development of skills of the individual so that he or she would willingly enter the social contract as an informed citizen; conversely, the individual was also taught to willingly consent to the system (a strand that was not altogether clear to the enlightenment thinkers). With the reconstitution of the university as the locus for the transmission of practical skills, knowledge ceased to simply impart civility; the university became the place to train the body to work and the mind to produce. Inquiry, the purpose of education, was relegated to the profession of those who made the academy their life; for the rest, the university is mostly another step on the ladder of mobility.

The age of mass production drove pedagogy toward the values of speed and efficiency. Our classrooms are a victim of a fordism of education in which the students read brief and scattered extracts and spend short, efficient periods (forty minutes, ninety minutes) learning as much information as quickly as possible. The form of presentation most adequate to the fordist classroom is structural-functionalism: complex social systems are broken down into their most salient features and these are presented as the system's essence. Complexity is squandered for the sake of clarification. Different disciplines simplify their complex materials along different axes and in concordance with their autonomous traditions: the ethical sciences chose pragmatism (and reduce the moral horizon of philosophy), the physical sciences chose operationalism (and reduce the ethical horizon of science), and the social sciences chose behavioralism (and reduce the contradictions of human life to fixed models) (Aptheker chap. 4). Rather than provide a summary and inadequate analysis of all the developments of the various components of American intellectual thought in the fordist classroom, I am going to concentrate on the formation of the social sciences' object of inquiry as well as its infusion into the classroom.

THE BUSINESS OF CULTURE

The functional model is the simplest way to offer students information as well as a key to the various times and places under investigation in the average social science classroom. To make it easier for the teacher, the world comes divided into geopolitical zones (continents and nations), but these are not the basis of the discipline's pedagogical divisions. Following G. W. F. Hegel, we divide the world into various "civilizational zones": West, China, India, Black Africa, Slavic Europe,

America, and Persia/Middle East. Each zone is treated as autonomous. Within a zone, our Hegelian hangover treats "society" as consensual, in which each of its members is determined by the zone's principal essence. These essences are not offered to say something about the zone; they are offered, rather, as an exhaustive and adequate description of the zone. The essence, further, is seen not as contradictory but as singular: a zone cannot have multiple and competing principles, but only one substantive essence. If criticisms are found within the zone, these might be acknowledged, but only as lesser forms of knowledge. In his *Lectures on the Philosophy of World History* (1822–23), Hegel surveyed the movement of the universal spirit (*Geist*) from the East to the West. Along the journey, Hegel commented on two civilizational areas that did not enjoy the benefits of Reason: the Amerindians and the Black Africans. Amerindia is dismissed as its essence is deemed to be "fantasy": Amerindians "are like unenlightened children, living from one day to the next, and untouched by higher thoughts or aspiration" (Hegel 165). Black Africa's essence is "nothingness," since Hegel deems its civilizational zone to be devoid of subjectivity: "history is in fact out of the question. Life there consists of a succession of contingent happenings and surprises. No aim or state exists whose development could be followed; and there is no subjectivity, but merely a series of subjects who destroy one another" (Hegel 176). History is glimpsed in Asia, but only in mangled forms. China's essence is "theocratic despotism" or Confucianism: too much of a patriarchal and bureaucratic state and an underdeveloped society. India's essence is "theocratic aristocracy" or caste hierarchy: too much of a disorganized and underdeveloped state system (N.B., Hegel's modern representative is Louis Dumont, who raised the following question: "Why should we travel to India if not to try to discover how and in what respects Indian society or civilization, by its very particularity, represents a form of the universal?" Dumont offered the caste system, personified by *Homo Hierarchicus*, as the essence of India). Persia's essence is "theocratic monarchy," which is the bridge between the imperfect East and the Reasoned West (Hegel 200). History begins its adolescence in Greece and then finds its magnificence in the Prussian state (whose essence, intoned Hegel, is Mediated Freedom or Equality).

Hegel's summary of the universal essences follows a body of information about the world provided by various agents of the colonial nations: the feudal Iberian and the capitalist Anglo-Dutch countries. Colonial knowledge arrogated all that is good to itself and allocated all that it deemed barbaric and unjust to its colonized subjects. If the colony had anything to offer to universal knowledge, it was in its ancient pasts, which were being reconstructed by colonial officials and their intellectual compradors. The ancient cultures of India, China, and Japan came to be the mark of value, and living Indians, Chinese, and Japanese were seen to be pale shadows of their cultural inheritance. The contemporary history and people of these fabricated civilizational zones were deemed irrelevant to human history and hence, their lives were left in the hands of the relevant peoples: European colonizers. Colonial thought produced a singular attitude toward other worlds, an attitude that carried the day until the 1960s: cultural absolutism. The tone of T. B. Macaulay's famous phrase from 1835 illustrates the arrogance of this position: "I have never found [a European expert on 'Oriental learning'] who could deny that a single shelf of a good European library was worth the whole native literature of India and Arabia" (Macaulay 241). West is Best, Forget the Rest (some of you may remember that T-shirt from the days of the Reaganist attack on the liberal university).

Cultural absolutism was not simply the arrogant will of the colonizer; its form was taken up by bourgeois Third World nationalists and their intellectual confreres. Frantz Fanon offers the emblematic criticism of this approach: "In an initial phase, it is the action, the plans of the occupier that determine the centers of resistance around which a people's will to survive becomes organized. It is the white man who creates the Negro. But it is the Negro who creates negritude. To the colonialist offensive against the veil, the colonized opposes the cult of the veil" (Fanon 47). Fanon demonstrates the manner in which the postcolonial nationalist simply inverts the normative judgments of the colonizer without conducting a ruthless and relentless criticism of the binary form that sustains colonial thought without colonialism. This Third Worldist intervention was the first salvo in the attack against cultural absolutism, but it was itself unable to demolish the absolutist form: now the other cultures are posed as coherent and superior to the "West."

Drawing from this Third Worldist intervention and from the progressive ideas put forth by the American anthropologist Franz Boas and his students, many intellectuals argued that each zone has its own ethical logic and it must be understood by that logic alone. One zone cannot be compared with another and no zone's normative logic may be used as a yardstick against the practices of another zone. At its best, cultural relativism allowed for the destabilization of the arrogance of colonial thought and Europe's ideological dominance. From under the heavy arm of Europe, other ideas and histories began to make their cautious entrance onto the world stage. However, relativism, like the Third Worldist intervention, was simply a continuation of the crisis: it failed to reframe the problem of ethics, moral universalism, and the hope for social justice. For one, relativism is unable to recognize the hand of colonial thought and imperialism in the construction of many of those ethico-historical artifacts that it took as the legacy of the various zones' cultural traditions. Further, relativism can be and has been freely appropriated by those who want to continue the imperial project, but without political colonialism: transnational corporations engaged in the economic conquest of the postcolonial states offer themselves a license to ill with the relativist argument that "those people" do not require high wages or fine standards of living, for they are used to (nay, require) the very opposite. A representative of American Cynamid (a transnational chemical company) responded to the 1984 Union Carbide massacre at Bhopal with this: people in the Third World don't mind death because they do not have the "North American philosophy of the importance of human life" (quoted in T. Jones 38). A well-regarded anthropologist wrote of the "filth, chaos, promiscuity, congestion; ruins, huts, mud, dirt; dung, urine, pus, humours, secretions and running sores" of Calcutta: "They are more like the natural environment which the Indian town needs in order to prosper" (Lévi-Strauss 134). A movie for children offered this as an early comment on the home of Aladdin: "It's barbaric, but hey, it's home to them." This is the perverse world of relativism that, for all its problems, appears to be kinder than the repulsive tone of cultural absolutism.

In Search of an Educational Principle

Cultural relativism and absolutism do not exhaust the terrain of intellectual thought: they share a fundamental premise whose foundations must be removed in the classroom if students are to gain a better understanding of difference in the postcolonial world. Their premise: culture is a homogeneous thing that is untouched by human hands. We need to be scrupulous in accounting for the way cultures are produced and how the very idea of culture appears in world history (for a nice introduction, see Williams 87–93). The principle for teaching must cease to be structural-functionalist (which has received extensive criticism as theory); it must be dialectical. To allow contradictions into the classroom, by presenting knowledge that has been relegated to distant and dusty storerooms or to the gallows, goes against corporate needs, but it is socially necessary. Multiculturalism need not simply mean relativism or the ceaseless inclusion of various elements from static models of cultures. Multiculturalism, if it is to remain relevant, must not simply mean curriculum enhancement. Multiculturalism must be seen as a process to fundamentally reconstitute American education, to renegotiate the partisan passivity imposed on students. The reconstitution must move in two directions:

1. The overlordship of trustees and provosts must be countered with the institutionalized resistance of teachers, graduate students, and undergraduates. Unions are an integral democratic force to rework the feudal way decisions are made on campus.

2. Faculty need to produce the philosophical space for students to engage critically with the forms of thought. The teacher must introduce the students to the isolation of our disciplines of study ("Islam," for instance); the combined and uneven production of the field of study and of the living traditions ("Islamology" and the practice of the faith); the historical connections between the various traditions and peoples (Ibn-Rushd, who worked on Plato, and Ibn-Sina, who worked on Aristotle; the traditions of mysticism whose authors, such as Maimonides, wrote across traditions); the multiple and contradictory traditions that develop within one overarching tradition of study and of life (the "Islam" of Al-Ghazzali, Ali Shariati, Mehdi Rezai [the nineteen-year-old martyr of the Iranian Revolution] and of the group entitled Women Living under Muslim Laws); the interrelationships of socioeconomic matters and cultural history (for example, the imperial domination of West Asia and Arabia, which spawned an anti-Western form of Islam); and finally, the massacre of the Left in the lands where Islam is dominant by an alliance between the imperial powers (Britain, France, the United States) and their local allies (the shah of Iran, Saddam Hussein, the Gulf "royal" families, and Suharto). These moments need to be offered in a class on the Al-Quran: a textual study of the book in an age when "Moslems" are the target of derision and violence is inadequate. Such a narrow approach may produce a very adept scholar of the Al-Quran, but it will not produce a citizen of the world.

Social science needs to inculcate the tradition of critical reason, in which the student questions all existing reality; social science needs to emphasize the social character of life and not the notion of a prehuman social existence as well as an overdeveloped sense of individualism; social science needs to promote the active participation of the students in the learning process and not just the passive acceptance of ideas; finally, social science needs to treat our reality as historical and as fraught with struggle on the basis of contradictory but creative ethical traditions (Hoare 51).

As we are indeed in the process of producing well-tempered citizens, we must consider the struggle to offer knowledges that do not replicate the bigotry of our inherited wisdom. Rather than take as self-evident our charge to produce "critical consciousness" (whose abstractness often mystifies it as a task), we might pose for ourselves the task of damaging the disenchantment of our youth and elaborating their doubt into productive (dialectical) directions. As technocrats of the humanities, we have a duty, an ethical and political responsibility, to disrupt the easy fictions of imperialism, which informs an uncritical pedagogy.

Works Cited

Aptheker, Bettina. *The Academic Rebellion in the United States.* Secaucus: Citadel, 1972.

Bernal, J. D. *The Social Function of Science.* New York: Macmillan, 1939.

Draper, Hal. *Berkeley: The New Student Revolt.* New York: Grove, 1965.

Dumont, Louis. *Homo Hierarchicus.* Chicago: University of Chicago Press, 1970.

Fanon, Frantz. *A Dying Colonialism.* New York: Grove, 1967.

Foucault, Michel. *Discipline and Punish: The Birth of the Prison.* New York: Vintage, 1979.

Golin, Steve. *New Left Notes,* 7 October 1966.

Hegel, G. W. F. *Lectures on the Philosophy of World History.* Cambridge: Cambridge University Press, 1980.

Hoare, Quintin. "Education: Programs and Men." *New Left Review,* 32, July–August 1965.

Jones, Gareth Stedman. "The Meaning of the Student Revolt." In *Student Power,* ed. Alexander Cockburn and Robin Blackburn. Baltimore: Penguin and New Left Review, 1969.

Jones, Tara. *Corporate Killings: Bhopals Will Happen.* New York: FAB, 1988.

Latour, Bruno. *Laboratory Life: The Social Construction of Scientific Facts.* Beverly Hills: Sage, 1979.

Lévi-Strauss, Claude. *Tristes Tropiques.* New York: Atheneum, 1974.

Macaulay, T. B. "Minute on India Education [2 February 1835]." In *Selected Writings,* ed. J. Clive and T. Pinney. Chicago: University of Chicago Press, 1972.

Sinclair, Upton. *The Goose-Step: A Study of American Education.* Pasadena: Upton Sinclair, 1923.

Williams, Raymond. *Keywords.* New York: Oxford, 1983.

Who's Afraid of Queer 1   y?

18

Ju   rstam

Like many emergent discourses, queer theory incites its fair share of criticism and skepticism. Most of the recent criticism of queer theory seems to
regard it as an elite academic practice performed mostly by white gay men who
are interested in the canonical work of other white gay men.[1] But when we agree
to render "queer" merely a synonym for "gay" we risk losing the entire critical
enterprise that queer studies has engendered, namely, a radical critique of iden-
tity-based politics, a history of sexual minorities and their practices, and a rejection of the homo-hetero binary model of sexual identities. Queer may soon lose
all affectivity as a word, a marker, or a threat (it may already have done so), but
this has more to do with the inevitable absorption of political dissent within late
capitalism into consumer culture than it has to do with the conflation of queers
and gays. Who's afraid of queer theory, I will ask, and why? And for what or for
whom does the queer in queer theory stand? Furthermore, what kind of cultural
work is presently possible under the heading of queer theory, and what spaces

for intervention has queer theory opened up? Is there such a thing as a queer pedagogy, and what is its relation to gay and lesbian studies and its pedagogies?

The institutionalization of queer theory has raised questions about its political affiliations and its increasing distance from queer cultures; as we begin to break down the pros and cons of institutional recognition, we should also attempt to account for what happens within the academy to discussions of the actual practices of queer sex. In "Thinking Sex," Gayle Rubin laid out in great detail the discursive foundations that hamper "radical thought about sex," and she called for "erotic creativity."[2] Samuel Delany in "Street Talk/Straight Talk" continues the call for a sexual discourse rather than simply a discourse about sex; he says, "what I am asking is that all of us begin to put forward the monumental analytic effort . . . needed not to interpret what we say, but to say what we do."[3] While queer theory has detailed elaborately and carefully the cultural constructions of heteronormativity, there has been less attention focused on the material practices of queer sexuality, practices that could lead to exactly the kind of "radical thought about sex" that Rubin called for a decade ago.

Rubin further suggested in "Thinking Sex" that feminism might not be or should not be "the privileged site for a theory of sexuality" (307). We might add that other political programs like socialism or liberalism may also provide hostile environments for theories of sexuality because they similarly impose moralistic codes of behavior on sex by assuming that there should be some continuity between what people believe in politically and what they do sexually. Of course, sexual behavior has proven to be rather impervious to such political programs, and we might question why we continue to want to prescribe political models for sexual activity. For example, the liberal democratic and feminist notions of mutuality, egalitarianism, and fluid exchange might be important to social arrangements, but why are they categories that we value in the realm of sexuality? What is queer sex? Is it dominated by notions of exchange rather than unequal desire, for example? What are the politics of certain sex acts? What is the relationship between queer sex and queer politics? How do we value fluidity over rigidity, androgynous sex over role oriented sex, gender-free sex over gendered sex, "give and take" over give or take? How do capitalist and socialist notions of the economy of desire thoroughly script our sexual morality? How can we keep sex queer? The study of sex, as theorists Foucault to Sedgwick have noted, is remarkably resistant to universalist theorizing; sex is also difficult to rationalize and quantify, and it is as difficult to say what people actually do sexually as it is tempting to say what they should do.

Questions about the relationship between sexuality and politics seemed to be at the center of a debate that was staged recently within the pages of the feminist journal *differences* (1996). In this issue, various feminist theorists attempted to account for the relation between feminism and queer theory; most seemed to suggest that there is a clear and problematic opposition between the aims and discourses of feminism and the aims and political commitments of queer theory. In the lead essay, Judith Butler argues that gay and lesbian studies has "no proper object" and that to assume that sexuality is the "proper object" of gay and lesbian studies is to create an unbridgeable and politically dangerous gap between feminism and other minority discourses.[4] She also argues that because "gay and lesbian studies" conflates sex and gender, feminism appears to have been superseded by gay and lesbian studies within the academy. What appears to be an analogical relationship between the two fields of inquiry, Butler writes, actually posits the erasure of feminism:

> And what passes as a benign, even respectful, analogy with feminism
> is the means by which the fields are separated, where that separation
> requires the desexualization of the feminist project and the appropria-
> tion of sexuality as the "proper" object of lesbian and gay studies. (6)

While Butler seems to be making a mostly rhetorical argument about "proper objects" and methodologies, I understand her to be arguing that feminism is a crucial site for the contestation of sexual identities because it has always paid careful attention to the relations between sex and gender, gender and race, race and sexuality, class and gender and sexuality, and so on. Rather than relinquish feminism to the antipornography groups headed by Catharine MacKinnon, Butler seems to think we should revive the feminist tradition in favor of sexual freedom. But the passage quoted above also suggests that when gay and lesbian scholars claim sexuality as their proper object, this entails a "desexualization of the feminist project." But the desexualization of the feminist project began years before gay and lesbian studies even appeared on the disciplinary map. Feminist debates about sexuality date back to the late 1970s and early 1980s and are chronicled carefully and historically within volumes like *Pleasure and Danger*, *Coming to Power*, and *Sex Wars*.[5] While it may be true that the sex-negative strand of feminism never achieved anything like cultural hegemony, this brand of feminist thought, as I will suggest later, cannot be ignored.

I agree with Butler that feminism should not be symbolically handed over to antipornography interests, and that people interested in the study of sex should not automatically situate themselves within gay and lesbian studies. However, an interesting elision has taken place within Butler's essay: while she takes great pains to identify the multiplicity of feminisms and the many different strands of political thought that might be grouped under the heading of feminist, she is not so careful to distinguish between versions or brands of gay and lesbian studies methodologies or aims, nor does she maintain a distinction between gay/lesbian and queer. "Against Proper Objects" begins by situating the debate between "feminist and queer theory," but the rest of the essay opposes feminism to "gay/lesbian studies." Since we are talking about methodologies and objects of study, would not the opposition therefore have to be between "women's studies" and "gay/lesbian studies" and feminism and queer theory?

Why does this matter? It matters because the history of women's studies has not at all been the history of feminism, and we should not expect that the history of gay and lesbian studies will be the history of queer theory or queer activism. Also, it was precisely within women's studies departments that the study of sexuality in the 1970s and 1980s seemed to take a moralistic turn and seemed to reject the kinds of sexual histories that queer theorists have claimed as their own (the history of butch-femme, for example, or intergenerational love, sadomasochism, or sex work). By conveniently ignoring this entire tradition of feminism produced within women's studies departments, Butler assigns feminist sex-negativity to MacKinnon alone and warns against the antifeminist tendencies of a queer movement run by conservative gay men.

So who are these queer theorists who are leaving an adequate analysis of gender out of their theories of sexuality? Some people seem to target Eve Kosofsky Sedgwick in particular for making sexuality and the study of sexuality in her work (but mainly in the introduction to *The Epistemology of the Closet*) the domain only of "antihomophobic inquiry." In a critique of Sedgwick's work, Biddy Martin takes Sedgwick to task for separating out the study of sexuality from the study of gender and then making gender into a relatively rigid system and sex into a more fluid one.[6] Butler follows up on Martin's critique in a footnote to "Against Proper Objects." She writes, "Sedgwick understands sexuality as the proper domain of lesbian and gay studies, or rather 'antihomophobic inquiry.' By separating the notion of gender from sexuality, Sedgwick narrows the notion of sexual minorities offered by Rubin." Both Butler and Martin seem to fear that sexuality becomes male sexuality in Sedgwick's scheme and gender remains tied to a stable definition of "woman" or "man." Butler goes on to suggest that Sedgwick's queer scheme also precludes the study of other sexual minorities.

However, it is in the introduction to *The Epistemology of the Closet* that Sedgwick suggests exactly how the hetero-homo binary sustains and enforces (and indeed is sustained and enforced by) the male-female gender binary. Taking up Gayle Rubin's astute observation that we lack a theory of "benign sexual variation," Sedgwick produces a list of obvious and even unremarkable ways "people are different from each other" (22) within the realm of sexuality. The list includes distinctions like "some people like to have a lot of sex, others little or none" (25). And its final distinction reads, "Some people . . . experience their sexuality as deeply embedded in a matrix of gender meanings and gender differentials. Others do not" (26). Sedgwick's list is a brilliant illustration of how impoverished we have allowed our thinking about sexuality, sexual practices, and their organization to become. Furthermore, far from categorically separating out sexuality and gender, she refuses to predict exactly what their points of convergences will produce. Gender as an erotic locus is not the same thing as gender as a marker of sexual difference. We may want to distinguish between social genders and sexual genders; butch would register as a sexual gender, for example, a place where sexuality does fold into gender identity sometimes as an inversion, sometimes as a more complicated fractal relation. Still, Sedgwick's account of the epistemologies of the closet may well prove not to be the best place to begin an inquiry into feminist theories of sex, but it most certainly does allow for an accounting of sexual minorities.

 Who's afraid of queer theory? Everyone, apparently. Marxists have a tendency to see queer theory as frivolous and "ludic,"[7] and some feminists, as we have noted, seem to see queer theory as a cover for gay male agendas that ignore the specificity of relations between sex and gender. And yet queer theory is still rather a recent academic arrival and certainly not one that has achieved such a degree of legitimacy in American universities that it may pose some threat to other programs like feminist studies or gender studies. The problem with queer theory, as I see it, is not a lack of political motivation nor a tendency to subsume all sexual minorities under the heading of gay and lesbian or all genders under male and female; the real problem with queer theory is that it fails to specify adequately the kinds of sexualities we are supposed to be studying. As Foucault says in volume 1 of *The History of Sexuality*, we need a history of the detail.[8] Furthermore, "queer" is in danger of stabilizing into an identity rather than remaining a radical critique of identity and a challenge to extend the study of sexuality and gender beyond the signifiers "gay" and "lesbian" and "man" and "woman" and into a domain of sexual and gender minorities.

In this essay I am trying to circumvent some of the conventional debates within gay and lesbian studies about discipline and method in order to address the limits of a discourse that fails to take into account what I am calling "the queer present tense."[9] Presently, in zines and community newspapers, in nightclubs and bars, queer communities look immensely more diverse than the theoretical work allows. It seems important to address the discrepancy between some gay and lesbian theory, which seems endlessly stuck in the repetition of psychoanalytic principles, and the theories of sexuality, gender, and self that circulate wildly in nonacademic spheres. Just as much queer theory in the 1980s took its cue from the queer activism of ACT-UP, so present-day queer theory must in part look to unofficial sources for a current history of queer modes of identification. While we argue endlessly about who studies whom or what and using what methodology and whether we should be reading texts or conducting surveys, sex, as in sexual acts and practices, and particularly lesbian sex, seems eclipsed once more by discursive practice. Specifying sexual acts and their histories allows us to break with identity discourses that have a tendency to render some minority sexual practices completely unintelligible and to conflate still others with criminality. We tend to make rather large and sweeping statements when it comes to an analysis of sexuality. Perhaps this is on account of an academic prurience about sorting through the details and minutiae of sexual lives. Perhaps it is also on account of what Gayle Rubin calls "vulgar Lacanianism,"[10] that we have become accustomed to talking sex and indeed thinking sex in increasingly abstract and increasingly symbolic ways. The true challenge of queer theory, I believe, is to put the sex back into sexuality, continue to define and make visible sexual minorities, and restore a sense of material practices to the discourse.

Obviously, accounting for the specificities of sexual practices has already begun, but by and large it has been left mostly to nonacademics like Joan Nestle and Leslie Feinberg, Pat Califia and Susie Bright to fill in the dirty details.[11] Is literature the practice and queer the theory? In other words, have we become all too comfortable with a division of labor that relegates the sexually explicit to the domain of fiction and the sexually abstract to the domain of academic theory? Can we combine the two? Because of what I would call a kind of squeamishness in the academy when it comes to "talking sex" as opposed to "thinking sex," we seem to discuss only the specifics of sexual practices that have already been made visible within a juridical system of crime and punishment. Sodomy, therefore, becomes a "proper object" (to use Butler's term differently) for queer contemplation, but a sexual practice like "tribadism" (the rubbing of the clitoris against a surface, fleshly or otherwise) receives little critical scrutiny. Penetrative sex when it involves penises and vaginas or anuses is a "proper object" of research either as a history of heterosexuality, reproductive sexuality, or anal eroticism, but penetrative sex when it involves fingers, dildoes, or fists seems not to command anything more than prurient interest. Are some sexual activities more symbolic than others?

FEMALE MASCULINITY: A QUEER PROJECT

The work of putting the sex back into sexuality and accounting for the existence of sexual minorities within queer theory is ongoing. In a book-length project on "female masculinity," I am currently analyzing over two hundred years of masculine presentation by female-born people and the kinds of sexual acts, practices, and identities that such presentations produce. Within my project, female masculinity is not a subset of a more general category that we might call "male masculinity"; rather, female masculinity represents a unique historical production of alternative and contested masculinities. Neither is this history, furthermore, simply the history of lesbianism (although we find it intertwined with that history); since lesbianism is a rather recent historical marker of sexual identity, it does not sufficiently describe a much longer history of the masculine woman. In pre-nineteenth-century texts, we often find the masculine woman in the role of a disruption to the even flow of heterosexuality; in this role she exploits the tensions produced by patriarchy between husbands and wives and inserts herself into the cracks of a flawed marital system. This is less a formation of sexual identity and more a social role with a clear sexual component and a marked gender identification.

The history of the masculine woman is more accurately termed the history of the tribade, the tommie, the invert, the female-to-male transvestite, the hermaphrodite, the female husband, the transgender subject. Pre-twentieth-century transgender identification occurred as cross-identification and most often took the form of transvestism and cross-gender passing. There are therefore numerous accounts of women who passed as men in the eighteenth and nineteenth centuries and of men who passed as women.[12] Turn-of-the-century sexology conveniently merged the phenomenon of cross-identification with sexual orientation and called this gender inversion. The history of the collapse of gender inversion into homosexuality has been well accounted for by George Chauncey, Esther Newton, and others;[13] most historians also claim that the model of gender inversion gave way more recently to a model of gay or lesbian identity that resists or reneges on so-called role playing. Apart from the fact that this genealogy has tended to erase the past and continuing importance of butch-femme identification within lesbian history, and that it is predicated on the notion of the desirability of gender normativity for gays and lesbians, it also ignores the ways gender transitivity has continued to matter greatly to other sexual minorities.

I will return to the question of transgender identification later, but I want to suggest here some of the ways a history of masculinity in women might provide a more nuanced and detailed account of sexual practice and a more flexible model of historical change than some linear histories within which one model of sexual and gender identification neatly gives way to another.

Esther Newton's classic essay " 'The Mythic Mannish Lesbian' " insisted that the mannish woman eventually dominated discourses about female homosexuality because the butch embodied an "active lust" at a time when "sexual desire was not considered inherent in women," and also because "gender reversal became a powerful symbol of feminist aspirations" (566). In other words, the mannish lesbian makes desire between women visible and potent and rescues lesbianism from the asexual pit of romantic friendship. Lisa Duggan's work on turn-of-the-century American lesbians has also noted the dependence of lesbianism on a model of sexual difference. In an essay on the sensational trial of Alice Mitchell for the murder of her young female lover, Duggan notes that the press commented on "Alice's 'masculine' characteristics and Freda's 'feminine' manner" (798).[14] She also shows how cross-gender identification and cross-dressing are main elements in this case and in others like it from the same period. Duggan summarizes the motivations and effects of cross-identifications for young women: "Through masculine identification they separated themselves from the family-based female world, defined their desire for other women as erotic, and declared their unyielding commitment to a new way of life" (809). In other words, the masculine woman saturated turn-of-the-century definitions of lesbian sexuality, and this was not simply because medical authorities forced a connection between gender inversion and so-called female perversion; masculine women became signifiers of a desire that had been rendered invisible, and they became the carriers and producers of a version of masculinity that had been rejected by the community at large.

While the most potent work in gay and lesbian studies manages to produce complex histories with nuanced understandings of the multiple origins of modern gay and lesbian identities, strains of an ahistorical approach to lesbian history do still make appearances within contemporary lesbian scholarship. Terry Castle's rather successful book *The Apparitional Lesbian* (1993) strenuously objects to recent currents in queer history. Castle seems to think that the constructivist approach to lesbian definition has needlessly obscured the meanings, realities, and history of lesbian desire. She argues that while women may not have used the word "lesbian" prior to the late nineteenth century, nonetheless other vernacular words like "tommy" and "fricatrice" did exist, and furthermore, "where there are words . . . there is identity."[15] Castle goes on to claim that "lesbian" is far from the unstable and incoherent signifier that queer theory makes it out to be; on the contrary, she claims, "I believe we live in a world in which the word lesbian still makes sense, and that it is possible to use the word frequently, even lyrically, and still be understood" (14). This approach to lesbian definition has the appeal of a commonsense attempt to cut through the theory and attend to the actualities of lesbian life; however, something definitely is lost in Castle's polemic. Having dropped the historicized notion of pre-identitarian sexual practices between women and having insisted on the stability of the term "lesbian" and all its colloquial synonyms, Castle proceeds to blot out crucial differences between tribades in the Renaissance, cross-identifying women in the early nineteenth century like diarist Anne Lister, women-identified women of the late twentieth century, and non-lesbian-identifying women like Greta Garbo who may appear as lesbian within elaborate representational homoerotic sexual codes. How can all these different versions of desire be comfortably accommodated under one definitional term? And furthermore, what are the effects of insisting that they all be labeled "lesbian"?

I am arguing here for specificity and detail in relation to sex in history. There are very good and clear reasons theorists resist the temptation to stretch terms like "lesbian" across a vast array of sexual phenomena. Valerie Traub, for example, in her work on early discourses on tribadism from the seventeenth century, emphasizes that "tribades were not lesbians"; rather, she astutely points out, associations made in this early literature between tribadism and enlarged clitorises "provide the raw material out of which the social categories 'lesbian' and 'heterosexual' would begin to be constructed."[16] Castle, on the other hand, allows for no such historical reckoning of the production of the category "lesbian." She willingly unites under this heading people who may identify as men, as transgender, as heterosexual. For example, in an extremely problematic chapter on diarist Anne Lister, Castle uses Lister's diaries to refute queer theorists' claims that "lesbianism" is a thoroughly modern notion. Castle quotes sexually

explicit passages from Lister's diaries and then merely points to them as evidence
of lesbian activity. But if we read the diaries closely, we discover that Anne Lister did not even identify with the terms of the day for same-sex erotic behavior.
Lister, in fact, rejected the label "sapphic" for herself and continuously refers to
her masculinity throughout her diaries: on the topic of "saffic regard," Lister
remarks, "I said there was artifice in it. It was very different from mine and
would be no pleasure to me."[17] Lister, a Halifax gentlewoman who kept explicit
diaries of her sexual adventures for ten years, articulates here her pleasure and
not her identity. She says that she is not "saffic" because that mode of lovemak-
ing affords her no pleasure; clearly then, "saffic" refers to some sexual practices
between biological women but not to others. Lister's lovers, furthermore, are
very different from her; they are mostly married, feminine women who are
unsatisfied by their husbands. What does it mean then to call both Anne Lister
and her lovers "lesbian" and to make lesbian signify some commonsensical
notion of regular sexual practices between women? Lister's explicit descriptions
of the sex she engages in with her various lovers completely underscores the
absurdity of such definitional attempts. Lister often fantasizes about having a
penis and while she energetically makes love to her partners, she does not allow
them to touch her sexually in the same way: she writes, "I do what I like but
never permit them to do so" (48). Lister was clearly tribadic and engaged in a
kind of masculine sexual aesthetic. We might ask, therefore, how is this "lesbian," or even how "lesbian" is this form of sexual practice?

Queer discourses about the history of sexuality stress the contingent nature of
sexual practices, sexual acts and their meanings, and sexual identities. They
stress, furthermore, the very different histories of sexuality and sexual trajectories marked out by class and race. An upper-class woman in Victorian England
could cross-dress with some impunity; a working-class woman might have to
pass successfully as a man when she cross-dressed; a black woman in nineteenth-
century America might consider it too dangerous to cross-dress. Anyway, an act
like cross-dressing means very different things to different people at different
historical moments, and, predictably, the sexuality inferred by the act of cross-
dressing cannot be considered "lesbian" in any uncomplicated way. The project
for queer historians, then, is no longer to find, document, and record the presence of gay men and lesbians throughout history, rather it is to judge the meaning of sex in any given historical location and to trace the development of
notions of identity and sexual selves from within discourses of acts and pleasures. The effect of the production of the homo-hetero binary at the turn of the

twentieth century was to commit a representational violence on the multiplicity of sexual practices in existence: the homo-hetero binary still continues to clamp down on sexual excess and insists on clear sexual distinctions between perverse and normal sexual behavior and between male and female sexualities.

This essay does not propose some simplistic celebration of material practices that will replace discursive practices, nor does it blindly call for a restoration of lost sexual variation; rather, I am suggesting that sexual practices and identifications in the here and now presently exceed the categorical imperatives of the homo-hetero binary, and many communities of sexual minorities already exist within far more complex epistemologies than some theoretical writing would lead us to believe. Furthermore, I would like to challenge the notion that descriptive enterprises or empirical research are necessarily less useful and more facile than philosophical or theoretical approaches to the study of sexuality. When I argue that we must put the sex back into sexuality, I mean that descriptive projects must necessarily round out purely abstract and theoretical projects because without some focus on the materiality of sex lives, we necessarily fail to engage with the body, pleasures, and their complex webs of association.

THE FUTURE OF TRANSGENDER STUDIES

Is there a way to use "queer," then, to begin the task of accounting for the sexualities and genders that fall outside the homo-hetero binary? And furthermore, can we use "queer" to account for the multiple sites and bodies in which gender and sexuality become inextricable? Queering gender, for example, makes us aware of how rarely gendering works as a process that produces men being men and women being women—if we are serious about diversifying gender, then it is time to account for, name, and ratify the multiple genders that we squash into the outdated categories of "men" and "women." Transgender theory currently promises to identify the significance and challenge of both cross-gender identifications and new gender formations. Work by transgender theorists like Susan Stryker on monstrous gender, Sandy Stone on virtual genders, and Jacob Hale on the philosophical analyses of gender concepts both normative and nonnormative takes gender trouble to a whole new level.[18] For Stryker, the monstrosity of the transsexual body serves to remind us of the unnaturalness of all gendered bodies. In her essay on "transgender rage," Stryker articulates a powerful and rageful identification with Frankenstein's monster, and she sends a word of caution to the medical profession: "As we rise up from the operating tables of our rebirth, we transsexuals are something more, and something other, than the creatures our makers intended us to be" (242). This element of "something more" and "something other" that for Stryker ensures the power of the monster to overthrow his maker allows for what Sandy Stone calls "a counter discourse" (295). Both Stryker and Stone note the ability of the transsexual to destabilize gender norms by calling attention to the remarkable plasticity of even "genetic naturals" (295). Stone points to the damage done by totalizing explanatory systems produced about transsexuals by nontranssexuals; such theoretical systems characterize "the" transsexual or "all" transsexuals, and such language ensures that, as Stone puts it, "there are no subjects in these discourses, only homogenized, totalized objects" (298). Stone suggests a word to remedy the damage: "some."[19]

The "someness" of identity and its composition of "something more" and "something other" makes categories like "man" and "woman" harder and harder to sustain but also reveals the grave need for an updated sexual and gender vocabulary. In his essay "Are Lesbians Women?" Jacob Hale finds that he quickly reaches the limit of what theoretical discourse can "know" about "gender in relation to sexuality" (118). In a long footnote, Hale makes the problem of articulation and identification all too clear: "Queer and transgendered discourses are produced by those of us who cannot communicate about our gendered sexual desires and practices without creating new languages, languages much more specific and more richly nuanced than those available to us from the dominant culture and from feminist, lesbian or gay cultures" (118). Hale notes also that academic discourses about sexuality, including his own, fall well behind the practices he observes and engages in within his sexual communities. Like Stone, Hale seems to call for a nontotalizing discourse about sexual and gender identity in order to acknowledge the inaccuracy and clumsiness of our sexual and gender classifications systems. So, in answer to his own question, "Are lesbians women?" Hale answers, "Some are, some are not, and in many cases there is no fact of the matter" (115). The answer of "some" for now serves to mark the instability of most identifications and hold the "truth" of sex at bay.

While transgender theorists come up with partial and contingent theories of sex and gender, transgender history, in the meantime, has been all but rendered invisible in fact by models of sexual identity that presume that cross-identification is merely an anachronistic model of modern lesbian and gay identity or else they assert that it represents a "third sex."[20] Transgender history, however, has emerged recently as an autonomous discourse partly because of the current visibility of transsexualism and partly because gender communities have distinguished themselves from the larger and more respectable, or at least more assimilated, gay and lesbian communities. Within transgender discourse, a discourse often confined to the edges of gay and lesbian conversation, people are actively recreating the protocols of gender identification and aggressively reclaiming what we might call a history of gender variance. The stakes of transgender studies are such that inevitably transgender becomes a fancy word for transsexual. But to presume that these terms are synonyms is to misunderstand the relation between gender construction and transsexualism. Certainly without the emergence in recent years of transsexual subjects who speak as transsexuals (as opposed to speaking as "real men" or "real women"), the notion of transgenderism could not have emerged; but transgenderism, I would claim, cannot be fully explained via transsexual subjectivity. The visibility of bodies that rescript their own gender codes through surgery and hormones allows for still other bodies to come into view as regendered but not assimilated into maleness or femaleness. These bodies seem in between (and some may be literally, since many transsexuals begin hormone treatments but never go through the surgery) and often do tremble on the verge of one gender or the other; but beyond the hegemony of binary genders, these "in between" genders actually become brave new bodies naming their own idiosyncratic relations to masculinity or femininity. In some embodiments, for example, female masculinity tips into maleness to the point at which transsexual identification becomes necessary and crucial; in others, the female body and its resistance to and intensification of masculinity make transsexual treatments undesirable.

In *Changing Sex: Transsexualism, Technology, and the Idea of Gender*, Bernice Hausman presents a rather rigid historical account of the production of transsexuality in which the transsexual emerges out of the development of medical technologies sophisticated enough to recreate the gendered body. Toward the end of her book Hausman attempts to stave off criticisms of her work that may be based on an emergent notion of transgenderism. She acknowledges that transgender discourse seems to counter her claims that transsexuals are produced solely within medical discourse and that this discourse actually suggests "a fundamental antipathy to the regulatory mode of medical surveillance."[21] Hausman manages to discount such an effect of transgender discourse by arguing that "the desire to celebrate and proliferate individual performances as a way to destabilize 'gender' at large is based on liberal humanist assumptions of self-determination" (197). This is an easy dismissal of a much more complicated and ongoing project. Transgender discourse in no way argues that people should just pick up new genders and eliminate old ones or proliferate at will because gendering is available as a self-determining practice; rather, transgender discourse asks only that we recognize the non-male and non-female genders already in circulation and presently under construction. Hausman's real stakes in this seemingly historical project slip out at the end of her chapter on "Transsexual Autobiographies." Having argued strenuously that transsexual autobiographies collude in the construction of notions of an authentic sex, Hausman attempts to ease off her critical tone and express some empathy for the transsexual condition. She comments earnestly, "Those of us who are not transsexuals may wonder what it is like to feel oneself in the 'wrong body' "(174)! The idea that only transsexuals experience the pain of a "wrong body" shows an incredible myopia about the trials and tribulations of many varieties of perverse embodiment. It neatly ascribes gender confusion and dysphoria to transsexuals and it efficiently constructs a model of "right body" experience that applies, presumably, to people like Hausman. Part of the motivation of a transgender discourse is to produce what Sedgwick calls in *The Epistemology of the Closet* "universalist" models of gender identity in which all gender identities fall under scrutiny rather than simply the unorthodox ones. Hausman resists a universalist model of gender identification and ensures that transsexual and pathology remain annexed while her book maintains the fiction of proper and normal genders.

However, I do not want to suggest here that transsexuality does not differ significantly from transgenderism. Gender dysphoria is one key to the distinction between transsexual and transgender. In the butch woman, for example, gender dysphoria can be less of an obstacle to sexual function and more of an incitement to claim her masculinity affirmatively.[22] For the female-to-male transsexual, gender dysphoria may well create the impossibility of continuing to inhabit a certain body. Female masculinity or butch transgenderism, in a way, presumes that gender comfort is simply not an option, that the body is never completely inhabitable, and that gender dysphoria actually articulates the dislocation of all gendered embodiment, but in its most extreme form. While someone like Hausman cannot quite account for what the relation between "invert," "transsexual," and "lesbian" might be, she can confidently assert, "transsexual is not a term that can accurately be used to describe subjects exhibiting cross-sex behaviors prior to the technical capacity for sex reassignment . . . there is not transsexuality without the surgeon" (116–17). This may well be so, but again, Hausman's totalizing statement manages to erase much more subtle connections and links between various historical forms of cross-identification. Within a contemporary

transgender discourse, for example, we may find that a literary figure like Radclyffe Hall and her novelistic creation Stephen Gordon represent both an early
form of lesbian identification and an early form of transgender identification.

The transgender butch, indeed, has long been a literary tragic hero. Whether it
is Stephen Gordon in Radclyffe Hall's *Well of Loneliness* discovering that "the
loneliest place in this world is the no-man's-land of sex,"[23] or the 1950s butch Jess
Goldberg in Leslie Feinberg's *Stone Butch Blues* (1993) finding herself out of time
and place in contemporary lesbian New York, the narrative of the transgender or
inverted butch has been one of loss, loneliness, and disconnection. The tomboy
butch Frankie Adams in Carson McCullers's novel *The Member of the Wedding*
(1946) perhaps describes most poignantly the meaning of being "unjoined": "This
was the summer when for a long time she had not been a member. She belonged
to no club and was a member of nothing in the world."[24] Frankie feels herself to
be a freak among normal people, an "I" who can never find a "we."[25] This sense of
being unjoined indeed pervades transgender literature. While critics tend to
place such novels in a lesbian canon and then reject them as part of a homophobic
imaginary of the trials and tragedies of stereotypical homosexual identification,
these narratives are also part of a transgender tradition that locates a tragedy of
unbelonging in the sphere of the tomboy, the mannish woman, the passing he-
she. Categorical statements about historical identifications do not really help us
unravel the tangle of identifications that eventually resolve themselves into recognizable axes of identity—what we now quickly refer to as GLBT (Gay, Lesbian,
Bisexual, Transsexual/Transgender) in our political efforts only brushes over the
surface of far more elaborate identities. The relation between GLBT and early sex-
ological classifications still poses many questions about the history of sexuality;
transgender studies promises a few answers.

QUEER PEDAGOGY

Teaching novels of gender variance, indeed teaching the topic of gender variance,
is a pedagogical challenge because it requires that the instructor hold apart definitions of transgenderism and definitions of gay and lesbian identity. For many students, unconventional gender is already the sign of homosexuality; gender and
sexuality become, for them, inextricably combined under the heading of
deviance. A focus on transsexuality as a topic may clear up some of the confu-
sions surrounding sexual and gender variation, but transsexuality as a discussion
focus all too quickly tends to become sensationalistic. On account of a burst of

media attention and talk show appearances, the transsexual body has become in recent times a fetish object for nonnormative physical expression. Students often become fascinated by the transsexual body, by what it might look like, by what it can and cannot do, by its potential to access and provide pleasure. A common talk show question leveled at transsexuals, for example, concerns postoperative orgasm. Such a question presumes, first, that the orgasm represents successful reembodiment; second, that changing one's sex is at base a sexual rather than a gender decision; third, that "normally" gendered bodies are always capable of orgasm. As Stone and Stryker suggest, however, the current fascination with the transsexual body in both talk shows and academic discourse can be helpful only if it reflects back on the artificiality of all gendered bodies. Teaching transgenderism involves, as much as anything, teaching the strangeness and transitivity of most gendered bodies while, on the one hand, holding onto the specificity of transsexual experience and, on the other hand, refusing to allow the transsexual body to bear the burden of representing paradigmatic gender transitivity.

Discussions of gay and lesbian studies pedagogy tend to focus on the sexualization of the classroom, questions about student-teacher dynamics, coming out issues, and problems related to homophobic student response.[26] A queer pedagogy, however, one that includes the discussion of a multitude of sexual minorities and minority genders, might avoid this particular nexus of concerns by refusing the schemata of identitarian institutional positions (lesbian teacher and heterosexual students, for example) and proceed eccentrically. By this I mean that the queer teacher may take up an eccentric position in relation to queer material and position herself as always implicated in *and* outside the topics she is teaching. Teaching material on transsexuality, for example, might mean refusing to simply identify as transsexual or as nontranssexual and rather focusing on what set of issues transsexuality raises and how all genders and embodiments look strange when subjected to medical and other voyeuristic forms of scrutiny.

Who's afraid of queer theory? Transgender studies represents one future trajectory of queer theory. The resistance offered to queer theory by some old-guard feminists and Marxists ensures that the history of the transgender subject in particular remains a tragic history, unrecuperable, unreadable, unjoined. My project on "female masculinity" imagines a queer future as a postmodern condition that does not loom in the distance awaiting the withering away of a persistent hetero-patriarchy but that resides here and now visible already in bold, gender-resistant bodies. Queer pedagogies are not confined to the classroom; rather, we might imagine a queer pedagogical practice as one that learns as much from unofficial as from official sources—queer theory informs such a pedagogy but so too do queer zines, films, videos, and a variety of popular knowledges.

Notes

1. This is more of a general opinion than the idea of one particular person. However, for an example of an essay that seems to regard queer theory suspiciously as a body of work by gay men and for gay men, see Elizabeth Weed, "The More Things Change," *differences* (special issue on "More Gender Trouble: Feminism Meets Queer Theory") 6, nos. 2–3 (summer–fall 1994): 249–73.

2. Gayle Rubin, "Thinking Sex: Notes for a Radical Theory of the Politics of Sexuality," in *Pleasure and Danger: Exploring Female Sexuality*, ed. Carole Vance (Boston: Routledge and Kegan Paul, 1984), 310.

3. Samuel Delany, "Street Talk/Straight Talk," *differences* (special issue on Queer Theory) 3, no. 2 (1991): 21–38.

4. Judith Butler, "Against Proper Objects," *differences* 6, nos. 2–3 (summer–fall 1994): 24.

5. Vance, ed., *Pleasure and Danger*; SAMOIS, eds., *Coming to Power* (Boston: Alyson Press, 1981); Lisa Duggan and Nan D. Hunter, *Sex Wars* (New York: Routledge, 1996); see also Alice Echols, "The Taming of the Id: Feminist Sexual Politics, 1968–1983," in *Pleasure and Danger*, ed. Vance, 50–72.

6. Martin writes, "Because her language is so compelling, my attention was caught over and over by the terms in which Sedgwick continues to cast gender throughout the introduction, as constraint, enmeshment, miring, and fixity, as she contrasts the excesses of sexuality, indicatively male, to 'the coarser stigmata of gender difference' (EC, 32)" (107). Biddy Martin, "Sexualities without Genders and Other Queer Utopias," *Diacritics* (special issue on "Critical Crossings," ed. Judith Butler and Biddy Martin), 24, nos. 2–3 (summer–fall 1994): 104–21.

7. See Donald Morton, *Materially Queer* (New York: Routledge, 1996).

8. Michel Foucault, *The History of Sexuality*, vol. 1, *An Introduction* (New York: Vintage, 1980).

9. "The Queer Present Tense" was the title of an MLA session arranged by Robyn Wiegman for the 1995 MLA. I presented an earlier version of this essay at that session.

10. Gayle Rubin, "Sexual Traffic: Interview of Gayle Rubin with Judith Butler," *differences* 6, nos. 2–3 (summer–fall 1994): 62–99.

11. See Joan Nestle, *A Restricted Country* (Ithaca: Firebrand, 1987); Leslie Feinberg, *Stone Butch Blues: A Novel* (Ithaca: Firebrand, 1993); Pat Califia, *Public Sex: The Culture of Radical Sex* (Pittsburgh: Cleis, 1994); Susie Bright, *Susie Bright's Sexual Reality: A Virtual Sex World Reader* (San Francisco: Cleis, 1993).

12. See accounts in Emma Donoghue, *Passions between Women: British Lesbian Culture, 1668–1801* (New York: HarperCollins, 1995); Dianne Dugaw, *Warrior Women and Popular Balladry, 1650–1850* (New York: Cambridge University Press, 1989).

13. See Esther Newton, " 'The Mythic Mannish Lesbian': Radclyffe Hall and the New Woman," *Signs* 9 (summer 1984): 557–75; George Chauncey Jr., "From Sexual Inversion to Homosexuality: Medicine and the Changing Conceptualization of Female Deviance," *Salmagundi* (special issue on Homosexuality: Sacrilege, Vision, Politics), nos. 58–59 (1982–83): 114–46; Martha Vicinus, " 'They Wonder to Which Sex I Belong': The Historical Roots of the Modern Lesbian Identity," *Feminist Studies* 18, no. 3 (fall 1992): 467–98.

14. Lisa Duggan, "The Trials of Alice Mitchell: Sensationalism, Sexology, and the Lesbian Subject in Turn-of-the-Century America," *Signs* 18, no. 4 (summer 1993): 791–814.

15. Terry Castle, *The Apparitional Lesbian: Female Homosexuality and Modern Culture* (New York: Columbia University Press, 1993), 10.

16. Valerie Traub, "The Psychomorphology of the Clitoris," *GLQ* 2 (1995): 98–99.

17. Ann Lister, *No Priest but Love: The Diaries of Ann Lister from 1824–1826*, ed. Helena Whitbread (New York: New York University Press, 1992), 49.

18. Susan Stryker, "My Words to Victor Frankenstein above the Village of Chamounix: Performing Transgender Rage," *GLQ* 1, no. 3 (1994): 237–54; Jacob Hale, "Are Lesbians Women?" *Hypatia* 11, no. 2 (spring 1996): 94–121; Sandy Stone, "The Empire Strikes Back: A Posttranssexual Manifesto," in *Body Guards: The Cultural Politics of Gender Ambiguity*, ed. Julia Epstein and Kristin Straub (New York: Routledge, 1991), 280–304.

19. In our introductory essay to *Posthuman Bodies* (Bloomington: Indiana University Press, 1995), Ira Livingston and I argued for the "someness" of identity: "How many races, genders, sexualities are there? Some. How many are you? Some. 'Some' is not an indefinite number awaiting a more accurate measurement, but a rigorous theoretical mandate whose specification, necessary as it is (since 'the multiple must be made'), is neither numerable nor, in the common sense, innumerable" (9).

20. See Gil Herdt, ed., *Third Sex, Third Gender: Beyond Sexual Dimorphism in Culture and History* (New York: Zone Books, 1994).

21. Bernice Hausman, *Changing Sex: Transsexualism, Technology and the Idea of Gender* (Durham: Duke University Press, 1995), 195.

22. Many transsexuals would completely reject the use of the term "gender dysphoria" since it is produced by a pathologizing medical literature on transsexualism. I am holding on to the term here because I think it usefully describes at least one aspect of cross-gender identification. "Gender dysphoria" should not be cast as the main cause of transsexualism but rather as an effect of the inefficacy of the binary gender system.

23. Radclyffe Hall, *The Well of Loneliness* (1928; reprint, New York: Anchor Books, 1990), 79.

24. Carson McCullers, *The Member of the Wedding* (New York: Bantam, 1946), 1.

25. See Elizabeth Freeman, "The 'We of Me': *The Member of the Wedding*'s Novel Alliances" for an intricate and nuanced reading of the construction of queer affiliation. *Women and Performance* (special issue on Queer Acts, ed. Jose Esteban Muñoz and Amanda Barrett), 8, 2, no. 16: 111–36.
26. See volumes like George E. Haggerty and Bonnie Zimmerman, eds., *Professions of Desire: Lesbian and Gay Studies in Literature* (New York: MLA Publications, 1995); Linda Garber, *Tilting the Tower: Lesbians, Teaching, Queer Subjects* (New York: Routledge, 1994).

Works Cited

Bright, Susie. 1993. *Susie Bright's Sexual Reality: A Virtual Sex World Reader*. San Francisco: Cleis Press.

Butler, Judith. 1994. "Against Proper Objects." *differences* (special issue on "More Gender Trouble: Feminism Meets Queer Theory") 6, nos. 2–3 (summer–fall): 24.

Califia, Pat. 1994. *Public Sex: The Culture of Radical Sex*. Pittsburgh: Cleis.

Castle, Terry. 1993. *The Apparitional Lesbian: Female Homosexuality and Modern Culture*. New York: Columbia University Press.

Chauncey, George Jr. 1982–83. "From Sexual Inversion to Homosexuality: Medicine and the Changing Conceptualization of Female Deviance." *Salmagundi* (special issue on "Homosexuality: Sacrilege, Vision, Politics"), nos. 58–59 (1982–83): 114–46.

Delany, Samuel. 1991. "Street Talk/Straight Talk." *differences* (special issue on Queer Theory) 3, no. 2: 21–38.

Donoghue, Emma. 1995. *Passions between Women: British Lesbian Culture, 1668–1801*. New York: HarperCollins.

Dugaw, Dianne. 1989. *Warrior Women and Popular Balladry, 1650–1850*. New York: Cambridge University Press.

Duggan, Lisa. 1993. "The Trials of Alice Mitchell: Sensationalism, Sexology, and the Lesbian Subject in Turn-of-the-Century America." *Signs* 18, no. 4 (summer): 798.

Duggan, Lisa, and Nan D. Hunter. 1996. *Sex Wars*. New York: Routledge.

Echols, Alice. 1984. "The Taming of the Id: Feminist Sexual Politics, 1968–1983." In *Pleasure and Danger*, ed. Vance, 50–72.

Feinberg, Leslie. 1993. *Stone Butch Blues: A Novel*. Ithaca: Firebrand.

Foucault, Michel. 1980. *The History of Sexuality*. Vol. 1, *An Introduction*. New York: Vintage.

Freeman, Elizabeth. "The 'We of Me': *The Member of the Wedding*'s Novel Alliances." *Women and Performance* (special Issue on Queer Acts, ed. Jose Esteban Muñoz and Amanda Barrett) 8, 2, no. 16: 111–36.

Garber, Linda. 1994. *Tilting the Tower: Lesbians, Teaching, Queer Subjects*. New York: Routledge.

Haggerty, George E., and Bonnie Zimmerman. 1995. *Professions of Desire: Lesbian and Gay Studies in Literature*. New York: MLA Publications.

Halberstam, Judith, and Ira Livingston, eds. 1995. Introduction to *Posthuman Bodies*. Bloomington: Indiana University Press.

Hale, Jacob. 1996. "Are Lesbians Women?" *Hypatia* 11, no. 2 (spring): 94–121.

Hall, Radclyffe. 1990. *The Well of Loneliness*. 1928. Reprint, New York: Anchor Books.

Hausman, Bernice. 1995. *Changing Sex: Transsexualism, Technology, and the Idea of Gender*. Durham: Duke University Press.

Herdt, Gil, ed. 1994. *Third Sex, Third Gender: Beyond Sexual Dimorphism in Culture and History*. New York: Zone Books.

Lister, Ann. 1992. *No Priest but Love: The Diaries of Ann Lister from 1824–1826*, ed. Helena Whitbread. New York: New York University Press.

Martin, Biddy. 1994. "Sexualities without Genders and Other Queer Utopias." *Diacritics* (special issue on "Critical Crossings," ed. Judith Butler and Biddy Martin) 24, nos. 2–3 (summer–fall): 104–21.

McCullers, Carson. 1946. *The Member of the Wedding*. New York: Bantam.

Morton, Donald. 1996. *Materially Queer*. New York: Routledge.

Nestle, Joan. 1987. *A Restricted Country*. Ithaca: Firebrand.

Newton, Esther. 1984. " 'The Mythic Mannish Lesbian': Radclyffe Hall and the New Woman." *Signs* 9 (summer): 557–75.

Rubin, Gayle. 1984. "Thinking Sex: Notes for a Radical Theory of the Politics of Sexuality." In *Pleasure and Danger*, ed. Vance, 267–319.

———. 1994. "Sexual Traffic: Interview of Gayle Rubin with Judith Butler." *differences* (special issue on "More Gender Trouble: Feminism Meets Queer Theory") 6, nos. 2–3 (summer–fall): 62–99.

SAMOIS, eds. 1981. *Coming to Power*. Boston: Alyson Press.

Sedgwick, Eve K. 1991. *The Epistemology of the Closet*. Berkeley: University of California Press.

Stone, Sandy. 1991. "The Empire Strikes Back: A Posttranssexual Manifesto." In *Body Guards: The Cultural Politics of Gender Ambiguity*, ed. Julia Epstein and Kristin Straub, 280–304. New York: Routledge.

Stryker, Susan. 1994. "My Words to Victor Frankenstein above the Village of Chamounix: Performing Transgender Rage." *GLQ* 1, no. 3: 237–54.

Traub, Valerie. 1995. "The Psychomorphology of the Clitoris." *GLQ* 2: 98–99.

Vance, Carole, ed. 1984. *Pleasure and Danger: Exploring Female Sexuality*. Boston: Routledge and Kegan Paul.

Vicinus, Martha. 1992. " 'They Wonder to Which Sex I Belong': The Historical Roots of the Modern Lesbian Identity." *Feminist Studies* 18, no. 3 (fall): 467–98.

Weed, Elizabeth. 1994. "The More Things Change." *differences* (special issue on "More Gender Trouble: Feminism Meets Queer Theory") 6, nos. 2–3 (summer–fall): 249–73.

Deconstructing the Family Album

19

Gregory L. Ulmer

The course is called "The Age of the Avant-Garde." The assignment is to compose an avant-garde family album. The experiment is to be carried out in three parts over the fifteen weeks of the semester: part 1—a theory to provide the rationale for such an album; part 2—a poetics to provide a method for composing the album; part 3—a specific experiment to test the theory and poetics in an actual version of the album.

The readings have changed each time I have taught the course, but the function of the readings remains the same: to put the students in a double bind; to confront them with a seemingly irresolvable dilemma. The most recent book used for this purpose is Jordan and Weedon, *Cultural Politics: Class, Gender, Race and the Postmodern World*. This book establishes nicely the problematic within which the project will unfold. The first thing we learn is that the very idea of an avant-garde family album is a contradiction in terms, for a prominent feature of most of the movements of the historical avant-garde is a rejection of, rebellion against, the bourgeois family. This rejection of the family is part of a systematic, holistic refusal of all the institutions of official Western civilization.

One of the chief goals of the course is to learn how to innovate, how to generate new ideas and methods, to understand through the example of the avant-garde how the creative process works. From the beginning, then, we work with the heuristic CATTt that I described in *Heuretics*. Every invention may be analyzed in terms of this heuristic: Contrast, Analogy, Theory, Target, and tale. At this stage we use the heuristic loosely, noting that the slot of Contrast (C) is filled by any and all of the practices of official culture. The innovators already know that whatever they are going to make, it will not resemble the existing, official, approved criteria for the practice in question. In our case, our album will not reproduce the conventions of the traditional family album.

We used the concept of the popcycle to establish a specific meaning for Family as a site of production. The popcycle refers to the relationship among the central educational institutions of society—Family, Entertainment, School (K–12), and Discipline (the specialized fields of knowledge). Each institution has a discourse that operates by its own logic, form, and means of proof. For some individuals Family might be replaced by Street, or Entertainment might be replaced by Church. Althusser characterized such institutions as constituting the state ideological apparatus, functioning to reproduce in the individual the values and beliefs of the dominant interests in the society. What Althusser thus characterized negatively as producing a potential conformity of thought, however, the literature on creativity characterizes more favorably by indicating that whatever happens to individuals during their entry into language from birth through the decade of the teens is the basis for their accomplishments in their careers thereafter (not to mention in their personal lives).

Early in the course we discuss the popcycle, locating our experiences of how it delimits and directs the circulation of ideas and signification through the society. Identity formation is constructed within this circulation. Children enter the world within the institution of the family, where they learn a native language. In our context the immediate question is, what is the nature of this experience? Is it that of the bourgeois family? Various studies have shown that many Americans no longer learn language in the traditional way—in a nurturing dialogue with a housewife mother, being read to every night from books. Instead, many children enter language by interacting with siblings and/or peers in the presence of a television set. Such children may experience little more than one minute per day of conversation with an adult, and have almost no contact with books. In addition, the language spoken on the television (English) may not be the one spoken in the home or place of day care.

Entertainment now has an equal share with the family in introducing children into language. As we know from our theories, the entry into language plays a foundational role in the formation of human identity. The popcycle suggests that the entry into language (theorized in psychoanalysis under the spectacularly named concept of "castration") is not limited to the entry into natural language, but continues with the entry into the other dimensions of discourse central to the civilization—writing, in our case, and now increasingly the use of electronic media. As many volumes of media criticism have shown, television is essentially about Family. The values of Family in general, and of a certain ideology of the dominant culture in particular, are reproduced in the programming flow of the television day. Here is the site of the problem to which much critique is devoted: the decline of the public sphere of literacy and its replacement by an electronic sphere that delivers consumers directly to markets. The unconscious is structured like a language; now that Entertainment (organized around a discourse of commercialism) participates equally with Family in the entry into language, the concern is that any possibility of the critical distance needed to support the individual autonomy of a conscious self has disappeared.

The popcycle indicates that the fears about the decline of the public sphere are misplaced, or rather that the function once performed by that sphere is displaced, in that the discourse of Entertainment is internalized as part of learning the native language. Having learned language within the discourses of Family and Entertainment, the children enter the third institution of the popcycle—School. The discourse of School helps clarify an important difference between the dual entry into language conducted up to this point: by the time they enter School, children have entered simultaneously into orality (maintained within Family) and electracy (emerging within Entertainment). They have the foundations of an oral culture from their homes and an electrate culture from television. This originary bilingualism is entirely new; its implications have not yet been taken into account.

In the popcycle each individual passes through the grammatological history of the civilization, experiencing within identity formation the conflicts created in the passage from one apparatus to another—orality, literacy, electracy. In School children enter into writing, literacy. The content of this literacy as well as the design of the practices of learning reproduce the dominant values of the culture. K–12 schooling, institutionalized in terms of local school boards and state laws, explicitly promotes a cultural literacy that does for the families collected within the community what Family does for the individuals collected within it. Text-books are to School what the album is to Family—a record of memory and identity. The community does not and cannot apologize for this bias, anymore than does a family for raising its children within a framework of its own beliefs. An expectation that a society should educate its people "in general" would indicate a misunderstanding, a false application of an enabling fiction of Discipline (the claim to universal truth within objective science) to the other discourses of the popcycle. At the same time, Discipline adds to the popcycle an ability to relativize official culture. It reveals, that is, that official culture establishes a hierarchy of norms that favors certain cultural traditions and subordinates others.

When students reach the university they are natives of the three discourses of the popcycle (they are trilingual). Few if any students who enter the university have been raised within the institution of the Street, in which the gang replaces blood relatives as the support group. "Blood," however, is still important at the level of proof. The Street with its tradition of the "school of hard knocks," however, is still reproduced within the popcycle. Many of my students, that is (and some of my colleagues), have internalized the look and style of the Street through the logic of fashion that structures Entertainment. Against the formulas of critique that characterized the ideological apparatus as reproducing a homogeneous identity in the image of the dominant values, the students find themselves constructed in terms of the fundamental discontinuities separating the three discourses they have internalized—orality, electracy, literacy. Critique is right about the contradictions informing modern existence, but grammatology locates these contradictions somewhat differently.

The family album project is a practice within the institution of Discipline in the University. Discipline has a relationship to School similar to that which Entertainment has with Family. With the nearly universal service status of radio and television, Family is the site of delivery of Entertainment, thus coming into a host-parasite relationship like that of the Discipline-trained specialist in tertiary schooling. Although television promotes the official idea of "family," the values of Family and of Entertainment are not entirely compatible, and even at odds, similar to the conflict of values separating School and Discipline. Murphy Brown versus Dan Quayle captured the conflict of values separating the diversity of families from the official version promoted on television. This divergence covers over a far greater disparity in the two discourses—the difference between orality and electracy (a difference in the very formation of identity).

The incompatibility between Discipline and School, meanwhile, is perhaps most evident in the fields of the liberal and fine arts, where the conflict between the purposes of School to reproduce the values of the dominant culture and the purpose of Discipline to promote critique has become sufficiently severe to attract the attention of Entertainment. The phrases "political correctness" and "culture wars" are the Entertainment labels for this conflict. Again, it is ironic that journalism (the specialized voice of Entertainment as knowledge) expresses the defense of official culture against Discipline. In reality, Entertainment (as the chief institutionalization of electronic technology until now) is one of the principal forces changing the formation of identity in electracy. Discipline, with its theories of the constructed subject that underlie the attacks on humanistic self-hood as an ideology, is simply stating the concept of identity that Entertainment is performing. The practice of identity formation emerging in electracy is anticipated and modeled by the phenomenon of celebrity and fame in Entertainment discourse. Critique rails against Entertainment, but historically they are on the same side: celebrity—made possible by media culture—is the prototype of the constructed subject theorized in critique.

Understanding the popcycle is the key to the family album project. The popcycle allows us to position ourselves at the center of this set of institutions and to recognize that all of them together constitute our Symbolic order. In this context the limitations of critique become apparent. Critique is so committed to the institution of literacy that it assumes the possibility of abstracting oneself out of the other founding discourses of language (orality and electracy). Critique engages in the external, abstract attack on traditional and commercial processes of signification, ignoring the fact that these significations are also inside, and intrinsic to the intelligence of the critics themselves, not to mention that of the citizens of the society. Learning the discourse of any one institution of the popcycle does not replace the others. Rather, each discourse supplements the others. Critique compounds the dilemmas of alienation and leads principally to a condition of fundamental confusion.

A positive way to state this limitation might be to say that critique is justified in its certainty about its own correctness within the frame of modernism, which valorizes an absolute segregation across the institutions, a compartmentalizing tendency of each medium and practice to find its own pure form. Critique, including its content and political themes, is a pure form. Ironically, critique is formalist in this sense of being conducted for its own sake, within the confines of specialized disciplinarity. Various individual critics have attempted to act upon

their ideals in other institutions, of course, but many have not, contenting themselves with career advancement through publications addressing other academics while claiming, despite their knowledge of the ideological apparatus, that
the classroom is a site of political "intervention." One lesson to learn from this
modernist arrangement is that critique is valuable precisely as the logic and
proof of Discipline, no more and no less, while each of the other discourses of the
popcycle has its own methods of logic and proof.

Critique cannot substitute for these other languages and practices. Critique
throughout the period of the Enlightenment has behaved as if its proper goal
were to make analytical logic the universal practice of thinking in every discourse of society. In the context of the popcycle, however, the goal may be
revised: each of the discourses is adequate to itself, within its own setting. The
failure of reason lies not with the style of cognition in each discourse, but in
their mutual isolation. The challenge of the family album project is to design a
practice capable of supporting the circulation of thought from one discourse to
the other, and to include Discipline in this process. The challenge, that is, is to
learn how to bring the two nested pairs of institutions into fruitful interaction
(Family and Entertainment on one side, with School and Discipline on the other).
This assignment does not reject critique (does not abandon the discourse of Discipline), but provides a grammatological adjustment intended to show how the
classroom might actually communicate with the home.

The complexity of the situation is indicated in the second dimension of the double bind structuring the family album assignment. The students must confront
not only the contradiction of a vanguard family album, but also the fact that the
book required as the source for their theoretical rationale of the project places the
avant-garde in a critical frame. In terms of the CATTt heuristic, the vanguard contrasted itself with the official institutions of modern industrial society (C), to
which it added an Analogy (A) of admired practices that it adopted as an alternative resource for its designs—the aesthetic creations of non-Western civilization.
Cultural Politics frames the history of the avant-garde in terms of the story of
primitivism, in order to make the point that the avant-garde simply reversed the
racist stereotypes of European colonial imperialism. The vanguard diagnosed the
ills of modernist Europe as alienation from the life of the body, emotion, nature,
and the like. Their search, as noted earlier, was not just for a different style of art,
but for a different style of life. The instrumentalization of the lifeworld that
resulted from the total triumph of scientific, positivist, rationalist values had to be

countered by an alliance with all those persons, behaviors, or formations marginalized and subordinated by this totalized, instrumental worldview. This meant celebrating, promoting, and embracing everything that Western dominant culture devalued—everything associated with savages, the insane, children, and women (outsider art). As Jordan and Weedon demonstrate, the vanguard inversion (celebrating the body of the Other as being wild and sexual, rather than condemning it for these same qualities) remains within the ideology of racism, sexism, and so forth.

This frame through which critique (represented by Jordan and Weedon) regards the vanguard reveals a certain naïveté within the arts about the ideological apparatus. The artists were like children themselves, who admired the objects produced within an alien society as if they were strange and wonderful toys. They disregarded the popcycle of culture that confined and directed the behaviors of these Others every bit as much as did the official culture of Western civilization. Like children or songwriters who think of birds as being "free," rather than as being determined by the laws of nature in a cruel struggle for survival, the artists idealized their own stereotypes. But this demystification does not reduce the complexity of the paradox. At the same time, critique's attack against primitivism may be seen as of a piece with the general imperialist superiority that Enlightenment civilization felt over against the civilizations of magic: critique is fundamentally committed to the epistemology of science and is no more capable of acknowledging the efficacy of the sorcery embraced by any number of vanguardists than is any other branch of science. Critique is itself ideological, is a "rhetoric" in Foucault's sense. Part of the paradox of the assignment is this situation in which critique itself is blind to the insights that it makes possible. The students have no firm ground, no point of certainty, no archimedean site of leverage that allows them in advance to know what they "should" think about the project.

Because this critical frame is included in our reading of the avant-garde, the students are not permitted simply to identify with the avant-garde and reproduce its solution to the problem of alienation—the adoption of the practices of the Other. At the same time, the popcycle context relativizes the judgments asserted by critique. Juxtaposing the attitudes of the avant-garde and of critique to the Other shows that the disagreement is over which period of Otherness one is to embrace: the past (vanguard) or the present (critique). Critique is as alienated from the official culture of the West as was the vanguard, but it identifies with the historically marginalized Others in their colonized degradation rather than in their precolumbian moment of power. In our context, these two positions constitute the terms of a problematic. Neither the vanguard nor critique has the solution to this dilemma; we have to take the project up in our turn. The same questions that the vanguardists and critics posed to themselves we must pose again in our turn from our own position. We do not claim to be avant-garde, neither in art nor in politics. The assignment acknowledges its place in the popcycle and asks of us that we use the understanding provided by our discipline knowledge to design a practice that would facilitate the circulation of this understanding through the society. The ethics and politics of grammatology are based on this belief in the transformative effects of learning (rather than simply a faith in education as an institution). The purpose of the paradox is to forestall the righteousness that often accompanies critique, and to redirect the critical attention onto one's own position.

The disciplines of criticism, according to this ethics, have as much responsibility toward the citizens of the society as do the other disciplines of knowledge such as agriculture or medicine or political science. The goal of critique to influence daily life, in other words, is an imperative within Discipline: this desire is the essence of this particular discourse, whose form is nothing other than problem solving. Is critique capable of learning, or does it know everything already? If our best disciplinary theories convince us that human identity is constructed within social institutions, our role should be to figure out how to act on that insight in practice. The question, however, is which practice.

The avant-garde family album is first of all a project of self-knowledge. It is a mystory (as I discussed in *Teletheory*). In the light of the popcycle the experiment turns out to concern the invention of a practice to help the family work productively with the flow of information circulating in the society. It is a way to draw on all the discourses at once, to think simultaneously in incompatible logics, rather than to replace all other modes of reasoning with the logic of Discipline. The method is to generate the design by composing an analogy with the materials assigned in the course. These materials are not in fact "models" but "relays." We experience for ourselves the risks taken by the historical vanguard since we are intervening in our own case, in our own experience of the different realities classified by the popcycle. We know that if we show this album to our family they might be upset, hurt, and worse. Perhaps it is not for the family that made me, but the one I will make in the future. When we take the project personally, the learning overflows the boundaries of the academy to engage holistically with our own identity formation.

The first demand in writing the theory is to break our old habits. The practical goal of the assignment is to learn to add the materials of the discipline to our thinking. The instructions ask the students to use the readings to generate their theory, to put their plans into the prosthesis of method, invented to give individuals access to the knowledge accumulated throughout the history of literacy. When the students complain that the disciplinary materials are not "clear," I know that they are reading them as if spoken in language of Family. If they complain that the discipline materials are boring, I know that they are looking at them as if they functioned as Entertainment. If they become anxious about making a mistake, I recognize their School training. None of these expectations fit the discourse of Discipline, which has its own mood.

The structure of the method is as follows: inventory what the avant-garde did; extrapolate to our own case. The solution to the problem is to work with a page divided into two columns. On the left side inventory the major moves of the vanguard; on the right side name each slot that must be filled in for our rationale. For example: (1) the vanguard felt alienated from the official values of their society; (2) the vanguard rejected these norms and looked to non-Western civilizations for alternative norms; (3) these alternatives called for the abandonment of the Western commitment to representational realism; (4) realism was to be replaced with the norms of a magical worldview, in which the arts are not a representation of life but participate directly in the conduct of life. "Extrapolation" names the move of invention, in which the students generalize a series of questions from the relay: they do not take the model literally. They do not conclude that they too must practice magic, for example; rather, they must find a way to make the album not a representation of an object but a way of living with a real family.

The expectation of the method is that the students will propose, at least initially, similar moves for themselves, extrapolated from the institution of Discipline (specialized arts) to Family. The relay from the vanguard proposes that we examine our own experience of alienation (to test the claims of alienation); that we experimentally replace the norms of our family practices with norms from an alien tradition (to identify the norms expected in each of the ideological slots valued by our families—for example, White, Anglo-Saxon, Protestant, Bourgeois, Heterosexual, Masculine, American), and replace or supplement them with the norms of the subordinated value in each case; and that we abandon our concern with a realistic representation of our family and replace it with procedures for using the media directly as means for interacting with ourselves, with other people, and with the other institutions we inhabit. One of the lessons learned from teaching this course any number of times is that while the students have little trouble following the procedure through its first two steps, they invariably miss the final two altogether.

Poststructural theory, of course, predicts this very problem—that it is easier to change the content of our thinking than its form. Indeed, poststructuralism in general and deconstruction in particular take the position that a change in thinking is possible only if it includes a change in the forms of representation. Thus, for example, the establishment of minority studies in the academy changes nothing if the forms and practices of academic writing remain unchanged. At the same time, needless to say, experimentation with form in the absence of alternative contents is equally meaningless. In our context, the students assume that the goal of the avant-garde album is a greater realism—to include all those things that the conventional album ignores; to go beyond the recording of ritual occasions such as weddings and birthdays to include documentation of spousal abuse, quotidian triviality such as how one brushes one's teeth, and any other area of experience they can think of that is currently underrepresented in the family record. The impulse is to become ethnographers of the home.

The positive legacy of the avant-garde, however, is somewhat different from this habit of realism. Part of the break with Western aesthetics is readily appreciated by the class. The vanguard break with the demands of craft, with the adoption of techniques such as automatic writing, collage, and various chance procedures, create the belief that here is art anyone could make. The point, of course, is that such practices make the category of "art" irrelevant. In wanting to break down the barriers separating art from daily life, the avant-garde showed how it was possible to popularize and democratize aesthetic practice. Aesthetics was for everybody, just as is physical health. It makes as little sense to reserve aesthetic performance to specialists in the arts as it would to reserve exercise to professional athletes. It follows that the vanguard album is not against professionalism as such, but opens a path of communication between experts and amateurs. The family album project embraces this lesson, being a practice for the amateur use of any and all media available to the private individual. The medium of our project may be confined to paper, including photo albums, writing, collage, photocopy, and the like. However, it may also extend to the audio and video taping equipment becoming ever more common in the home, and even the computer with its tools of graphic design and connection to the World Wide

Web. The theory and poetics of the vanguard album are general enough to be applied to whatever tools the family cares to use, however low- or high-tech.

At this point I have discussed only the first part—the theory—of a three-part project. Perhaps I have said enough to give a sense of how I design assignments to relate to social issues outside the university. Much more could be said about the second part—using various practices of the experimental and independent arts as relays from which to extrapolate a poetics for amateurs—and the final part, the experiment itself, in which the students traverse their own paths through the popcycle. Instead of the lengthy account such a description might require, let me instead relate the metaphor I use to introduce the popcycle to the class. The popcycle operates in the manner of the Enigma machine used by the German military to encrypt all its communications during the Hitler era. The history of the Enigma machine supplies a certain allegory of the use of the popcycle in my pedagogy.

The Enigma machine was essentially a typewriter that automated electronically the process of encryption. The message was typed into the machine and passed through a series of four rotors. The first three rotors displaced the original letter through the alphabet, creating an extraordinarily complex number of possible variations. The fourth rotor was a reflector that sent the message back through the other three rotors. For anyone who knew the original settings of the rotors, the encrypted message could be typed into another Enigma machine and the output would be the decoded communication. In my allegory, the popcycle with its four institutions corresponds to the four rotors of the Enigma machine, with the reflector rotor being the discourse of Discipline. The initial settings are the norms of official culture that determine the codes of each discourse.

An additional part of the history is the fact that the Allies broke the German code even before World War II started. For us, the writing of a mystory corresponds to this cracking of the code. Specifically, Alan Turing working for British Intelligence made a breakthrough in decryption when he proposed to take advantage of the pattern created in the encrypted messages by the German tendency to use stereotyped formulations in their posts. The repetitions of these stereotyped phrases (such as always beginning with the title or rank of the officer in charge, and other such protocols of military address) created patterns that drastically reduced the permutations in the information and allowed the British to guess the original settings of the encrypting rotors. Similarly, the stereotypes issuing from each of the discourses of the popcycle may be lined up, matched, and their pattern mapped as the key to understanding one's own identity as constructed within these institutions. The family album project is a version of this larger mystorical genre, the mystory being to an individual learner what history is to a given community. Or, we might say that in each of us is played out this war of encryption between the Nazis and Allies: every message the Enigma Engine of official culture encrypts, the mystory of the Allies may decipher.

The allegory further suggests that the composition of a mystory is not an end in itself, but just the first step in a plan of action. When the Allies deciphered the German communiqués, their work had just begun. For us, the composition of a vanguard family album is not the end of our learning, but a way to sustain learning beyond the limits of education as an institution. Since I have made so many unsupported assertions so far, it might be appropriate to break off this discussion with one more, stated as a proposal or goal rather than as a claim. What is the mystory for? It is to become the practice of the new institution forming around the Internet. The Internet, that is, is the institutionalization of computing in the same way that cinema institutionalized film and television institutionalized video. These latter institutions, however, were the vehicles of Entertainment, which has emerged as the challenger to School and literacy as the vehicle of collective cognition. Or rather, the insight of grammatology is that Entertainment has as much to offer to electracy as does Discipline; in electracy myth and critique (the methods of Entertainment and Discipline respectively) will not be the enemies that they were during the era of literacy.

The final relay of the assignment, provided to guide the design of the experiment, is *Mixed Blessings*, by Lucy Lippard. At this point in the course the students are prepared to appreciate the syncretic aesthetics demonstrated in the survey of multicultural practices covered in this study. Multiculturalism proves to be one solution to the paradox confronted at the beginning of the course: the contradiction-in-terms represented by a vanguard family album. Lippard compiles an extensive review of works that combine avant-garde and experimental practices with the traditional materials of the ethnic backgrounds of the artists. Far from turning against their family traditions, these multicultural artists research their heritage and bring its themes and forms and symbols into contact with the modernist devices of the specialized arts. Amateur and outsider makers are treated alongside individuals with degrees from the most prestigious art schools.

As an alternative to the primitivism of the historical avant-garde (first world artists appropriating the past traditions of colonized peoples), the multicultural artists reappropriated the inventions of the primitivists (the collage-montage styles of modernism) on behalf of the present condition of those cultures still marginalized. Lippard makes it clear, however, that separatism is not the best answer to the melting-pot model of subjectivation: the polarity of apartheid/melting pot is a false opposition. Rather, the relays show us a poetics of syncretism, in which the materials of different cultures enter into unpredictable combinations with one another to form hybrids across the divisions of orality-electracy-literacy. The final instruction for the album is not only to research the ethnic traditions of one's given heritage, but to self-consciously explore the resources of other heritages as well. In place of the binary dialectic of Western and Other, the vanguard album proposes a new practice in which families open their habits to the states of mind of other cultures, in the same way that they have welcomed other cuisines into their kitchens.

This last analogy offers a vehicle for this difficult and controversial lesson. We watch a tape of *The Frugal Gourmet* showing how to make chili. Our poetics in general, and the final design of the experiment in particular, amount to a style of making that Plato associated with sophistry and dismissed contemptuously as mere "cooking." The use of cooking, with its lists of ingredients and recipes for combining them, has the added advantage in my context of a relay for how to introduce an actual family to a broader interest in cultural syncretism. Do you like chili? It is a syncretic dish—a hybrid of several different cuisines. Food and music, as Lippard notes, tend to travel well across the borders of different communities. World music is perhaps an even better image than cooking to give a glimpse of the hybrid practices emerging within electracy. In our post-primitivist albums we begin to experiment with adding still more aspects of world cultures to our options for living, to our lifestyles and state of mind.

The new album is post-primitivist because its makers do not disavow their own heritage in turning to other traditions. As Gilles Deleuze once advised, the strategy is to find the minority within oneself. The relay for this search is the work of African American artists, who show how to perform the double-consciousness of recovering a traditional culture nearly destroyed by the middle passage, and renovate it through the inventions of modernism. These artists appropriate vernacular methods of representation, especially those found within the traditional crafts and religions. My students recognize their own alienation from their traditions in these relays, and the extent to which the melting pot erased their collective memories of all the details that might ground them in a tradition. The post-primitivist album is not simply a victory of tradition over modernism, but a syncretic hybrid of tradition and the vanguard. The goal is not to confine us to our respective heritages but to learn what might be missing from the worldview this heritage supports. A tradition other than our own might then be added to our mix to address this lack. Such is the experiment, in any case.

The necessity of postmodernism (for lack of a better term) in our moment is driven by the inability of modernism to deal with the institutional equivalent of miscegenation inherent in an emerging world culture that is developing its own discourse, different from any one of those organizing the popcycle in the era of literacy. The Internet promises to be the vehicle of a new dimension of the pop-cycle—the dimension that I have theorized in terms of chora, a special place or space of mediation, or rather, syncretism. What the essay is to School, the treatise to Discipline, the melodrama to Entertainment, or the snapshot to Family, so is the mystory to this potential, but still unrealized, discourse whose site of application is the World Wide Web. Choragraphy, then—that is what has my attention: not yet, but coming soon.

Detours: PPS

Pedagogy and a Public Scene

20

John P. Leavey, Jr.

What if we were to ask about the demands of pedagogy not as a matter of the intellectual, nor as a nostalgia for a pure democratic space, but as a matter of refusal and the communal in the apostrophe (the politics of friendship, in Derrida's terms)?[1] Within a class, there must be the address that turns from the class as class, as public in the class, toward the public as public disappearing over the horizon in the address: depellation.

Against a classroom as client server, as the contractual exchange of knowledge, as social factum and market for obtaining entry into the labor market, or as atmospheric learning in the enlightenment of knowledge, there is the classroom of apostrophe and translation.

DETOUR: APOSTROPHE AND TRANSLATION

Apostrophe—the discourse of turning away in order to address, a discourse of interruption and interruptive address. Also the address of prosopopoeia.

Translation—"more than one tongue,"[2] even in one tongue ("we speak the same tongue, and yet I do not understand you"),[3] interruption in order to address.

290

On the public scene, translation and apostrophe are never far away.

These telegraphic lines meet up with the phone call to Joseph K., a call demanding his attendance at a Court of Inquiry.

(But first another voice calls, the voice of apostrophe that interrupts Kant's *Critique of Judgment* [§ 8] and sets going the apparatus of sensus communis. This is the universal voice [*Stimme*] to which the aesthetic judgment appeals in its demand for universal assent [*Einstimmung*] without resort to the concept. Judgment interrupts its judgment to translate its voice into that universal voice of assent, the possibility of assent that the appeal requires as possible, that is, more than one voice: the voice of judgment that must impersonate everyone turns away to check the universal voice without the concept. Against the concept, the universal voice always opens on a public scene [judgment here is a public scene, not a philosophic one].)

The phone call beckons Joseph K.

What if we were to read *The Trial* as an attempt to define a public scene?[4] And if we were to read it as such, what would it mean for a pedagogy that recognizes its public responsibilities?

The chapter of the first interrogation presents us with questions left open, even for Joseph K., who suffers in this first interrogation from being off the mark, late for the interrogation, early in the incident of the secret sign, in any case, never on time. Time's lag does not let one be on time. Discursus interruptus, the limp of time.

A phone call informs K. that he must come "that next Sunday" for "a short inquiry" (31), a message that he neither agrees to nor not, as he does not answer. According to the narration, "his mind was made up to keep the appointment on Sunday, it was absolutely essential, the case was getting under way and he must fight it" (32). K. is given an address, but no time. He goes there on Sunday, with the assumption "that the house would be recognizable even at a distance by some sign which his imagination left unspecified, or by the unusual commotion before the door" (34). That, however, is not the case. When Joseph arrives at Juliusstrasse, he goes to the tenement of the address, but he does not have a room number, a lack that annoys him, and there is no commotion or sign.

Having walked up to the first floor, K. decides to begin his "real search" (36) for the Court of Inquiry. The real search takes a curious turn here. One might expect him to ask for the Court and to abandon the method of the street: to recognize it, as in the street, "by some sign" or "commotion." But K. comes upon a different strategy. With a reason without explanation, he continues the recognition scene with an apostrophe:

> As he could not inquire for the Court of Inquiry he invented a joiner
> called Lanz . . . and so he began to inquire at all the doors if a joiner
> called Lanz lived there, so as to get a chance to look into the rooms. (36)

An implied apostrophe is required in this search without reason, not in the sense
of the unreasonable, but in the sense that no reason can account for the search
itself. This is not a search that can be inquired after, nor a search for what can be
inquired after. Vision and hearing had already failed once, in the street, where
the "house" of the Court should have been recognizable by some sign or movement. The Court of Inquiry is public, not secret, not private. We are dealing then
with a public space that is not public (it cannot be inquired after, and there are
no signs of it in any case on the outside). What will be this public space that is
not public? What will be the means of access? For K., access is by means of apostrophe: the invented address, the address that is not and as invention must interrupt, the address that turns one away from the one addressed in order to address
another: K. asks if Lanz is there in order to check out the space, a space opened
by the apostrophic question that names the space Lanz and that K. will turn from
in the interruptive question. K. will ask for Lanz in order to see what he cannot
inquire after. In the detour of the address, a turn to the address, the glance of the
eye will be the guarantee of success. K. will recognize the space.

K. continues to ask for Lanz, continues to look, continues to fail to see and
find, until he does not recognize the publicless public: the Court of Inquiry that
cannot be inquired after.

In the end K. scarcely needed to ask at all, for in this way he was conducted
over the whole floor. He now regretted his plan, which at first had seemed so
practical. As he was approaching the fifth floor he decided to give up the search,
said good-bye to a friendly young workman who wanted to conduct him farther,
and descended again. But then the uselessness of the whole expedition filled him
with exasperation; he went up the stairs once more and knocked at the first door
he came to on the fifth story. The first thing he saw in the little room was a great
pendulum clock, which already pointed to ten. "Does a joiner called Lanz live
here?" he asked. "Please go through," said a young woman with sparkling black
eyes, who was washing children's clothes in a tub, and she pointed with her
damp hand to the open door of the next room (37).

K. does not give up his quest, and although he enters the meeting hall, he
does not recognize it as the Court of Inquiry. He had to leave; the air felt "too
thick." He "stepped out again and said to the young woman, who seemed to have

misunderstood him: 'I asked for a joiner, a man called Lanz.' 'I know,' said the
woman, 'just go right in' " (37). His return to remind the woman and to repeat
his original request, not for the Court, but for Lanz, produces a curious result.
She sends him back in to be led to the other end by a young boy. The woman
says, " 'I know [Ja] . . . just go right in. . . . I must shut this door after you,
nobody else must come in' " (37).[5]

Within the meeting hall, the place for a political or a socialist meeting,[6] there
is the complementary incident of the "secret sign," an incident that is itself an
apostrophe to the defense that K. was engaged in. K. notices what he supposes to
be a sign exchanged between the Examining Magistrate and a member of the
audience. K. recognizes that as soon as he remarks on the sign as a sign, he must
give up any hope of further testing its significance; any remarking will be premature and will delay any confirmation of meaning. The apostrophe:

> "The Examining Magistrate sitting here beside me has just given one
> of you a secret sign. So there are some among you who take your
> instructions from up here. I do not know whether the sign was meant
> to evoke applause or hissing, and now that I have divulged the matter
> prematurely I deliberately give up all hope of ever learning its real
> significance. It is a matter of complete indifference to me, and I pub-
> licly empower the Examining Magistrate to address his hired agents
> in so many words, instead of making secret signs to them, to say at
> the proper moment: Hiss now, or alternatively: Clap now." (44)

Sound, noise, speech do not suffice to settle this premature apostrophe, the apostrophe of interpretation. The attempt to empower publicly with words does not
"succeed" but continues the interruptive structure.

Kafka "designates" this untimely space twice: once as a political/socialist
gathering and once as the "public" space of education. The chapter ends on the
designation of this public space in the analogy of the students: "Behind him rose
the buzz of the audience, which had come to life again and had begun to discuss
the apparent situation like expert students" (48, modified).

DETOUR: TRANSLATION

How then to come upon such an untimely space, a space neither transcendent nor
immanent, a space that cannot be inquired after, a space just before or just after,

too early or too late for the space of signs (representation, hermeneutics, semiotics, pedagogy, politics as forms of representations, nations, states, nation-states, etc.)?

One "intervention" would be translation. The woman, recognizing (or not) the detour of K., recognizing (or not) the interruption of the apostrophe, translates one interruption with another: Yes, go through to another room. If you name this public space Lanz, yes, she seems to be saying, if your inquiry for the Court of Inquiry can only be such an apostrophe, I can only prematurely empower you to go through and to speak in the other room. Her translation addresses but interrupts, yes, relates without establishing the relation. K. speaks. She speaks. They speak the same tongue, and yet they do not understand each other? The fault between the two speakings (like Kant's judgment) falls on the bridge of translation.

Detour: Geopedagogy

Untimely, too early or too late, so Kafka defines translative, pedagogical, public space. *The Trial* might be read as the difficulty of such a place taking place, and Deleuze and Guattari's *What Is Philosophy?* as the call for its place.[7]

Translative space, as Deleuze and Guattari remark on a different subject, can be made timely ("reterritorialized") only too quickly because "We lack resistance to the present" (108). In one sense, politics and teaching are timely activities (they apparently occur in the here and now), and translative space as a resistance to the timely would be a resistance to such a politics and teaching. But this too simple tabulation assumes that resistance is not a political or pedagogical act, and that resistance arises after the here and now of the timely. The expected relations of timeliness and of the place of the utopic are overturned in Deleuze and Guattari's argument of the event of the concept.

One way to resist the present is to confide in the future, Deleuze and Guattari argue in *What Is Philosophy?* If philosophy is the creation of concepts and as creations signed, then, and in order to "avoid" what Deleuze and Guattari term the first and the third ages of the concept, the encyclopedia and commercial professional training, there is "the more modest task of a pedagogy of the concept, which would have to analyze the conditions of creation as factors of always singular moments" (12). Geophilosophy would be one result of such a pedagogy, a pedagogy that recognizes the contingency of reason[8] in geography's "wresting" of "history from the cult of necessity in order to stress the irreducibility of contingency."

Geography apostrophizes history, in a Nietzschean apostrophe: "History today still designates only the set of conditions, however recent they may be, from which one *turns away* in order to become, that is to say, in order to create something new" (96, my emphasis). The apostrophe of geophilosophy—philosophy in the milieu of the chance of a conceptual creation somewhere, a chance that therefore cannot arise from history and a somewhere that cannot arise from a transcendental place—that apostrophe allows one to sign again and for the first time, to sign a concept, to create in the singular moment of signing, and in its turning from the universal voice open the singularity of creation. Against the present, the untimely in the timely; one turns from the universal subject and from packaging to the untimely place taking place—Event. Deleuze and Guattari designate this space "utopia" and find in this untimely space the space of politics, a space in which "communication, exchange, consensus, and opinion vanish entirely."[9] Their confidence is this apostrophe that interrupts what is confided in turning from that confidence to the future in the poor word "utopia," in the deterritorialization of the earth in the political, in the untimeliness of the political:[10]

> It is with utopia that philosophy becomes political and takes the criticism of its own time to its highest point. Utopia does not split off from infinite movement: etymologically it stands for absolute deterritorialization but always at the critical point at which it is connected with the present relative milieu, and especially with the forces stifled by this milieu.

And in the revolution:

> But to say that revolution is itself utopia of immanence is not to say that it is a dream, something that is not realized or that is only realized by betraying itself. On the contrary, it is to posit revolution as plane of immanence, infinite movement and absolute survey, but to the extent that these features connect up with what is real here and now in the struggle against capitalism, relaunching new struggles whenever the earlier one is betrayed. (100)

Revolutionary utopia, a turn from absolute territory in the connection to the here and now, marks out a politics of detour. The apostrophe of translation and the politics of detour turn in the nowhere (a classic utopian term) that is the

revolution that connects against the present in the place of the event's taking
place.

D E T O U R :   P P P S :   D E P E L L A T I O N

If *What Is Philosophy?* explores that place *The Trial* opens and if the event of the
concept, too early or too late—what opens the discursive and not its result—
depells the present in politics' and pedagogy's turn from that connects to, then,
contrary to common sense, politics and pedagogy are the apostrophe of translation's place. Politics and pedagogy, a series one of the other, too early and too late
to the present, interrupts the here and now in the apostrophe whose chance creates a publicless public space (nowhere). Without foundation or end, without
finality of meaning or recognition of place, translation takes place in the turn of
those without(s).

PPPS modestly wrests from . . .

N O T E S

1. Jacques Derrida, "Politics of Friendship," trans. Gabriel Motzkin and Michael
    Syrotinski, with Thomas Keenan, *American Imago* 50, no. 3 (1993): 372, 377, 382. The
    cited apostrophe, "O friends, there is no friend," "reaches like the heritage of a
    boundless rumor across the philosophical literature of the West, from Aristotle to
    Kant, to Blanchot, from Montaigne to Nietzsche, who reverses it" (354).
2. Jacques Derrida, *Memoires, for Paul de Man*, trans. Cecile Lindsay, Jonathan Culler,
    Eduardo Cadava, and Peggy Kamuf, rev. ed. (New York: Columbia University Press,
    1989), 15 (modified).
3. Gilles Deleuze and Félix Guattari, *What Is Philosophy?* trans. Hugh Tomlinson and
    Graham Burchell (New York: Columbia University Press, 1994), 110 (modified).
4. Franz Kafka, *The Trial*, trans. Willa and Edwin Muir (New York: Schocken, 1974).
5. The relation of this chapter to the chapter "In the Cathedral," which takes up "Before
    the Law," is not reducible to allusion or parallelism. I would argue that, at the least,
    one is the detour of the other, a series of detours.
6. The designation "socialist" was used first and then changed to "local political" in the
    manuscripts of Kafka.

7. Complementarity of disciplines is engaged here only by means of detour: one detour for another: literature, philosophy. Kant's universal voice runs up against its own translation in Kafka.

8. The encounter between friend and thought was needed [for the birth of philosophy]. In short, philosophy does have a principle, but it is a synthetic and contingent principle—an encounter, a conjunction. It is not insufficient by itself but contingent in itself. Even in the concept, the principle depends upon a connection of components that could have been different, with different neighborhoods. The principle of reason such as it appears in philosophy is a principle of contingent reason and is put like this: there is no good reason but contingent reason; there is no universal history except of contingency.

   What Is Philosophy? 93.

9. Philosophy takes the relative deterritorialization of capital to the absolute; it makes it pass over the plane of immanence as movement of the infinite and suppresses it as internal limit, turns it back against itself so as to summon forth a new earth, a new people. But in this way it arrives at the nonpropositional form of the concept in which communication, exchange, consensus, and opinion vanish entirely. It is therefore closer to what Adorno called "negative dialectic" and to what the Frankfurt School called "utopian." Actually, utopia is what links philosophy with its own epoch, with European capitalism, but also already with the Greek city.

   What Is Philosophy? 99.

10. "The word utopia therefore designates that conjunction of philosophy, or of the concept, with the present milieu—political philosophy (however, in view of the mutilated meaning public opinion has given to it, perhaps utopia is not the best word)." *What Is Philosophy?* 100.

Renegotiating the Pedagogical Contract

Jeffrey Williams

21

In a recent ECU English Department newsletter—so aptly named *The Museletter*—the chair announced, sportscaster-like, that English was indeed the champion in the contest of faculties, at least in one measure:

> English is still #1 again this term, and we appear to be in good shape going into the Spring 1996 semester as well. With 18,090 weekly student credit hours for Fall 95, the department once again has generated more credit hours than any other unit on campus, easily surpassing the Schools of Business and Education (with 17,830 and 15,262 hours, respectively) as well as, within the College of Arts and Sciences, the departments of Biology (15,336) and Mathematics (15,893). Even though overall University enrollment was down slightly this term, English had more students in its classes (and generated more student credit hours) than last fall.

Hooray, we've won? The chair goes on desultorily, more to the point and not quite reassuringly, "As many of you are aware, this increase in the number of students we teach, at a time of declining personnel lines University-wide, has placed a strain on departmental resources. This situation is being tightly managed, however."

While almost sublime in its breeziness over what are palpable and most likely adverse changes in teaching demands and prospective work conditions, this kind of administrative rhetoric and the situation it recounts, I'd surmise, are familiar if not commonplace in most departments in most universities, particularly in the "liberal arts" and particularly in state colleges and universities. As we have been hearing for a while, state budgets are strapped and legislators want to know where their money is going, and they have targeted universities especially, since the profit from higher education is largely intangible and they are suspicious of, if not hostile to, the liberal tradition of the university, and more generally since entitlement to public programs such as education (as well as health, welfare, and so on) has been recast as a kind of dependent relation akin to freeloading (if not addiction) rather than as a public franchise or right.[1] In North Carolina—paradoxically, a state that is fiscally sound and growing— we've heard that "UNC Must Do More with Less in the Future, Legislators Say,"[2] and we've recently undergone a mandated state audit on "Faculty Workloads and Secondary Employment Practices," which recommended more formal procedures for accounting for work time (and expressed dismay at the lack thereof). How all of this plays out on campuses is in an intensified pressure toward greater "productivity,"[3] a not very masked code for teaching more, greater teaching loads, less time allotted for research leaves or course abatements, more students in courses, and more "outsourcing," or use of cheap, part-time lecturers—those practices that the chair's column finesses—for, in categories that an audit would recognize, the primary measure of productivity is quantitative, in the bottomline number of FTEs (full time equivalencies), the current administrative acronym of choice for students taught. One can't definitively measure the effect on Jill or Johnny of reading, say, "The Yellow Wallpaper," and her or his ensuing thinking on gender roles and equality, but one can graph the total student hours generated by a department, and the funding contingent on them, on a spreadsheet.

This turn toward accountability and productivity records a substantial reorientation in the rationale of the university, from the rubric of liberal education and the disinterested pursuit of knowledge to its more functional and direct preparation of a workforce—its role in sorting and circulating "human resources," as Evan Watkins points out.[4] Along with this, it also signals a significant shift in the professional prospect of professors, from that of researcher and specialist on the vanguard of knowledge to that of teacher/ service manager processing more product, that is, students, as they have recently been labeled. This shift in professional prospect was the topic of the recent National Conference of

State Legislatures, about which the *Christian Science Monitor* succinctly noted, " 'Publish or Perish' Becomes 'Teach or Perish': Many Legislators Want Professors at State Universities to Teach Longer Hours and Research Less."[5]

It's worth stressing that the cutback in public funding for higher education is not simply a move to scapegoat universities — although it's no accident either[6] — but forms one component of the general rollback of public entitlement and franchise, especially of liberal state institutions and programs, whereby the state has become a more direct vehicle for corporate policies and practices, reconstituting the public sphere overtly as an instrument to facilitate the "free market" and the agenda and transactions of corporations in that market. This construction of the state and negotiation of the social contract are blatantly ideological in that the expansion of corporate interests presumably comes to profit us all, but in actuality the past twenty years have witnessed a vast concentration of wealth in the upper 5 percent of the population, the evisceration of the welfare state, the greatest degree of poverty since the Great Depression, and the economic decline if not desperation of the middle class.[7] This probably isn't news to most of us, but my point is to underscore that what's happening to the university is a question not of an economic downturn that somehow will right itself like the weather — in fact the economy has been stable and growing, if you listen to the Federal Reserve — but of corporate protocols and the far-reaching reconfiguration of life under the present restructuring of global capital. The university is not by any means an ivory tower isolated from the economic determinations of the world, but functions as a crucial institution reflecting and abetting the present reconstitution of the public sphere.

I've sketched out this general context of the university and its economic embattlement to place a different spin on the question of pedagogy and the public sphere. The usual way to see pedagogy, as I take it, is as a methodology or set of practices that defines our work as teachers — what we teach and how we teach it, and how we deal with and affect students, whether by dispensing knowledge or spurring their co-participation in learning.[8] On this view, work on pedagogy thus forges a social contract, with its prime signatories stipulated as teacher and student. Given the context I've sketched, though, the pedagogical contract is now under enforced renegotiation as an employment practice, not on terms of our own devising and placing us — college teachers — in a functional and service position in relation to the state and to corporate interests. The state and the present redrawing of the public franchise stipulate our material pedagogical contract, bluntly effecting a speedup, that fewer of us process more students, and that we overtly play an instrumental role in the manufacture and distribution of human resources.

II.

Of late, there has been a profusion of work in literary studies taking up the question of pedagogy, crossing over to and drawing on the otherwise rarefied zone of theory and espousing a left or radical politics. This discourse on pedagogy by and large invokes the standard sense of the pedagogical contract, that we can catalyze and generate social change via our relation with students. This possibility—to reach the minds of the young to effect social change—is perhaps the great hope of education and why it is cast as having significant stakes, from Socrates on. The explicit political staking of the terrain of pedagogy counters the residual humanist assumption that the classroom is a neutral, duty-free zone, fostering the disinterested search for objective truth, or the more deterministic view that education serves as a central space of ideological reproduction.[9]

You can see this turn to an avowed radical pedagogy in a number of venues in literary studies, in such wide-circulation journals as *College English*,[10] or in *College Literature*, which has consistently foregrounded the crossover between literature, theory, and pedagogy in a series of special issues on topics such as "The Politics of Teaching Literature," "Literary Theory in the Classroom," and "Cultural Studies: Theory, Praxis, Pedagogy."[11] You can also see it in a number of recent collections dealing with the intersection of contemporary theory, politics, and pedagogy, as indicated by their aggregate titles, such as *Pedagogy Is Politics: Literary Theory and Critical Teaching*, edited by Maria-Regina Kecht (1992), *Reorientations: Critical Theories and Pedagogies*, edited by Bruce Henricksen and Thais Morgan (1990), *Theory/Pedagogy/Politics: Texts for Change*, edited by Donald Morton and Mas'ud Zavarzadeh (1991), and this one, among others.[12]

On the face of it, then, this mass of work seems to signal an unabashed celebration of pedagogy and its political potential. However, beyond its efficacy in prescribing teaching strategies and practices, this turn to pedagogy represents a site-specific revision of literary studies, largely on the discursive terrain of theory and the disciplinary terrain of the higher faculties that the discourse of theory speaks for.[13] For attention to pedagogy—to place this in the context of the internal hierarchy of literary studies and its subfaculties—is not quite a new invention, since such a concern has always been there in underfields of the literature faculty like rhet/comp, not to mention in "applied" disciplines like education, which have historically been cordoned off from the higher faculties of the arts and sciences.[14] Pedagogy has typically been consigned to the "service" wing of literature departments—to composition programs in English, as well as to introductory language courses in foreign language departments, which in their utilitarian roles generate the vast majority of student hours—whereas theory for the most part has occupied a more elite space attached to the pure literature faculty. (The division between "applied" and "pure" research falls out on the same lines as the high school split between practical courses like shop, accounting, and cosmetology and college prep courses like world lit or physics, or between statistics or engineering and mathematics or biochemistry in college, in the hierarchy of disciplinary knowledge.)

Given these coordinates, what does the turn to and theoretical upgrade of pedagogy do? What effects does it have and what needs does it answer? And why now? To pose a no doubt schematic genealogy of contemporary critical practice, the "new" pedagogy answers the recent impasse in literary studies sometimes characterized as the end or death of theory. That is, it provides an antidote to what is frequently perceived as the overprofessionalization and ahistoricity—in short, the social inconsequence—of high theory, which dominated academic-intellectual discourse these past twenty or so years. (Whether or not this representation of theory is entirely accurate, there is a way in which theory, for all its purported conceptual radicality, reinstated a banking model of the classroom, in Freire's formulation, stressing a difficult subject matter to be accumulated and the performance of a teacher with occult knowledge to transfer to worthy novices.) When the ever more insistent question of relevance (and its more utilitarian coding in accountability) pressed up against the rarefication of theory, pedagogy became the home of politics, somewhat in the manner of Dorothy's discovery in *The Wizard of Oz*, that had been there all along. To put this another way, the most viable location for doing politics within the institutional field that constitutes literary studies moved from theory—from the various contestatory discourses of the 1970s, thought of in their best light as politics by other means[15]—to the more concrete space very literally in front of us, at least for a few hours each week. Thus, the new pedagogy gestures to shift from a decidedly professionalist discourse, opening out into an extraprofessional, "public" space beyond the professional space, albeit circumscribed by the otherwise institutional limits of the classroom. In short, it projects a bridge from the intraprofessional location of theory to an extraprofessional vista.

Within the discursive economy of the institutional field, I would take the turn to pedagogy as a symptom of the changing conditions and exigent ideological needs of that field. Coded as a greater or renewed conscience of academic-intellectuals and as accessing a direct channel to political efficacy, the new pedagogy represents a renegotiation of the insistent, frequently embarrassing, and constitutively vexed question of the public need for and utility of the professional study of literature, as well as the general question of the relation of the academy to the public sphere. In other words, it speaks to a professionalist concern and legitimation, to reinvoke a public purpose and thereby to relegitimate its threatened professional status—intensified by contemporary fiscal and ideological pressure for accountability. I say this to countervail what often seems to me the self-congratulatory tenor of the invocation of politics and pedagogy, as if we have finally discovered and gained the grail of actually existing politics.[16] If only it were quite that simple. Not to put too fine a point on it, but like the tropisms of plants, intellectuals respond to rather than determine their socio-institutional conditions of existence. The parameters and effects of academic-intellectual work are not autonomously governed by intellectual self-definition or desire, but mediated through and negotiated within the space of their socio-institutional and professional situation.

In different ways, the various ascendant practices that have come to prominence in literary studies most recently—cultural studies, the invocation of the concept of materiality (notably in the category of the body) in residual high theory (i.e., Judith Butler), and what Michael Bérubé calls "public access" or the recent reinvention of the figure of the public intellectual—likewise respond to the current construction of the socio-institutional field. Whatever the actual political valence they carry, along with pedagogy they all discursively project the vista of politics, of engagement with the questions of history and social relevance that theory and previous professional practice have been charged with lacking. Cultural studies does this by recasting the object of literary studies (from its presumably elitist bias to a more democratic range of popular objects) and by its attention to the modes of cultural production (from aesthetic—the verbal icon—to sociocultural concerns), materiality by reorienting the basis of theory from language and linguistic models of signifying practices to include the grail of material affect, "public" criticism by ascribing an extra-academic audience of presumably "common readers" and real folks, and pedagogy by ascribing an extraprofessional, intra-university constituency of students. Each of these moves assumes the discovery of a lack, which it then solves by the assertion of a species of political efficacy.

I would argue that within their specific socio-institutional location (again, beyond the radical prospect they pose, their effects are circumscribed by the apparatuses of progressively more commercialized publishing, more competitive conditions for the production of academic discourse, and the socio-configuration of the university, which is more directly cast as a corporate "partner," as I've mentioned) these practices function crucially as different versions of professional-institutional relegitimation, to renew the credentials of the humanities and professional practices in the humanities in troubled times. In other words, they do indeed offer a response to the public sphere, though not in quite the ways that they announce. This isn't to dismiss the political possibilities of these moves and practices, for they can indeed exceed their institutional functions and determinants, but those possibilities are very much bounded by their scene of production, and the expression of a desire to have political effect frequently substitutes for if not obfuscates that effect.[17]

Broadly, theory through the seventies and early eighties functioned to provide an intra-university rationale for the potency of the humanities, particularly in relation to the social sciences. It reoutfitted the humanities, shedding the touchy-feely aura and methodology of literary appreciation for the techno-difficulty and expertise of social scientific methodology.[18] That is what professions do: claim an occult knowledge that only their accredited members have access to, attribute an incontrovertible need for what they provide, and therefore establish a monopoly on dispensing the knowledge to fulfill that need. (Think of medical doctors, as opposed, say, to midwives.)[19] Within this professionalist economy and by its logic, the extant practices of cultural studies, bodytheory, public criticism, and pedagogy in turn rewrite the professionalist prescription and renew its public license. They project a more tangibly "relevant" and accessible public rationale, precisely set against the "excesses" of the intra-academic purview of high theory.

Specifically, in a significant way the attention to pedagogy offers a renewed professionalist rationale for the higher literature faculty in the face of recent legislative and media charges—as in the headlines I've recounted—that professors spend too much time on their own hyperspecialized, pet research projects (say, deconstructing Herman Melville) and not enough time in the classroom ("where they belong," teaching Herman Melville). The recent spate of work on pedagogy discursively puts professors back in the classroom and thus claims a certain utilitarian cachet. The revived discourse on pedagogy, in this sense, becomes our public alibi, establishing our whereabouts and work time in the classroom.

Again, this isn't to discredit the focus on pedagogy out of hand, but to stress that its current reappraisal is more complicated than simply upgrading or explicitly politicizing curricula and classroom practices, and serves multiple and contradictory ends.

In its narrowly professionalist dimension—its cross-breeding with theory codes it inextricably as such—the new pedagogy has a profoundly conservative function and reaffirms rather than reconfigures the current distribution of academic knowledge production, since it retrenches the higher faculties and their threatened privileged status by appropriating the utilitarian cachet of the lower faculties—those consigned, in blunt material terms, in sheer hours of work time, to teaching in composition and other "service" courses—which constitutes the division of labor that thereby enables "research" (and literally frees time and resources) for the higher faculties. The assertion of professionalist interest participates in the maintenance of hierarchical job relations—the classing—of university labor. For left academic-intellectuals, it's imperative to renegotiate this facet of the pedagogical contract, as well as to radicalize the pedagogies we espouse and recommend.

III.

I don't mean to take up the typical line of anti-professionalist argument here, that professions are irretrievably self-interested if not something of a scam, for our professional position does allow for a degree of relative autonomy. A side effect of professional relegitimation is that it works to enforce professional isolation and self-determination—to maintain control of the profession's dispensing of services, against external mandates—which pragmatically opens a space for anomalous and, one hopes, oppositional work.[20] Still, that prospect is limited largely to those of us who have a fully franchised professional position, that is, those who have secure and research-oriented jobs, generally in the higher faculties. And even for those so privileged, that position negotiates a structural complicity in the instrumental class divination and state service of higher education. To put it mildly, the professional position is conflicted.

The pedagogical contract, then, occurs at the intersection of a vexed set of interests and registers the ambivalence of our position. It records the negotiation among state interests (circulating human resources, as well as the ideological reproduction of bourgeois values and, bluntly, producing class distinction), professional interests (maintaining privilege and prestige, as high academics, as well as simply maintaining secure employment), student interests (which are usually not progressive but aim to acquire cultural capital in order to secure a berth on the social ladder), and a more abstract public interest (oppositional critique of inequitable practices, altruistically to build a better society—or, on the traditional view, to conserve the extant social order). Part of the current legitimation crisis of the profession has been precipitated by the refiguring of university administration as a direct vehicle of state interest and corporate imperatives (the tight managing that my chair's column alludes to), rather than as an outgrowth or organic articulation of faculty. As Stanley Aronowitz notes, there are two senses of academic freedom: first, of individual faculty members to speak and write freely, without fear of coercion or retribution, which is the way it is most frequently defined; and second, the deeper and more long-sighted sense, "the rights of the faculty as a collectivity to retain sovereignty over the educational process."[21] In the corporate takeover of the university,[22] this second sense has been effaced, thus skewing the previous balance of power among these competing interests.

One way to see the current revision of pedagogy, within this web of interests, is as an attempt to reconfigure student interest (in a sense, slightly patronizingly for their own good) to serve a public interest (of our choosing). This revision carries with it the aura of transgression of state interest in its espousal of radical critique, although that transgression for the most part functions symbolically, since the actual material relation of students in the university incontrovertibly ties to their marking as nascent members of the (advanced) labor pool, that is, serving the interest of the corporate state. As Evan Watkins shows in *Work Time*, regardless of the pedagogy we practice, whether passively transmitting canonical knowledge or proactively spurring radical critique, students are circulated through literary studies in order to be distinguished for the labor pool:

> For just by virtue of being taught in English, any text—"radical" or "conservative" or whatever—is already caught up in the social constructions of class, of race, and of gender. And they are caught up in ways that may or may not at all be congruent with the direction of values "in" the text or "in" the concrete labor of teaching the text or "in" the effort of ideological analysis to expose their secrets. For as part of the social organization of work in English, these texts occur in the midst of the social circulation of people.[23]

In other words, the radicalizing of pedagogy—reorienting student interest explicitly toward a genuinely public rather than corporate-state interest—might perform a good faith intervention, but it is essentially a mission of conversion (from career interest to the greater good of public interest) and it is materially circumscribed by the administrative parameters of higher education—such as grading, admissions policies, and so on.

As I suggested at the beginning of this essay, an alternative way to read the pedagogical contract is in its literal material relation as an employment practice, which directly engages the blunt terms of corporate-state interest enforced on us, as service technicians dispensing and overseeing the production of symbolic resources (educated students), as well as, from the standpoint of students' interests, to provide them appropriate credit and accreditation—which is, as one hears demystified student-consumers put it, what they're paying us for. The rude intrusion of these material concerns and interests prompts the crisis renarrativizations of the field, recorded in the struggle over our professional recoding as teachers rather than as researchers or intellectuals who happen to teach. A crucial way to resist these interests, then, is to struggle for the ground of the pedagogical contract as employment, radicalize our labor practices, resist administrative mandates for downsizing, speedup, and the like, and reform the inequitable distribution of labor that presently constitutes the university.

These are a forbiddingly tall order, but there are a number of avenues where we might start: within our departments, to resist downsizing and speedup and not to take such changes as inevitable, since they are a deliberate and strategic implementation of policy (after all, and which bears repeating, the job crisis is not about a lessened demand for teachers, but about the greater extraction of labor from teachers' work); within our universities, to protest administrative imperatives and corporate rationales; publicly, in venues like letters to the editor, in speaking, and in lobbying (as Linda Ray Pratt recounts in her experience with AAUP in Nebraska);[24] in support and organizing work for unionization, for faculty and for graduate students, as is ongoing at Yale and many other places;[25] and in any other sites where one can intervene and by any other means one can invent. It is imperative that we recognize and oppose the current assertion of corporate-state interest in its dominance of higher education. Frankly, I don't know how successful these interventions will be—I have hardly been successful at my university and in my department—but I don't think we can discount whatever means we have available to us.

However, these interventions still represent a petitionary relation with university administrative interests and with the corporate-state, not a decisively radical break or revolutionary relation.[26] They propose the pragmatic negotiation of extant circumstances within the present configuration of power, and so offer at best reforms of some of the instrumental aspects of higher education. Recall that university education, while it might hold the potential of fostering a revolutionary class, still is predicated on the inequitable distribution of wealth, on, as Marx noted, "defraying the cost of the education of the upper [and I would add, at present, professional-managerial] classes from the general tax receipts."[27]

Without cynicism, then, I'd say that it is an open question whether the extant system of higher education, of "liberal" or humanistic education, is radically recuperable. However, I would stress that we still need to see education as an expansionary project, as the locus for change and for reconfiguring and asserting a public interest. I say this especially in response to recent reactions to the job crisis, including suggestions that we downsize graduate programs, admit fewer students, and so forth.[28] While we no doubt have an obligation to fair advertising in recruiting students into the professional armature of literary studies, we need to reenvision the project of education, of public education, beyond enacting stopgap repairs. We need to reclaim the utopian prospect for education, not just in the things we teach within the present configuration of the institution, but in making a new institution, in inventing and enacting new institutional arrangements. We need a vision of and proposals for new schools and for new structures of labor in them, aiming at fulfilling the promise posed by a genuinely public education. We might have to give up some of the perquisites of our professional positions — despite what seem constitutive irritations, to be a tenured university professor in contemporary America is indeed a privileged and quintessentially bourgeois life (think of the places we live in and culture we consume) — but I would rather teach in a school where everyone was paid a fair and equitable wage, what we now call secretaries and graduate assistants, along with assistant or endowed professors. In the current crisis of education, why are there no proposals for radicalization in this sense, in terms of labor hierarchies, as well as in terms of actual access to education? To steal a line from Paul de Man announcing the moment of high theory, that is the task of literary criticism and theory — at least that purports a radical vista — in the coming years.

NOTES

1. See Nancy Fraser on the rhetoric of dependency versus rights, especially chapters 12 and 13 of *Unruly Practices: Power, Discourse, and Gender in Contemporary Social Theory* (Minneapolis: University of Minnesota Press, 1989).

2. Associated Press trailer, *Daily Reflector* (Greenville, NC), 20 December 1994, B3.

3. The productivity issue seemed to flame into existence in the early 1990s; see, for instance, Robert L. Jacobson, "Colleges Face New Pressure to Increase Faculty Productivity," *Chronicle of Higher Education*, 15 April 1992, A1; and "Public-College Officials Struggle to Respond to Growing Concern over Faculty Productivity," *Chronicle of Higher Education*, 11 November 1992, A17. For a site-specific case that received prominent news coverage, see "UConn Devises a Point System to Rate Professors' Productivity," *New York Times*, 10 January 1993, 29. This question of productivity goes hand in hand with those of accountability, on which see Allan M. Winkler, "Explaining What Professors Do with Their Time," *Chronicle of Higher Education*, 15 July 1992, B1; and William F. Massy and Robert Zemsky, "Faculty Discretionary Time: Departments and the 'Academic Ratchet,' " *Journal of Higher Education*, January–February 1994, 1. See also the AAUP report in response to these changes, "The Politics of Intervention: External Regulation of Academic Activities and Workloads in Public Higher Education," *Academe*, January–February 1996, 46–52.

4. See Evan Watkins, "The Educational Politics of Human Resources: Humanities Teachers as Resource Managers," *minnesota review*, n.s., 45–46 (1996): 147–66. See also idem, *Work Time: English Departments and the Circulation of Cultural Value* (Stanford: Stanford University Press, 1989).

5. By Laurel Shaper Walters, *Christian Science Monitor*, 27 February 1995, 13. See also Larry Gordon, "For Profs, Teach or Perish?" *Los Angeles Times*, 10 January 1993, A1.

6. As Ellen Messer-Davidow notes, "The attack on the academy from without and within is only half of the strategy to break what conservatives believe is a liberal monopoly of higher education. The immediate goal is to transform the higher-education system into a free-market economy by weakening liberal institutions and strengthening conservative ones." "Manufacturing the Attack on Liberalized Higher Education," *Social Text* 36 (1993): 49.

7. For a sampling of some of the various statistics, see Holly Sklar's report on the minimum wage, "Link the Minimum Wage to Congressional Pay," *Z Magazine*, March 1996, 41–42; and Noam Chomsky, "Class War: The Attack on Working People," *Southern Humanities Review* 30, no. 1 (1996): 1–20.

8. Although the ends of conservative and progressive pedagogy obviously differ, both define pedagogy largely in terms of what and how we teach. As Robert Con Davis puts it, "the attempt by Paulo Freire, Pierre Bourdieu, and many others to theorize

but also to initiate radical social change through pedagogy, *through what students are taught and how they are taught it*" (my italics). "A Manifesto for Oppositional Pedagogy: Freire, Bourdieu, Merod, and Graff," in *Reorientations: Critical Theories and Pedagogies*, ed. Bruce Henricksen and Thais E. Morgan (Urbana: University of Illinois Press, 1990), 249.

9. While he allows for a certain autonomy for ideological apparatuses, Althusser identifies schools as the most significant modern zone of ideological reproduction. See "Ideology and Ideological State Apparatuses (Notes towards an Investigation)," in *Lenin and Philosophy and Other Essays*, trans. Ben Brewster (New York: Monthly Review, 1971), 152–57.

10. For instance, see Ronald Strickland, "Confrontational Pedagogy and Traditional Literary Studies," *College English* 52 (1990): 291–300.

11. It's worth noting that, while these journals represent significant and respected venues in literary studies, by and large most elite journals (say, *Critical Inquiry* or *New Literary History*) still deal with theory as a metaphysical entity, leaving arguments on teaching to the "pedagogical" or "applied" journals (say, *College English* or *CCC*, which are institutionally supported by "teachers'" organizations such as NCTE). One oft-cited exception, *Yale French Studies'* special issue on "The Pedagogical Imperative," speaks of pedagogy in anything but practical terms.

12. All three titles are published by the University of Illinois Press. Others include *Order and Partialities: Theory, Pedagogy, and the "Postcolonial,"* ed. Kostas Myrsiades and Jerry McGuire (New York: State University of New York Press, 1995), which stems from work in *College Literature*, and the first such deliberate treatment, *Theory in the Classroom*, ed. Cary Nelson (Urbana: University of Illinois Press, 1986). For a relevant review, see Michael Bernard-Donals, "Situating Theory in the Classroom," *minnesota review*, n.s., 41–42 (1994): 298–309.

13. The case presented by cultural studies complicates this claim, since cultural studies, at least in its mythic origin, casts its roots in adult education in Britain and thus projects an organic connection to pedagogy. However, by my surmise CS has largely been absorbed into and mediated through the formation of literary studies in the contemporary U.S. academy and functions as an upgrade of current theory—rather than as an outreach to, say, high schools or community colleges.

14. To give one telling example of how this bias operates, to attain Phi Beta Kappa standing, a college of arts and sciences cannot house lesser disciplines such as education (or hotel management, for that matter), but only the purer traditional disciplines, such as history, philosophy, biology, and their cognates.

15. How genuine or effectual those politics were remains another question. Terry Eagleton provides an apt comment on this question of the displacement of radical politics in "Discourse and Discos," *TLS*, 15 July 1994, 3–4.

16. For a pointed critique of the "radical panache" and liberatory claims of high theory, see Barbara Foley, "Subversion and Oppositionality in the Academy," in *Pedagogy Is Politics: Literary Theory and Critical Teaching*, ed. Maria-Regina Kecht (Urbana: University of Illinois Press, 1992), 70–89.

17. Evan Watkins argues pointedly that the primary role of education, despite the purported radical content of courses, is in the present circulation of labor (*Work Time*, 26 ff.).

18. For a fuller elaboration of the advent of theory and its professionalist function, see my "The Posttheory Generation," *Symplokē* 3, no. 1 (1995): 64–73.

19. See M. S. Larson, *The Rise of Professionalism: A Sociological Analysis* (Berkeley: University of California Press, 1977), 86–89.

20. As Noam Chomsky underscores and demonstrates in the model of his own practice, our professional position garners "the leisure, the facilities, and the training to seek the truth lying hidden behind the veil of distortion and misrepresentation, ideology, and class interest through which the events of current history are presented to us." "The Responsibility of Intellectuals," in *The Chomsky Reader*, ed. James Peck (New York: Pantheon, 1987), 60.

21. Aronowitz goes on: "Matters such as the establishment, expansion, retention, or elimination of departments and programs; the hiring and dismissal of faculty; the assignment of positions to programs and departments; and workload and class size are only a few of the crucial decisions that were traditionally addressed by faculty and have been gradually assumed by administration and boards of trustees." "Higher Education: The Turn of the Screw," *Found Object* 6 (1995): 91.

22. Lest this seem alarmist, see Lawrence C. Soley, *Leasing the Ivory Tower: The Corporate Takeover of Academia* (Boston: South End Press, 1995) for a detailed and decidedly grim account.

23. *Work Time*, 26.

24. "Going Public: Political Discourse and the Faculty Voice," in *Higher Education under Fire: Politics, Economics, and the Crisis of the Humanities*, ed. Michael Bérubé and Cary Nelson (New York: Routledge, 1995), 35–51.

25. Cynthia Young, "On Strike at Yale," *minnesota review*, n.s., 45–46 (1996): 179–92 provides a useful narrative of a unionizing drive, albeit unsuccessful, and there are others to be gleaned, such as the unionization of graduate students in the SUNY system several years back.

26. See Paul Smith on the limitations of such petitionary measures, in "A Memory of Marxism," *Polygraph* 6–7 (1993): 101.

27. "Critique of the Gotha Program," in *The Marx-Engels Reader*, 2d ed., ed. Robert C. Tucker (New York: Norton, 1978), 539.

28. As Andrew Ross argues, "We should not be in the business of producing a job bourgeoisie, which is the traditional career academic model. And so it is imperative not

to accept the shrinkage injunction that has been presented as a response, in some left circles, to the job crunch. Graduate education must continue to be an expansionary project, if only because it is one of the few places where the work of training a generation of radical intellectuals can occur." Jeffrey Williams and Mike Hill, "Undisciplined: An Interview with Andrew Ross," *minnesota review*, n.s., 45–46 (1996): 82.

Contributors

TIMOTHY BRENNAN is an associate professor of English and comparative literature at the State University of New York at Stony Brook. He is the author of *Salman Rushdie and the Third World: Myths of the Nation* and *At Home in the World: Cosmopolitanism Now*.

RACHEL BUFF is an assistant professor in the history department at Bowling Green State University. Currently she is collaborating with Jason Loviglio on a collection of essays concerning pedagogy and cultural studies.

MARIA DAMON teaches contemporary poetry and poetics at the University of Minnesota. She is the author of *The Dark End of the Street: Margins in American Vanguard Poetry* and a member of the National Writer's Union.

JEFFREY R. DI LEO teaches in the philosophy and comparative literature departments at Indiana University, Bloomington. He is editor in chief of the theory journal *Symplokē*.

HENRY A. GIROUX is the Waterbury Chair Professor of Secondary Education at Penn State University and the director of the Waterbury Forum for Education and Cultural Studies. His many books include *Border Crossing*, *Disturbing Pleasures*, and most recently, *Fugitive Cultures: Race, Violence and Youth*.

JUDITH HALBERSTAM is an associate professor of literature at the University of California, San Diego. She is the author of *Skin Shows: Gothic Horror and the Technology of Monsters* and coeditor with Ira Livingston of *Posthuman Bodies.* She is currently finishing a book project on female masculinity.

DONALD K. HEDRICK is a professor of English at Kansas State University, where he helped found and direct the graduate program in cultural studies. His current work centers on early modern valuation and on dissident appropriations of Shakespeare.

MIKE HILL is an assistant professor of English at Marymount Manhattan College. He is the editor of *Whiteness: A Critical Reader* and is currently at work on *After Whiteness* and a book on the discipline of literature and eighteenth-century crowds.

PETER HITCHCOCK is an associate professor of literary and cultural studies at Baruch College of the City University of New York. He is the author of *Working-Class Fiction in Theory and Practice* and *Dialogues of the Oppressed.*

AMITAVA KUMAR teaches in the English department at the University of Florida. He has published a collection of poems, *No Tears for the N.R.I.* His book *Passport Photos* is forthcoming.

NEIL LARSEN teaches in the modern languages department at Northeastern University in Boston. He is the author of *Modernism and Hegemony* and *Reading North by South,* and is currently at work on a book about national and postnational cultures.

JOHN P. LEAVEY, JR., has translated several volumes of Jacques Derrida's texts, including *Glas,* and has published numerous articles and *Glassary.* He teaches at the University of Florida.

GEORGE LIPSITZ is a professor of ethnic studies at the University of California, San Diego. He is the author of *Rainbow at Midnight: Labor and Culture in the 1940s,* as well as *Time Passages, A Life in the Struggle, Dangerous Crossroads,* and *The Sidewalks of St. Louis.*

JASON LOVIGLIO is a Ph.D. candidate in American studies at the University of Minnesota, and is completing a dissertation on the cultural history of talk radio. He is currently teaching American studies and English at the University of Massachusetts, Boston.

CHRISTIAN MORARU teaches in the comparative literature department at Indiana University, Bloomington, and is the author of *The Poetics of Reflection.* An associate editor of *Symplokē,* he is currently completing a book on contemporary American fiction and critical theory.

JOHN MOWITT teaches in the department of cultural studies and comparative literature and in the department of English at the University of Minnesota. He is the author of *Text: The Genealogy of an Antidisciplinary Object* and the forthcoming *Percussion: Drumming, Beating, Striking.*

VIJAY PRASHAD is an assistant professor of international studies at Trinity College. His research interests include modern Indian history, South Asian American politics and society, and issues in contemporary global labor politics.

BRUCE ROBBINS teaches English and comparative literature at Rutgers University. He is the author of *Secular Vocations: Intellectuals, Professionalism, Culture* and the editor of *Intellectuals: Aesthetics, Politics, Academics* and *The Phantom Public Sphere*. He is also a coeditor of *Social Text.*

GAYATRI CHAKRAVORTY SPIVAK is the Avalon Foundation Professor in the Humanities at Columbia University. Among her publications are translations of *Of Grammatology* by Jacques Derrida and *Imaginary Maps* by Mahasweta Devi, as well as her own *In Other Worlds, The Post-Colonial Critic, Outside in the Teaching Machine*, and, forthcoming, *Obtuse Angling in Various Mainstreams.*

CAROL STABILE works in the department of communication at the University of Pittsburgh and is a member of the Metro-Pittsburgh Labor Party Chapter and the Pittsburgh Socialist Educational Collective.

RONALD STRICKLAND is an associate professor of English at Illinois State University. He has written frequently on pedagogical and curricular issues and is the coeditor, with Christopher Newfield, of *After Political Correctness: The Humanities and Society in the 1990's.*

GREGORY L. ULMER is a professor of English and media studies at the University of Florida, and the author of *Heuretics: The Logic of Invention, Teletheory*, and *Applied Grammatology*. He is currently working on the theory and practice of distance education as moderator of the Electronic Learning Forum.

ALAN WALD is a professor in the English department and program in American culture at the University of Michigan. He is the author of five books about literary radicalism in the United States, most recently *Writing from the Left*. He is also the editor of the University of Illinois Press series *The Radical Novel Reconsidered.*

JEFFREY WILLIAMS is the editor of the *Minnesota Review* and *PC Wars: Politics and Theory in the Academy*. His book *The Theory Market* is forthcoming.

Index

Sex: lesbian, 261; and "no-man's-land of sex,"
270; penetrative, 262; queer, 257; and sex-
ual variation, 260
Sexton, Anne, 37
Shakespeare, W., 36, 65–73, 128, 155, 175, 234
Silko, Leslie Marmon, 103
Silone, I., 141
Simpson, David, 26
Sir Gawain and the Green Knight, 155
Sixties, 80, 83, 127, 129, 133
Slobin, Mark, 42
Slochower, Harry, 135
Smedley, A., 137
Sokal, Alan, 50–51, 225
Spencer, Herbert, 230, 236
Spengler, Oswald, 226
Spicer, Jack, 34
Spivak, G. C., 24, 99, 104, 106, 110, 112n.,
114n., 121, 237
Spoken word, 37
Stalin, J., 103, 132
Steady, F., 97, 106–7
Stone, Sandy, 266–67
Strikes, 18; French, 146; Homestead, 217, 219;
Mayday 1970, 247; of Staley and Caterpillar
workers, 146; Yale TA, 162, 214, 248, 307
Stryker, Susan, 266
Student, 19, 25, 30, 34, 49; alienation, 288;
awards, 172; and classroom community, 126;
and disenchantment, 248; evaluation forms,
139, 143, 171; expenses, 167; gaining con-
trol, 133, 138; graduate, 233; less privileged,
214; as participants, 165; and student-cen-
tered pedagogies, 72, 118; writing, 42, 43,
58, 67
Students for a Democratic Society, 130, 217
Subaltern, 88
Sudarkasa, Niara, 97
Survey paradigm, 58–59; and "field coverage,"
168–69; and the "standard course," 133,
136; and U.S. history survey, 202
Sykes, Charles, 180
Symploke, 242

Taggard, Genevieve, 135
Taylor, Charles, 100

TESOL, 170, 201
TESOL Quarterly, 170
Testimonio, 36
Texeira, Mary, 92
Theater, 70, 102
The Empire Strikes Back, 230
Theory: and abstraction, 122; in activist feminist writing, 100; condemnation of, 153;
critical, 56; as critique and auto-critique,
166; feminist theory course syllabus, 106;
and grammatology, 283; high, 99; and the
interruptive question, 292; and limitations
of critique, 280–83; in the 1960s and 1970s,
130; as object of pedagogy, 82; and pedagogy, 77; and poetics of the vanguard, 286;
politics of appropriation of, 113n.; and the
politics of detour, 295–96; politics of production of, 96; radical politics in, 152; and
the renewal of public license, 304; and sexual practices, 261; social, 11; social significance, 26; theory of, 80; and theory czars,
150; transgender, 266–70; trickle down theory, 94; underpinning teaching, 171
Thies, Kaye, 107
Thomas, Clarence, 188
Thompson, E. P., 151–53
Trade union, 14, 16, 143
Transnational world, 87, 89, 91, 98
Traub, Valerie, 264
Tribadism, 261–62
Trilling, Lionel, 184
Trotskyism, 132, 136, 145
Turner, Victor, 71
TV Guide, 41
Tzara, Tristan, 226

United Nations, 104, 111n.
United States: anti-intellectualism, 212; Border
Patrol, 92, 98; cultural Left, 132; imperial-
ism, 99, 104, 112n.; imperial policy, 79, 91;
public school system, 210
Unlearning, 5, 127–33, 136, 140, 217–18
Upward mobility, 10, 22, 25, 203
U.S.-Japan Women's Journal, 110

Vaid, Sudesh, 106